GW01606017

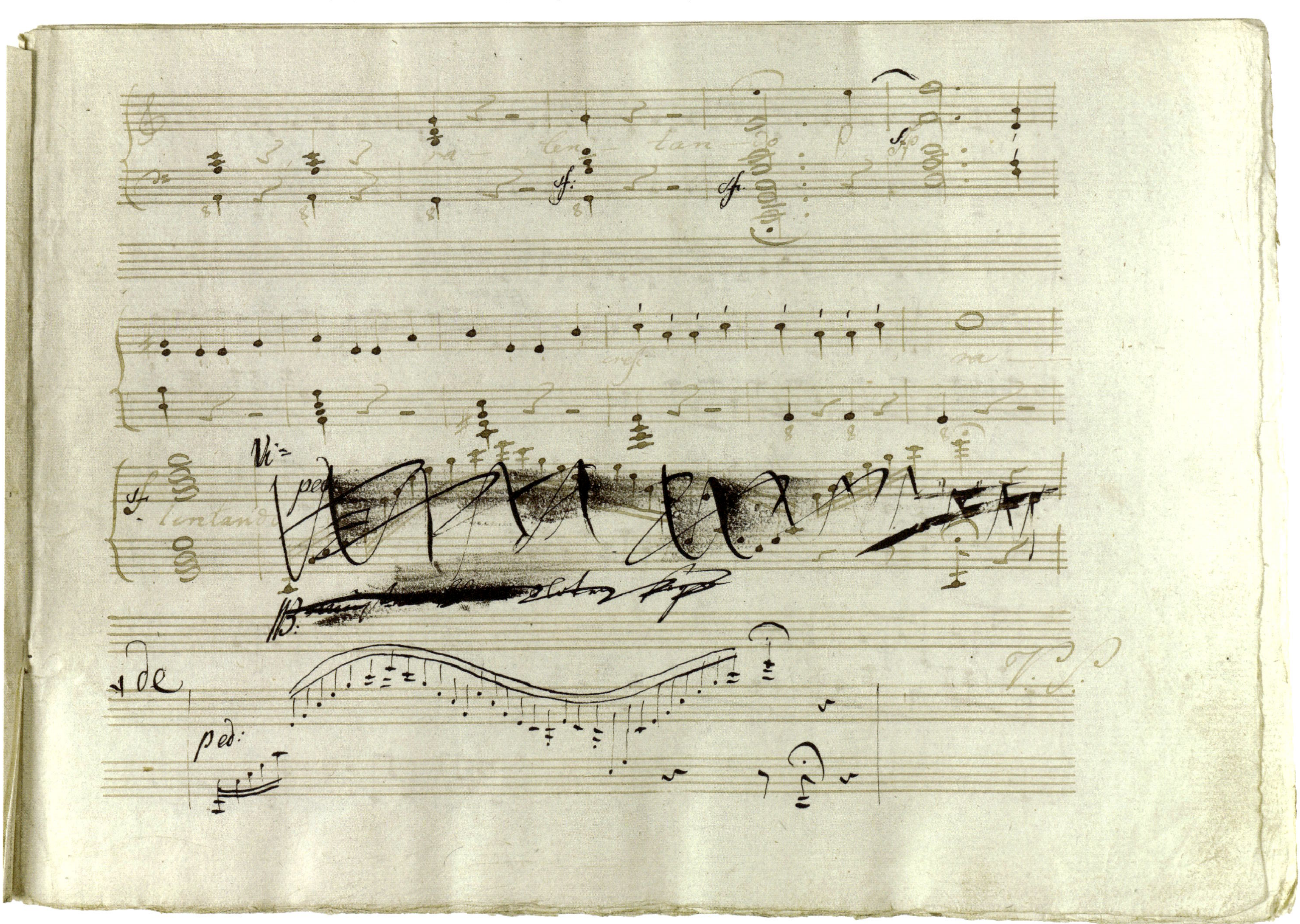

Ludwig van Beethoven. Sonata for violin and piano No. 9 in A major, op. 47, 'Kreutzersonate'. 1802/03. Courtesy of the Juilliard Manuscript Collection

BEETHOVEN MOVES

EDITED BY
ANDREAS KUGLER
JASPER SHARP
STEFAN WEPPELMANN
ANDREAS ZIMMERMANN

KUNSTHISTORISCHES
MUSEUM VIENNA

HATJE
CANTZ

Foreword

Sabine Haag
General Director of the Kunsthistorisches Museum Vienna

Ludwig van Beethoven and the Kunsthistorisches Museum would seem to make for a surprising pairing, yet the universal significance of their respective realms means that there is in fact a solid basis for bringing the two together, if only temporarily.

In 2020, the Kunsthistorisches Museum is playing its own part in the bonanza of concerts, exhibitions, symposia and commemorative events taking place to mark the 250th anniversary of Ludwig van Beethoven's birth. In cooperation with the Archive of the Gesellschaft der Musikfreunde in Wien, we have prepared a most unusual tribute to this great exponent of Viennese Classicism, whose popularity remains undimmed to this day. Reaching well beyond the field of music, his humanist messages have influenced the history of art and culture. The early loss of his hearing contributed decisively to his image as a tragic genius.

Both the universal and the unique appeal of his epoch-making music and also the way in which he has been set up as an iconic figure mean that Beethoven can be approached from any number of different angles. High culture and pop culture, business and politics all use him as an almost inexhaustible source of inspiration – sometimes with the intention of exploiting him for their own ends.

While other exhibitions are dealing with Beethoven's life, his patrons and his few rivals, or are focusing on his genius and the creative process, our exhibition follows a different, yet complementary path. Playing with associations between different art forms, with performance art and with modern and contemporary art, we deliberately skirt around a 'void' at its centre. The exhibition extends into our own times and is conceived as an imaginative meditation on the composer and his oeuvre. The expressive power of Beethoven's music is thereby invested with visual form, so that his music is not only heard but also 'seen'.

This elaborately planned exhibition does not feature a single work from the holdings of the Kunsthistorisches Museum. However, it is itself showcased in the Museum's Picture Gallery, in the context of several centuries of art and culture and surrounded by hundreds of works which chronologically extend precisely up to Beethoven's lifetime – and which, to some extent, may be said to lead to that life.

Characterized by personal impressions and imaginative topical essays, the present book serves as a fitting companion volume to an equally unusual exhibition, the organization of which I was delighted to support throughout the whole process, using all the available resources, after unexpectedly inheriting this project from Eike Schmidt, my formerly designated successor as Director General.

I should like here to express my gratitude to the exhibition's four curators – Andreas Kugler, Jasper Sharp, Stefan Weppelmann and Andreas Zimmermann – who, coming from four different perspectives, managed to develop an original and ambitious concept in a short space of time. Without them, the initial, vaguely formulated idea of a Beethoven exhibition would have remained wishful thinking, would never have come to life. Significantly, their emphasis was not on music theory or music history but on seeking to take an open-minded and associative approach to the universal story of Beethoven as a creative and suffering individual.

If visiting the exhibition itself or leafing through the accompanying catalogue at home inspires people to engage with Beethoven's life and to listen to or play – yes, even play – his music, then this will be an elegant, personal and indeed possibly very intimate way of filling the above-mentioned void at the heart of the exhibition. And this will be precisely what we have been aiming for.

AYŞE ERKMEN

esile rüf

2020

JASPER SHARP When we were asked to curate the exhibition about Beethoven we were given very little time, a little less than a year – which for an exhibition of this size in a museum of this size is extremely short. We were not given any specific direction in terms of what form it should take – simply that the Kunsthistorisches Museum as the most important museum in Austria should celebrate this adopted son of Vienna in a very grand and public way on the occasion of his 250th birthday.

ANDREAS ZIMMERMANN One of you once remarked that the Kunsthistorisches Museum with its collections spanning five thousand years is in a sense the pedestal for the figure of Beethoven. That's a nice image! I don't know if it's a coincidence or if there is some sort of historical explanation, but the point is that Beethoven lived at very much the same time as that first generation of artists – those born around the years between 1760 and 1780 – who are not represented in the museum at all. And that whole generation – which includes Turner, Friedrich, Goya and Beethoven – may be said to stand for that opening into modernity which the Kunsthistorisches Museum failed to pass through. The fact that we're doing this now is, in my view, a unique opportunity for our institution.

JS It's always said that Beethoven is one of those once-in-a-generation figures who broke with everything that came before. You could argue that what the museum represents is precisely that 'everything'. Yes, it's not the world of music, but it is the context, the baggage. I think part of the nervousness that everyone shares about this exhibition is that Beethoven is someone from outside the world of art history and that this exhibition about him is going to take place in a museum called the 'Art History Museum'. That is the thing that most people find difficult at first.

AZ But don't we keep emphasizing, at every possible opportunity, the universal scope of our collections? Well, Beethoven happens to be such a universal figure! In that sense the two really are very well matched.

STEFAN WEPPELMANN When the idea for this exhibition first came up, one of the very first things I started to think about was how our museum's rooms could actually function as its venue. Another was the challenge of assembling and showcasing so many different media there, including ephemeral media such as Tino Sehgal's new work and moving images – not the kind of stuff you'd expect to find in the holdings of the Kunsthistorisches Museum! Apart from the topic of Beethoven, I also found it very exciting to have this opportunity to break free from the conventional mould that normally circumscribes my work as an art historian. From a certain point on though, the project developed its own momentum and I ceased to ask myself the question: 'Just why are we doing this exhibition?' For it was the exhibition itself that now began to make demands. You may have noticed how I said 'we' just now. You see, for me it was so nice to be able to mount an exhibition as part of a team of four, applying a methodology (if we can speak of a methodology in this context) that brought together and drew on four very different backgrounds. That – to return to Beethoven – is probably no coincidence either, since he is a crystallizing point for such a wide range of topics.

JS One thing that was very important for us at the beginning, and also maybe something of a relief, was the understanding that this should not be the type of Beethoven exhibition that people would expect. That this wasn't the classic biography in exhibition form. There wasn't enough time to do that, the Kunsthistorisches Museum was perhaps not the right place to do that, and it was also already happening in Bonn. The fact that Bonn is putting on such a comprehensive exhibition freed us up somewhat to think a little differently, a little more intuitively, which I think made the whole process much more thrilling for us. And it enabled us, as I said, to do things that people aren't expecting. They come expecting to see an image of Beethoven in the first room or on the poster or in the last room and he doesn't appear anywhere in the exhibition.

ANDREAS KUGLER Well, the fact is that cultural history exhibitions do often find themselves in the situation of orbiting a void at their centre, because the subject as such is not physically there and can't be put on display – quite the opposite of an art exhibition. Although we do have Beethoven's music 'on show' here and there, this analogy is to some extent also applicable to our exhibition. Navigating the space around an empty centre, moreover, means that the curator has to consider how the visitors can be stimulated to think further and exchange ideas about the exhibition once they have left its premises. Now that is true of any exhibition, but it is especially so in this case.

AZ Yes, and that element of the unexpected ties in nicely with Beethoven. In many cases his music took audiences by surprise, even overwhelming them. His works very often operate (not just in terms of their opening but structurally too) with an element of suspense – indeed, in a sense, they are out to shock.

AK Because of all the factors we've touched on so far, this project gave me the opportunity to approach Beethoven in a way that actually made sense, namely, with a very open mind. While some of the ideas I originally came up with were bold, I was never concerned with startling the public or breaking with tradition as such. Rather, I wanted to use this combination of exceptional rooms with exceptional works of art to be thought-provoking. The associative aspect appealed to me from the very start – something that is so highly productive when experiencing art. Beethoven's uniqueness lies, among other things, in the fact that he is so exemplary – it is not merely a question of his not fitting in or of his towering over everyone else. So much of what is fundamental to the appreciation of music, the fine arts and literature can be keenly experienced, perceived or meditated over by engaging with Beethoven.

AZ You are right to speak of 'associative aspects' and of 'being thought-provoking', but these concepts are after all closely related to that of the unexpected. So all that fits together very well.

AK However, it is not a question of provoking, seeking after effect or trying to shock as if that were all that mattered; these are just fascinating subsidiary phenomena of any encounter with art. The idea of a 'net' of associations – casting a net is a nice metaphor because it implies covering a large space, but it is also a dangerous one if you think of how all the strands are tightly woven, though that's not what I'm referring to here ... Yes, it was the idea of an associative net that seemed so promising to me from the word go. If such a net is cast very widely, then its meshes will fasten almost imperceptibly on the 'hooks' that are to be found in the personal experience and emotions of every visitor. The net cast by the exhibition may then be said to merge with the vast 'web' of feelings and sensations that visiting our exhibition and reading this book will arouse.

JS I think Beethoven belongs to a very small group of people of whom the world is so aware that you can mount an exhibition about them and not even say what year they were born and what year they died because that's not what it's about. Shakespeare, Beethoven ... they are part of our common consciousness, so you can delve into them in a somewhat oblique way. They are so utterly familiar in so many ways that it is no longer about re-emphasizing their familiarity. This enables you to do quite a nuanced exhibition, as we are doing. You can even introduce Beethoven in the first room without him being there in any way, just in the completely abstract form of music and some notes on a piece of paper, and I think it's fascinating that this is what we have chosen to do.

AZ When I told Tino Sehgal during his first visit here how fantastic it was that he had agreed so quickly to create a work for us, he replied: 'It's not such a big deal, you know! When I heard about the exhibition, my first thought was: Beethoven? He's kind of halfway between Karl Marx and Jesus.' That was a clear recognition of the universal, almost demigod-like status of Beethoven.

JS I would add Diego Maradona to that group. And then it's probably complete. *(laughter)*

SW Although we did in fact refuse to put Beethoven on a pedestal – which would have meant approaching the monument piously to decipher and elucidate the inscription on its plinth, as it were – although, or rather precisely because we took such a down-to-earth approach, we nevertheless did end up treating Beethoven as a monumental figure one simply has to look up to. We achieved this paradoxical feat precisely because we didn't think of Beethoven as standing on a pedestal. Yet, at the end of the day, there he is back on that very pedestal.

JS But I hope we have been successful in taking him off this pedestal in the exhibition.

AK That's an important point because it is so typical of the reception of Beethoven – though there are others of whom it is also true – that the number of times he has been put on a pedestal is matched by the number of times his lofty status has been called into question. These constantly alternating efforts to elevate and topple him fit in so well with the nature of his music. Now, this tendency to turn composers into heroes or demigods was especially pronounced in Europe, invariably steered by vested interests of various kinds. It's quite strange, though, because music – especially over the last few decades – has, more than any other art, become so bound up with people's private lives. I mean the way in which people are reminded of specific moments or encounters by a certain song or a piece of music that was then playing in the background. This is of course true of any art form, but music grips you most intimately because it is not palpable or concrete, because it comes over you at once and affects your mood.

JS This question of the private and the public and the profile is very interesting. Thinking about the exhibition, there are some moments which are exuberant, showy and public. But then when you walk into the second room, you feel as if you are somewhere incredibly private and intimate and closed. Then you burst out of it again, and in the fourth room it's suddenly very immediate. Here both of these things come together: it's kind of private and collective at the same time. The tension between the public and the private is something that runs through Beethoven's life and his reception – and it runs through the exhibition, and the book to a certain extent, in terms of people's takes on him.

SW I should like to add a few remarks about something that I often notice as part of my 'baggage', in a positive but sometimes also negative sense – namely, the methodology I am obliged to apply to the items of a collection or exhibition. Art historians tend to always follow a specific approach when engaging with such objects. Those approaches are often based on the secondary literature and, therefore, on the previously accumulated knowledge and opinions of others. This means that the scope is very narrow and that one in fact ends up discovering no more than what one already knew, which is to be paraded yet again or reinforced through the exhibitions one subsequently curates. Here, in contrast, we may dare to look and listen to things in a completely unprejudiced manner. Before this exhibition my knowledge of Beethoven was hardly very deep; indeed, it was restricted to the five or six pieces that anyone coming across his music in popular culture is more or less familiar with. When I started work on the programme, I did what I always do when I'm involved in an exhibition – that is, I bought relevant books. The idea behind this was: 'Now I can prepare myself and read up on the subject so that I am well versed in it and actually able to produce something.' However, I didn't manage to read a single line of those books because so many other things of a purely logistic nature got in the way and demanded my attention. It was perhaps precisely for that reason that I was able to approach the topic from a kaleidoscopic perspective.

JS I won't lie: I had a lot of moments during this process when I felt like a complete fraud doing a Beethoven exhibition. I think what's been interesting about this constellation is that we have real experts on Beethoven in the group, who can give us assurance about the path and the instinct. And I think it's very interesting to have a couple of voices – or at least mine – in the group who are almost there representing the interest of people who don't know a huge amount about Beethoven, because exhibitions are often done by people who know everything and they cannot see the wood for the trees in terms of what actually interests people. We are not just curating for the Beethoven experts, but we are also not just curating for the layperson. Hopefully, we are putting together an exhibition that everyone can find a way into and everyone can find a way out of.

AK If I may chip in here, what one experiences when listening to Beethoven's music is both its complexity – which ultimately proves too much for the listener – and a spontaneous exuberance that sweeps one along or sometimes also an intimacy that opens one up – above all to oneself. That is truly exemplary, for the effect is the same as when reading great literature or viewing artistic masterpieces. Beethoven's music now thrusts itself on the listener, now embraces him. This is expressed so emphatically in the music that, as soon as we had reached agreement on taking a liberal and openminded approach to the composer, our ideas just flowed forth one after the other. What we then sought to do was to relate the major conceptual leaps in the exhibition's programme and the extensive selection of artworks on display to Beethoven's music and his autograph manuscripts. It is even possible to draw a parallel with Beethoven's own working method. As a young man he was already famous for his improvisations, yet at the same time he took greater trouble than any other composer before him to elaborate on, deepen, vary, weed out, replace and restructure his ideas. All this material he put together – that is, 'composed' in the literal sense of the word – in countless sketchbooks, which he himself had bound. It is precisely this tension between improvisation and composition – the latter to be carried out with painstaking conscientiousness, despite the huge time pressure – that one also finds in curating and that makes it such a wonderful job.

AZ My goodness, let's not start comparing ourselves to Beethoven, though!

AK No, of course not! It was just meant to stimulate further discussion.

AK The exhibition follows a very clear and well-known narrative, which is, however, by no means the most important thing. By this narrative I mean the story of the great pianist and composer who arrives in Vienna and impresses himself upon the public consciousness, achieving iconic status. In the second chapter we encounter a man whose progressive hearing loss not only isolates himself increasingly from those around him but also robs him of the sensory experience of his own music, yet who all the same continues to pursue his path as an artist. After that we have the theme of *A Political Artist in Revolutionary Times*, to cite the title of a book by William Kinderman that will be published later this year: Beethoven as an artist who, inspired by the Enlightenment and the French Revolution, sees the world – and I really do mean the world, comprising both society and nature – in a new light, who has this notion that it is possible to establish a new rapport with the world, a new kind of fellowship with mankind.

JS The narrative structure of the exhibition came pretty quickly. The same can be said about the selection of objects. In every room there was one key object, which started to give physical shape to that room and brought the atmosphere with it. In the first room this was Jorinde Voigt's group of drawings, followed a little bit later by Rebecca Horn and the Rodin. Similarly, in the second room, the floor and the Goyas came in right at the beginning and set the mood. In the third room, it was really Guido van der Werve's film of the icebreaker and the presence of Caspar David Friedrich and Turner. And then we added a few pieces around them. I think we have a really nice overall balance between works that were made with Beethoven in mind and works that were made with anything but Beethoven in mind, but which lend themselves very well to the mood and the atmosphere that we are trying to create. We also felt right from the beginning that part of our experience with Beethoven is the live experience and the sharing of this remarkable experience with total strangers. And that is how we got to the final chapter – the work by Tino Sehgal.

AK The fact that in the final room one experiences a direct encounter with Beethoven, on the same level – thanks to Tino Sehgal's wonderful idea that Beethoven's music has no beginning and no end, that it has no need for a stage or anything similar separating it from the audience – this is the culmination, as it were, of the idea behind our exhibition, namely, that everyone is invited. This may all sound very melodramatic, and it is of course true of any encounter with art that everyone is entitled to respond as he or she wishes. But we hope that in the first room people will already feel that this is the guiding principle of our exhibition, perhaps in a more obvious way than in other similar events – and it is manifested quite explicitly in the final room.

AZ There's nothing wrong at all in it sounding somewhat melodramatic. Indeed, I would describe the whole exhibition as relatively rich in pathos. For first the scene is set, in most poignant fashion, by Rooms 1 to 3, followed by Tino Sehgal's highly moving and emotional work. I have no problem with the use of pathos and of a light heroic manner because both concepts are characteristic of Beethoven's persona and of his times. The same goes for the cliché of the suffering artist – like so many clichés, it is one which carries more than a grain of truth. I am referring here to how Beethoven suffered on account of his failing health, of his misfortunes in love, of social conditions, and to how he clearly incorporated all that suffering into many of his works, which in turn goes a long way towards explaining the provocative nature of his music. If some people find themselves, so to speak, provoked at times by our exhibition, then it will have achieved one of the things we wanted it to do.

JS It's also an unashamedly theatrical exhibition in the way it's put together. It's a series of tableaux. Even the fourth and final gallery will be a tableau vivant. The whole thing has a quality of different worlds which actually all work on their own, in isolation from everything else, but hopefully they will also work as a string of experiences together. I've rarely been part of an exhibition that has such strong changes of mood from one gallery to the next. Again, for some curators this is what they do all the time, but we don't have the chance to do this very often in the Kunsthistorisches Museum. Perhaps the exhibition will feed a little bit into future practices going forward. Different ways of doing things are always interesting for us to explore.

AZ All this has a lot to do with Tino Sehgal and the use of the unexpected as a structural principle – something that, to a certain extent, he shares with Beethoven. Museums in general and museums for Old Masters in particular are very predictable places. People visit them knowing more or less what to expect. With the present exhibition this is really not the case: it begins in an unexpected manner and comes to an end in quite a different way.

JS We are very much in control of many aspects of the exhibition: the thickness of the fabric, the height of the pictures, which picture it is, the label that goes next to it. But there is a huge element of the exhibition – the fourth room – which is a completely unknown entity. What is going to happen in there? We have no idea, it's out of our control. That happens so rarely but it is so faithful to the subject matter that we are dealing with. We will have all sorts of encounters in the exhibition and it's going to feed us all the way through: unexpected things, annoyances, problems, goosebumps, emails from people, letters, conversations – it's going to be something really fascinating for better and for worse. Every time I think about it, I gasp and think: 'Our work is only halfway done when the show opens. Then comes the life of the exhibition beyond.'

AK This reference to how we shall have to deal with people's expectations regarding the exhibition brings us conveniently to the accompanying book. For in both exhibition and book we refuse to submit to the notion that a story must have some sort of conclusion to wrap things up.

AZ At the very start of our project, Stefan once used the term 'kaleidoscope' and that is in fact the only specific term that occurred to me when trying to collect my thoughts in preparation for this conversation. The exhibition and the book are, if I may put it thus, two kaleidoscopes both of which provide, in different ways, fragmentary reflections of a universal object: I mean Beethoven of course. This same underlying approach means that the exhibition and catalogue have a lot in common. But that is probably where the similarities end.

JS We decided right from the beginning that it didn't make sense to simply replicate the exhibition in book form. That was never really a serious consideration. We bounced around ideas for the catalogue for quite a few weeks, thinking: 'We know we have to do this, but how are we going to do it?' In the end, it was the idea of a choir of voices, a multitude of people with different levels of experience, coming from different backgrounds and different places. In order to give it some structure, we sat down – I think Andreas Kugler began first – and made a list of all of the emotions, ideals, qualities and characteristics that were in the exhibition, in different artworks, in the rooms, in the atmospheres. We set them up in opposition to each other, direct opposites such as freedom and confinement. When we invited people to contribute for the catalogue and write about Beethoven, we gave them this list of terms and expressions, moods and approaches, which they could draw upon – or not. Some people did it very directly, some people were more interested in specific objects in the exhibition, and other people disregarded everything and did their own thing. There were some very expected contributions that came in, but also some very unexpected ones. That was the way in which the shape of the catalogue developed: it came from the exhibition itself, but not by holding up a mirror to it, more like by holding up three mirrors to it.

SW Nor did we make any attempt to use the catalogue to provide a running commentary on the exhibition. The works on display are not discussed at all. Our approach was somewhat plateau-like. There's a book by Deleuze and Guattari entitled *A Thousand Plateaus*, in which a structure is developed on the basis not of linear evolution but of a horizontal arrangement of objects and interrelationships, like an expanding network. In that sense, the catalogue is actually an extension of the exhibition ...

AZ Structurally!

SW ... as if one were somehow still visiting the exhibition. That is why there was also this nice idea of having a photo essay, which allows us yet again to approach the subject from many different angles. Users of the catalogue – I deliberately said 'users', not 'readers' – really are given the opportunity to encounter themselves on its pages. At least I hope this is what we have achieved. It is what we were aiming for, at any rate.

AK What you have both just mentioned is something that the catalogue sets out to achieve, by – among other things – not having the various textual and visual contributions clamped together under individual chapter headings and not assembling a construct out of several such chapters. Rather, we have used photos of key works in the exhibition quite sparingly as structural elements instead of chapter headings. There is a strong link to the exhibition in the sense of seeking to keep the catalogue as open-ended and undefined as possible, though this should by no means be interpreted as indifference on our part. Admittedly, we have to put up with the fact that there is no way we can unequivocally refute allegations that such an element of indifference is present. For the underlying idea is that all the catalogue is meant to provide is opportunities or offers that users, readers and visitors to the exhibition can either take up or reject. This freedom has a snag – namely, that we have made our subjectivity a definite fixture – but we do try to offer that subjectivity unobtrusively, almost provisionally, so that it is easy for people to accept or reject it as they wish.

AZ I think that's something very important. This is not a book that presumes to lay down the law and to be taken as gospel. Rather, it operates with a substantial bunch of contrasts and even contradictions – and it invites people to partly reject its contents and to not quite know what to make of them. This highly uncanny effect that the book achieves in places dovetails quite nicely with the structural features of Beethoven's works. What I found so wonderful about the whole book project is that Beethoven is clearly a figure who elicits opinions from all kinds of people approaching him from the most diverse backgrounds.

AK All that is so liberating for the museum and for our notions of education as such. Seen from those angles, Beethoven does indeed represent a splendid opportunity. He can serve as a model for similar constellations of ideas and ways of experiencing art.

AZ It is particularly important that both in the book and in the exhibition we have made no attempt whatsoever to perpetuate the instrumentalized hero-worship that has been characteristic of past decades. Instead, the project's kaleidoscopic nature, its multiple refractions should – such is our hope – enable a great number of people to access it in different ways. Even if such access results in bewilderment here and there – that's also fine.

SW It's worth noting that the genre of exhibition catalogues hasn't been around for so long. It began with those big ephemeral art exhibitions of the post-war years. On the one hand, the organizers wanted to explain in learned fashion how all the works on display had come together and how they should be appreciated, and on the other hand they wanted to make a record of the whole event – apart from these two factors there would actually be no need for exhibition catalogues. Now, we never set out to create an exhibition catalogue as such – a most important point, in my view. Moreover, we stepped back – not simply by saying that we were happy to invite a Japanese car dealer or a child to provide contributions but by leaving it up to the contributors themselves to decide what they wanted to provide. A wonderful example is how we approached a contemporary composer, expecting that, fired up by Beethoven's music, he would write an illuminating essay on how music is composed. And then, contrary to those expectations, what we got back from him was a kind of Dadaist artwork! Amazing! If you study that piece closely, you can see how the intellectual sparks really were flying when the author was working on it. Having such things in the catalogue is so enriching.

JS And to go back to the idea of the book as a *Projektionsfläche*, a projection surface: I hope that it's the type of book that makes you want to pick up a pen and write something yourself. It invites people in to think about it and be part of it, to realize that their own thoughts about Beethoven are part of something bigger.

AK I very much like to imagine that, after returning home from the exhibition, people will – because we don't in fact do this either in the exhibition or in the book – look up a particular artist on Wikipedia or of course listen to Beethoven's music. But one could also imagine – it would almost be the ideal situation – someone being prompted by a visit to the exhibition or by reading the book to think of something else that matters to him or her – a picture, say, or a piece of music – and to engage with it actively. Now what could be more beautiful than that?

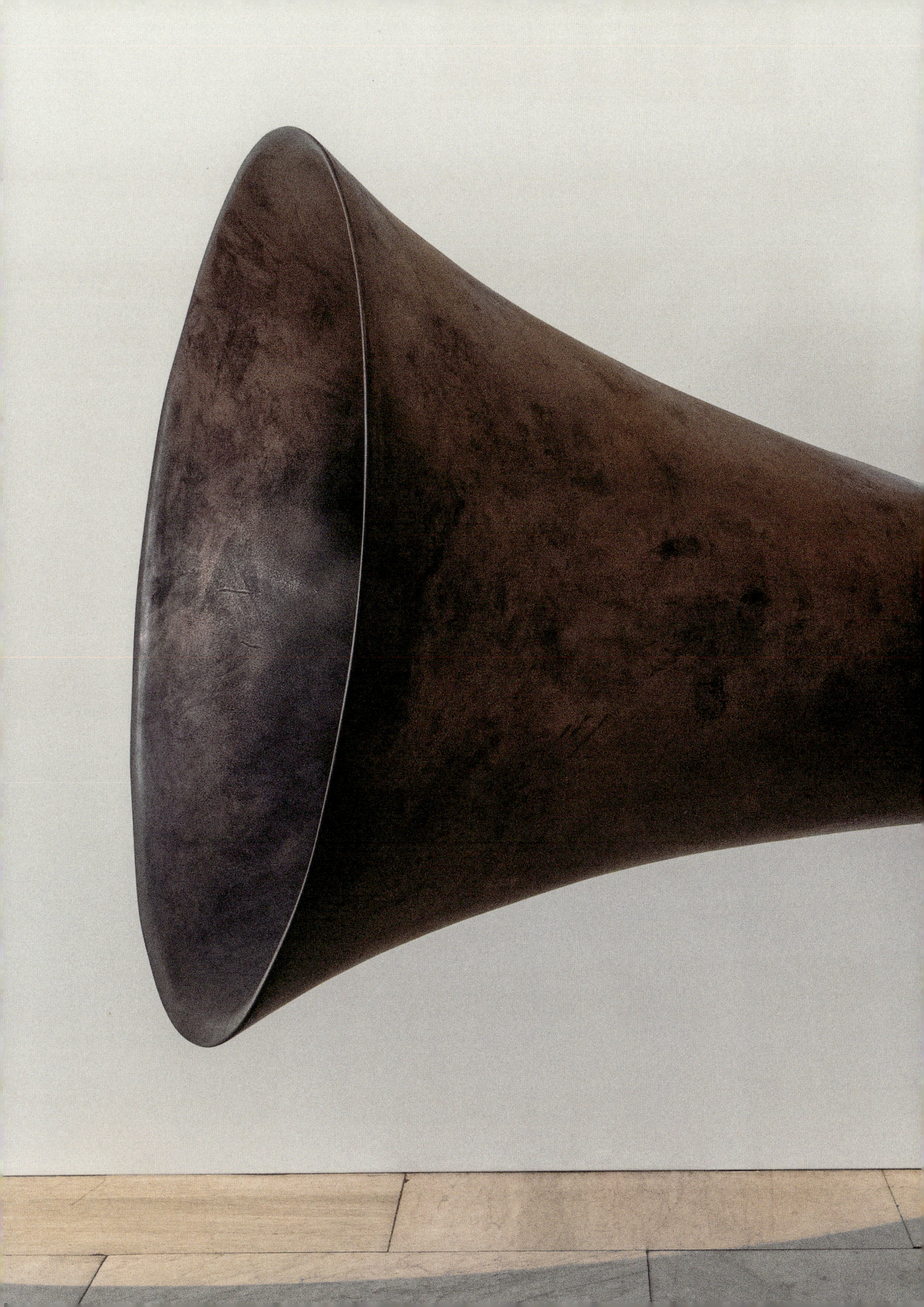

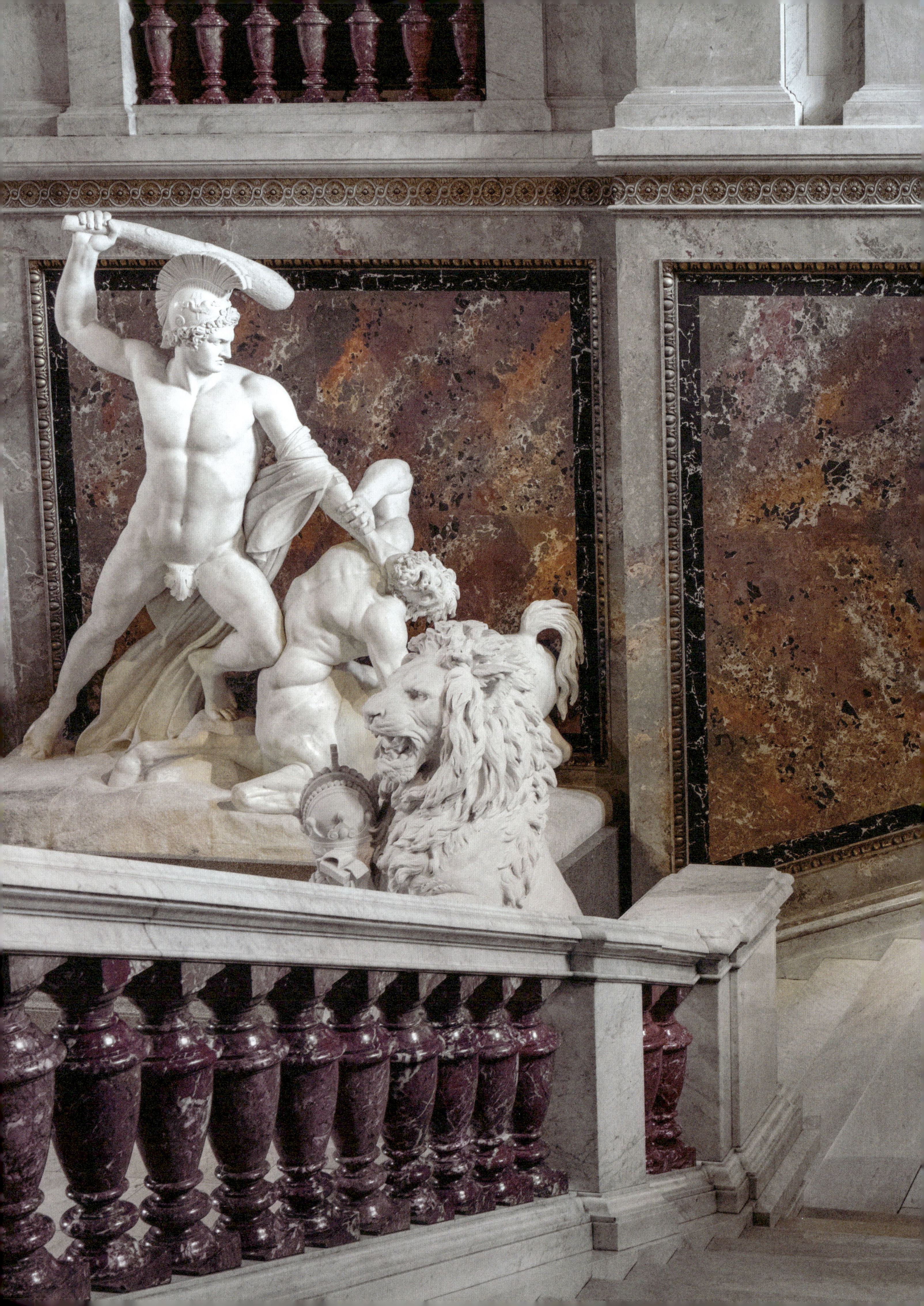

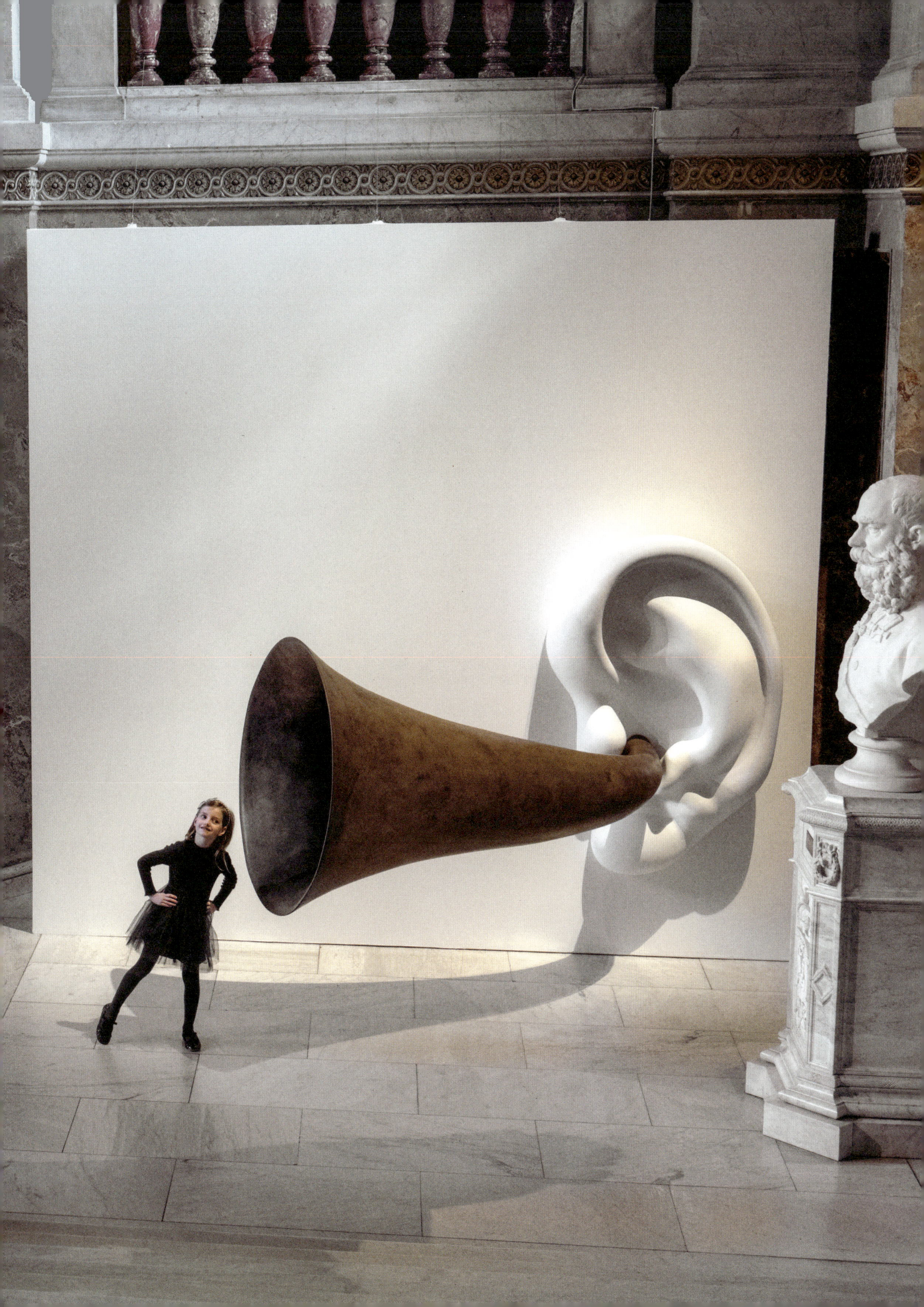

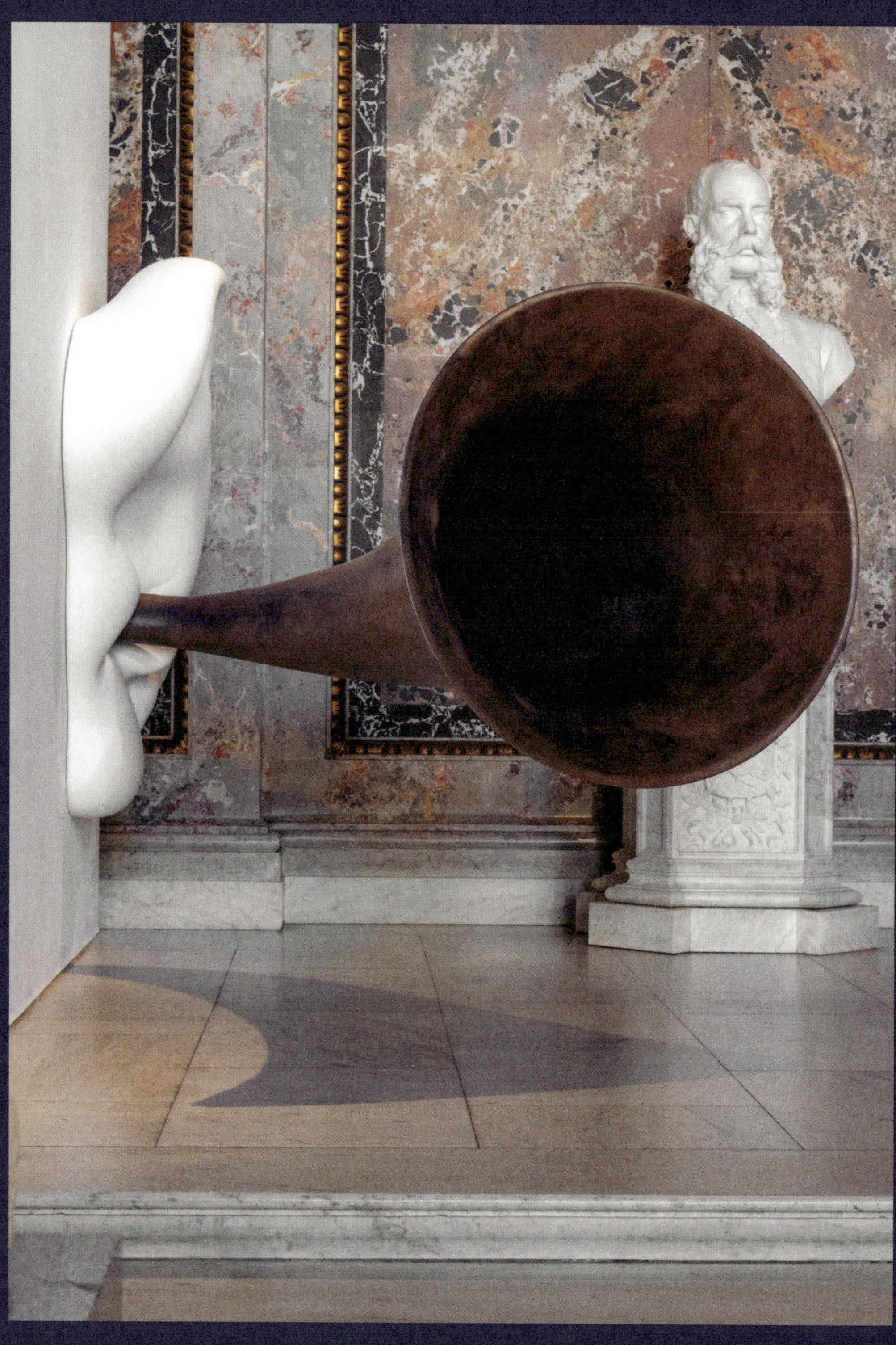

JOHN BALDESSARI, BEETHOVEN'S TRUMPET (WITH EAR) OP. # 132, 2007

JAN AND ALEIDA ASSMANN

A Conversation about Beethoven Framed around Ten Questions

One

Aleida Assmann: Mozart did not live to see the turn of the nineteenth century; his biography remains anchored in the eighteenth. What distinguishes Beethoven, who lived almost thirty years in the nineteenth century, from his predecessor?

JAN ASSMANN The opportunities that Beethoven enjoyed in Vienna were quite different from those that Mozart had had. By his time, in addition to the aristocratic circles in which Mozart had moved, there had also emerged a middle-class musical culture – an educated, enlightened and politically engaged *Bürgertum* that was itself involved in musicmaking and reacted with great intensity to Beethoven's music. The world changed completely after Napoleon arrived on the scene; there was a widening of political horizons. People discovered the concept of nations but also a new feeling for humanity. Beethoven's star rose: he became the musical hero of the new epoch, which found its ideals and hopes expressed in his music.

TWO

AA: Were there any specific defining experiences in Beethoven's life and, if so, what were they?

JA: Yes, absolutely. I should like to single out just three here. The first defining experience was undoubtedly his mother's death. It meant that the seventeen-year-old Beethoven had to assume responsibility for the whole family, including his younger siblings, because their father succumbed to alcoholism. Half of the father's salary was paid over to the son, who was now expected to be the family's breadwinner. The young Beethoven was then working as an organist and viola player at the court orchestra in Bonn.

A second defining experience was of a political nature: the French Revolution and Napoleon's subsequent victories. The ideals of liberty and equality filled him with enthusiasm and swept him along in their wake.

A third defining experience was the onset of deafness when he was twenty-seven years old and the inexorable progression of that severe malady. From 1802 onwards, Beethoven knew that his condition was incurable. It estranged him from his fellow men. Isolation aggravated his sense of insecurity and drove him to despair. Yet, remarkably, all this hardly impaired his creative powers. On the contrary: the more desolate his own situation, the greater, the more innovative and ambitious were the works that he defiantly wrested from his fate. This very defiance is clearly discernible in the bitter and unflinching expression on Beethoven's face in the likenesses of him that have come down to us.

THREE

AA: To whom was Beethoven originally indebted for his fame? By whom was it proclaimed and propagated?

JA: There were various factors at work. One was the revolutionary spirit of the age emanating from France. More than any other composer, Beethoven captured its essence in his symphonies, particularly the 'Eroica' and the Fifth. This immediately made him famous throughout Europe. In 1804, the French were anxious to secure his services.

Music printing further paved the way to enduring fame. In the nineteenth century, music publishing houses sprang up like mushrooms, since there was a new market for their products. The middle classes read and strove for self-improvement; they also bought sheet music, which proved to be a lucrative source of income for Beethoven in his lifetime. His renown, therefore, was consolidated not only by concerts but also by printed sheet music and the domestic musicmaking that it served.

Another important factor was the emergence of a vibrant European press. Newspapers and journals now began to employ music critics, who kept track of and evaluated new developments across national borders.

FOUR

AA: Beethoven's music reaches out in so many directions. In the lieder we find an intimate, lyrical tone, while the symphonies are addressed to all mankind. His music can mobilize politically, but it can also be sacral and religious. Is there some unifying link between all these elements or are they a symptom of a mind torn in several directions?

JA: Certainly not a symptom of that. Beethoven sought not only to operate in all musical genres but also to revitalize these and, in so doing, always to surpass what had been achieved before. He developed his own style in such disparate genres as the symphony, chamber music, piano music, ballet music, opera, the oratorio and the settings of the Mass. Within each genre, too, Beethoven's music displays a tremendously wide amplitude of expression. This is especially evident in the markings used to indicate tempo and mood, which range from the pianissimo of 'innigster Empfindung' (utmost intimacy of feeling), through 'espressivo', 'mit Andacht' (with devotion) and 'mit Ausdruck' (expressively), all the way to prestissimo, fortissimo and sforzato over every other note. Beethoven was able to realize himself everywhere – both in his intimate, private works and in the public works with their broad and mighty sweep.

FIVE

AA: How important for Beethoven were the place and milieu in which he lived? What did the provincial town of Bonn have to offer him? What about the metropolis Vienna?

JA: The provincial town of Bonn was able to offer him the electoral court of the archbishopric of Cologne, that is, the same kind of milieu as Salzburg in Mozart's case and the even more provincial Esterházy court in Haydn's. It was in Bonn that Beethoven's career as a wunderkind was launched: he gave his first public performance as a pianist at the age of seven. This was followed by service in the court orchestra and studies under the direction of the court organist Christian Gottlob Neefe, himself a composer of some reputation, who recognized his genius: 'If he carries on like that, he may become a second Mozart.' Neefe was far more than just a music teacher. He was a member of the Illuminati and familiarized his pupil with the ideals of the Enlightenment. In addition, he was in charge of a reading society to which the young Beethoven also belonged.

The move to Vienna meant for Beethoven – as it had meant for Mozart twenty-one years earlier – leaving behind the narrow confines of provincial life for the wide space of a metropolis. There, in addition to aristocratic and imperial patrons, he found a far broader, musically much more cultured middle-class audience than that which any German city would have been able to provide.

SIX

AA: Let us stay on the same subject. There is a traditional and quite indisputable link between music and nationhood. I am thinking here of Italy, France, England and Russia. What did Beethoven bring to the tradition of 'German music'?

JA: Beethoven almost certainly wanted to be a European composer first and foremost, and not so much a German national composer – rather like Schiller, whose plays dealt with the history of practically every European nation. It was not until after his death that Beethoven, like Schiller and Goethe, was appropriated for nationalist purposes as the German national composer par excellence. Later composers, by the way, were very much inclined to think along national lines. Schönberg, for example, once wrote that, thanks to his invention of the twelve-tone technique, he had 'guaranteed the supremacy of German music for the next hundred years'. There thus emerged this idea of a tradition that extended back from Beethoven to Bach, even though such a way of thinking would have been quite alien to those composers. Beethoven operated within, and felt himself to be part of, a wider European context – quite the opposite, incidentally, of Schubert, who was a Viennese composer from top to toe, yet whose compositions were at the same level as Beethoven's.

SEVEN

AA: This goes to show yet again how right the EU was to choose Beethoven's choral setting of Schiller's Ode to Joy as its hymn, thereby highlighting the European dimension of Beethoven's music! Which brings me to the next question: Did Beethoven belong to any movement? Did he have any lodestars? A guru even? What was his credo?

JA: His deafness alone was sufficient reason for Beethoven not to join any association. But he most certainly did have lodestars. Napoleon was, without doubt, a political one, even though Beethoven was bitterly disappointed by Napoleon's coronation as emperor and revoked the dedication of the Third Symphony, which was originally to have been entitled 'Bonaparte'. As for his musical lodestars, those were Handel, whom he came to regard as the greatest composer of all time, and Bach, whose *Well-Tempered Clavier* he had studied with Neefe and whom he once referred to as the 'god of harmony'.

With regard to his 'credo', that would always remain the Freemasons' philosophical religion into which he had been initiated by Neefe. There are three axioms that he copied out from Schiller's essay 'Die Sendung Moses' (The Mission of Moses) and that were considered at the time to be the quintessence of ancient Egyptian wisdom. Beethoven had them framed and mounted under glass and kept them on his desk where he could see them every day: 'I am that which is.' – 'I am everything that is, that was and that will be. No mortal man has lifted my veil.' – 'He is only and solely of Himself, and to this only One all things owe their existence.'

EIGHT

AA: Never mind Egypt and the Freemasons – those three axioms sum up very neatly the credo of a Romantic religion of nature. Apropos of romanticism – in an ode by Keats it says: 'Heard melodies are sweet, but those unheard | Are sweeter.' How may one describe the relationship between heard and unheard music in Beethoven's case? While he always continued to compose, did he not at some point lose his audience?

JA: I am sure Beethoven would have subscribed wholeheartedly to those wonderful verses. Indeed, some melodies in the late string quartets and piano sonatas are of fascinating beauty; we often find in his late works such indications as 'dolce', 'cantabile', 'mit innigster Empfindung' and so on. Perhaps Beethoven, who could no longer hear his own music, was trying to make up for his sensory deficit linguistically by writing in these highly expressive directions for performance. Since he could 'hear' music only in his mind, he wanted to make quite sure that the heart was also involved. The motto of his *Missa Solemnis*: 'Von Herzen – möge es wieder – zu Herzen gehen!' ('From the heart – May it return – to the heart!') surely applies to all his works.

There were moments of happiness in which Beethoven, his deafness notwithstanding, was emotionally at one with his audience. When improvising, Beethoven would enter a state of rapture, moving to tears those listening to him. There are many eyewitness accounts of that. Now Handel, Bach and Mozart were great improvisers, too, but their playing was not described in terms of emotional ecstasy. At the other end of the spectrum, however, we find such extremely harsh works as the *Große Fuge*, op. 133, for string quartet, which proved to be too much for many contemporary listeners.

NINE

AA: How can one account for the truly sacral veneration of this composer? It is frequently said that a 'religion of art' emerged in the nineteenth century – that the old religious ties were replaced by a new form of worship in the 'temples of the Muses', namely theatres, museums and concert halls. Is the veneration of Beethoven also a religious phenomenon?

JA: That is one aspect in which Beethoven and Handel resemble each other. Both were revered like gods in their lifetime – there is no other way of putting it. After they died, this veneration very much took on elements of religious worship, both in England in Handel's case and in Germany and Austria in Beethoven's. Music does, after all, affect the human soul directly, without the mediation of language and intervention of the intellect. That may be one reason why composers in particular command such intense veneration – one has only to think of Bach, Mozart and Wagner.

TEN

AA: The link between music and emotion is very important and also very old. It is precisely for that reason that music is a central vehicle for the communication of religious traditions and messages. In an age of increasing secularization, music itself becomes, if you like, a medium and object of religious experience. And now for my last question: of the composers who came after Beethoven, which one is most indebted to him?

JA: Well, there's the rub – none of them! They are *all* overshadowed by him, especially the composers of symphonies. But of course music after Beethoven is inconceivable without Beethoven. In fact, they are all his successors, whether they seek to cut themselves loose from his legacy or to overcome it.

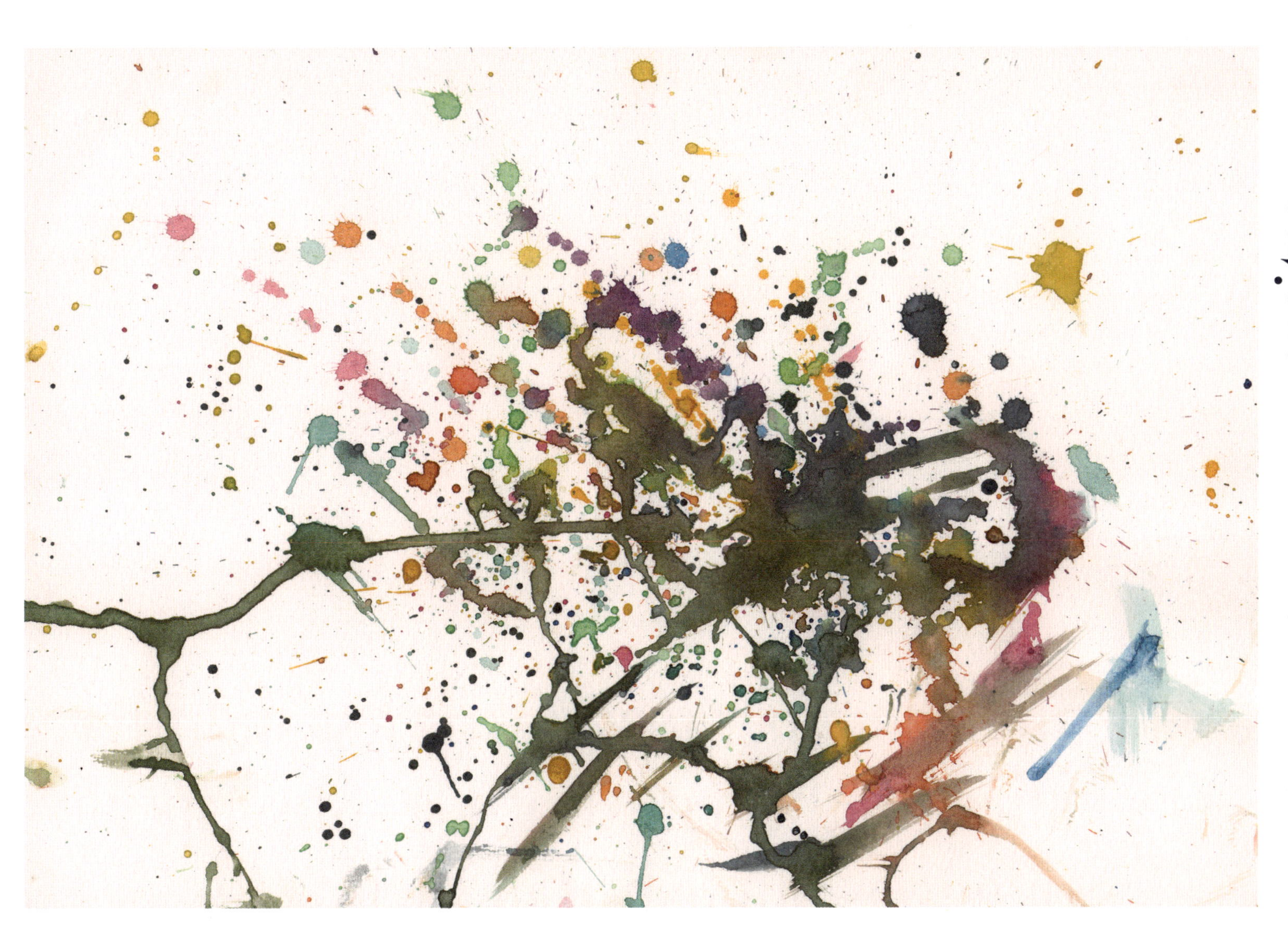

MAGDALENA GRAUSAM

Piano Sonata No. 23 in F minor, op. 57, 'Appassionata'
2019

BIRGIT LODES

Messiah with Spider and Sword: Stories about Beethoven’s Childhood

In September 1827, just a few months after Beethoven’s death, a subscription offer was published in Vienna for ‘Ludwig van Beethoven’s biography, based on original materials and authentic documents’, advertised as the ‘complete life story of our artist-hero’, who is further on also referred to as the ‘great hero of music’.[1]

The term 'hero' denotes a then relatively new concept that was developed in Beethoven's lifetime; it was to be promoted ever more emphatically after his death and in the course of the nineteenth century,[2] and to this day it is very much alive – the notion of Beethoven as the notoriously nonconformist hero who is familiar with suffering, yet who succeeds in overcoming and thereby creatively transmuting it. His 'divine' works – especially those with a 'per aspera ad astra' narrative, such as the Fifth or the Ninth Symphony, but also works like the Third Symphony, 'Eroica'[3] – are deemed to substantiate that notion. Moreover, Beethoven's biographers discovered elements of nonconformism, even quirkiness, in his life, alongside suffering and struggle – one has only to think of the *Heiligenstadt Testament* of 1802. However, when writing the biography of a famous hero it is necessary to relate episodes from his childhood, too, which naturally leads us to ask about the circumstances of that stage in Beethoven's life. Providing relevant answers was, and even today remains, no easy task, especially since the source material is very scanty: in contrast to, say, Mozart's childhood, there are practically no sources of a private nature on Beethoven's first thirteen years. None of the more extensive accounts by contemporaries were written down until after the composer's death, that is, until after the passage of at least fifty years.[4] The lapse of time since the events narrated left its mark upon these accounts, as indeed did the knowledge of Beethoven's subsequent personal and artistic trajectory.

THE LONGING FOR AN IMAGE FROM THE MESSIANIC HERO'S CHILDHOOD

In the Christian Museum in Esztergom there is a silver snuffbox with a portrait miniature on the lid that is meant to depict the three-year-old Beethoven (fig. 1). The caption reads: 'L. v. B. / 3 Jahre', while the painter's signature on the bottom right, partly covered by the frame, gives a (putative?) date of origin: '... pinx. 1773'.[5] The text on the inside of

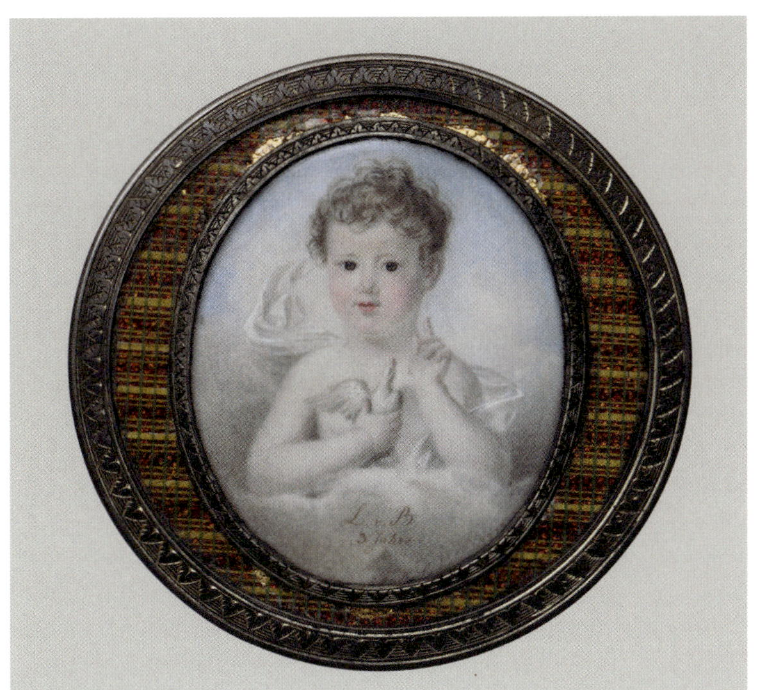

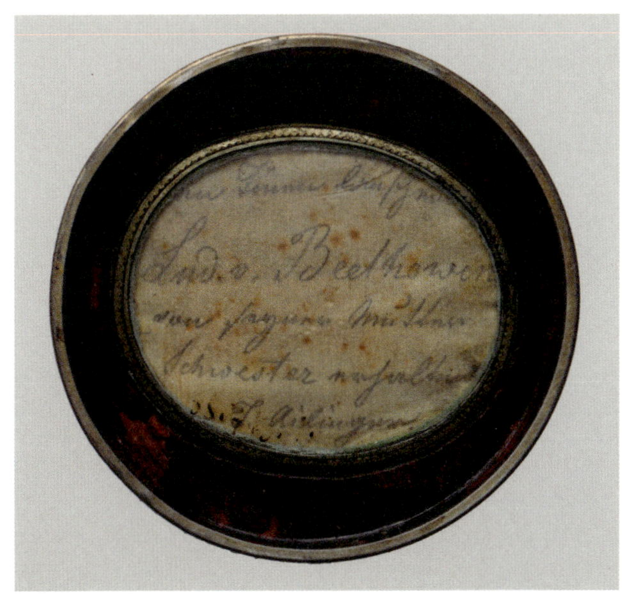

Fig. 1a, b [Anon.], *Portrait of Beethoven at the age of three*, early 19th century. Miniature painting in tempera on the lid of a silver-mounted snuffbox. Esztergom, Keresztény Múzeum, inv. no. 55.719.1. From the estate of the Hungarian-born Mileva Nákó, Princess San Marco

the lid explicitly states the iconographic scheme and the picture's alleged provenance: '[d]en Tönen lauschen[d?] / Lud v. Beethowen / von seyner Mutter / Schwester erhalten / I. Aichinger' ('Harkening to music / Lud v. Beethowen / received from his maternal aunt / I. Aichinger'). Since an obscure boy aged three would hardly have been painted in this way, László Zolnay, who was the first to bring this picture to light in 1971, concluded that it was not an authentic portrait but, rather, 'an early fruit of the Viennese cult of Beethoven' dating from the first third of the nineteenth century.[6] Like all portraits that purport to show Beethoven as a child, this one, too, owes its origins to an idealized, retrospective view from the vantage point of a later age.

Furthermore, it is worth noting that this miniature painting makes no reference whatsoever to music: instead, the portrait operates with the iconographic attributes of a memorial picture or perhaps even of images of Jesus.[7] For instance, the dove held by the boy in his right hand[8] and his nakedness except for a cloth are reminiscent of well-known, traditional depictions of the infant Jesus (cf. fig. 2). The other (in this case left) hand is suggestive of the sign of blessing made by Christ, though here it has been transformed into a more rhetorical gesture, the finger pointing skywards to indicate upward motion and more especially the path to heaven. Indeed, clouds frequently appear in the memorial pictures painted around 1800 to commemorate those who had died in infancy or youth.

Thus, in the early nineteenth century Beethoven was portrayed as an infant in a manner that draws on the features of traditional depictions of Jesus. It is even possible that an existing memorial picture was passed off as a portrait of Beethoven. At any rate, the portrait was furnished with bogus provenance information, for none of the sisters of Beethoven's mother, who died in 1787, survived into adulthood. The iconographic scheme tells us a lot about how the composer was perceived at the time: so natural was it to see in him a great and god-like artist-hero and a messianic Saviour that it was pos-

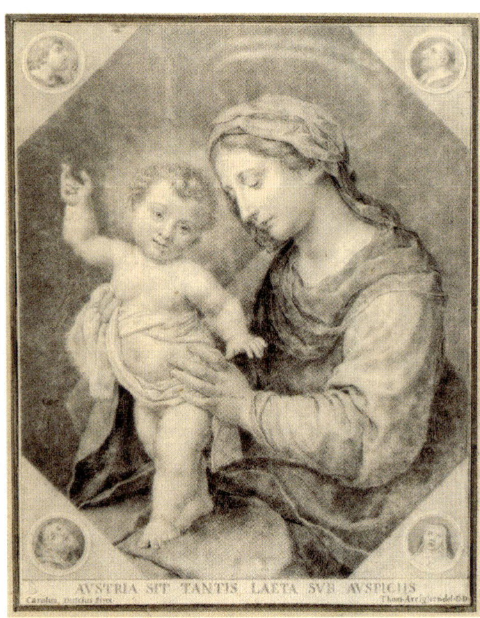

Fig. 2 Tommaso Arrighetti, *Madonna with the Christ Child Blessing*, c.1760/70. Chalk drawing, 28 x 21.7 cm. Vienna, Albertina, inv. no. 1319

sible for the absence of portraits from his childhood to be made up for by something resembling an image of Jesus.

While the modern conception of a hero entails, among other elements, the hero's transfiguration into a 'bringer of salvation',[9] it is interesting that Beethoven himself was the first to draw parallels every so often between his fate and that of Jesus. It was above all after his death, though, that the sacralization of Beethoven became a compelling trope, even leading to a pictorial representation of his birth that was modelled on the Nativity.[10]

THE SPIDER AND MUSIC, OR: THE SOLITUDE OF A GENIUS

Even in Beethoven's lifetime, an anecdote about his childhood was published that, to a certain degree, has endured into our own times:

> Anecdote.
> In the letters on the effect of music on animals (in the 19th and 20th issues of the first volume of this periodical), spiders are disposed of so summarily that I shall take the liberty of repeating some anecdotes about them from Quatremère Disjonval's *Araneology*.[11]
> Even at the age of seven, a boy destined by his parents for a musical career was already astonishing his listeners with his violin-playing. He would normally practise in a small attic room, all by himself – though not quite all by himself, since the garret also sheltered an uncommonly large house-spider. The boy noticed that the spider would abandon its web and draw near to him as soon as he started playing on his violin. It did so every time. Little by little, performer and listener got so used to each other that the latter would leave its corner and crawl at first onto the stand, then from there onto the artist and, finally, onto his bowing arm. The boy's interest in this phenomenon played no small part in spurring him to diligence, thereby helping him to make progress. One day, his aunt, who had taken the place of his late mother, led a visitor into the attic who was to appraise the young violinist's talent. The boy started playing; the spider did not fail to show up and duly crawled onto his arm. At that moment, the boy's aunt stepped forward, knocked the spider down onto the floor with a slipper and instantly trampled it to death. The horror-stricken youth fainted on the spot.
> (That boy artist is now the so famous *Beethoven*. Anyone wishing to verify the truth of this episode may make enquiries of his teacher at the time, Citizen *Le Mierre* in Paris.) (sent by D. Hager from Altenburg).[12]

This anecdote, which conveys so vividly Beethoven's sensitivity, his ability – already manifest in his childhood – to speak through music and, above all, his solitariness, was very often recounted in early biographies of the composer and in encyclopaedia articles about him. Interestingly, at the very beginning it makes no bones about its French provenance and source. It is evident that the above-mentioned character traits would fit in well with the image of any famous musician or composer. As time went by, the pre-existing spider anecdote was frequently adapted to fit Beethoven more closely – for example, by introducing a mother instead of an aunt, dropping the Parisian teacher and even having Beethoven smash his violin to pieces at the end, as a result of which he became a pianist.[13]

The spider motif is no fortuitous detail in the legend of an artist. Indeed, it traces its origins to antiquity, when spiders were regarded as a token of true art because they would, allegedly, crawl over an artwork (say, a still-life) if it looked deceptively enough like the real thing.[14] Moreover, according to the Grimm brothers' German dictionary, it is said precisely 'of someone who is extremely isolated and forlorn' that 'he keeps company with spiders'.[15] Legend thus has it that the early death of the great Mannheim composer Anton Fils was due to his 'having bizarrely taken it into his head' to 'eat spiders'.[16] On the other hand, the solitary state is a prerequisite for being able to follow one's 'genius', that is, 'an innermost divine voice in the heart that can reveal to us what is secret'.[17]

With its tropes of sensitivity and solitariness, the above anecdote offered two essential qualities that a nineteenth-century musician and composer marked by the stamp of genius simply had to possess. While these traits were by no means restricted to Beethoven, they were assiduously deployed – especially after his death – to build up his image and thus established themselves as a counterpoint of sorts to the narrative of the outgoing, universally liked wunderkind à la Wolfgang Amadeus Mozart.[18]

While the content of the spider anecdote is generic, the point in time at which it came into being is characteristic: in June 1800, shortly after Beethoven's first benefit concert ('Akademie') on 2 April 1800 had won him public acclaim as a performer and composer. The relevant periodicals reported ecstatically on that event (with the *Allgemeine musikalische Zeitung*, for example, describing it as 'probably the most interesting benefit concert held in a long time'[19]), and in the musical community there was thereafter not a shadow of a doubt that Beethoven was the rightful heir of the Classical composers Mozart and Haydn. This new aura also resulted in increased demand for Beethoven's works among publishers; in June 1801, he was to observe with pride how each of his works was coveted by 'six or seven publishers, nay more'.[20]

However, his growing fame and the increasing demand for his works gave rise not merely to anecdotes: it was at this very time that the first portrait of Beethoven, then aged twenty-nine, was commissioned. The likeness of the fêted composer, based on a drawing by Gandolph Ernst Stainhauser von Treuberg, was published in 1801 both in Vienna and (as a re-engraving) in Leipzig; a further re-engraving appeared in a supplement to the *Allgemeine musikalische Zeitung* in 1804.[21] Furthermore, various objects of everyday use were manufactured bearing the portrait (see fig. 3).

That the story of Beethoven as a solitary boy practising in an attic room was still bearing pictorial fruit at the end of the nineteenth century is shown by a lithograph by Théodore Gérard that appeared in 1894 in a periodical intended for French-speaking children (fig. 4). Even in the biographical texts of antiquity it had been standard practice not to relate specific details from a person's childhood but to project back into those early years whatever had come to be typically associated with that person in his or her later life: a case in point is Hercules strangling serpents in his cradle.[22] This practice continued in biographies of artists well into modern times. Shortly before the Beethoven lithograph was printed, a children's picture-book about Napoleon had appeared with, as its very first illustration, an image showing the hero alone, without his siblings (as in Beethoven's case), and, what is more, sitting symbolically on a lion's skin in the room where he has just been born, which is hung with tapestries depicting Homeric heroes. Isolation has always been the hallmark of a hero genius – a familiar trope not least thanks to the stories about the childhood of Jesus of Nazareth.[23]

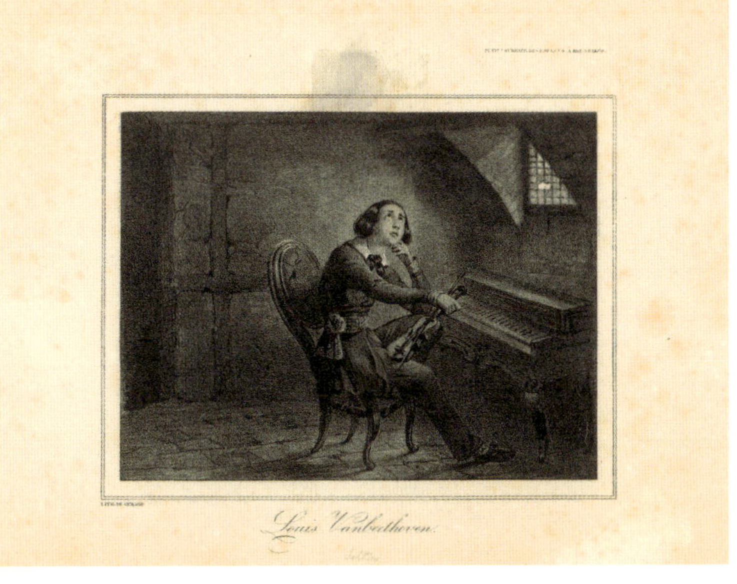

Fig. 4 Théodore Gérard, *Beethoven as a Boy in an Attic Room of his Parents' House*, mid-19th century. Lithograph from *Petit Courrier des Enfants à Bruxelles*, 2/11 (1894), plate before col. 481

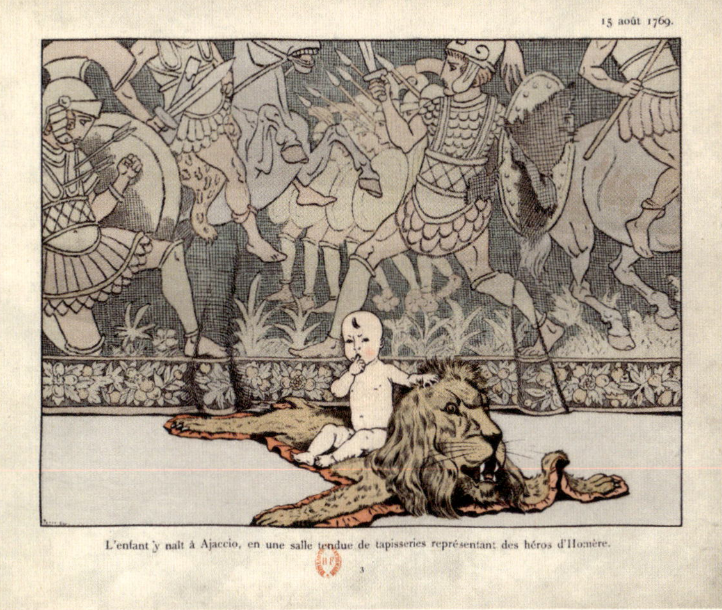

Fig. 5 Jacques Onfroy de Bréville, *The Newborn Napoleon in his Birth Room*, from Jules de Marthold and Jacques Onfroy de Bréville, *Le Grand Napoleon des Petits Enfants* (Paris, 1893), 3

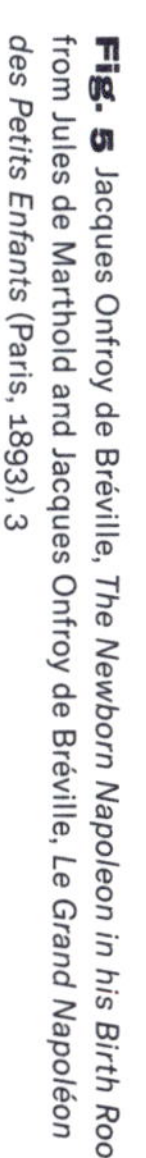

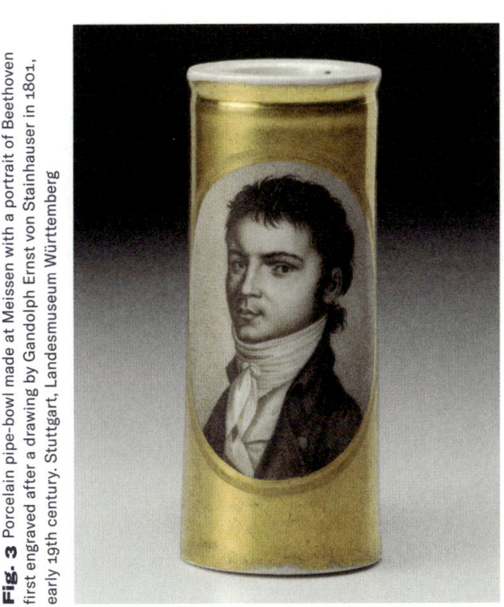

Fig. 3 Porcelain pipe-bowl made at Meissen with a portrait of Beethoven first engraved after a drawing by Gandolph Ernst von Stainhauser in 1801, early 19th century. Stuttgart, Landesmuseum Württemberg

CLUES ABOUT BEETHOVEN'S CHILDHOOD

Anecdotes and legends – and the associated visual representations – are therefore clearly not a reliable means of establishing true facts about the lives of heroes, especially from their childhood years, of which so little is known. It is ultimately irrelevant to probe the truth content of such stories,[24] since they either fall into the pattern of typical artist legends that are almost lacking in individual traits or they retrospectively project onto childhood the idealized notions of a later epoch.

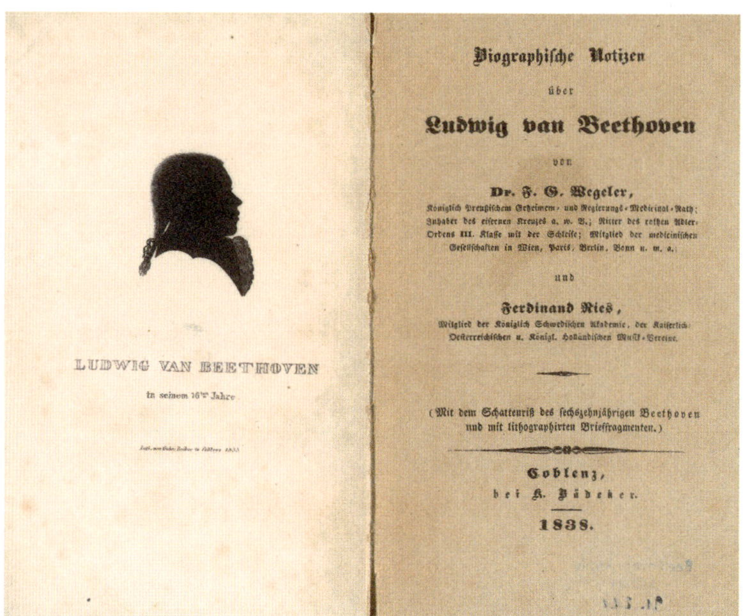
LUDWIG VAN BEETHOVEN

in seinem 16ten Jahre

Biographische Notizen

über

Ludwig van Beethoven

von

Dr. F. G. Wegeler,

Königlich Preußischem Geheimem- und Regierungs-Medicinal-Rath; Inhaber des eisernen Kreuzes a. w. B.; Ritter des rothen Adler-Ordens III. Klasse mit der Schleife; Mitglied der medicinischen Gesellschaften in Wien, Paris, Berlin, Bonn u. m. a.

und

Ferdinand Ries,

Mitglied der Königlich Schwedischen Akademie, der Kaiserlich-Oesterreichischen u. Königl. Holländischen Musik-Vereine.

(Mit dem Schattenriß des sechszehnjährigen Beethoven und mit lithographirten Brieffragmenten.)

Coblenz,
bei K. Bädeker.

1838.

And yet some original documents have survived that do enable us to gain an insight into certain aspects of Beethoven's childhood. There is, for example, the record of a princely payment made after the twelve-year-old Ludwig had performed at the court of Prince Willem of Orange-Nassau at The Hague (where many years earlier the ten-year-old Mozart had also starred) – one of the few attempts by the boy's family to exhibit him, Mozart-like, as a touring wunderkind.[25] There are also various newspaper reports about his first performances as a pianist, the publication of his first works and more besides.[26] The events on which contemporary sources shed light revolve mostly around the site of Beethoven's primary initiation into social and musical life, namely the Electoral court of Bonn, where Beethoven grew up in the tradition of a court musician's family – at first under Elector Maximilian Friedrich and then, from 1784 onwards, Elector Maximilian Franz. Beethoven's grandfather had been a distinguished bass singer in the Electoral choir and had also served as Kapellmeister; his father had been a tenor there; and his mother, Maria Magdalena, was the daughter of a head cook at the court of the Archbishop-Elector of Trier, where the Bonn *Hofkapelle* often performed. Ludwig's earliest teachers were likewise court employees. In 1782, at the age of eleven, he himself entered service in the *Hofkapelle*, at first on an unpaid basis and then from 1784 as a regularly appointed court musician. As an organist and viola player he had many different responsibilities, acquiring in the process the most varied and valuable musical experience.[27] Naturally, Ludwig's brothers Caspar Carl and Nicolaus Johann also received a musical education.[28]

A picture of Beethoven (fig. 6) has even survived from these eminently formative early years as court musician: it is the first and only authentic portrait from his Bonn period (and the only one before the above-mentioned 1801 portrait that was reproduced on a pipe-bowl). It shows Beethoven in the gala uniform worn on Sundays and feast days. The master-baker Gottfried Fischer describes it as follows, noting also the mandatory sword:

> Sea-green tail-coat; short green breeches with buckles; white or black silk stockings; shoes with black bows; white silk waistcoat with floral pattern and flap pockets; chapeau; the waistcoat trimmed with genuine gold cord; hair worn in curls with a pigtail; cocked hat; sword worn under his left arm, with a silver belt.[29]

It strikes me as symptomatic that this portrait, despite being the earliest and the only one from the first twenty-nine years of Beethoven's life, is hardly ever reproduced for public consumption. The role of a court musician is after all not the one that we (wish to) principally associate with Beethoven. Rather, what springs to mind when we think of 'our' Beethoven – the prototype of the great hero-artist of the nineteenth century – is the messianic and heroic, but also solitary and suffering, composer. And that image is served far better and more satisfyingly by legends and anecdotes.

CONCLUSION

Messianic infant, musically gifted animal lover, lonely hero, suffering conqueror – and dutiful court musician: this ragbag of tropes and narratives conveyed by contemporary images and anecdotes about Beethoven as a child provides an instructive compendium of individual cases that can help to shed light on essential aspects of the biographical genre as such, and of the composer's childhood in particular. Each epoch fashions its own image of Beethoven's childhood – an image that, owing to the meagre extant sources, depends very much on later speculation. In the process, even hard facts can be construed in the most diverse ways, and certain features are simply dismissed altogether because they do not fit in with the preconceived image that is typical of its time.

The above-mentioned processes are most clearly noticeable in early biographical material, where it was still a question of inventing images and finding suitable tropes by trial and error. However, we also encounter them in the later, source-based biographies. To give just one example: Beethoven's father Johann, who throughout the nineteenth century had been portrayed in an almost exclusively negative light, was rehabilitated in Ludwig Schiedermair's biography in accordance with the tenets of racial theory.[30] (In fact, as a result of excessive drinking, Johann van Beethoven had been unable to meet his professional obligations in the later years of his life.) In 1810, the rumour was even set afloat that Ludwig van Beethoven was the illegitimate son of the King of Prussia;[31] and it is a stock element in legends about artists to use mysteriously obscure origins and disavowal of the biological father to prove that a given subject is of more exalted, royal descent.[32]

The most recent biographies, fictional accounts and films about Beethoven of course also transmit tropes, which occasionally – and this is

Fig. 6 Joseph Neesen, *Beethoven at the age of sixteen*, silhouette. This has survived only as a lithograph by the 'Becker brothers' on the title page of the book by Wegeler and Ries, where the caption 'in his 16th year' is given: Franz Gerhard Wegeler and Ferdinand Ries, *Biographische Notizen über Ludwig van Beethoven* (Coblenz, 1838)

what makes the situation particularly exciting – are derived from areas that are quite different from those of the nineteenth century: from, say, psychology, cultural studies or gender studies. Significantly, despite the rejection of hero-worship now generally characteristic of biographical writing, even the latest biographies of Beethoven continue to resound with the main recurring theme from the nineteenth century, namely, the motif of the solitary artist who suffers yet triumphs.

Relaying and adapting stock elements on the one hand, establishing new constructs on the other – both these are in the nature of biographical texts and both processes make biographies come alive. As a result, we will ourselves no doubt have occasion, over the years, to revise our mental picture of Beethoven's life – almost certainly including his childhood – in some way or other.

1 [Ludwig van Beethovens Biographie nach Original-Materialien und authentischen Urkunden ... die ganze Lebensschilderung unsers Kunst-Heroen ... diesen großen Tonhelden...] 'Herausgegeben von mehreren Freunden und Verehrern des Verblichenen.' ('Published by a number of friends and admirers of the deceased'), in *Archiv für Geschichte, Statistik, Literatur und Kunst*, 18 (1827), 651. The biography was never published.

2 See Melanie Unseld, *Biographie und Musikgeschichte. Wandlungen biographischer Konzepte in Musikkultur und Musikhistoriographie* (Cologne, 2014), particularly 244–87.

3 See, for example, Scott Burnham's study with the telling title *Beethoven Hero* (Princeton, 1995).

4 The standard sources on Beethoven's childhood are: Franz Gerhard Wegeler and Ferdinand Ries, *Biographische Notizen über Ludwig van Beethoven* (Coblenz, 1838; with a supplement by Wegeler in 1845); and Gottfried Fischer's memoir, which is based on the reminiscences of his sister Cäcilie (written down from around 1838 to the mid-1850s) and has been published by Margot Wetzstein as *Familie Beethoven im kurfürstlichen Bonn. Neuauflage nach den Aufzeichnungen des Bonner Bäckermeisters Gottfried Fischer* (Bonn, 2006).

5 The surname probably reads 'Ludwig' or 'Ludvig'. (László Zolnay had suggested Adalbert Suchy as the artist – an attribution that now seems untenable for stylistic reasons, among others.) I am grateful to Patrick Fiska and Brigitte Huck for their expert opinions. The item awaits a thorough investigation *in situ*.

6 László Zolnay, 'Ein unbekanntes, Beethoven als Kind darstellendes Porträt', in: *Studia Musicologica Academiae Scientiarum Hungaricae*, 13 (1971), 307–10 (esp. 310).

7 I am grateful to Werner Telesko, Dagmar Eichberger and Michael Viktor Schwarz for their helpful suggestions.

8 Cf., for example, the so-called Admont Madonna (c.1300) or the Merciful Infant Jesus in the former Poor Clares' Convent of Our Lady of the Angels (Klarissen-Kloster St. Maria, Königin der Engel) in Vienna.

9 See, for example, Werner Telesko, *Napoleon Bonaparte. Der 'moderne Held' und die bildende Kunst 1799–1815* (Vienna, 1998), especially the chapter 'Napoleon als neuer "Heilsbringer"' (Napoleon as a new 'bringer of salvation'), 174–216.

10 Friedrich Geselschap, *Beethoven's Birth*, c.1895 (watercolour study for a painting that was never executed); additional material may be found in the exhibition catalogue *Mythos Beethoven*, ed. Rainer Cadenbach (Bonn, 1986), particularly in the chapter 'Sakralisierung', 99–138; ibid., 114, where there is also a reproduction of the watercolour.

11 The reference is to the treatise by the French physicist Denis-Bernard Quatremère d'Isjonval (also spelt Disjonval) entitled *Araneologie oder Naturgeschichte der Spinnen* (Frankfurt, 1798).

12 *Allgemeine musikalische Zeitung*, 2 (1800), cols. 653–54.

13 As retold by Wilhelm Christian Müller in 'Etwas über Ludwig van Beethoven', *Allgemeine musikalische Zeitung*, 29 (1827), cols. 34554 (346–47).

14 See, for example, Ernst Kris and Otto Kurz, *Die Legende vom Künstler. Ein geschichtlicher Versuch* (Vienna, 1934), 17.

15 ['er hält umgang mit den spinnen' sagt man von einem, der im höchsten grade vereinsamt, verlassen ist] Jacob Grimm and Wilhelm Grimm, entry for 'Spinne' (spider) in *Deutsches Wörterbuch*, http://woerterbuchnetz.de/cgi-bin/WBNetz/wbgui_py?sigle=DWB [last accessed: 14 Nov 2019].

16 [sein bizarrer Einfall, Spinnen zu essen] Christian Friedrich Daniel Schubart, *Ideen zu einer Ästhetik der Tonkunst* (Vienna, 1806), 141.

17 [eine innerste göttliche stimme im herzen, die uns geheimes offenbaren kann] Grimm and Grimm, entry for 'Genie' (genius) in *Deutsches Wörterbuch*, URL as in n. 15 [last accessed: 14 Nov 2019].

18 See the recent study by Jonas Traudes, *Musizierende 'Wunderkinder'. Adoration und Observation in der Öffentlichkeit um 1800* (Vienna, 2018).

19 [wahrscheinlich die interessanteste Akademie seit langer Zeit] *Allgemeine musikalische Zeitung*, 2 (1800), col. 49.

20 [Auch habe ich auf jede Sache 6, 7 Verleger und noch mehr.] Letter of 29 June 1801, quoted from Ludwig van Beethoven, *Briefwechsel. Gesamtausgabe*, ed. Sieghard Brandenburg, 8 vols. (Munich, 1996–98), i, 79, no. 65.

21 *Allgemeine musikalische Zeitung*, 6 (1804), 15 Feb. On this portrait, see also Silke Bettermann, *Beethoven im Bild. Die Darstellung des Komponisten in der bildenden Kunst vom 18. bis zum 21. Jahrhundert* (Bonn, 2012), 134–37.

22 Kris and Kurz, *Die Legende vom Künstler*, particularly 17, 41.

23 See Albrecht Koschorke, *Die Heilige Familie und ihre Folgen. Ein Versuch* (Frankfurt, 2000), 20.

24 See Kris and Kurz, *Die Legende vom Künstler*, 20, and Unseld, *Biographie und Musikgeschichte*, 117–19 (where the point is made even more emphatically).

25 Michael Ladenburger, 'Ludwig van Beethoven – ein typisches Wunderkind?', in the exhibition catalogue *Beethoven und andere Wunderkinder*, ed. Ingrid Bodsch, Otto Biba and Ingrid Fuchs (Bonn, 2002), 11–28 (esp. 15, 17).

26 John D. Wilson, 'From the Chapel to the Theatre to the Akademiensaal: Beethoven's Musical Apprenticeship at the Bonn Electoral Court, 1784–1792', *Beethoven Studies*, 4 (Cambridge, 2020), ed. David Wyn Jones and Keith Chapin, 1–23 (forthcoming).

27 For details of the repertoire of works that were performed at the court, see the results of the research project 'The Music Library of Elector Maximilian Franz' (coordinated by the author of the present essay) at: https://musikwissenschaft.univie.ac.at/maxfranz.

28 The Twelve Minuets, WoO 12, which were previously attributed to Beethoven, have been identified as being by his brother Caspar Carl, who, in addition to composing, was also active as a piano teacher until 1800.

29 [See grüne Frackrock, grüne, kurze Hoß mit Schnalle, weiße p. oder schwarze Seide Strümpf, Schuhe mit schwarze Schlöpp, weiße Seide geblümde West mit Klapptaschen, mit Shappoe, das West mit ächte Goldene Kort umsetz, Fisirt mit Locken und Hahrzopp, Klackhud, unter linken Arm sein Dägen an der linke seite mit einer Silberne Koppel.] Wetzstein, *Familie Beethoven im kurfürstlichen Bonn*, 76. The translation of the quotation is based on Martin Geck, *Beethoven*, transl. Anthea Bell (London, 2003), 6.

30 Ludwig Schiedermair, *Der junge Beethoven* (Leipzig, 1925), but above all the second edition (Weimar, 1939); idem, 'Ludwig van Beethoven. Der große Sohn der Stadt Bonn', *Ewiges Deutschland. Monatsschrift für die deutschen Volksgenossen*, 4 (1939), 266–67.

31 Alexandre-Étienne Choron and François Joseph Fayolle, *Dictionnaire Historique des Musiciens*, i (Paris, 1810–11), 60; likewise in later editions and also in Friedrich Arnold Brockhaus, *Conversations-Lexikon*, from the third (1814) to the seventh edition (1830). Beethoven was aware of the rumour but did not take any action against it. See the entries in his conversation books for the years 1819/20 and an emphatic letter of 28 December 1825 from Franz Gerhard Wegeler to the composer in: Beethoven, *Briefwechsel. Gesamtausgabe*, vi, 196–99 (no. 2100).

32 See Kris and Kurz, *Die Legende vom Künstler*, 58–64; Koschorke, *Die Heilige Familie*, 188–92. Cf. what the Bible tells us about the childhood of Jesus of Nazareth.

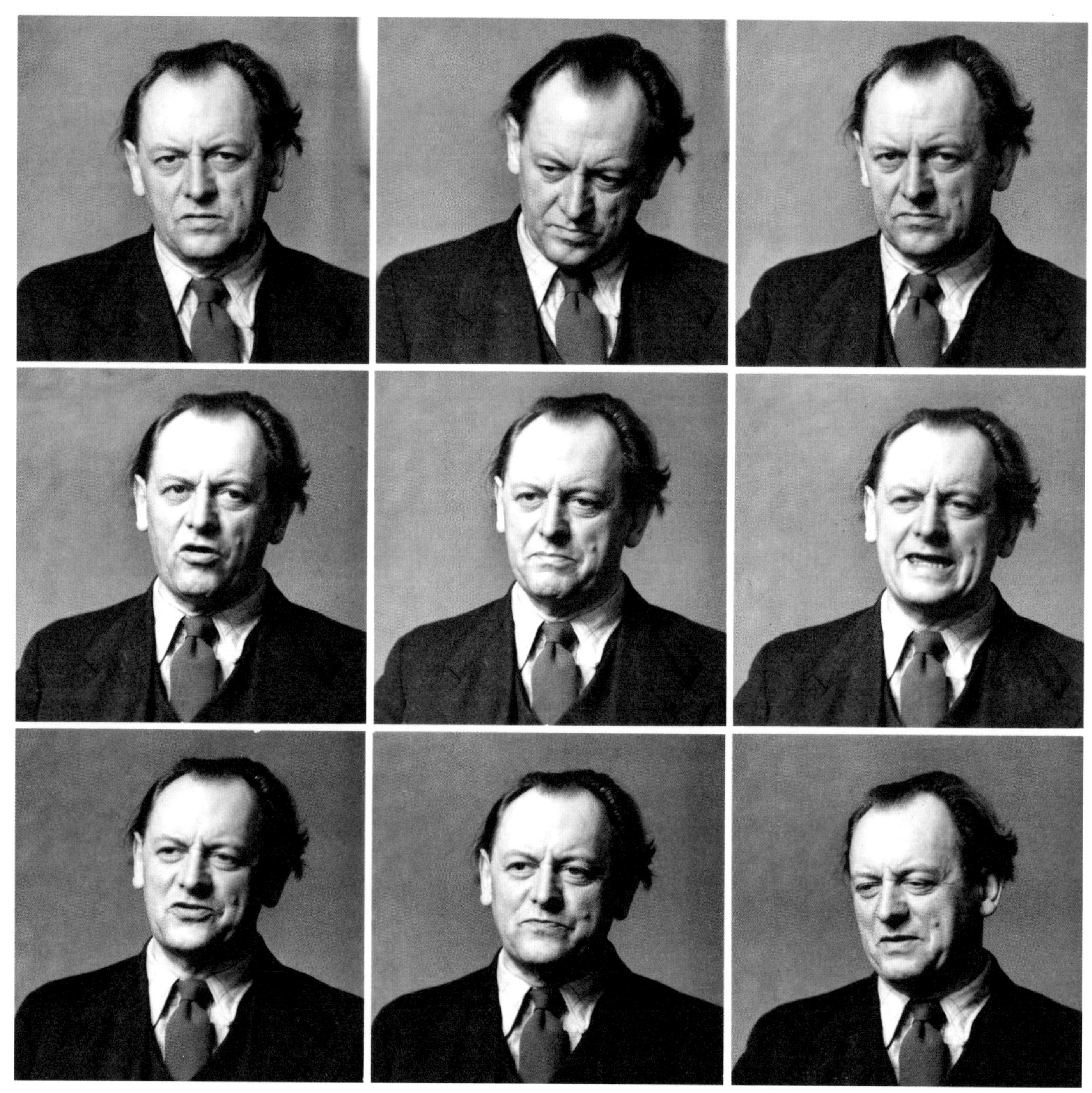

Ursonate is a poem written and performed by Kurt Schwitters that has a similar structure to a classical sonata or symphony. It consists of four movements: First Part, Largo, Scherzo and Presto. Each movement has its own rhythm, theme and tempo, which is to be performed meticulously when the poem is spoken.

ERNST SCHWITTERS

Ur Sonata Performed by Kurt Schwitters [Series I] 1944

SUSANA ZAPKE

Beethoven: A Prophetic Hero of Music and his Devotees

> I am that which is. I am everything that is, that was and that will be. No mortal man has lifted my veil. He is only and solely of Himself, and to this only One all things owe their existence.[1]

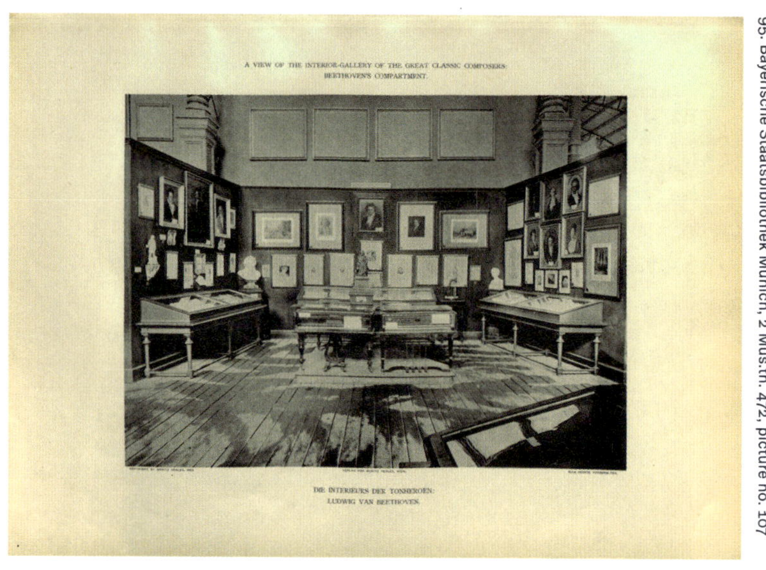

Fig. 1 View into the Beethoven room of the exhibition *Die Intérieurs der Tonheroen*, Vienna 1892. Photograph in: Siegmund Schneider, *Internationale Ausstellung für Musik- und Theaterwesen Wien 1892* (Vienna, 1894), 95. Bayerische Staatsbibliothek Munich, 2 Mus.th. 472, picture no. 107

HEROES OF MUSIC AND THE WORSHIPPERS OF THEIR RELICS

The *Internationale Ausstellung für Musik- und Theaterwesen* (International Exhibition of Music and Theatre) in the Vienna Prater from 7 May to 9 October 1892 exhibited in its combined German and Austro-Hungarian section a choice selection of 'Interiors with the relics of the heroes of music'.[2] Wolfgang A. Mozart, Ludwig van Beethoven, Carl Maria von Weber and Giacomo Meyerbeer, Robert Schumann and Felix Mendelssohn-Bartholdy, Franz Liszt and Richard Wagner were each represented. A single room was dedicated to the relics of Ludwig van Beethoven. Large display cases contained items such as the invitation to his funeral on 29 March 1827, the invitation to the reburial of his earthly remains on 22 June 1888 and numerous sketches of his works including the 'Marcia funebre sulla morte d'un eroe' (from op. 26) and the beginning of a cantata, *God is immaterial.*[3] The Musikverein, distinguished representatives of Viennese aristocracy and individuals such as the Viennese publisher Carl August Artaria had placed a number of manuscripts and objects at the disposal of the exhibition.[4] Two fortepianos that had belonged to Beethoven took up a prominent position in the middle of the room (fig. 1). On the left can be seen the fortepiano from the workshop of Thomas Broadwood in London that was donated to the composer by its maker in 1817. Beethoven had expressed his thanks for this 'honourable gift': 'I will regard it as an altar upon which I will offer my most beautiful spiritual offerings to the god Apollo.'[5] To the right of the Broadwood stands the Érard piano with four pedals from the year 1803, which had initially pleased Beethoven, but after repeated modifications had been declared 'unusable' by the composer.[6]

With this international event the City of Vienna went to the expense of presenting the very first music exhibition, positioning itself officially as the city of music *par excellence.* One day after the opening on Sunday, 8 May 1892, the *Neue Freie Presse* accordingly wrote:

> Music is the second mother tongue of our city. It speaks from the murmurings of her ancient river, weaving its yarn passionately yet tenderly in the river's green tributaries; within its old, grey walls young melodious songs blossom, the air is filled with singing and the playing of instruments. In their graceful poise, our women and girls are the slender carriers of this musical *fluidum* that trembles through all the veins and nerves of the towns on the Danube. The immortal composers, once the envy of all Europe, have long since gone from us, but even if Beethoven no longer storms through our streets with his wild genius, arousing people's minds and hearts, if Mozart and Schubert no longer benignly gild the cramped rooms of the old town houses with the magical glow of their treasures, we are still anointed with a drop of the spirit of these immortals, and their culture remains alive within us.[7]

The emerging *topos* of Vienna as the city of music is exposed here in its purest and most naïve form. Music is revealed in feminine shape, enchanting the senses and nerves of the city dwellers like Klimt's water snakes. These slender women and girls are contrasted with the 'great men' Schubert, Mozart and Beethoven, whose genius must stand proxy for the immortality of a city gilded by their fame. In 1892 Vienna was already looking back into the past, creating the city's image retrospectively. Some years earlier, in 1870 and 1877 respectively, the city had formally celebrated the centenary of Beethoven's birth and the fiftieth anniversary of his death. The many examples of Viennese musical euphoria include

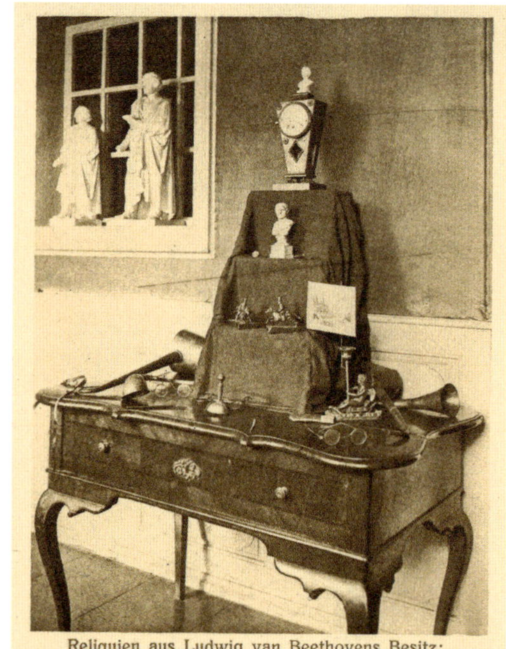

Fig. 2 Relics from Ludwig van Beethoven's personal possessions. Postcard, publishers of the Beethoven-Haus in Bonn. Private collection

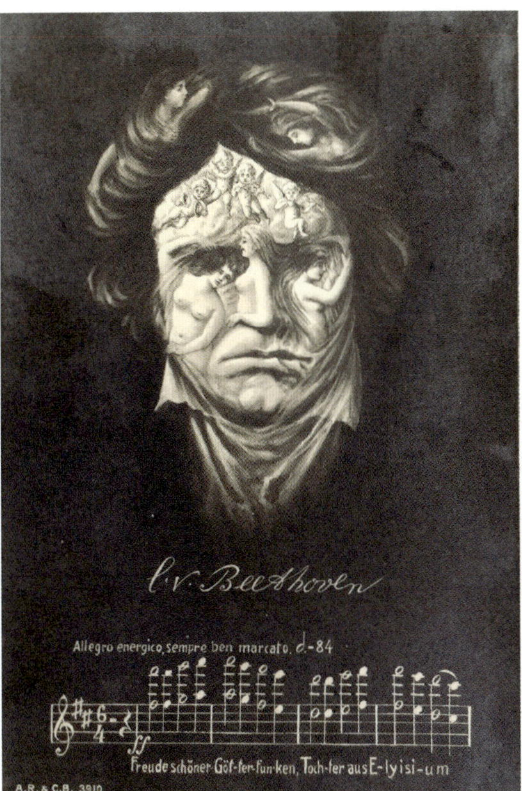

Fig. 3 Ludwig van Beethoven. Postcard, c.1900. Private collection

prominent monuments, such as the statue made by Caspar von Zumbusch following a generous donation from Franz Liszt and unveiled on Beethovenplatz on 1 May 1880.[8] However, the cult of the genius and the worship of art lead not only to the erection of monuments, but also to the diligent collecting of 'relics' – a trait that set in immediately after Beethoven's death and continues to this day (fig. 2).

In his brilliant 1918 dissertation on the religion of genius, Edgar Zilsel, a philosopher of the Vienna Circle, offered the following explanation for this phenomenon:

> It is clearly evident that we treat the relics of our great men – their signatures and locks of hair, their pens and snuff boxes – with a devotion similar to that shown by the Catholic Church to the bones, artefacts and garments of the saints, or by the Greeks to what are presumed to be the bones of Theseus and other mythical heroes. [...] However, not only does the outward form, the ritual of genius worship, resemble that of a religious cult, our reverence towards our figures of genius is also closely related to religious fervour [...].[9]

This ritualized worship of the genius and the reverence associated with it became the corner stone of the concept of a national German culture in which Beethoven was to play a pivotal role. The celebrants of this religious ritual, the worshippers of relics, were the property-owning and educated middle classes (*Bildungsbürgertum*), whose political and economic status was less secure in Germany and Austria than in France, England or Holland. In this respect the cult of genius-worship surrounding Beethoven exercised a compensatory function in that it offered an ideal surface upon which the middle classes could project their own search for social identity. In Beethoven the middle classes also recognized the determined self-made man, the model for achieving independence and social recognition beyond the privileges of class by hard work. From this grew an idealized, male-dominated dialogue *inter pares* between the genius and the bourgeoisie within a society of equal 'great men'.

THE SLEEPWALKER AND REASON

The genius of these great men is often juxtaposed by female figures who take the form of imaginary auspicious figures ensconced upon an Isle of the Blessed to embody the prophetic gaze of genius in a utopian Elysian realm (fig. 3).

To what extremes this transformation of Beethoven's music and its influence into allegory can be taken becomes apparent in the numerous attempts made at pictorial representation of his works. In Alois Kolb's etching *Neunte Sinfonie,* the *transitus* – whether as resurrection in a religious sense or enlightenment in a secular sense – is the central theme of the allegorical transformation of the work. The rise of the somnambulists – a concept that also turns up in Richard Wagner's essay on Beethoven from 1870 – into the kingdom of the clairvoyant is vividly depicted here (fig. 4). 'We now compared the musician's work with the face of the somnambulist

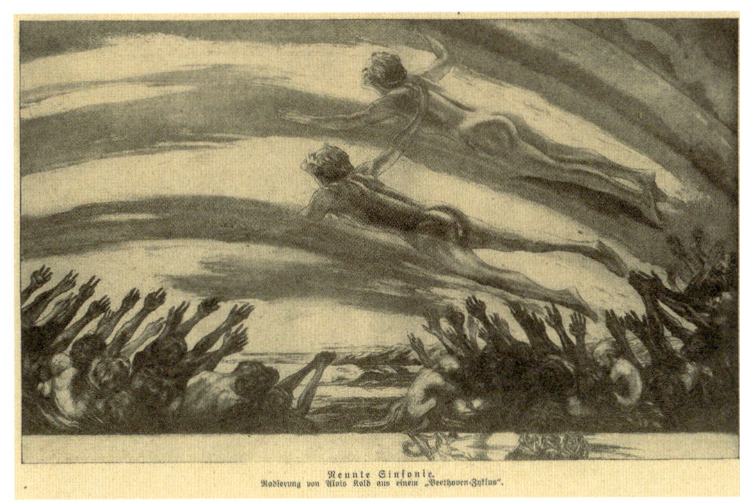

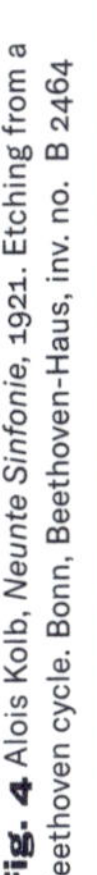
Fig. 4 Alois Kolb, *Neunte Sinfonie*, 1921. Etching from a Beethoven cycle. Bonn, Beethoven-Haus, inv. no. B 2464

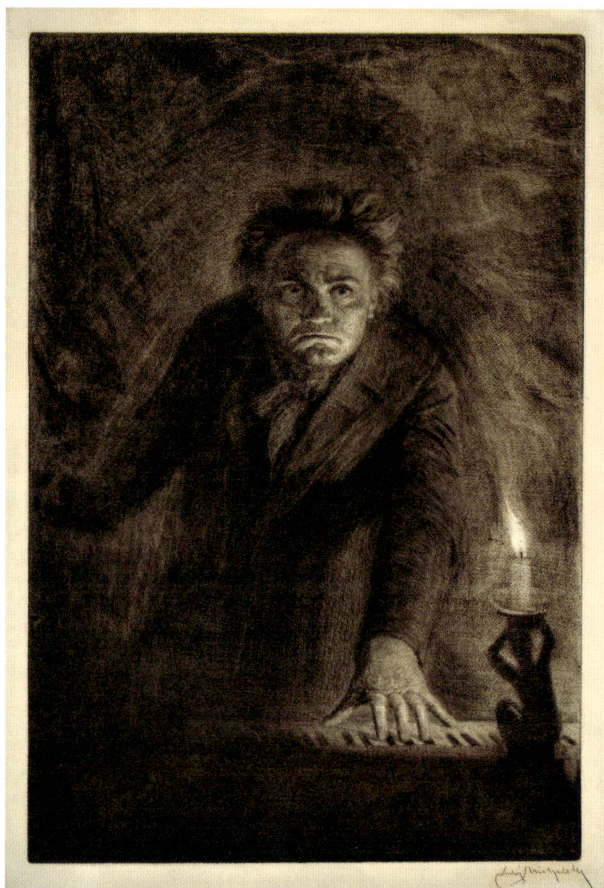

Fig. 5 Ludwig Michalek, *Ludwig van Beethoven*. Etching, 1927. Muggia, Biblioteca Beethoveniana, Collezione Carrino

who has become clairvoyant'[10] is the Wagnerian metaphor that finds its immediate counterpart in Kolb's pair of lovers, rising with closed eyes but prophetic vision into the universe, beneath them a vale of tears filled with desperate figures. The redemptive power of music that divides the world into an earthly realm and a hereafter, a dystopian and a utopian space, is portrayed clearly and concisely. However, the aura of this prophetic vision harbours reverential aspects, a deference towards the unfathomable, the enlightened insight, that is apparent in the physiognomy bestowed upon Beethoven in some portraits (fig. 5). The determined, reverential expression shown in Ludwig Michalek's portrait leads us to the inner character of the man, a spiritual essence is to be read in the physical appearance, much in the tradition of the physiognomic interpreter of the soul Johann Caspar Lavater. Whether with this introspective expression the genius plays simultaneously upon the keyboard of the imagination and of reason – however the latter may be defined – is an open question. In his *Caprichos*, Francisco de Goya y Lucientes proclaims that when reason sleeps, imagination can only give birth to monstrosities,[11] whereas Arthur Schopenhauer describes the sleep of reason as the *conditio* of a somnambulistic musical language that reveals the profound meaning of things: '[...] the composer reveals the innermost essence of the world and pronounces the deepest wisdom in a language that his reason cannot understand'.[12]

In Michalek's portrait, shapes born out of the imagination can be seen in the candlelight surrounding Beethoven's face, emerging more from musical thought than from the chord that has been struck. His piercing gaze has something of the look of the possessed – of someone who does not see music as a frivolous *divertissement*, as an end in itself, but rather as the search for truth, as the language of wisdom. Thus his gaze is turned inwards, like that of a sleepwalker: the somnambulistic state permits insights into the unconscious that would not be possible when awake. And while music is seen in this context as a process that is beyond the grasp of rational understanding, the pictorial allegory serves an attempt at translation that can only lay claim to an approximate, yet never perfect reciprocity.

Certain works of Beethoven such as the 'Moonlight' Sonata – the *Sonata quasi una Fantasia* in C sharp minor, No. 14, op. 27,2 – served much more frequently than others as objects of heightened interpretation. Combined with the motive of the blind girl, the motive of moonlight exactly corresponds to the clairvoyance of the introspective gaze:

'I wish to play her the moonlight that she has not been granted to look upon,' Beethoven is supposed to have said. For in a certain way the blind person is also a sleepwalker, who experiences the world through a unique form of perception in which the sense of hearing is sharpened in order to compensate for the lack of vision (fig. 6).

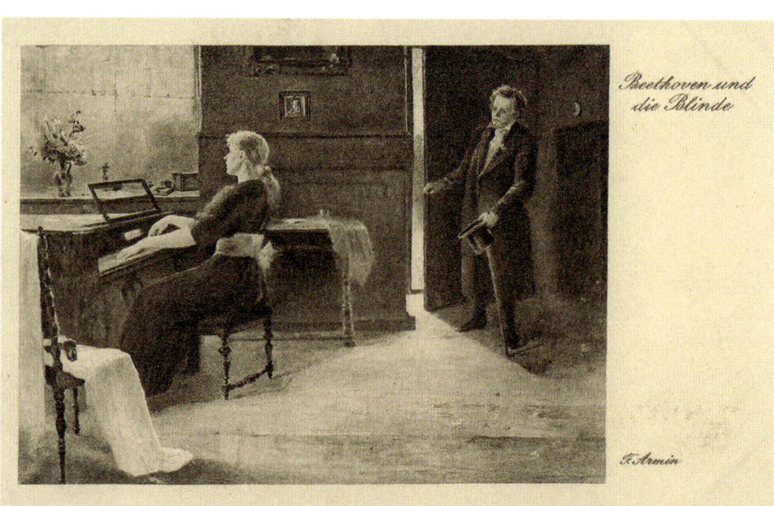

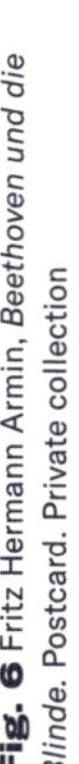

Fig. 6 Fritz Hermann Armin, *Beethoven und die Blinde*. Postcard. Private collection

FAITHFULNESS TO THE ORIGINAL

Beethoven's personality and above all his music appeared alien to his contemporaries. Correspondingly the picture of the misanthropist, the reclusive artist vacillating between genius and madness has been a constant throughout the whole history of the reception of his works. Behind the obsessive attempts at an interpretation of his appearance, behind the repeated descriptions of his character that hang on every wrinkle in his face, every nuance of hair colour and gesture, behind the sometimes very basic attempts at explaining his works allegorically, lies the elusive wish to appropriate Beethoven's spiritual world. No other composer has been subject to such a wealth of projection in the sense of a spiritual, demagogic interpretation of the world. He is a chosen one, a martyr, a Christ on the Mount of Olives, a revolutionary artist, a frustrated lover, a morose *citoyen*, a sensitive, suffering individual: 'For you, poor Beethoven, there is no external happiness, you must create everything within yourself, only in the ideal world will you find joy,'[13] Beethoven himself wrote in 1810, having just turned forty.

The 'ideal world' of his music is, as Mauricio Kagel has already implied, an immaterial category that can ensure continuity and living topicality only through an individual appropriation of the work – through the subjectivity of the musician. In his composition *Ludwig van*, which was premiered in 1970, the year of the second centenary of Beethoven's birth, Kagel appears to be suggesting a reversal of the concept of faithfulness to the original. Faithful are those who dedicate themselves unquestioningly to a work's alterity, and reproduce the distillate of Beethoven's music through the prism of their own imaginative and expressive power.

1 These three inscriptions from an Egyptian temple allegedly lay framed on Beethoven's desk. See Ludwig Nohl, *Aus Beethoven's Leben* (Leipzig, n. d.), 546.

2 [Intérieurs mit den Reliquien der Tonheroen.] See Siegmund Schneider, *Die internationale Ausstellung für Musik- und Theaterwesen Wien 1892* (Vienna, 1894), 87–164, regarding Beethoven: 95–100.

3 While it was not possible to confirm the existence of this cantata at hand of a list of works, it was listed thus in the exhibition catalogue. The fragment was a loan from Sir George Grove from London. The text is taken from Brahman literature and is written in his conversation notebooks; ibid, register of photographic reproductions, n. p.

4 See Theophil Antonicek, *Die Internationale Ausstellung für Musik- und Theaterwesen, Wien 1892*, Vienna 2013, http://www.dtoe.at/Texte/ausst92haupt.pdf [last accessed: 11 Oct 2019].

5 [Ich werde es als einen Altar sehen, auf dem ich dem Gott Apollo meine schönsten geistigen Opfergaben darbringen werde.] 'Beethovens Beziehungen zu Großbritannien. Der Klavierbauer Thomas Broadwood', ed. Beethoven-Haus Bonn, online: https://da.beethoven.de/sixcms/list.php?page=museum_internetausstellung_seiten_de&sv%5binternetausstellung.id%5d=31568&skip=9 [last accessed: 11 Oct 2019].

6 The Érard piano was owned by Beethoven's brother Johann, who bequeathed it to the Landesmuseum in Linz in 1843. The Érard brothers produced state-of-the-art fortepianos in Paris that differed from Viennese pianos in their double escapement action and their four instead of two pedals.

7 [Die Musik ist die zweite Muttersprache unserer Stadt, sie spricht aus dem Rauschen ihres alten Stromes, webt feurig und zärtlich in ihren grünen Nebenhängen, in den altersgrauen Mauern blühen junge melodische Lieder auf, die ganze Luft ist vom Klingen und Singen erfüllt, und unsere Frauen und Mädchen sind in ihrer schwebenden Anmuth die schlanken Trägerinnen dieses musikalischen Fluidums, welches alle Adern und Nerven der Städter an der Donau durchzittert. Längst sind die unsterblichen Tondichter, um deren Besitz uns einst Europa beneidete, von uns geschieden, aber wenn auch Beethoven nicht mehr in wilder Genialität durch unsere Straßen stürmt, alle Geister und Herzen aufregend, wenn auch Mozart und Schubert nicht mehr lächelnd mit ihren Schätzen die engen Zimmer der alten Stadthäuser wie mit zauberischem Schimmer vergolden, sind wir doch mit einem Tropfen vom Geiste dieser Unsterblichen gesalbt, und ihr Cultus ist in uns lebendig geblieben.] Johannes Opp, 'Eröffnung der Musik- und Theater-Ausstellung', in *Neue Freie Presse,* 8 May 1892, 1–2.

8 See Werner Telesko, 'Die Musikdenkmäler und ihre Stellung innerhalb des Denkmalkults der Habsburgermonarchie des 19. Jahrhunderts', in *Imago Musicae XXV,* 2012, 107–28.

9 Edgar Zilsel, *Die Geniereligion. Ein kritischer Versuch über das moderne Persönlichkeitsideal, mit einer historischen Begründung,* ed. with an introduction by Johann Dvorak (Frankfurt a. M., 1990), 53.

10 [Wir verglichen nun das Werk des Musikers dem Gesichte der hellsehend gewordenen Somnambule.] Richard Wagner, *Beethoven. Mit dem nicht veröffentlichten Schluss der Schrift von 1871* (Berlin, 2015), 46.

11 [El sueño de la razón produce monstruos. La fantasía abandonada de la razón produce monstruos imposibles: unida con ella, es madre de las artes y origen de sus maravillas.] Francisco de Goya y Lucientes, *Caprichos,* no. 43 (Madrid: Museo del Prado). Edith Hellman, *Trasmundo de Goya* (Madrid, 1983), 221.

12 [... der Komponist offenbart das innerste Wesen der Welt und spricht die tiefste Weisheit aus, in einer Sprache, die seine Vernunft nicht versteht.] Arthur Schopenhauer, *Die Welt als Wille und Vorstellung* (Ditzingen, 1986), i, 344.

13 [Für Dich, armer Beethoven, gibt es kein Glück von aussen, du musst dir alles in dir selbst erschaffen, nur in der idealen Welt findest du Freude.] Letter from L. v. Beethoven to Ignaz von Gleichenstein, 1808, in: Emerich Kastner (ed.), *Ludwig van Beethovens sämtliche Briefe* (Leipzig, 1910), 126.

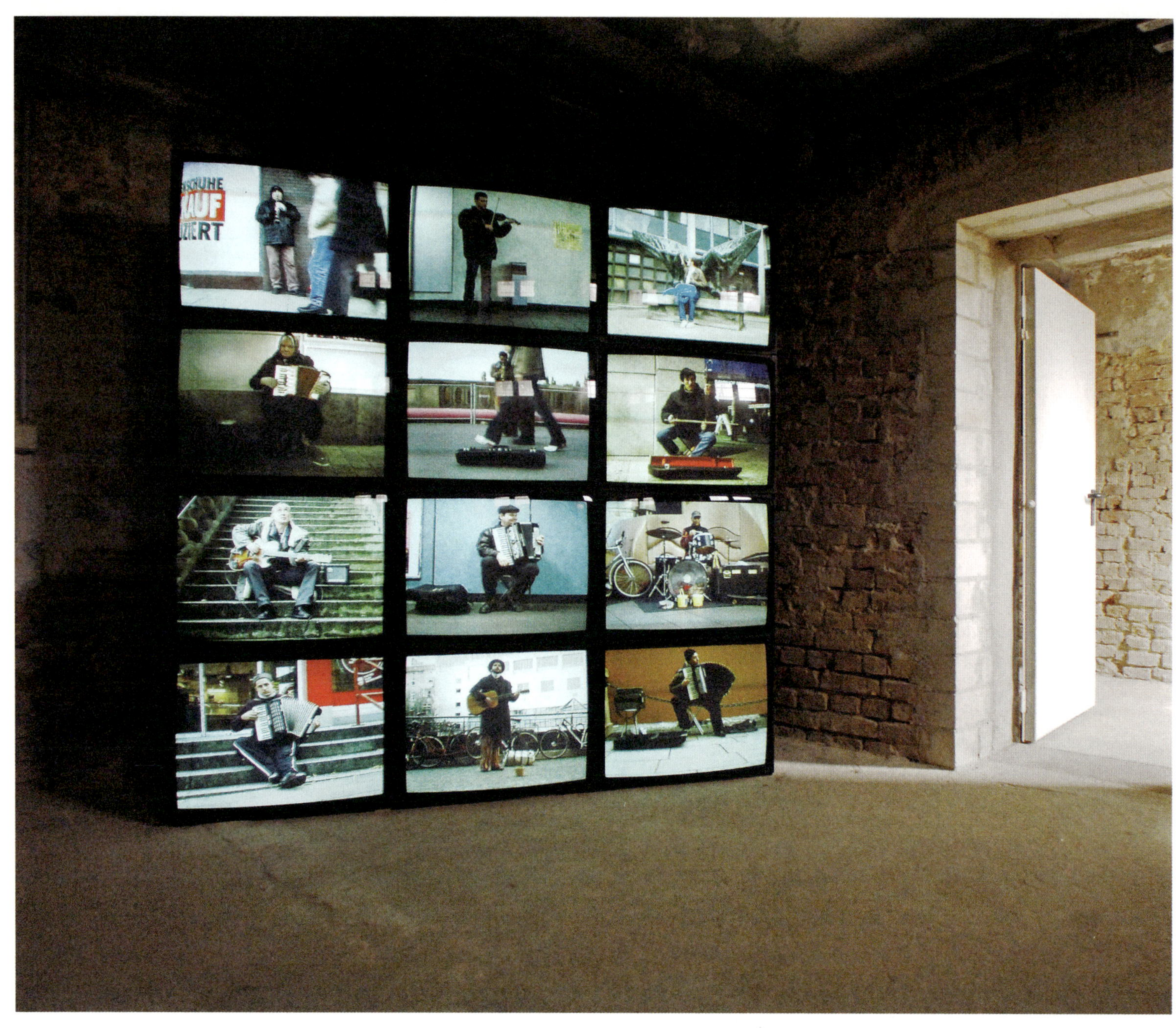

In this film installation, Aminde brings together the recordings of various street musicians, each playing only a single note, to form a noisy orchestra. Usually these performers would go unnoticed by passers-by on the street. Together, however, they form an irritating cacophony that captivates our attention, showing that music still has the ability to provoke.

ULF AMINDE

Life is not a Musical Request Show 2006

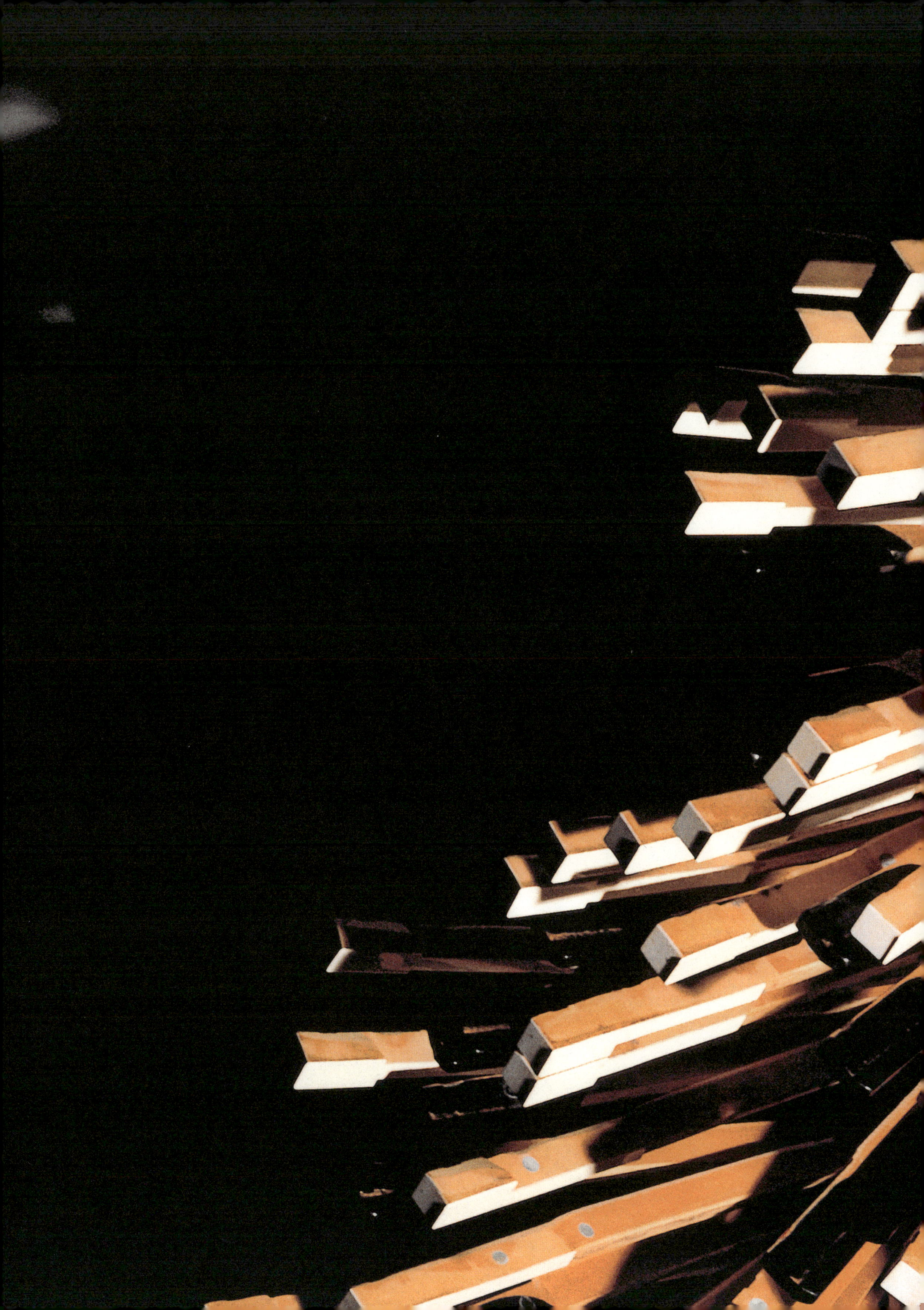

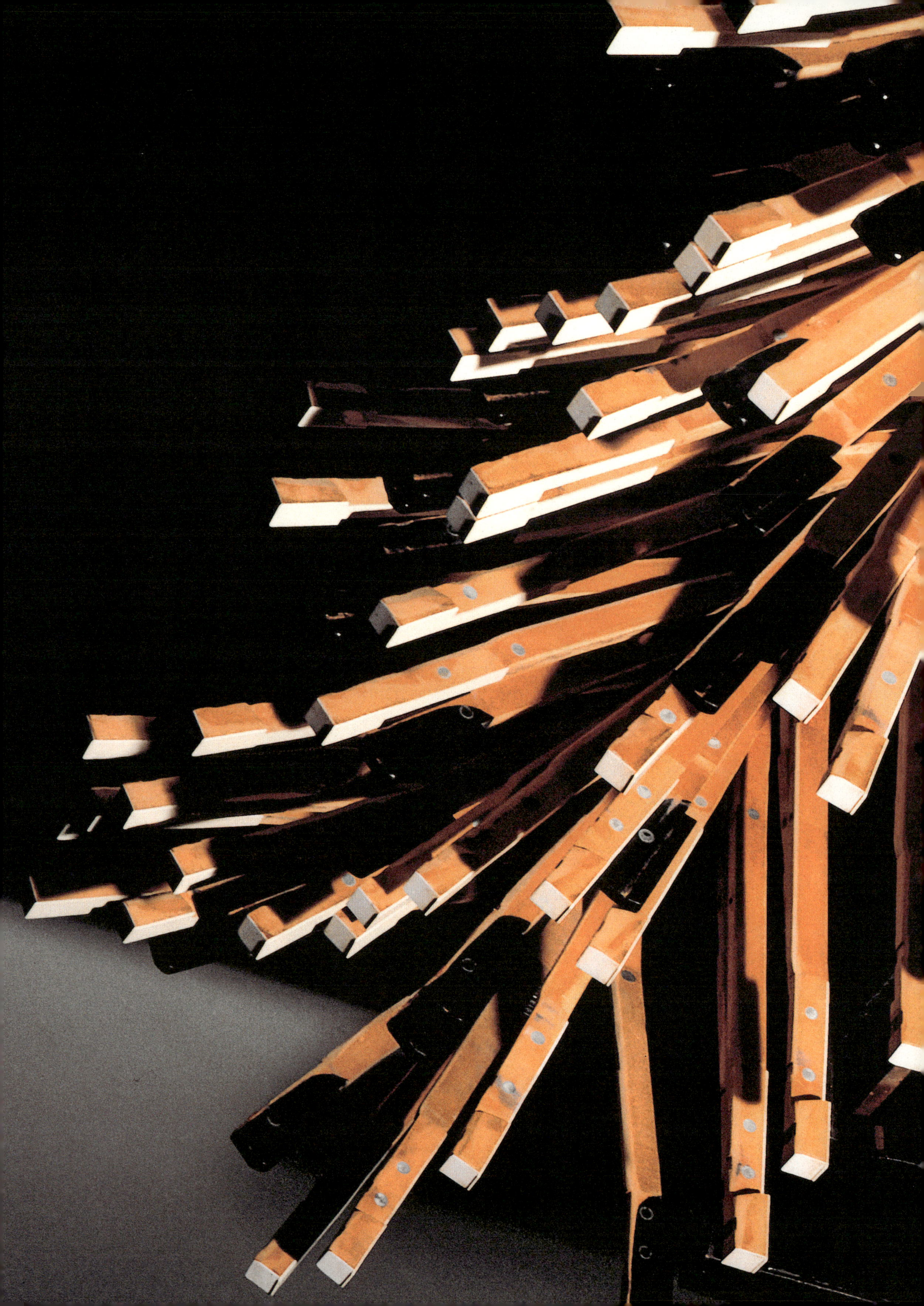

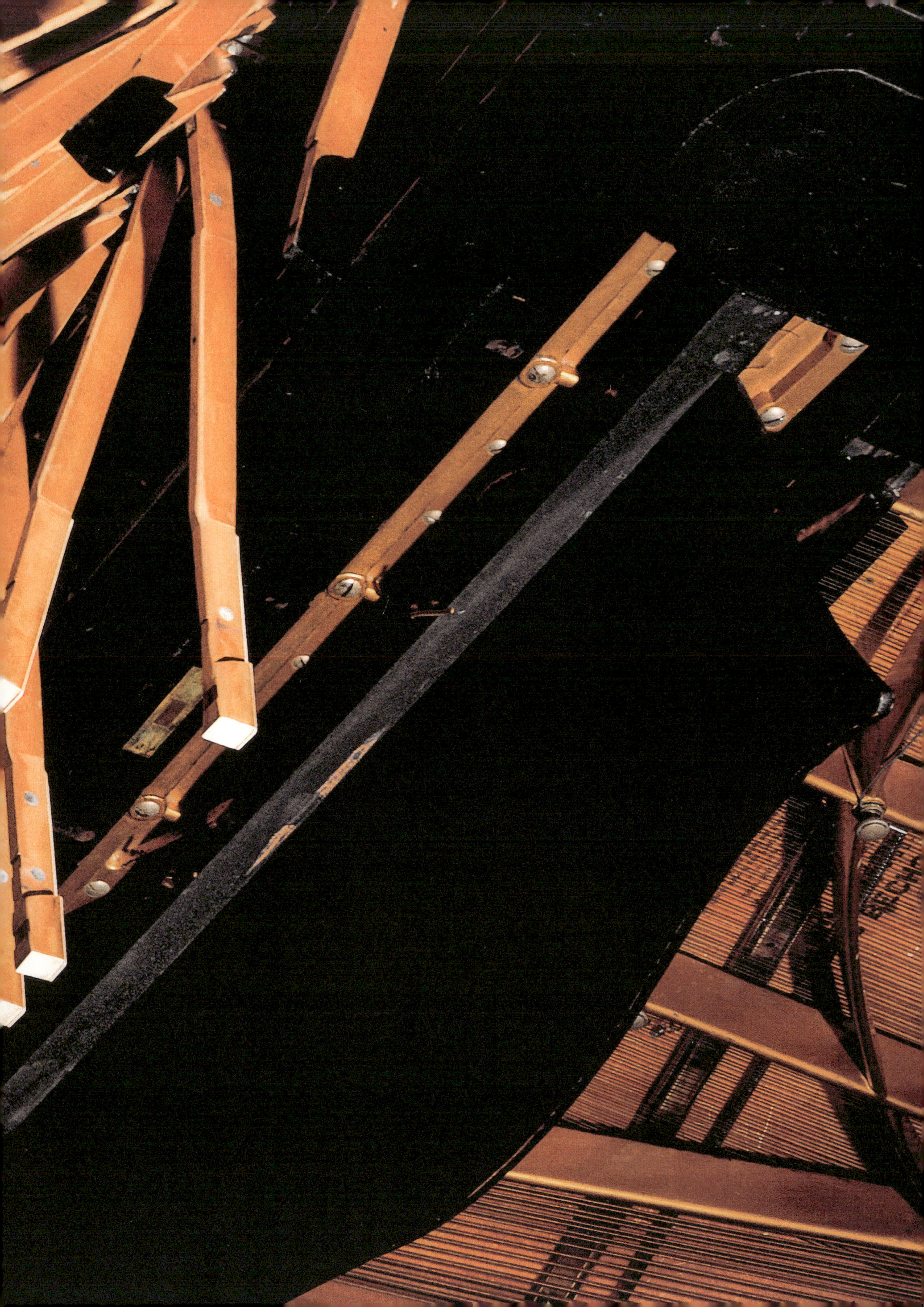

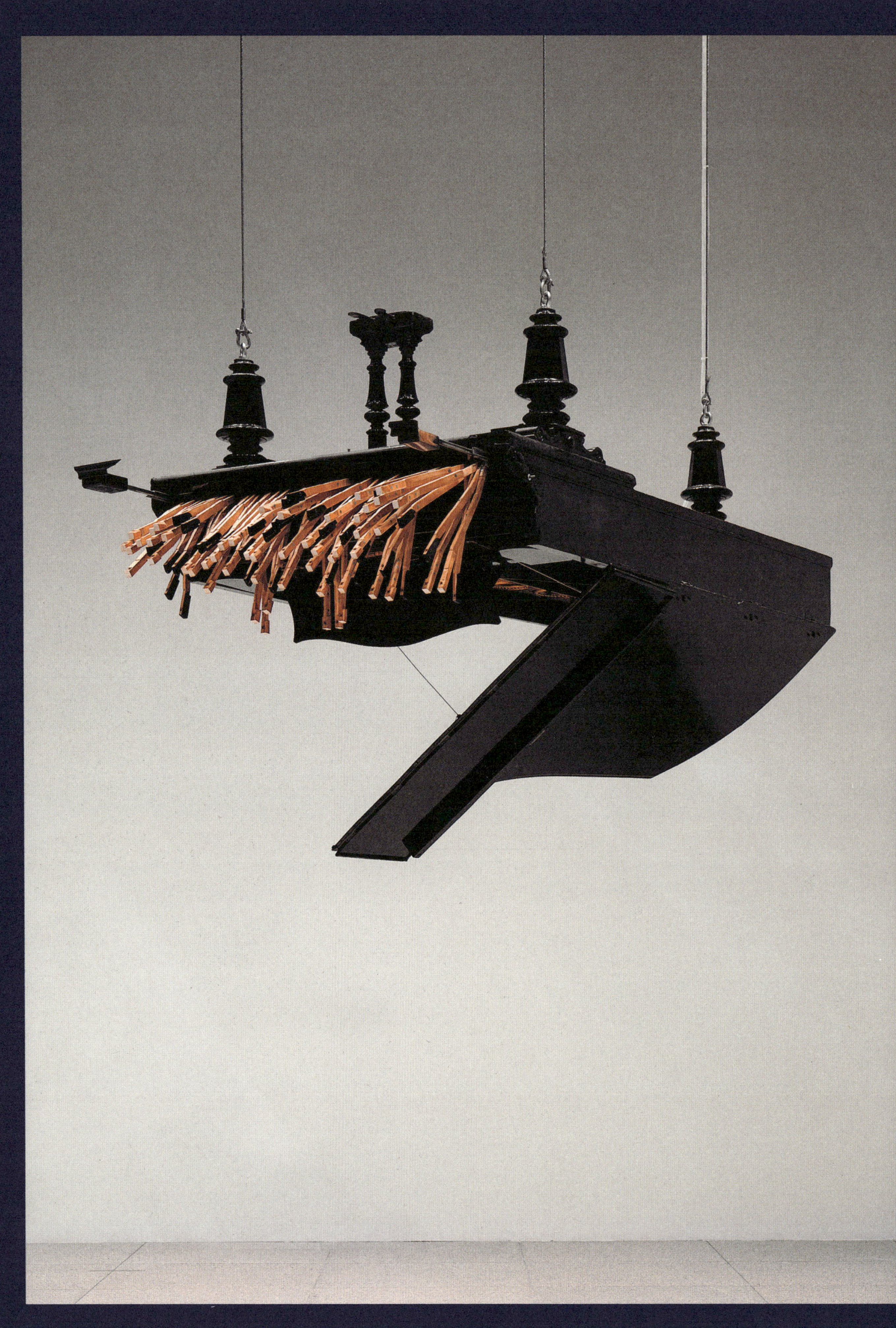

REBECCA HORN, CONCERT FOR ANARCHY, 1990

VEA KAISER

Loss of the Senses

O people, should you read this one day, reflect that you have done me wrong, and the unhappy man may take comfort at finding one of his own, who in spite of all of nature's obstacles has done everything in his ability to be accepted into the ranks of worthy artists and human beings.*

Who are we if we are stripped of the thing that constitutes us?

At the age of nine, I had piano lessons every Thursday in a dark, quiet room in my primary school. I remember one lesson in which I was supposed to learn how to play a simplified Beethoven theme from my piano book, but I found it impossibly difficult. When I complained, my teacher, a sensitive South Korean woman, replied that I was never allowed to frown while playing Beethoven, because in comparison with him no one had the right to complain. In my memory she began crying quietly at the idea that such a great composer had gradually lost his hearing. Whether this really happened or I constructed the memory as appropriate to the emotion involved, I can no longer recall.

However, it is indisputable that I have approached Beethoven differently since then. Namely with infinite, unquestioned and uncontested respect. Not only because of the greatness of his composition, but chiefly out of regard for the fact that he neither went mad nor gave up – even though he was aware that he was losing the very sense that enabled him to express himself, that allowed him to create the art that he carried within himself, and thus to become the person he was.

Probably the oldest story about a man who is robbed of everything in order to test his essential core is that of Job. He lives as a well-to-do and pious man in an unknown country, but God, on Satan's prompting, sees to it that he loses all his possessions, his children and his health. In spite of all these blows of fate Job does not abandon his faith but remains pious. Job's story is on the one hand the primal narrative of theodicy, but on the other hand it is also the primal narrative of the theory that one can take everything from a person but his faith.

Faith is an activity, not an ability. Moreover, it is something for which one needs neither a particular disposition nor any kind of aid or a special sense. Faith is a decision that one takes or fails to take. The only requirement for faith is one's own will.

It is often said that faith and art are united by their participation in some kind of metaphysics. When humanity began producing art, it explained it to itself with reference to the intervention of the muses or other divine entities. Today there is hardly an area of life as secular as art; unlike the faithful, however, no artist has yet arisen from sheer will alone. Countless are those who would like to be artists, who want to make works of eternity, who have within them an almost compulsive will and who are fundamentally prepared to give everything for it. And yet the number of those who achieve precisely that is relatively small. We think we know about all the species and the laws of our world. We have been to the deepest spot in the sea and even on the moon, but we do not know what enables those who feel called upon to make great art to actually make great art. We work with makeshift expressions such as talent or genius so as not to have to admit that the 'gift' – much discussed but in no way measurable, yet impossible to ignore when it appears – is one of the greatest mysteries of human history.

Obsession with art or the calling to pursue it is like an illness for which there is no cure, an urge which never fades and which is thus a fundamental part of anyone with the good luck or the misfortune to be permeated by it. No artist who feels that urge to expression within themselves can ever be kept from it. And that is precisely what makes artists' biographies so attractive: that in constantly changing variations they tell how neither poverty nor happiness in love, or suffering in love, illness, political upheavals, persecution, exile, children or other twists of fate can part the artistically obsessed from their art. Isn't it the characteristic of true artists not to be able not to yield to the urge to express their art and, through it, to communicate with others? The artist becomes an artist by creating art. The will alone is not sufficient, because to create something, to translate something from the world of ideas into the world of objective being, takes the ability that the Greeks described as a gift from the gods. The world of being is the world as perceived by the senses. In order to create for it, one needs senses. More than that, in fact: one needs senses that are more pronounced than those of the majority of people. Or, as Beethoven wrote about his sense of hearing: 'that which I have to a more perfect degree than others are supposed to have, a sense which I once possessed to the greatest perfection, a perfection such as few in my possession enjoy or ever have enjoyed.'

Hence, once again: who are we if we are stripped of the thing that constitutes us?

During the summer, I myself was granted a small insight – ludicrously minor and not actually worth mentioning, yet terrible for me – into the horror of not being able to pursue my own creativity as the result of physical impairment. Because of a multiple fracture and ruptured tendon in my hand I was unable to write as I had always been used to doing. It was harmless, of course, especially because I knew it was only temporary, and yet I suffered terrible nights because I could not press on with my work on a new novel. The physical pain that the injury caused me was not burdensome for a second. It remained entirely irrelevant in light of the fear of being robbed of my means of expression. I quickly came to terms with it. I found other possibilities, aids and slaves to carry on writing without writing. I surprised myself with a degree of creative problem-solving of which I would not have thought myself capable. Because the inability to use one's hand has always been the content of the deepest anxieties and nocturnal nightmares of the writing fraternity, the motif appears probably more frequently in literature than people in the real world lose a hand or an arm. After all, literature also serves the purpose of pervading the fears of its creators. And what fear can be greater than losing the means of one's own acts of creation? In John Irving's novel *Last Night in Twisted River* a character chops his hand off after taking blood thinners so that he can die. In *The Fourth Hand* a journalist has to come to terms with his hand being eaten by a lion. And in Roberto Bolaño's magnum opus *2666* one minor character is a painter who owes his fame to a self-portrait at the centre of which he has installed his own amputated painting hand.

In Bolaño's novel, the severed hand is a metaphor for subordinating everything to art, in extremis even one's own ability to produce art. In the Irving novel, by contrast, the hand as a primary tool of the writing fraternity represents life itself: a writer who loses it loses their livelihood. The journalist whose hand is eaten by the lion is given a second chance, however, when he receives the transplant of the hand of a dead man. On the abstract level these two figures therefore stand for the two possibilities of carrying on in the face of adversity or capitulating to fate. And who could blame anyone for doing the latter? Even Beethoven reflected: 'I was not far from ending my own life – only art held me back, it seemed impossible to me to leave the world before I had achieved everything for which I felt I had been put here.'

He carried on. He decided to bring forth what impelled him onwards. He remained himself, even though he was losing the very sense that he needed in order to exercise the very thing that constituted him.

Although the Argentinian writer Borges went completely blind in his fifties, he became director of his country's National Library at this time, and until the end of his life he remained a writer, a reader and a librarian. 'I had always imagined paradise as a kind of library,' he said, followed by the bitter and ironic observation that that same paradise had been handed to him precisely when he was no longer able to enjoy it in the sense in which it was intended. But his lack of eyesight changed nothing about the fact that he had arrived in paradise. And consequently he went further than the rest of the world, for whom entrance to paradise, the sphere of the celestial, a share in some kind of metaphysics, is denied in their lifetime. Because, even if we cannot understand it, that seems to remain the privilege of art.

A privilege that no loss of the senses can take away.

* All quotations from: Ludwig van Beethoven, *Heiligenstädter Testament*, Autograph Transcript, Hamburger Staats- und Universitätsbibliothek, ND VI 4281.

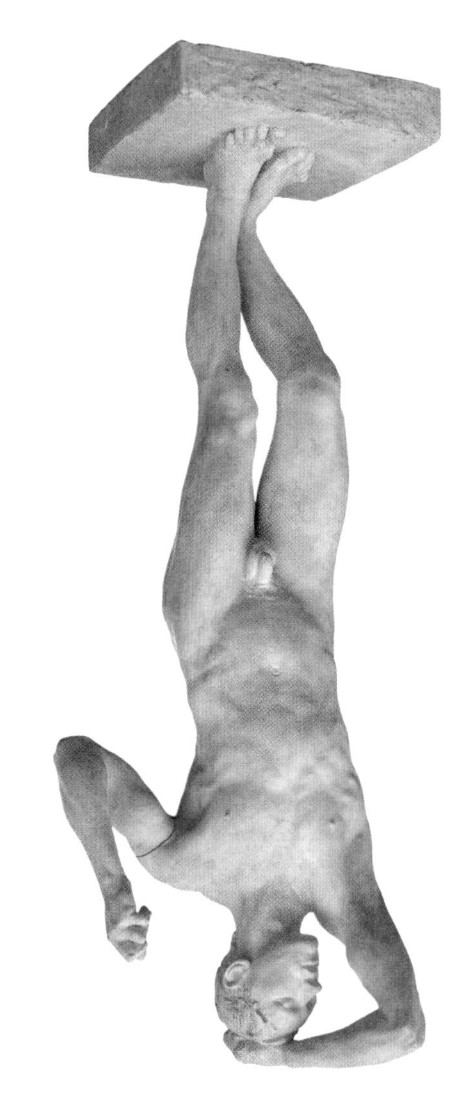

AUGUSTE RODIN

L’Âge d’airain (The Age of Bronze)
1887

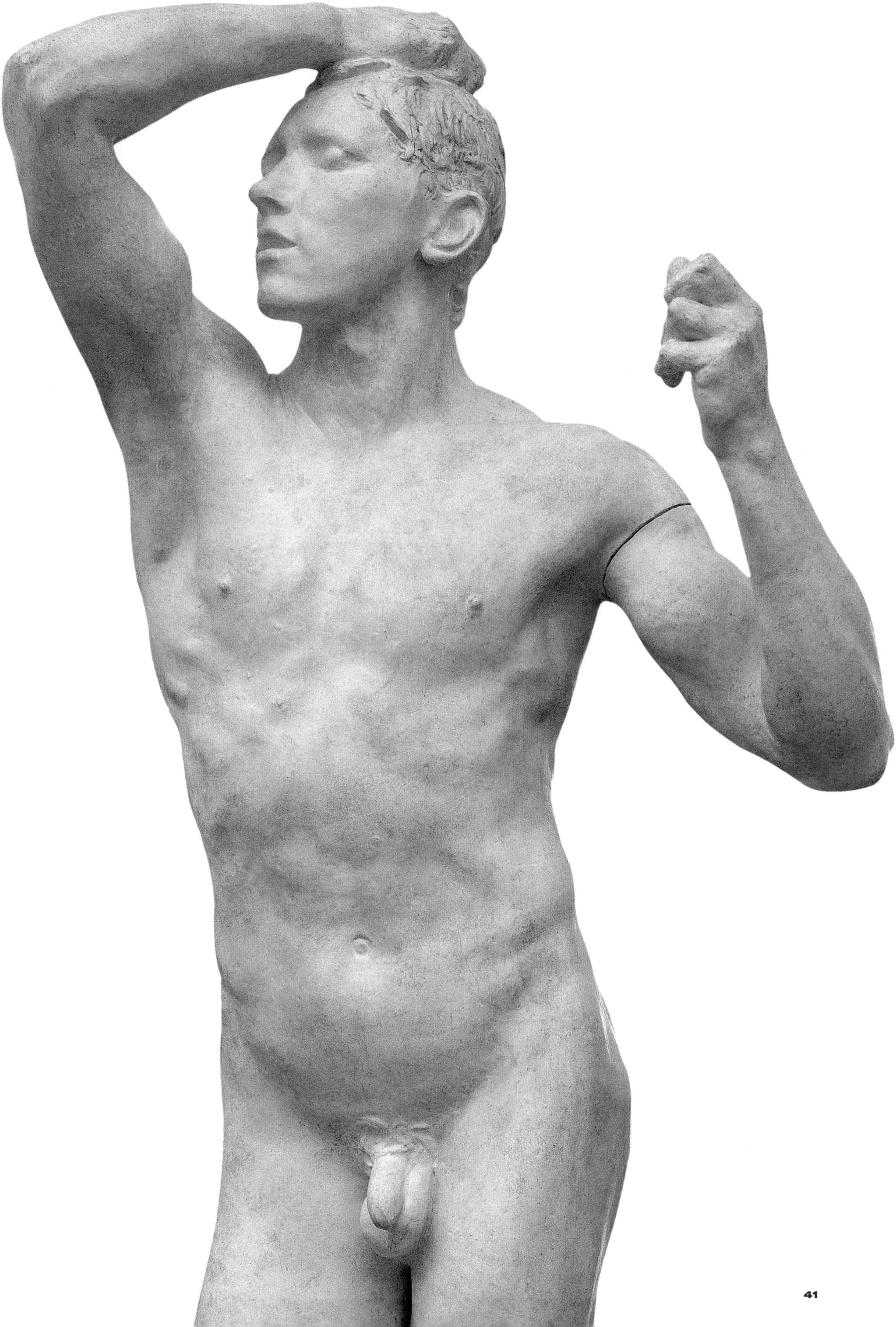

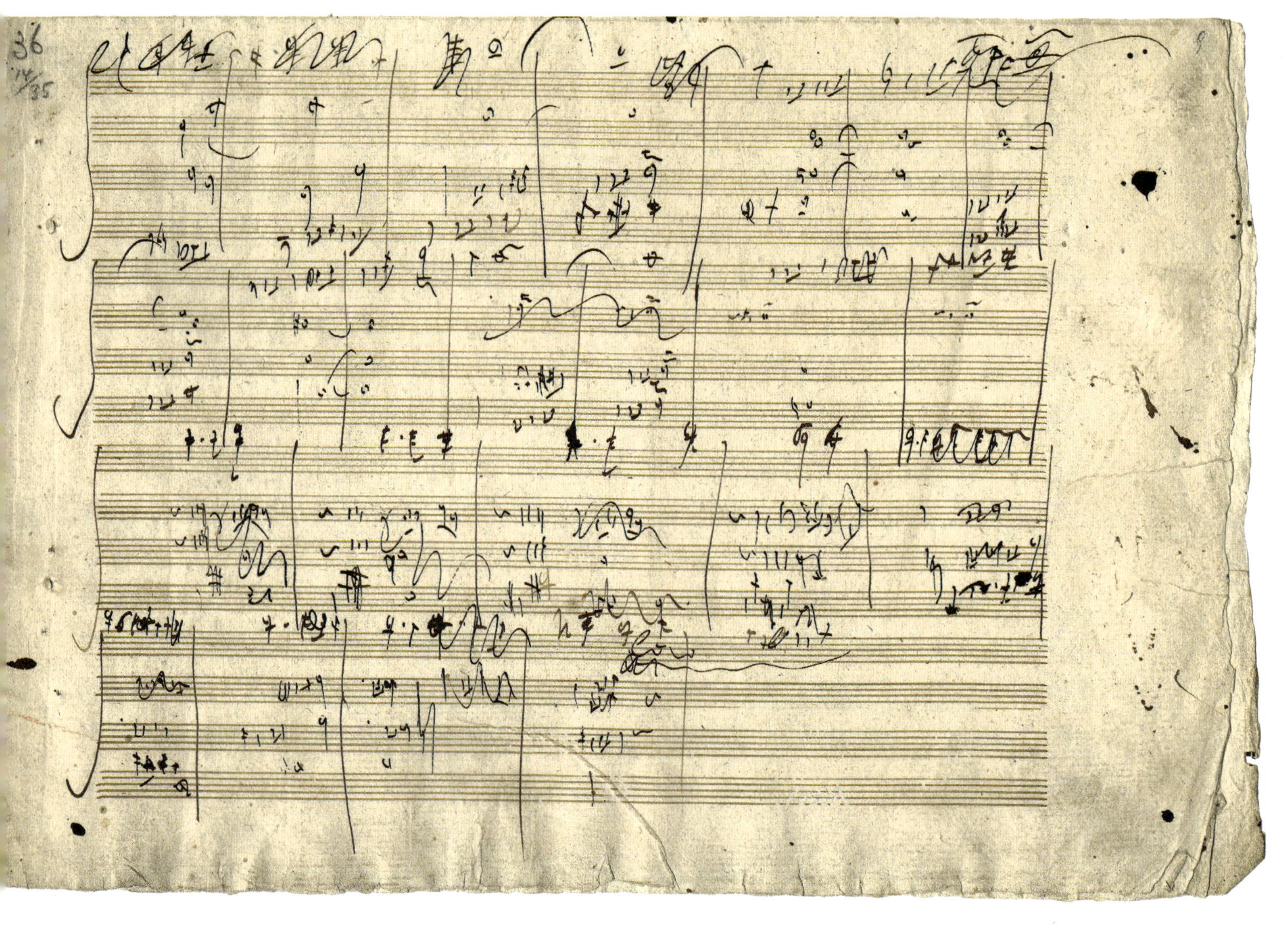

LUDWIG VAN BEETHOVEN

Sketches for String Quartets (in F major, E minor and C major), op. 59, autograph 1806

BEAT WYSS

From Wunderkind to Marketing Pioneer

There is probably no other artist who has been portrayed as frequently as Ludwig van Beethoven. It is not immediately obvious, though, why this composer and virtuoso pianist should have captured the imagination of visual artists to such an extent. After all, the art of the man they have celebrated in their sculptures and paintings – sometimes in monumental fashion – possesses a purely immaterial existence, namely in the ear and within the inner world of feeling.

The sensory experience of a musical performance lasts only for as long as the music is playing; it wanes as soon as the musicians fall silent. The audience's ensuing applause – that ineffably barbaric custom which masquerades as gratitude – in fact serves no other purpose than to drown in a cacophony the emptiness that sets in once the musical delights are over. Such applause cannot but grate on a sensitive ear, which, at the end of a concert, pines for the music that has just died away.

The way visual artists have reacted to Beethoven is not unlike that of the noisy audiences. In paying homage to him, they have been cultivating an ideal that, conveyed as it is through stilted iconography, must remain unattainable: the ideal of unconditional existence as a genius and of being revered by society almost like a figure of lore without needing to win over all those patrons and admirers by offering them tangible goods. The short, pockmarked man with frizzy hair who in his social interactions invariably displayed a lack of tact, politeness and empathy had no need to court popularity. He was after all Ludwig van Beethoven, a wunderkind in direct line of descent from Mozart. Like his predecessor, who achieved so much so soon, Beethoven was a genius and genius does not need to prove anything – an idea already mooted by Lessing who, in his tragedy *Emilia Galotti*, had the court painter Conti remark: 'Wouldn't you agree, Prince, that Raphael would still have been the greatest genius in the realm of painting even if he had suffered the misfortune of being born without hands?' Lessing's aperçu describes Beethoven's situation perfectly: the composer became deaf, but his genius was never called into question on account of that physical disability.

A genius of the modern sort does not smile in portraits. That would be an admission of weakness, as if the subject had felt obliged to ingratiate himself with the public by affecting bonhomie. If we study the many portraits of Beethoven created after his death, we may readily detect the same attitude in all of them. Beethoven does not look out at one from the canvas; rather, his gaze is directed inwards. Sometimes the eyelids are even closed, as if every waking thought of his were taken up by the music surging inside his head. Like an electric charge, all this energy causes the luxuriant hair to stand on end as in a sunburst. Fittingly, the genius's face bears an expression of grim aloofness, his forehead clouded by the pathos of inspiration.

However, it is this very remoteness that whets the public's desire to get up close to the genius and to appropriate, cannibal-like, some physical part of him. Beethoven on his deathbed became the centre of a spectacle that dragged on for several days as the musical world gathered to pay its last respects to a renowned colleague. The room in which the 56-year-old Beethoven died on 26 March 1827 was not guarded very strictly and soon turned into a magnet for eager relic-hunters. The officially appointed watchmen earned a little on the side by turning a blind eye to locks of hair being cut from Beethoven's head – and duly pocketing tips. Even before the autopsy, which was to establish cirrhosis of the liver as the cause of death, the dead man's beard had been shaved off so that a cast of the face could be taken for the death mask. According to eyewitness accounts, there was not a hair left on Beethoven's head when the coffin was borne out of his lodgings in the Schwarzspanierhaus near the Schottentor and drawn in a carriage to the Church of the Holy Trinity (Alserkirche), through streets that were lined by as many as twenty thousand people – almost half the population of Vienna at the time.[1]

The veneration of the genius was marked by a truly Catholic fetishism. The relics strengthened admirers, male and female alike, in the belief that they were now able to commune with the *Missa Solemnis* in all its epic grandeur.

Of course, not all the devotees of Beethoven's music displayed such cannibalistic slavishness. The members of the profession knew their man, warts and all. Thus, in 1828 the music publisher Anton Diabelli purchased from Beethoven's estate an unfinished piano work with the opus number 129 to which the maestro himself had given the title *Alla ingharese quasi un capriccio*. Diabelli completed the brisk rondo, which today belongs to the most popular virtuoso pieces for the piano, and christened it *Die Wut über den verlorenen Groschen* ('Rage over a lost penny'). This was meant ironically, for Beethoven's relationship with money was the talk of the town in Vienna. The composer had swung between miserliness (for example, towards servants) and bouts of extravagance (say, in the consumption of wine). In choosing his own title for the rondo,

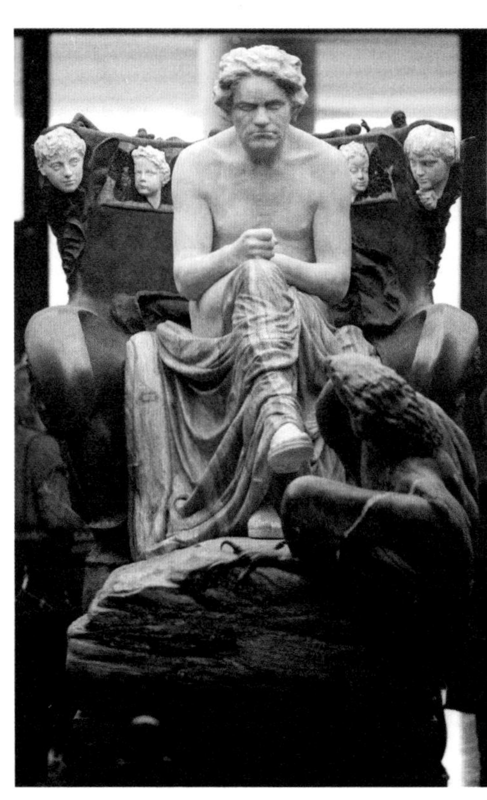

1

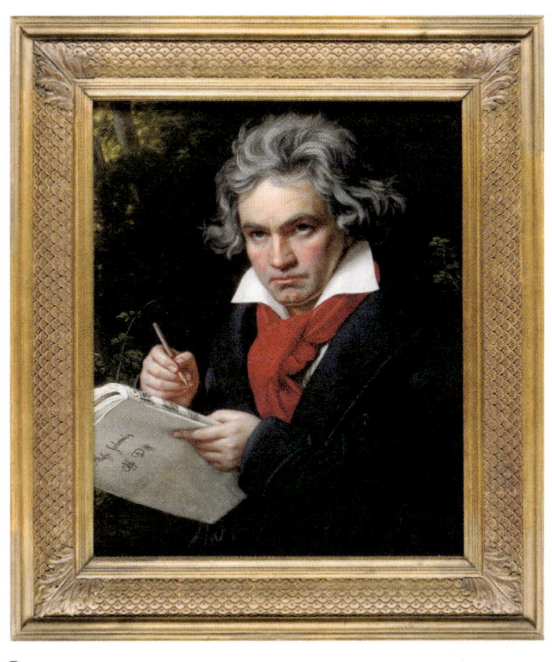

3

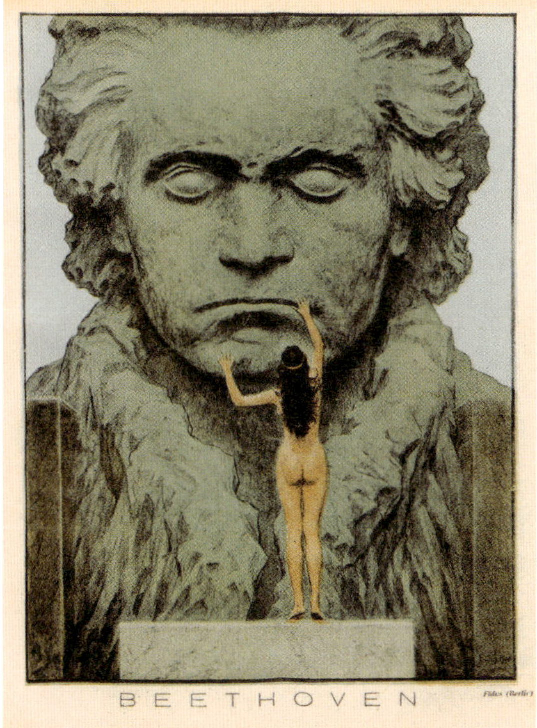

5

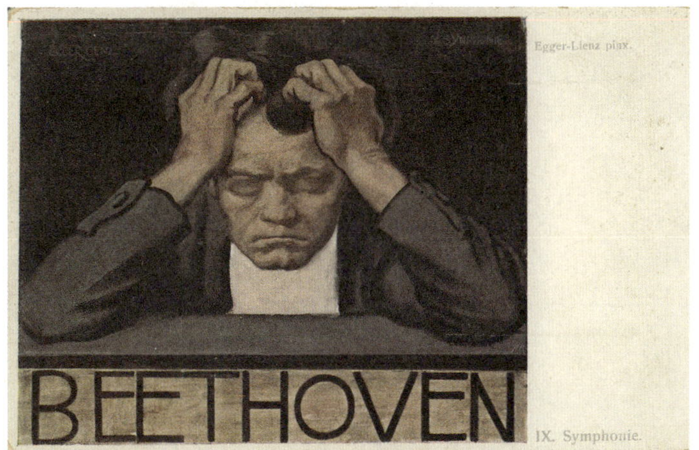

4

Diabelli may also have been thinking of the scandal that ensued in 1818 when Beethoven was charged with tax evasion. 'All meine Noten bringen mich nicht aus den Nöten' ('All my notes cannot extricate me from want'), our genius once felicitously quipped on that subject. Beethoven's constant fear of falling into penury was not entirely unwarranted. In all his life he never held a permanent post; indeed, his professional circumstances mirrored those of European society at a time of upheaval. Until the French Revolution, musical culture had been sustained by the Church and the court, but now these structures were clearly disintegrating. In the wake of economic liberalization, art was expected to pay its own way as a commodity. Visual artists had perceived the commercial nature of their work ever since the fifteenth century and had succeeded in turning it to profit: now was the time for music, too, to sell itself, though its immateriality continued to be a problem. A first step in overcoming that was the reproduction, through printing, of sheet music for amateur music-making in middle-class homes. As far as multiple exploitation of his works was concerned, Beethoven displayed a good deal of cunning. In 1805, having simultaneously sold the rights to his String Quintet in C, op. 29, to Artaria and to Breitkopf & Härtel, the composer became entangled in a lawsuit which he eventually lost.

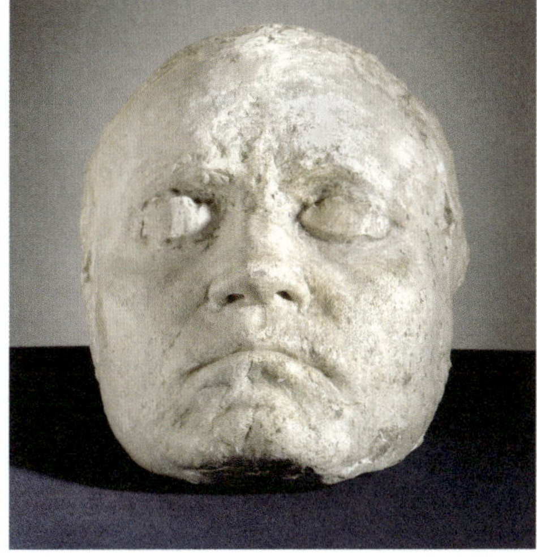

2

If one studies the careers of the two wunderkinder Beethoven and Mozart, the peculiar antagonism between modern genius and princely courts becomes apparent: an artist of the genius type had trouble adjusting to life at court with its strict regulations. Thus, Mozart at the age of 21 resigned his position as *Konzertmeister* (leader and conductor) of the orchestra of the Prince-Archbishop of Salzburg because fame and fortune beckoned in the form of performances to be given in Milan and Vienna. A slightly later attempt to hold down a job in his home town of Salzburg – this time as court organist – ended after twenty striferidden months with the infamous kick dealt out to him by the Prince-Archbishop's chief steward, Count Arco. Genius can thrive only within the atmosphere of a liberal art market.

Mozart had been dead for almost a year by the time Beethoven arrived in the city of Vienna in October 1792 – a move that had unintended consequences for the young man. For it was an eastward retreat away from the floodwaters of the Revolution and into the Habsburg metropolis, which was to become a bastion of conservative restoration. While Napoleon's troops were busy occupying the Rhineland, the palaces of the Viennese aristocracy were still aglow with all their ancient splendour. Their enfilades, framed by glistening silk tapestries, baroquely painted sopraportas, chandeliers and stuccoed vaults, would have been little better than hollow museums had they not been animated by a merry-go-round of elegantly dressed ladies and self-assured cavaliers exchanging pleasantries to the festive

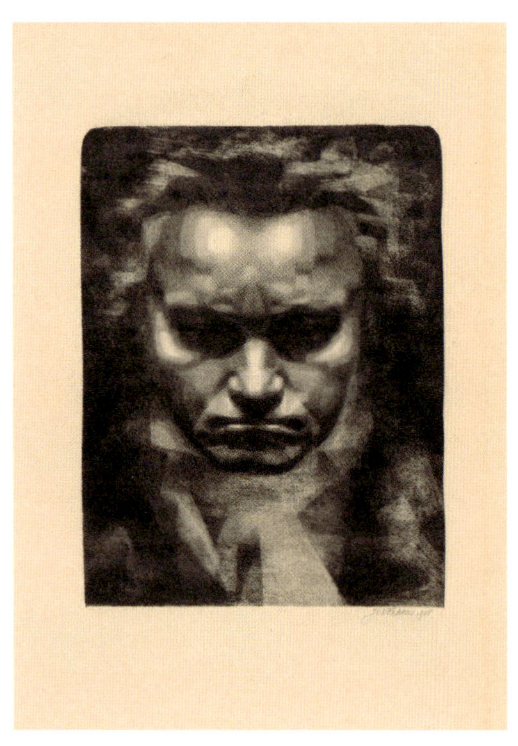

7

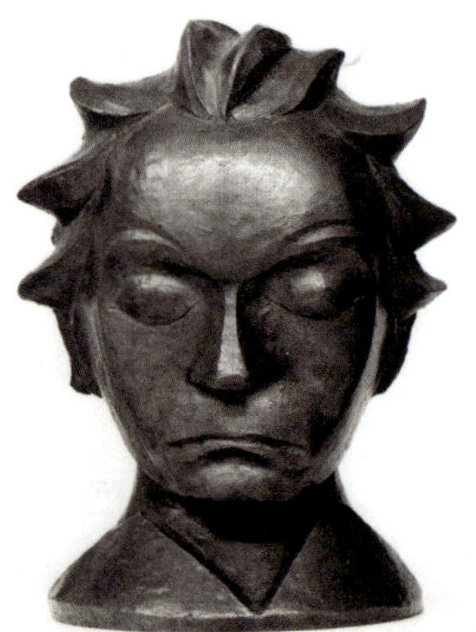

8

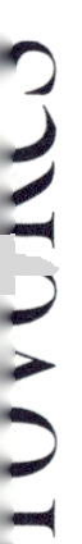

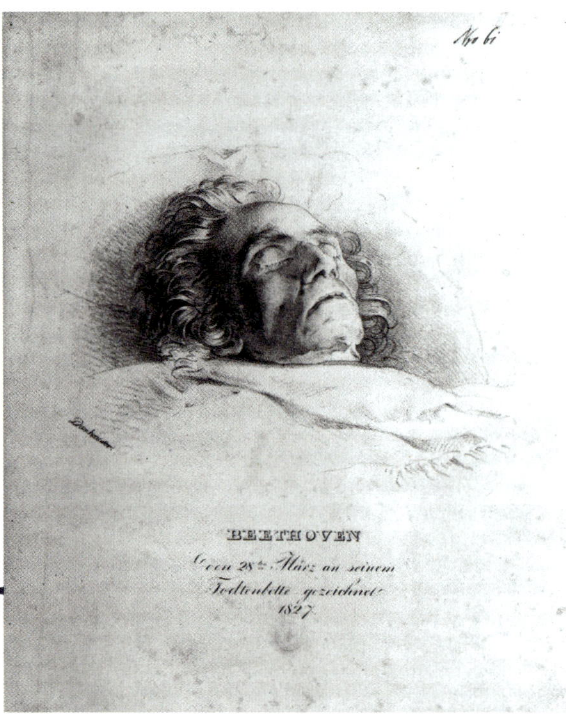

6

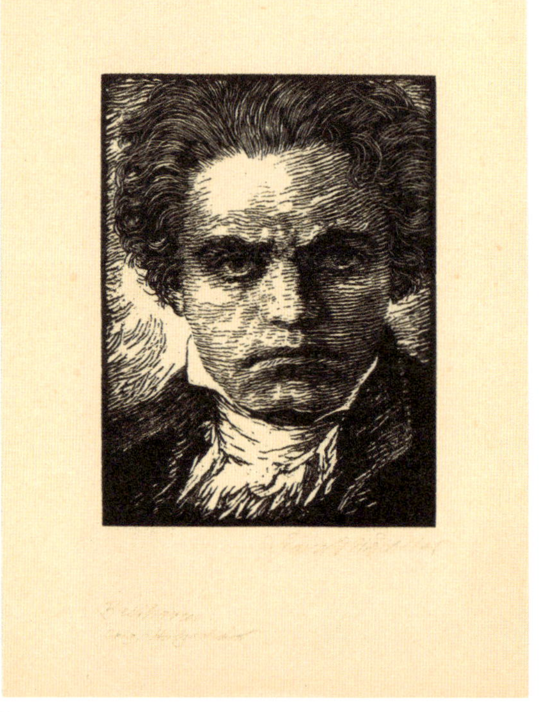

9

sounds of music. It was a society that depended on virtuosi like Beethoven who, worshipped as geniuses, were able to feed the vanity of their listeners by performing for them.

Beethoven found a patron in Prince Karl Alois Lichnowsky, who had once been a benefactor of Mozart's and was no mean pianist himself. This relationship between prince and artist was on a different level from court culture. A shrewd Beethoven knew how to play various patrons off against one another in order to increase his own market value. Thus, in the autumn of 1808 he spread the rumour – which was actually true – that Jérôme Bonaparte, youngest brother of Napoleon and recently crowned King of Westphalia, had invited him to take up a position at the Kassel court with an annual salary of 600 gold ducats. Three patrons of the arts teamed up hastily so as to retain their genius in Vienna: 1,500 florins were offered by Archduke Rudolph, 700 by Prince Lobkowitz and 1,800 by Prince Kinsky to make up a combined annuity of 4,000 florins and persuade Beethoven to stay. This business model anticipated certain elements of modern sponsoring in that it allowed the artist – treated in this case as a sacred genius – great freedom so that he could achieve commercial success, which in turn redounded to the benefit of his sponsors. The modern patron of the arts is, as it were, a holder of shares in genius. There was just one snag, namely, the fact that even the aristocracy was not immune to the economic pressures of the new era. Thus, Lobkowitz was able to pay his part of the annuity only up to 1811, when he was declared bankrupt. The debts incurred in maintaining a luxurious lifestyle were not so easy to sweep under the (Persian) carpet in the bourgeois age. After Prince Ferdinand Kinsky was killed in a horse-riding accident, Beethoven had to file a lawsuit in order to compel the nobleman's heirs to honour their financial obligations. As a result of Austria formally declaring itself bankrupt in February 1811, Archduke Rudolph, too, had to tighten his belt: after all, a Habsburg was expected to set a good example at a time of national hardship.

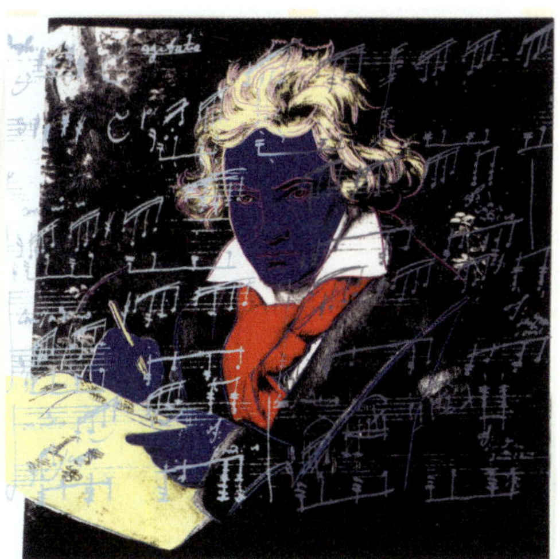

10

Attended by prominent figures from the world of European politics, the Congress of Vienna in 1815 brought new cultural life to the city, though Beethoven's music was not to the taste of Prince Metternich, the key player in the remoulding of Europe along the lines of conservative restoration. Nor was Beethoven's music held in particularly high esteem by the Austrian imperial family. Still, this did not cause him to die a pauper. His nephew and sole heir was able to retire into domestic life as a gentleman of leisure thanks to the property he inherited.

A further generation would, however, have to pass from the face of the earth before musicians finally succeeded in really striking it rich. The prerequisite for this was created by Emil Berliner with his Gramophone Company. By means of the shellac-based record, which was invented in 1896, and the imperishable label His Master's Voice, he was able to distribute music to all corners of the world. In this new medium, Beethoven proved to be a reliable brand from the very outset.

If we regard Mozart and Beethoven as pioneers of the modern music market on the slippery terrain of aristocratic patronage, then their legitimate heirs are the stars of pop culture. Among these we may also recognize that 'cult of relics' which found its way into art with Beethoven's death. The estates of Elvis Presley and Michael Jackson were deftly safeguarded by their agents and continue to be exploited commercially. Those two places of pilgrimage, Graceland in Memphis and Neverland in California, are like monumental reliquaries in which fetishes from the singers' lives are preserved. The iconic likenesses of the two stars, however, can certainly not be said to have been executed in the Beethoven style: the smiles they offer their fans are too affable, too seductive even. Yet the face of Michael Jackson in his later years, pale and flattened by operations, does resemble a death mask. This takes us back to how a plaster cast of Beethoven's face with a sullen expression became the prototype of all posthumous portraits of the composer.[2]

1 *Wien Geschichte Wiki*, 'Bevölkerungsgeschichte' (Population history): www.geschichtewiki.wien.gv.at/Bev%C3%B6lkerungsgeschichte [last accessed: 4 Nov 2019].

2 I am indebted to the biography by Kirsten Jüngling, *Beethoven. Der Mensch hinter dem Mythos* (Berlin, 2019), by which I was greatly stimulated.

Figure captions:

1 Beethoven monument by Max Klinger at the Gewandhaus. Photo: Klaus Mehner, 1989

2 Ludwig van Beethoven mask. Recast after the mask taken by Franz Klein in 1812

3 Joseph Karl Stieler, *Beethoven composing the* Missa Solemnis, 1820. Bonn, Beethoven-Haus

4 Albin Egger-Lienz, *Ninth Symphony*, after 1900, postcard

5 Design for a Beethoven temple, *Fidus*. Illustration in the magazine *Jugend. Münchner illustrierte Wochenschrift für Kunst und Leben* 8, 1903. Heidelberg, Universitätsbibliothek

6 Josef Danhauser, *Beethoven on His Deathbed*, 1827. Berlin, Staatsbibliothek zu Berlin

7 Jan Fekkes, *Beethoven*, 1918. Amsterdam, Rijksmuseum

8 Ernst Barlach, *Beethoven*, 1926. Güstrow, Ernst Barlach Foundation

9 Leopold Wächtler, *Portrait of Beethoven*, c.1930. Leipzig, Graphikantiquariat Koenitz

10 Andy Warhol, *Beethoven*, 1987

Mahler

Ludwig van Beethoven, comic-strip artist

Excellency!

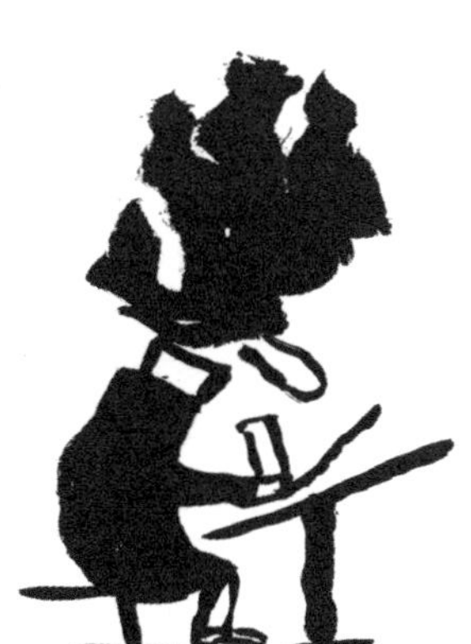

It is possible that a number of your ever-unique poems, adapted by me into drawings, will soon be published, among them „RASTLOSE LIEBE".

How highly I would value a general comment from you on the art of drawing as such or on the adaptation of your poems into picture sequences!

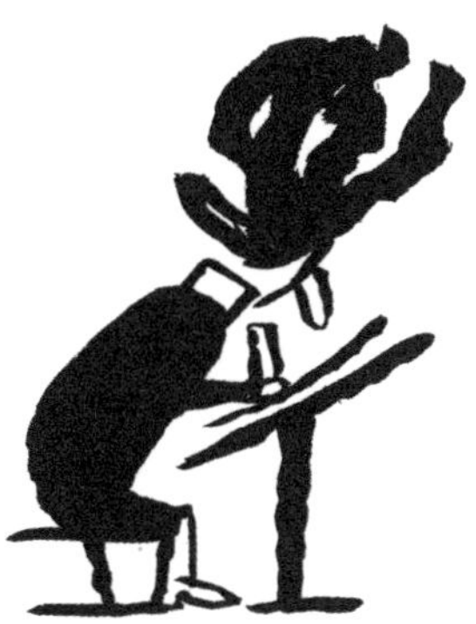

Right, this is it!

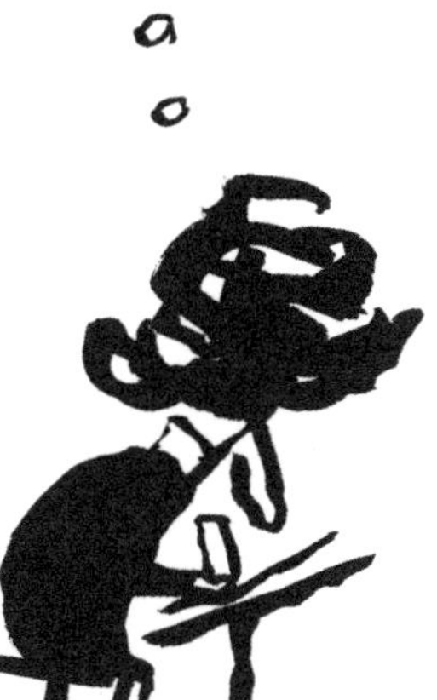

Now a request to Your Excellency: I have created a grand GRAPHIC NOVEL, the fee for which is just 50 euros.

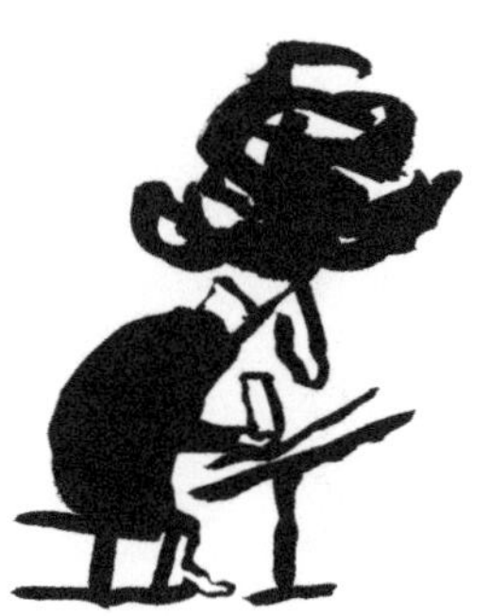

I have drawn so much, yet EARNED almost nothing at all.

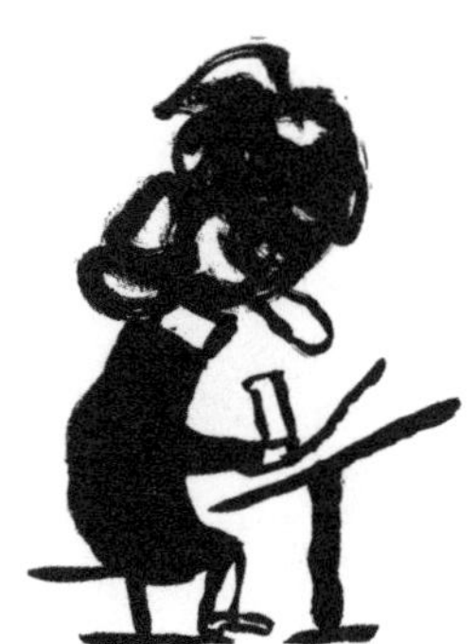

My request is that Your Excellency should draw the attention of His Serene Highness to this matter.

More Expression!

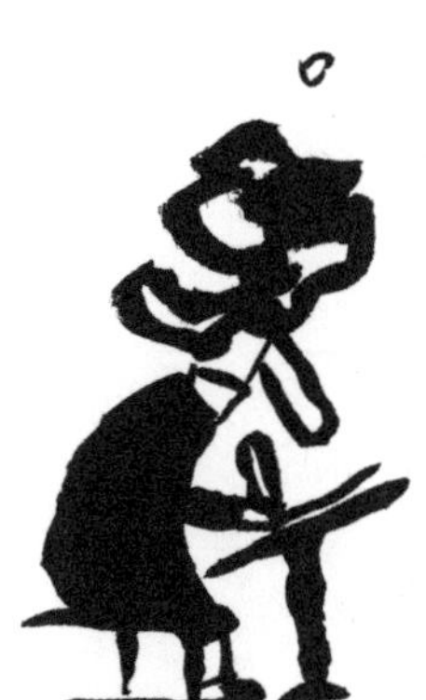

The veneration, love and high esteem that I have felt for the unique and immortal Goethe ever since the days of my youth are something that cannot be conveyed in words, especially by a BUNGLER like me, who has cared only to master the art of comics.

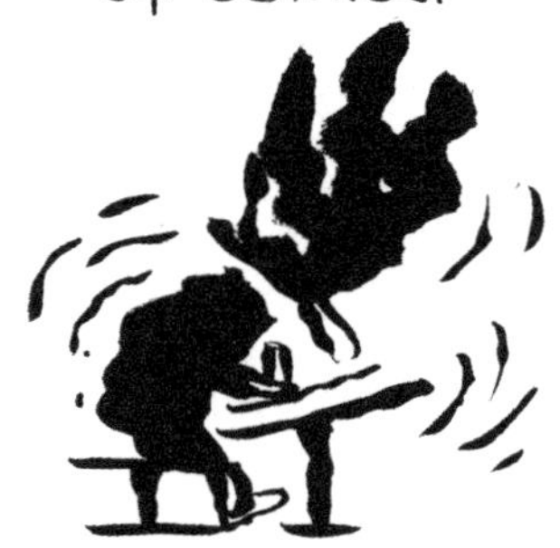

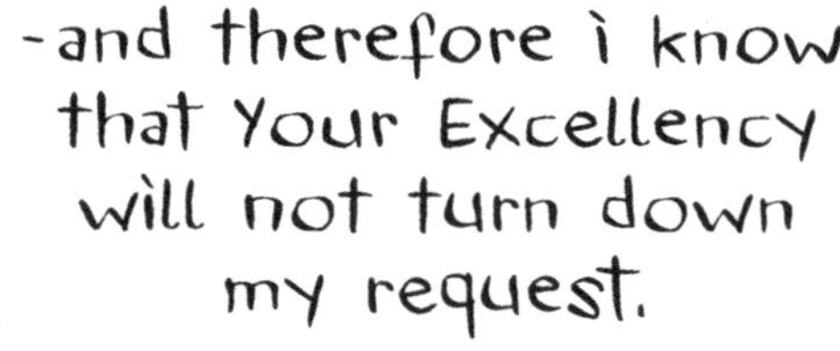

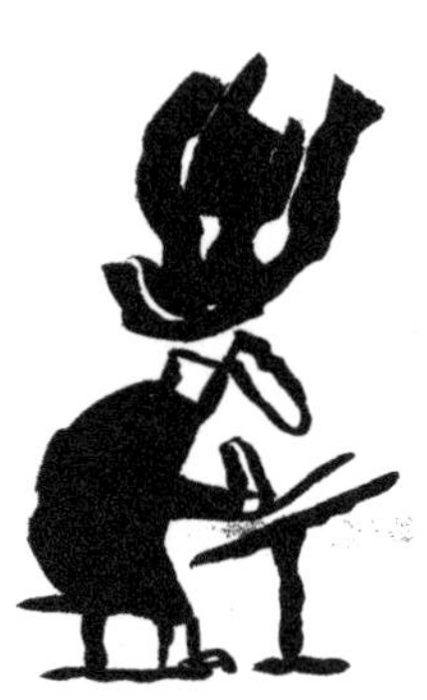

I remain, Excellency, with the sincerest and most unbounded respect,

BEETHOVEN

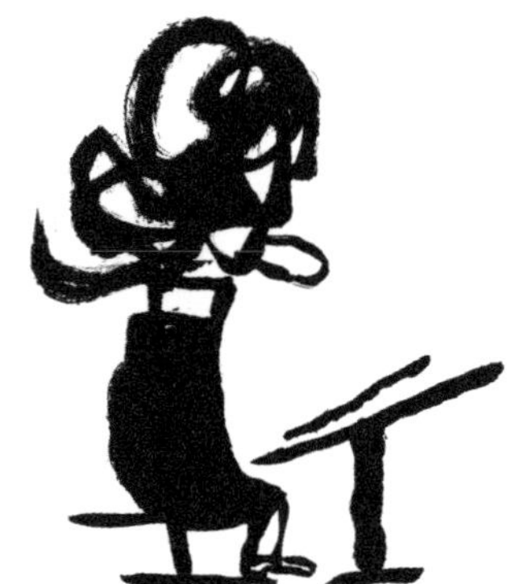

Source:

Letter from Beethoven to Goethe, Vienna, 8 february 1823.

The words „tones", „composing", „music", and „grand Mass" have been replaced by „drawings", „picture sequences", „graphic novel" and so on.

mahler

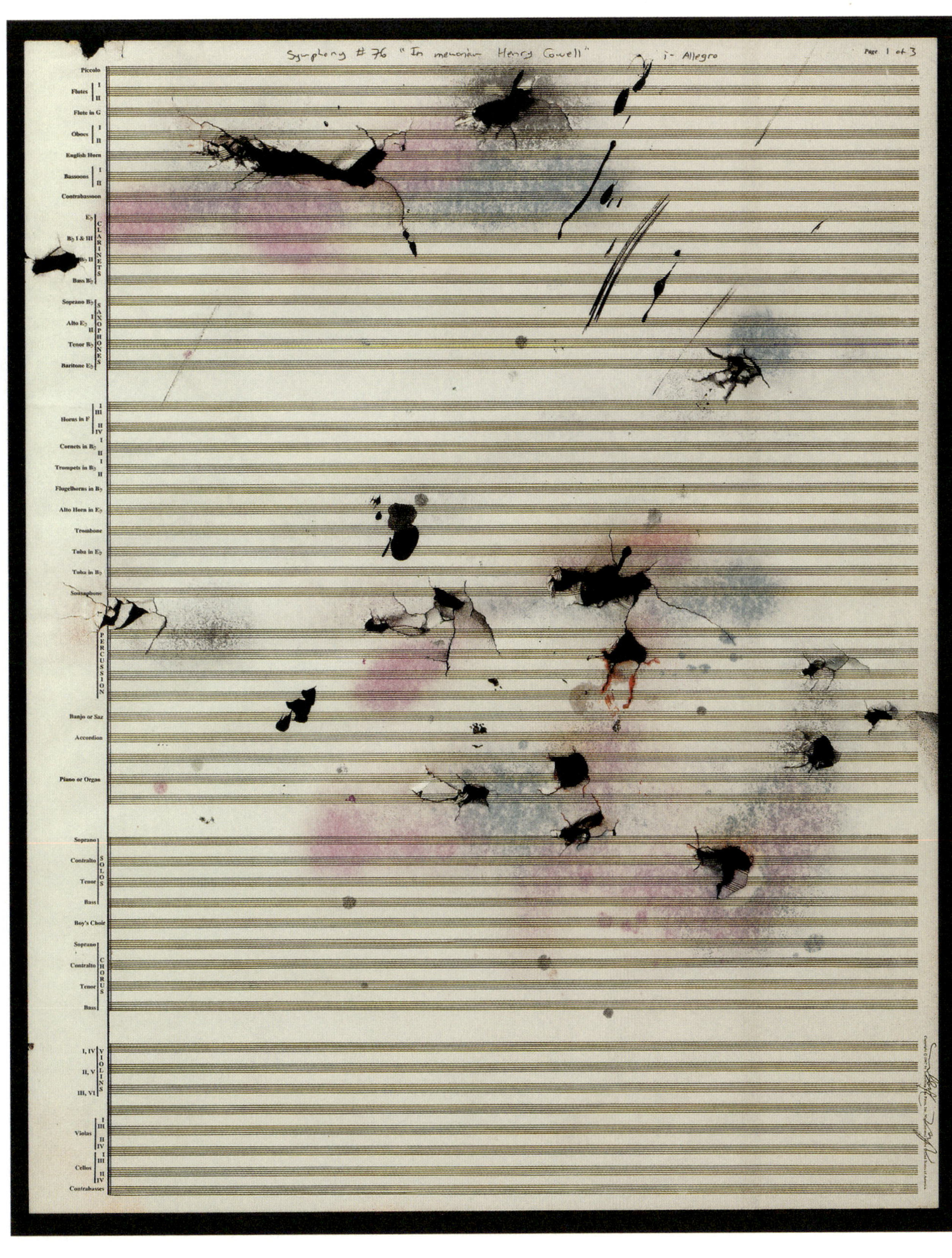

DICK HIGGINS

Symphony No. 76 in Memorian Henry Cowell: Allegro / Funeral March / Triumphal Jig 1968–1991

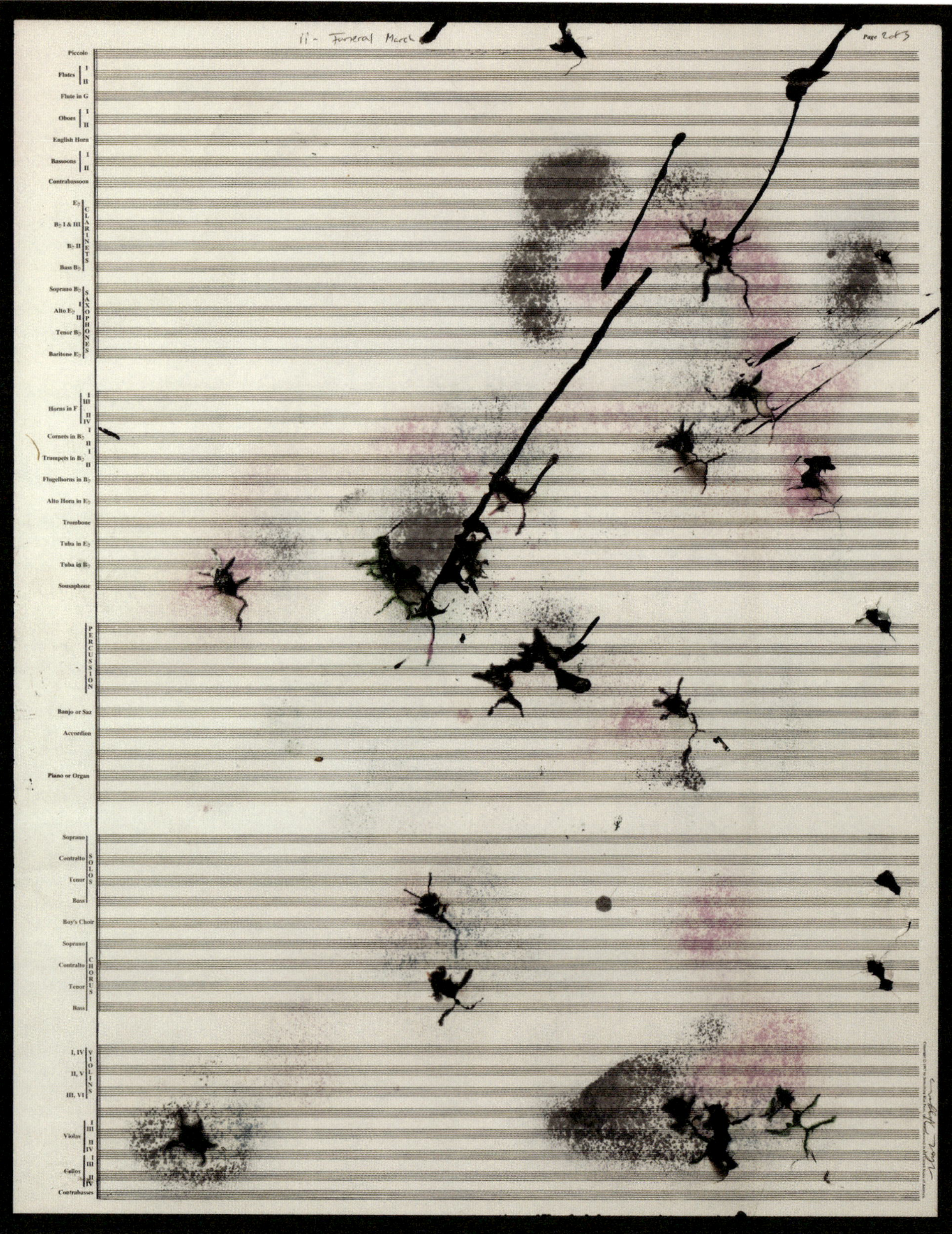
ii - Funeral March
Page 2 of 3
Piccolo
Flutes I II
Flute in G
Oboes I II
English Horn
Bassoons I II
Contrabassoon
CLARINETS
E♭
B♭ I & III
B♭ II
Bass B♭
SAXOPHONES
Soprano B♭
Alto E♭ I II
Tenor B♭
Baritone E♭
Horns in F I III II IV
Cornets in B♭ I II
Trumpets in B♭ I II
Flugelhorns in B♭
Alto Horn in E♭
Trombone
Tuba in E♭
Tuba in B♭
Sousaphone
PERCUSSION
Banjo or Saz
Accordion
Piano or Organ
SOLOS
Soprano
Contralto
Tenor
Bass
Boy's Choir
CHORUS
Soprano
Contralto
Tenor
Bass
VIOLINS
I, IV
II, V
III, VI
Violas I III II IV
Cellos I III II IV
Contrabasses

In 1968, after the death of the greatly loved and respected American composer Henry Cowell and in protest against the Vietnam War, Dick Higgins commissioned a police officer to fire a machine gun at a few hundred orchestral score sheets. He later made copies of the score sheets and had an ensemble play the bullet holes as notes, thereby turning an act of destruction into one of creation.

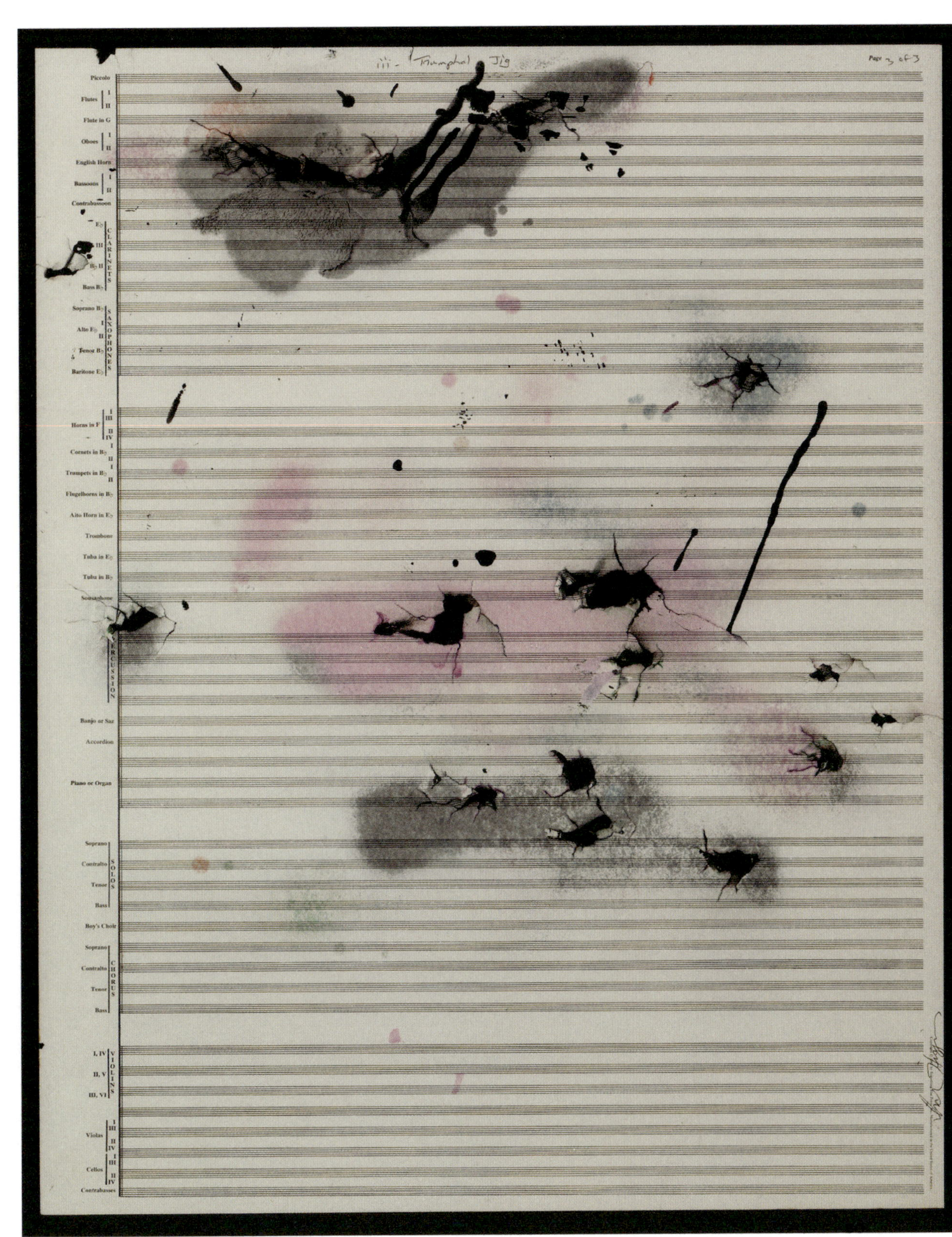

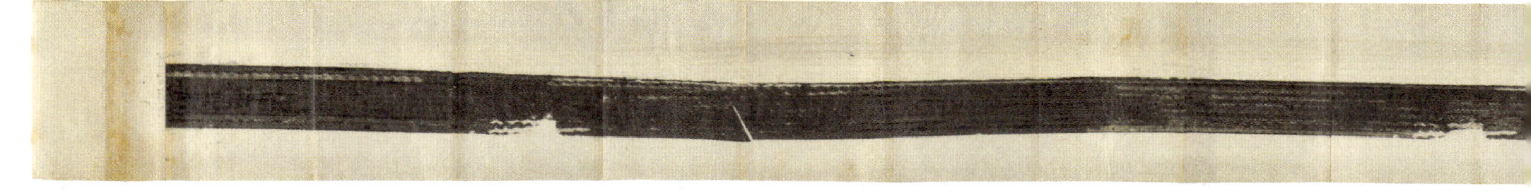

ROBERT RAUSCHENBERG

Automobile Tire Print
1953

In 1952, John Cage had written the piece *4'33"*, the score of which contained three movements but not a single note. During the premiere, pianist David Tudor indicated each movement by closing the piano fallboard, opening it only between movements. The sound of the silent concert hall was the performance. One year later, Rauschenberg directed Cage to drive his car over twenty sheets of paper. Both works raise questions regarding time, performance and the artist's role in the creative process.

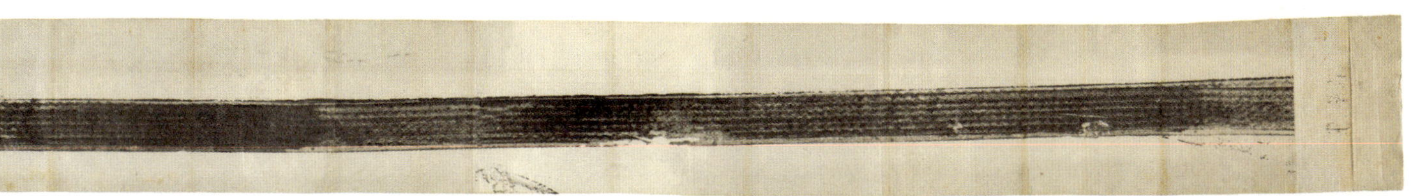

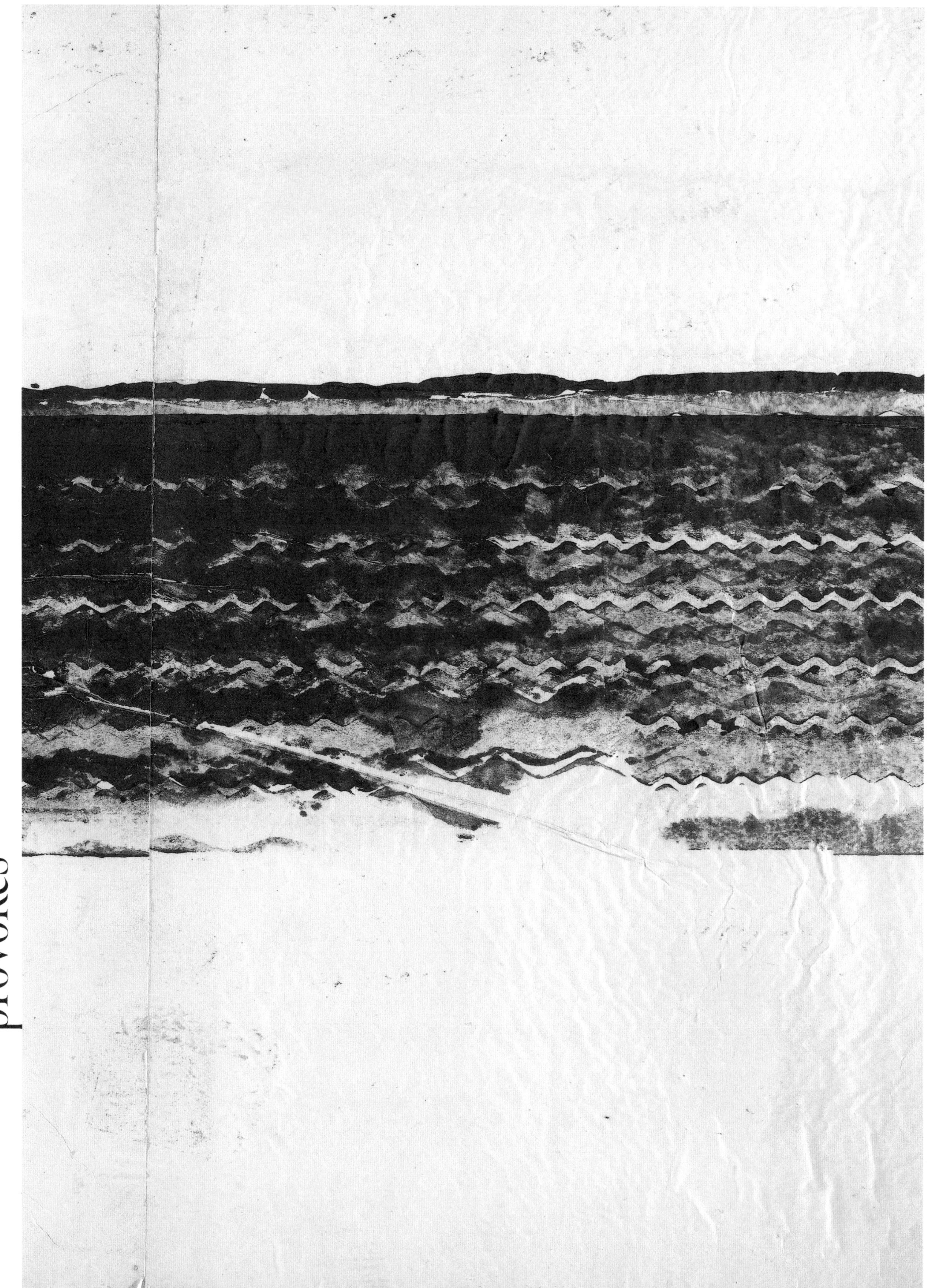

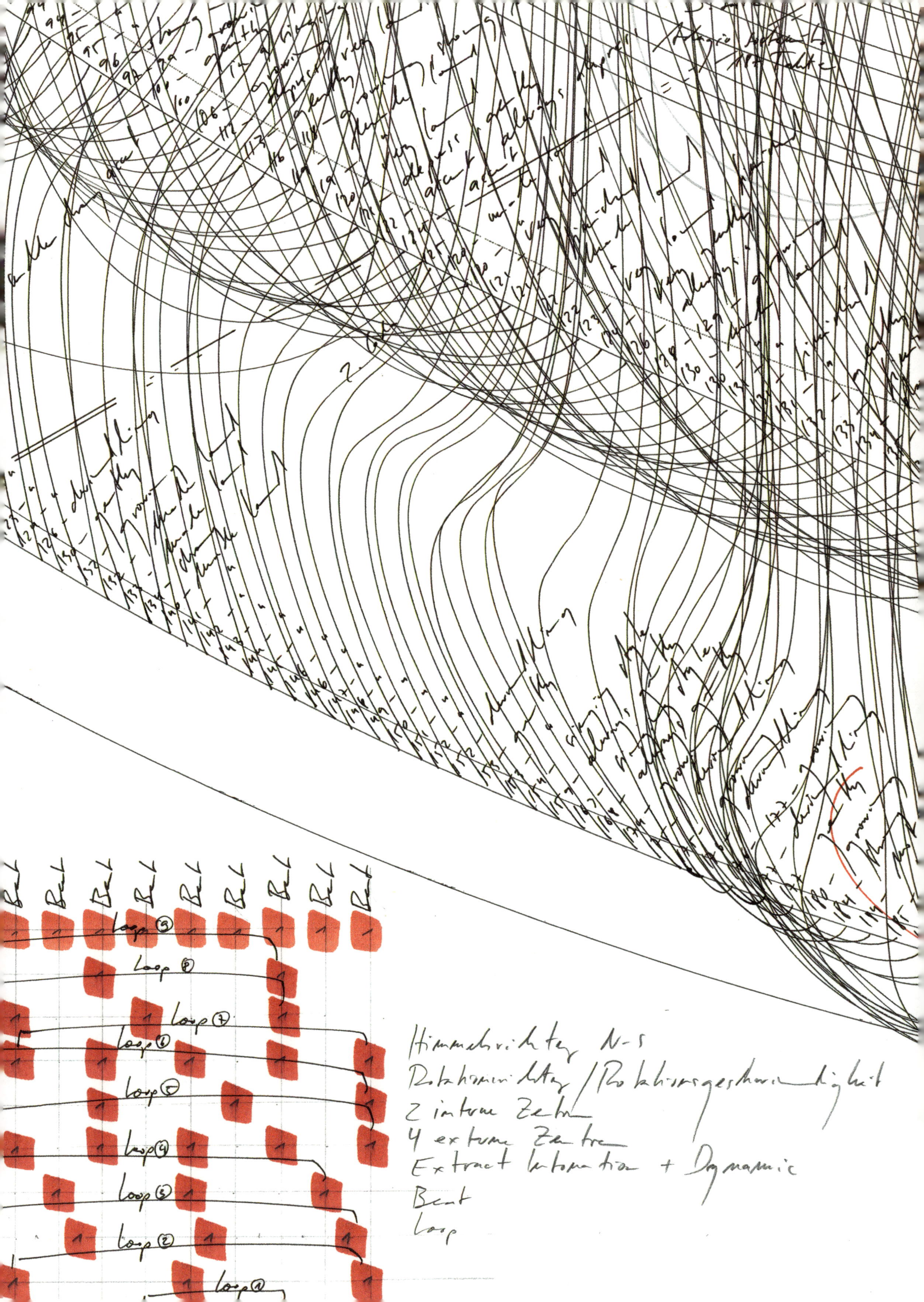
Beat
Loop 9
Loop 8
Loop 7
Loop 6
Loop 5
Loop 4
Loop 3
Loop 2
Loop 1
Himmelsrichtung N-S
Rotationsrichtung / Rotationsgeschwindigkeit
2 interne Zentren
4 externe Zentren
Extract Intonation + Dynamic
Beat
Loop

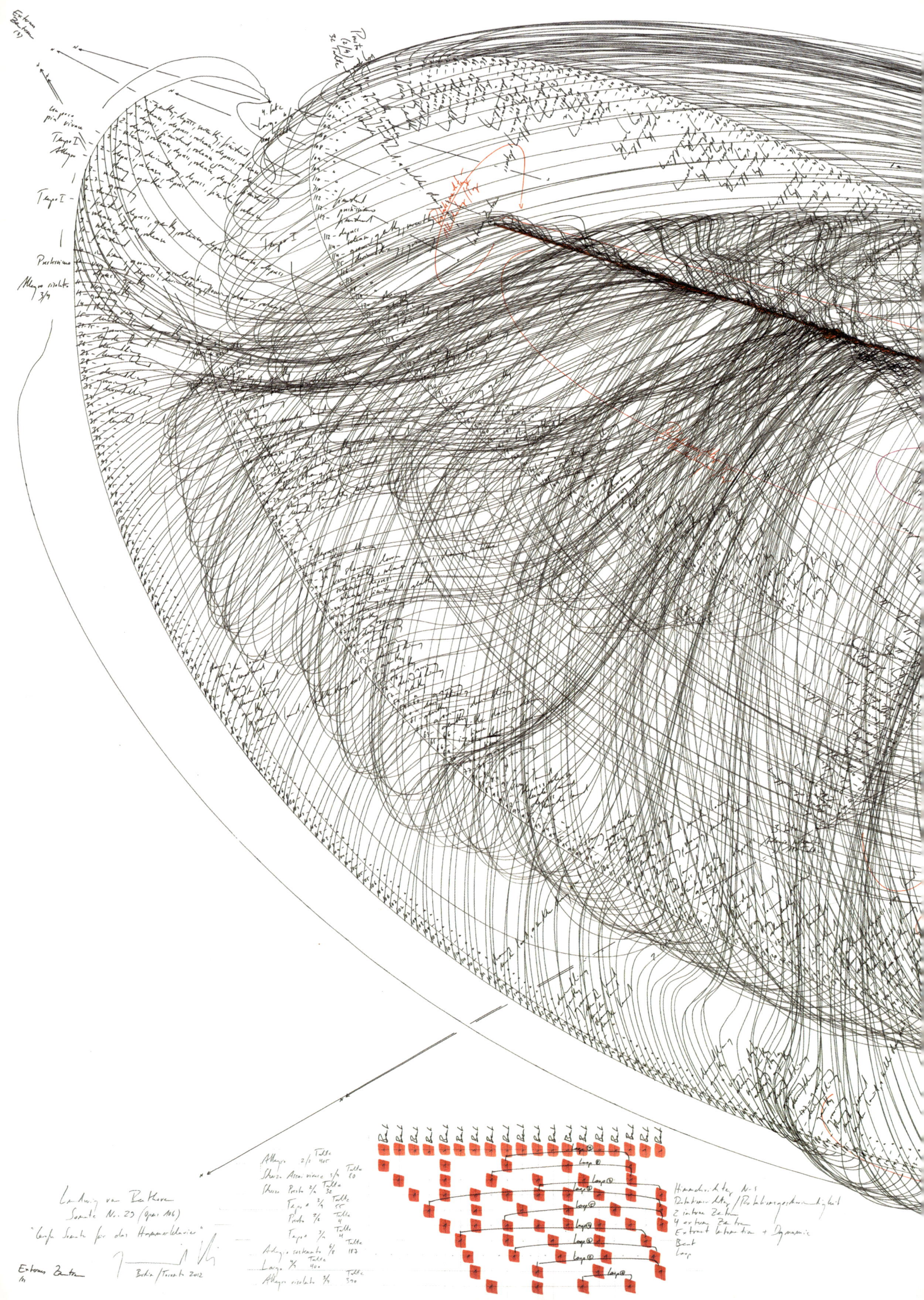
Ludwig van Beethoven
Sonate Nr. 29 (Opus 106)
"Große Sonate für das Hammerklavier"
Berlin / Toronto 2012
Externes Zentrum
Allegro 2/2 Takte 405
Scherzo Assai vivace 3/4 Takte 80
Scherzo Presto 2/4 Takte 32
Tempo I 3/4 Takte 55
Presto 2/2 Takte 4
Tempo I 3/4 Takte 4
Adagio sostenuto 6/8 Takte 187
Largo 4/4 Takte 40
Allegro risoluto 3/4 Takte 390
Himmelsrichtung N-S
Rotationsrichtung / Rotationsgeschwindigkeit
2 interne Zentren
4 externe Zentren
Beat
Loop

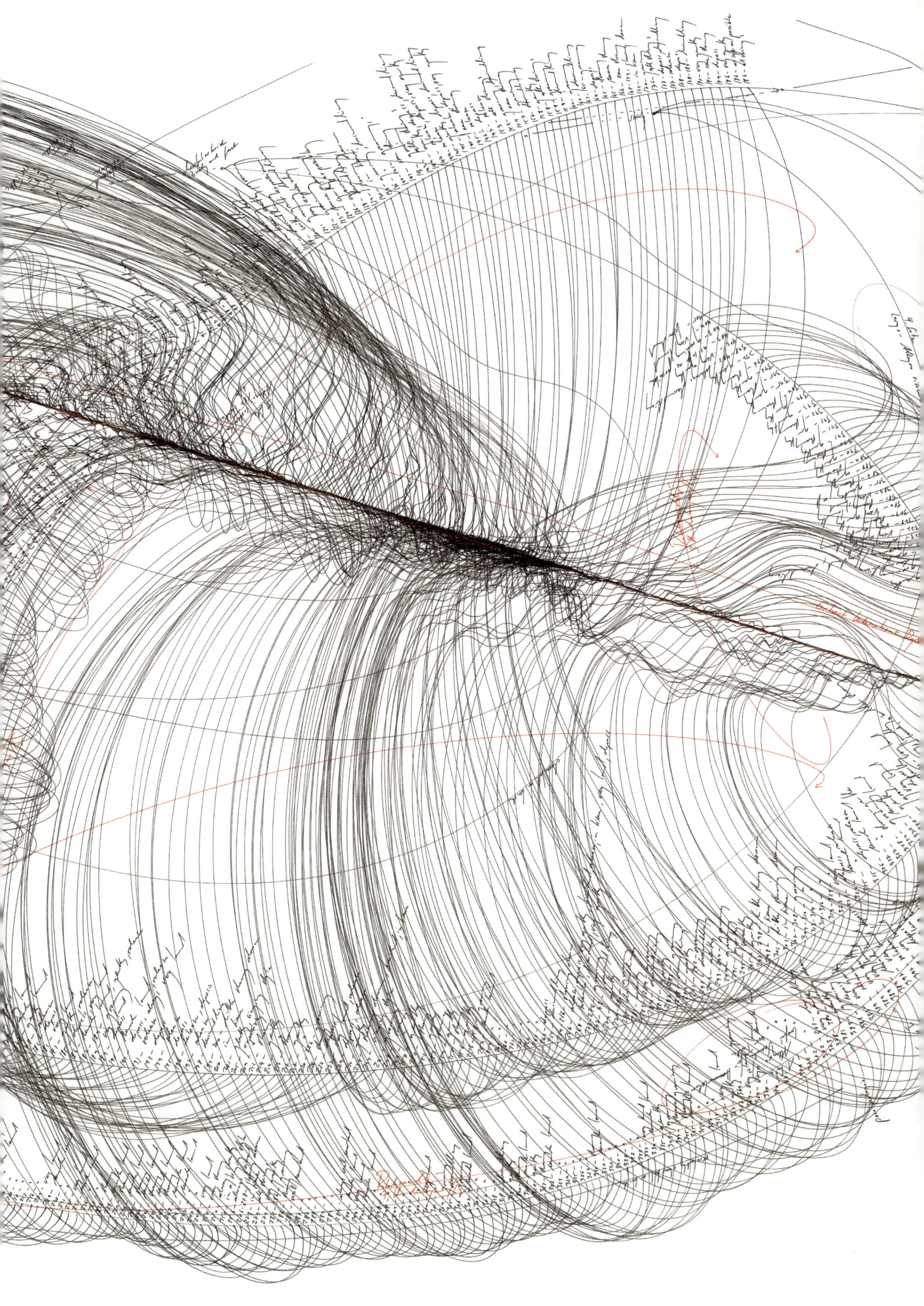

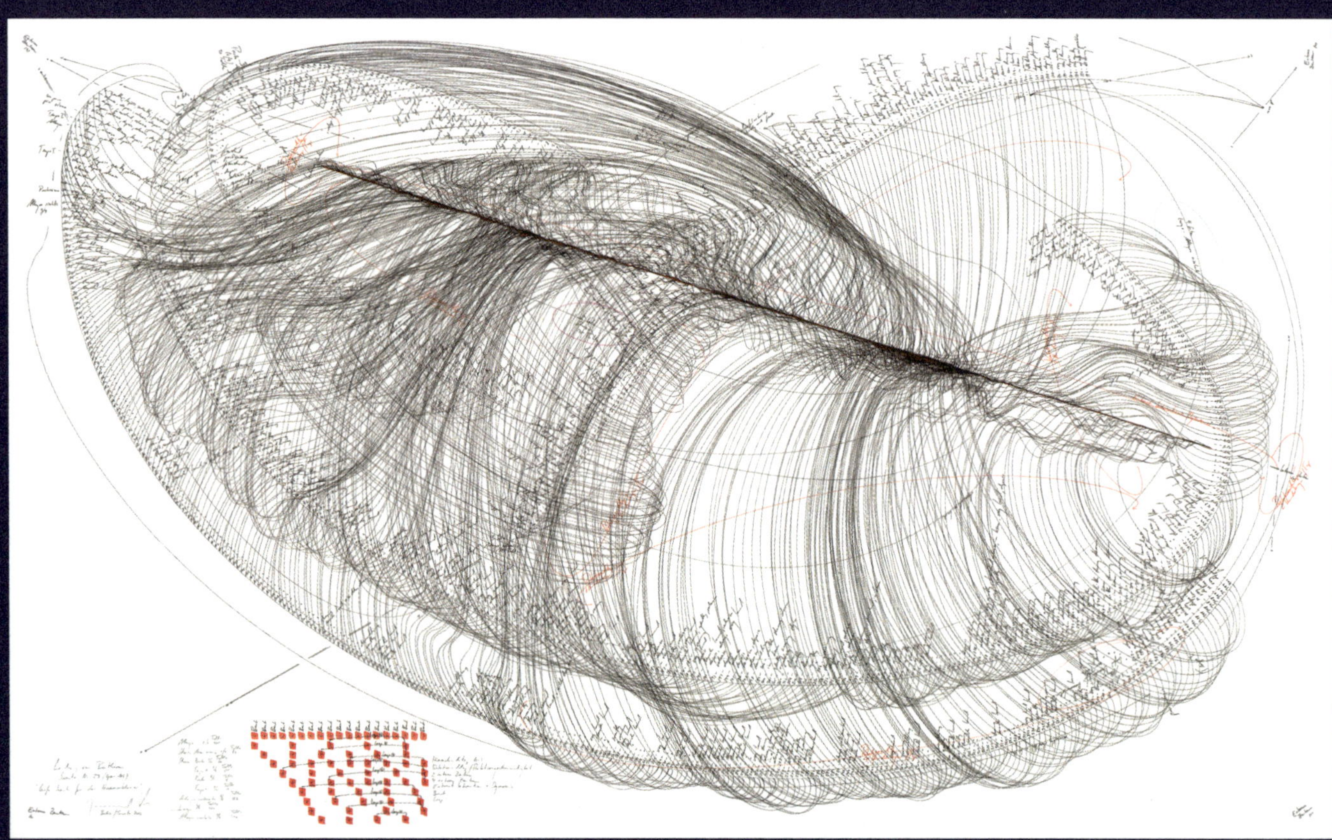

JORINDE VOIGT, LUDWIG VAN BEETHOVEN SONATA 29, 2012

CLEMENS GADENSTÄTTER

Iconosonic Beethoven

Culture, with all its historic connotations, inevitably intrudes upon our perception as a normative force. It sets standards, teaches us how to see a thing and what it is supposed to mean. It shapes all future perceptions and it influences how we view past experiences. Though cultural history can potentially expand our horizons, over the course of time it also entrenches us within the standards it imposes upon us – it becomes a prison for our perception.

As an antidote we have invented art, which in its turn becomes part of our cultural history. Consequently, art is also in constant danger of being consumed by that history. Art questions the perceptive norms of its time, extends them, turns them upside down – at least that is what I expect from art.

Beethoven has been consumed by cultural history and has been spat out again, fighting back against this misappropriation. Sometimes he – or rather his music – succeeds, but sometimes it doesn't. The machinery of cultural history (or rather the culture industry, to use Adorno's apt term) has turned Beethoven's sound-worlds into set pieces that can only imprint themselves upon our perception in a grossly simplified manner – devoid of the works' context, without differentiation and above all without the ramifications of Beethoven's fresh struggle with the very substance of music that every piece represents.

These are the set pieces that I refer to as iconosonics. I use the term to signify musical figures, structures, gestures, timbres that have come to represent aspects of our world, areas within our emotional life, across almost all stylistic borders. Storms, suffering, pain and grief, joy, rejoicing, the twittering of birds: all these phenomena are represented by the same or similar set pieces in the works of Vivaldi, R. Strauss and of course Beethoven. They have even retained their validity into the twentieth and twenty-first centuries. We have no difficulty imagining the sound of thunder, but we are also able to imagine the sound of a lightning flash – the very flash of light itself – because composers have projected this flash into the acoustic plain and there it has become entrenched. Iconosonics influence not only our understanding of sound phenomena, they also impact upon our acoustic imagination.

As entrenched perceptive *topoi,* we are no longer able to hear (perceive) their actual qualities, but rather react to them by assigning them prelearned meanings. This entrenchment of perceptive categories acts as a block to HEARING in an absolute sense. It sets in motion reactions and emotions in accordance with old patterns.

In my compositions I reverse the path briefly outlined above – the path that leads to acquired, ingrained forms of perception, reception and comprehension. I attempt to shift the listener from a mode of pre-determined reaction to that of actual HEARING. And this other way of hearing can perhaps allow a different way of experiencing, a new sensibility, even a hitherto unknown emotion to unfold.

I do not want to depict the world, instead I work *with* – or rather *away from* – entrenched modes of depiction. Such a re-forming of elements and acoustic structures rather than merely working with them may lead us to where we can begin to HEAR in an all-embracing sense, where we can experience the polyvalence, the multidimensionality of every phenomenon, every context, every structure. This also triggers our understanding of these phenomena and structures, where the phenomenon and its perception can free themselves from entrenched imprinting while at the same time retaining the imprints' shadows that allow us to experience the phenomena as our own. This method may lead to a place where we can undergo experience in the light of new perceptual categories, where we may learn to experience our own selves in a different way, to experience other selves as possibilities within us ... and probably much else besides.

Artistic acquisition begins by changing the context in which these iconosonics are perceived. When that which is pre-existent, foreign to us – though it may define us – is placed within a context unique to a specific work, it thereby loses its predetermined significance without being itself manifestly altered – though of course its former meaning still resonates, producing the necessary frictional energy I mention above. This is the case with all acoustic phenomena: the bowed sound of the violin, any interval, any noise – and the complex gestures of iconosonics. No phenomenon exists which is not in some way pre-defined: from our perspective there only exists that which comes to us from outside – that which is foreign to us. Through the conditioning of our perception, as part of our growing up, our learning, we feel as if it is 'in us'. Placed within a new context, we make phenomena our own in the sense of a consciously experienced perception of outward occurrences. And in a first step as a composer I make these externally defined objects my own.

Composing is thus an act of re-forming these pre-existent phenomena and equally pre-fixed contexts that have conditioned my – and in a broader sense *our* – perception. Such work as an act of transformation tears the fixed phenomenon from the chains that the history of our perception has laid upon it, revealing its specific qualities, concealed nuances, other possibilities and levels of meaning. We can experience the familiar, that which defines us, in all the dimensions and possibilities that its collective use has driven out of it.

In extreme cases I can try to present such iconosonics, phenomena created by other composers that have become narrowed in their frame of reference over time, in such a way that the context of the works from which they are taken is lost and they are experienced merely as signs, emblematic representations of parts of the world or sensations.

This takes place through a process of simplification, constriction and a trivialising 'pruning' of the music into a simple, appellative, collectively effective signal – for instance with phrases from the music of Ludwig van Beethoven.

Thus I make fragments of Beethoven's *oeuvre* my own – in various works, and in a particularly prominent manner in *Figure – Iconosonics I*.

In the face of the greatness of the incredible music and the endless variety of experimental approaches that this composer brought into the world, it may perhaps appear inappropriate to regard

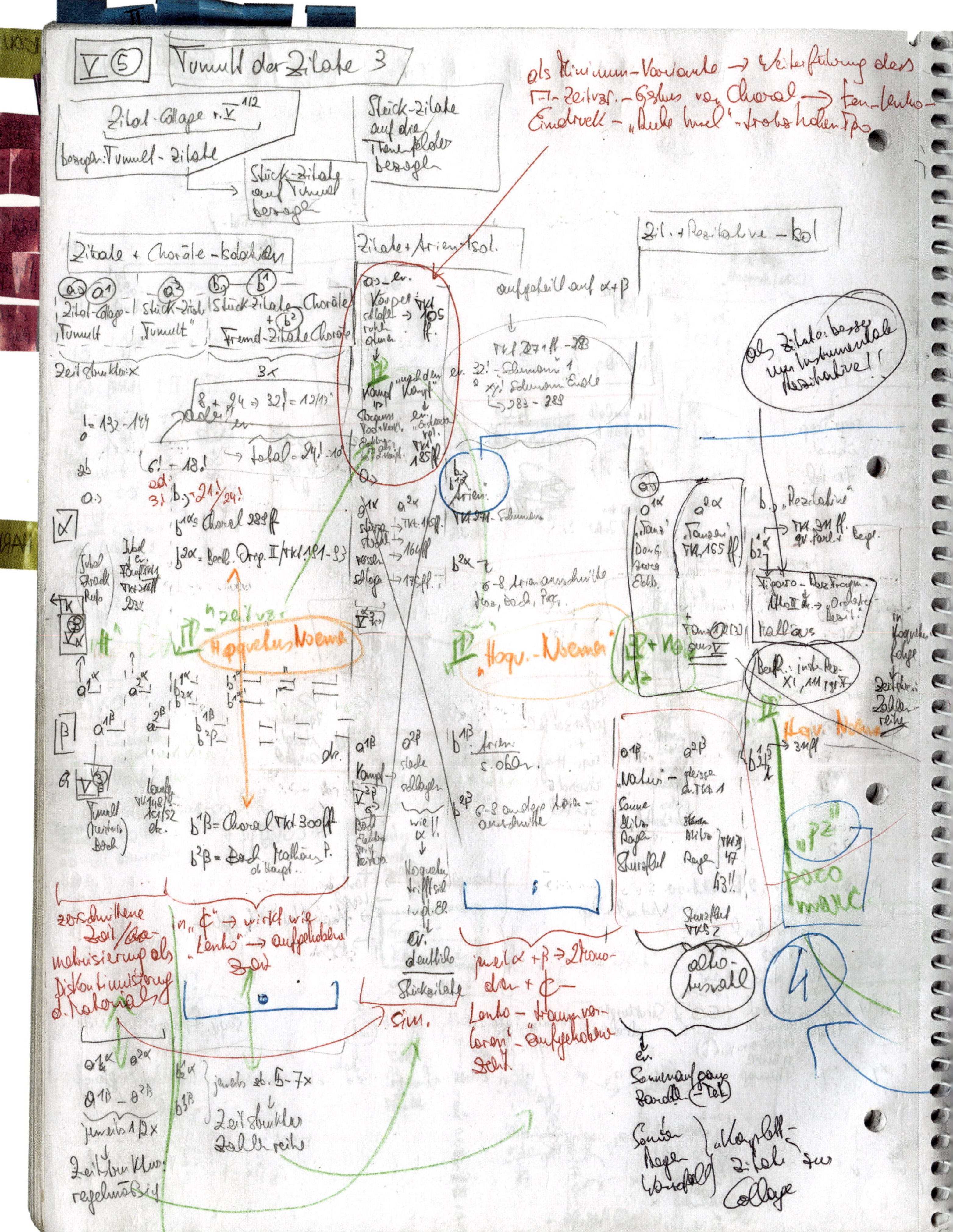
V 5
Tumult der Zitate 3
Stück-Zitate auf die Themenfelder bezogen
Stück-Zitate auf Tumult bezogen
Zitate + Arien-Isol.
sim.
POCO marc
Sonnenaufgang

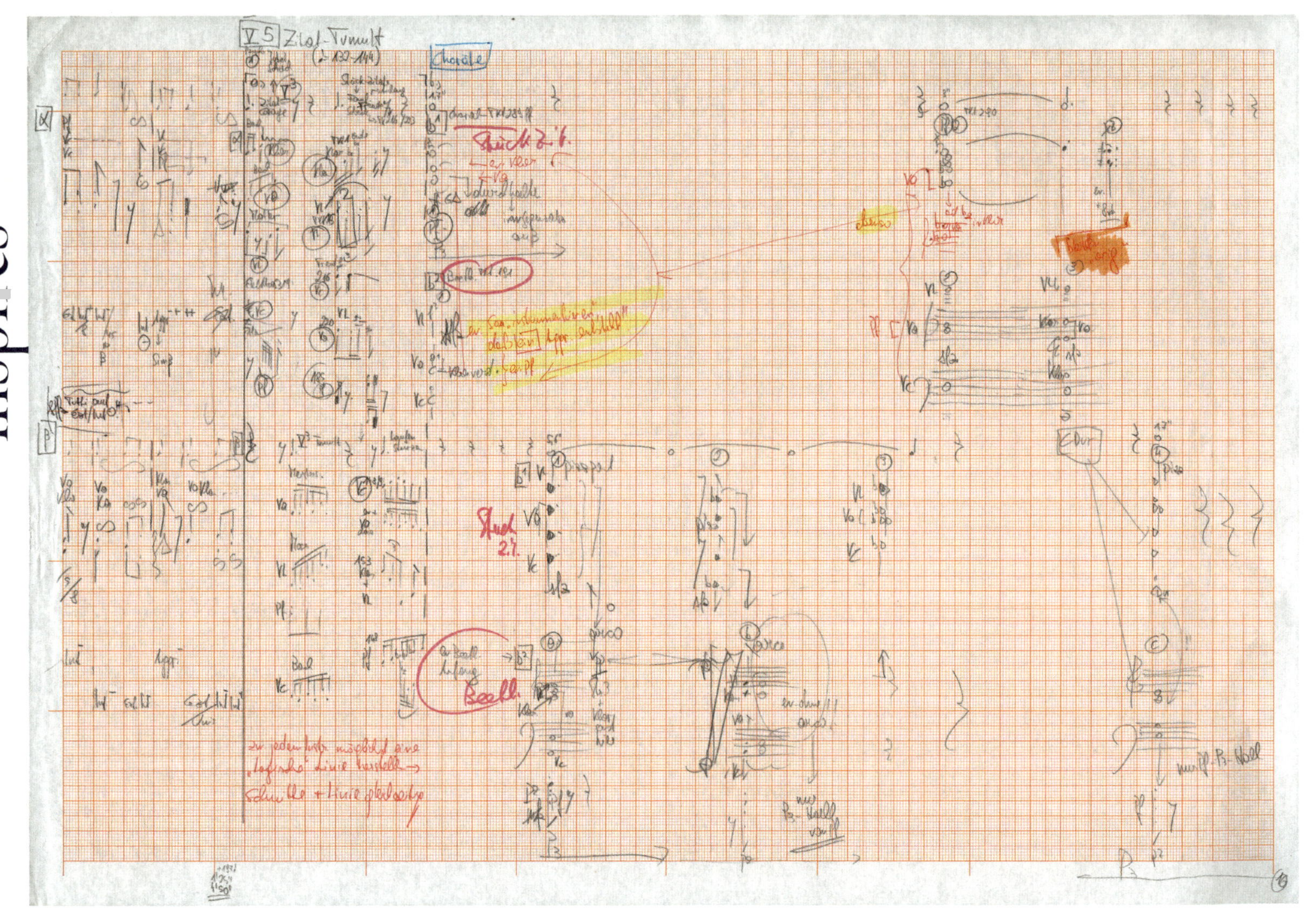

fragments of Beethoven's works as iconosonics, as signals for certain feelings or as acoustic depictions of certain worldly phenomena, and to turn these into 'set pieces' of our perceptual history, of our normalized way of thinking. However, Beethoven's music has been trivialized by our society, reduced to a pre-determined level of significance and experience: it has been turned into a banal substitute for European unity, to a cut-and-dried depiction of fate – a decorative copy of an experience of 'nature'. We are supposed to experience all these things in such and such a way – in this banal form – ideally all at once: such has been the training of our perceptual history.

Beethoven's music has itself been made into a 'figure'.

My work tries to allow those aspects of the music that have hitherto not in themselves been apparent to come to the fore. It seeks to expound upon the possibilities that are now open to us in the changed circumstances prevalent two hundred years after Beethoven's birth: those ways of understanding that he could not even guess at but that now offer themselves to us. Of course, I apply this same process to all the other objects upon which I set myself to work. Beethoven is just one of many iconosonics.

This process of appropriation is essentially different from a mere 'quoting' of the music of Beethoven, or anyone else. The specific contexts in which these Beethoven iconosonics appear as something new and different – as, for instance, in *Figure – Iconosonics I* – represent the first step in the work process. The fragments of Beethoven's music appear as 'maxima' – as isolated qualities in which, to varying degrees, other building blocks are embedded.

On a certain level, the end of the third movement of the String Quartet, op. 132 ('Heiliger Dankgesang eines Genesenden an die Gottheit, in der lydischen Tonart') that is woven or rather worked into *Figure – Iconosonics I* represents my music's closest approach to tonality, to the modes of listening and understanding inherent in the work's formal organization: an approach to the colours and types of feeling that such modes of listening can be deliberately made to trigger.

This approach is both criticism and deviation from those labelled or entrenched ways of experiencing music. Tonality is no longer the only possible harmonic world (a world that Beethoven thoroughly shook up). It stands in contrast to other worlds, and at the edges of these worlds arise energies that can change these worlds: when fire and water meet there is a hiss, steam rises, and wet ashes are all that is left – and none of these phenomena can be experienced when fire and water are merely juxtaposed.

Modes of articulation and instrumental playing techniques are contextualized as alterities that deviate from the musical shapes surrounding them and refer to something else.

The sharply accentuated *tenuto* that begins at the same time forms a musical figure that synthesizes disparate elements: the sharp cutting accents and the quiet prolongation of the sound. This element of synthesis is developed further in *Figure – Icosonics I* and pursued to other extremes.

The abandonment of polyphonic techniques is reworked to become an intermediary step towards 'absolute unison'.

Dynamic contrast becomes a level of dynamic flexibility in which the crude contrasts are differentiated in various degrees throughout the course of the work.

On other levels the Beethoven fragment within the context of the work is assimilated, throwing its particular light on the work as a whole. As such it cannot be separated from the corpus of the work.

Clearly the fragment from Beethoven's quartet remains what it is, but at the same time is has been transformed to become to an integral part of my quintet. It is simultaneously 'just Beethoven' as well as becoming my own unique material and part of my compositional world.

This two-faced nature of the work (though there are probably many more facets to the music than this) makes it possible for us to hear that which is familiar in a different way, and opens up the possibility of experiencing that which is unknown in the light of that which is familiar.

This adaptation of foreign material as a working hypothesis and central artistic premise occurs on all levels with all objects, structures and techniques and is taken to extremes in the adaptation of fragments of 'foreign' musics.

In the case of Beethoven, however, this is done with specific reference to a composer who is for me perhaps the most central composer of all: the composer who reinvents his *Instrumentarium* for each new work – building a different piano in each sonata – the composer who introduced *Empfindung* as an adaptable musical category into music.

Not the obliteration of feelings (this occurs automatically), but a re-working, a re-forming of our feelings: this is central to his music. We hear ourselves anew in this music. And to allow us to hear this apparently familiar music renewed, with new energies, meanings and qualities: this is the goal of the notated compositional thread of my work. In this respect the intrusion of Beethoven into the piece *Figure – Iconosonics I* and my attempt to appropriate this music is a form of homage that reverently yet confidently pays its respects to the composer who has made such a way of thinking, such a form of artistic activity possible in the first place.

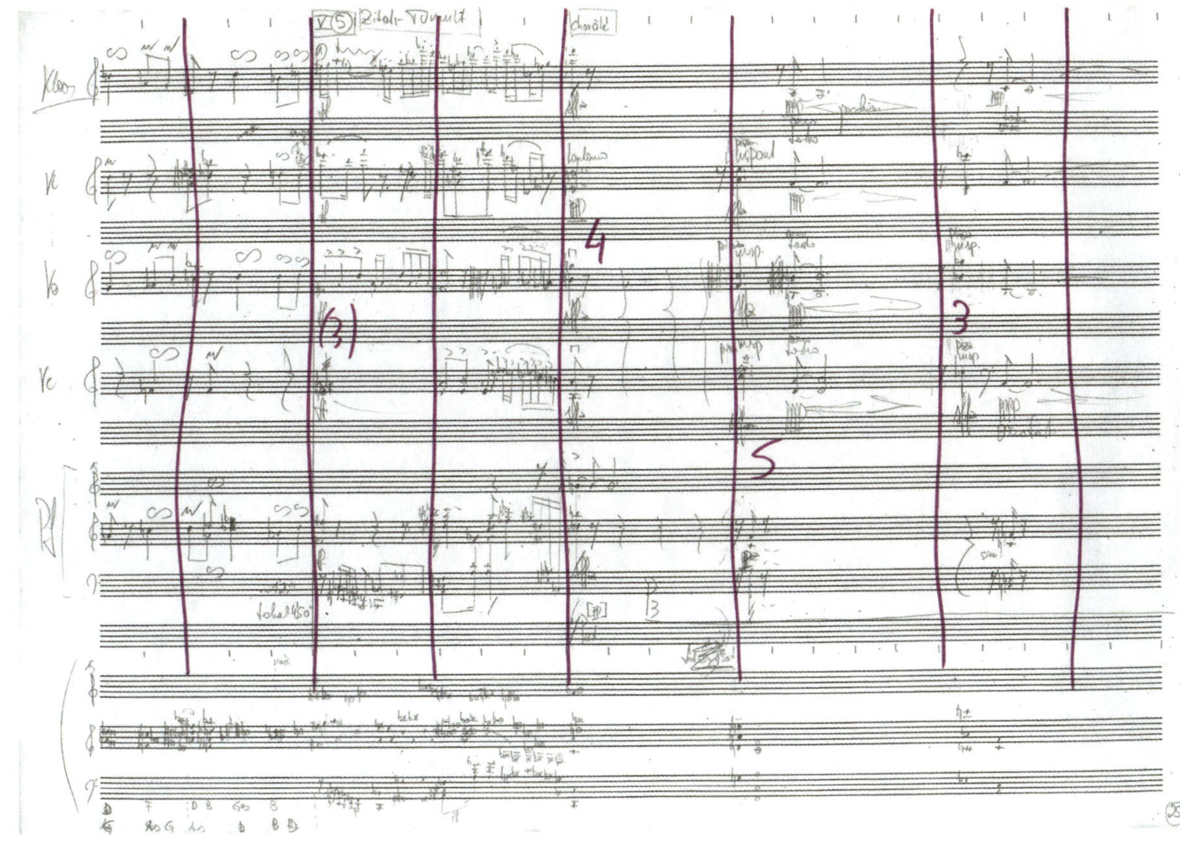

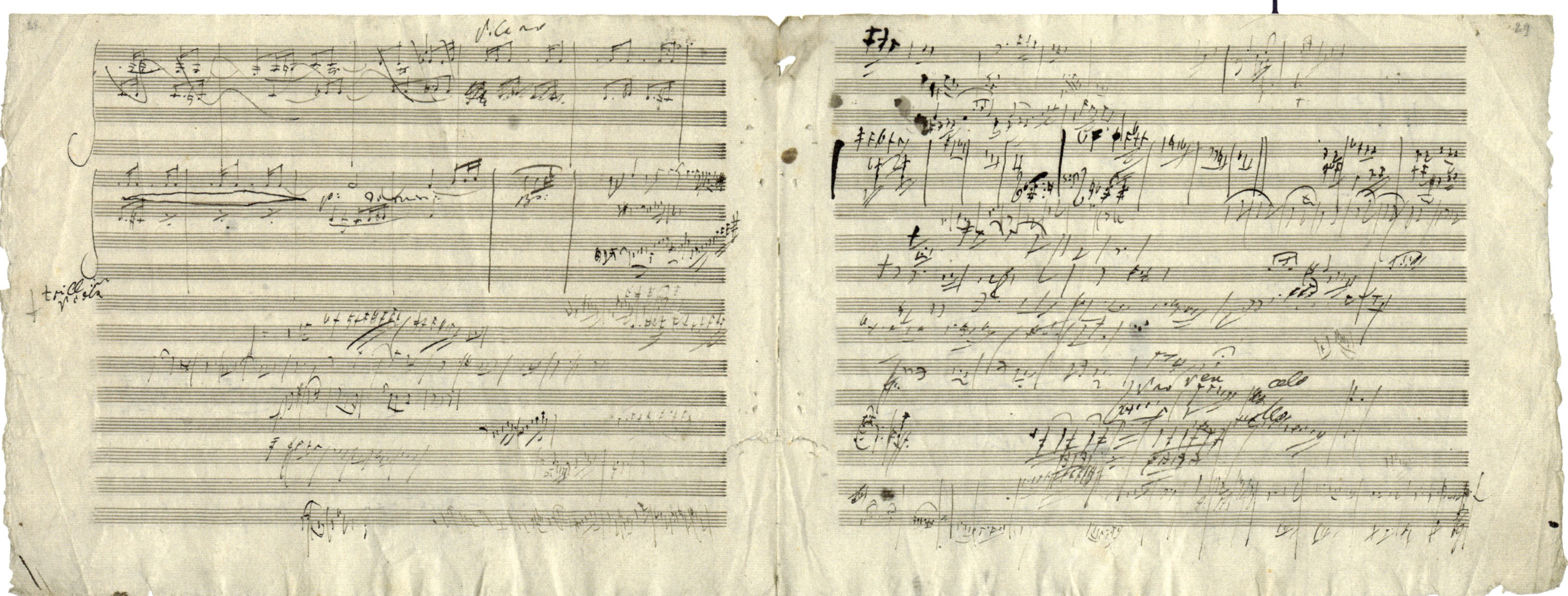

LUDWIG VAN BEETHOVEN

Sketches for String Quartets (in F major, E minor and C major), op. 59, autograph
1806

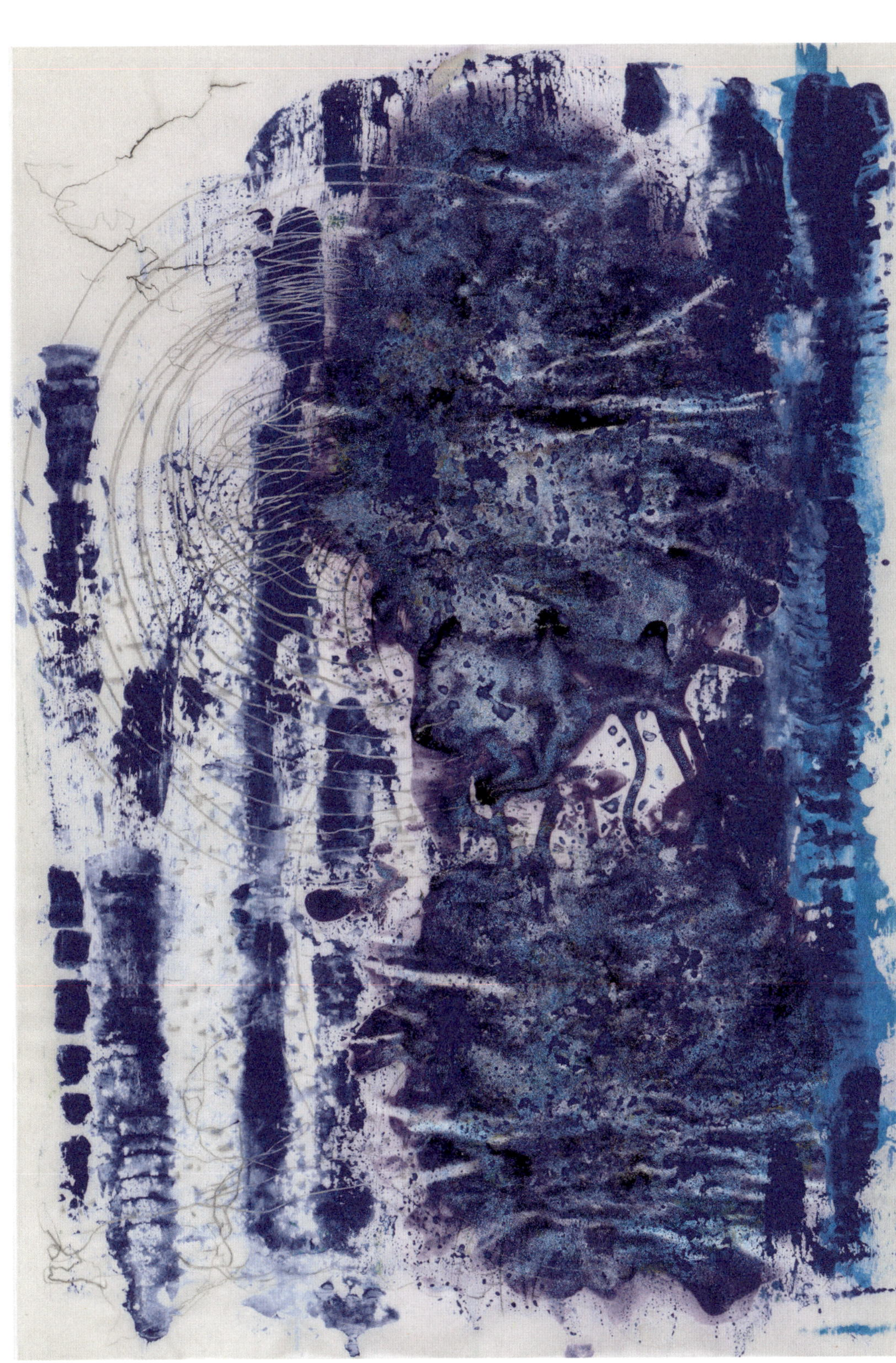

MARCELLO MERCADO

Bestiary of the Minds of the 21st Century: Genomic Opera 2015

My process involves converting fragments of genetic information mined from different organisms (mammals, insects, fungi etc.) into audio files using mathematical algorithms. The audio files are then translated into visual patterns via 3D printing, which form part of a new musical score. It is music to be seen and touched.

HIROSHI NAITŌ

Architectural Intention

inspires

Wilhelm Furtwängler, the famous conductor of the Berlin Philharmonic, once described Beethoven's music as being born of 'such steely calm and clarity, such an indomitable striving for mastery, the shaping of all matter to absolute completion'.[1] This is in fact the very essence of what architecture must aim for, and it aptly expresses the creative challenges that architectural intention must forever grapple with.

An elderly man of means wished to donate a new hall to one of Japan's national universities and asked me to design the building. The man had missed the chance to attend university himself in his struggle to make it through the hard times following the Second World War. As part of his legacy, he wanted to leave something behind for those young people who were now entering their higher studies. This hall was to be that gift. He was following a similar example from before the war: the entrepreneur Yasuda Zenjirō, founder of the Yasuda *zaibatsu*, had made his fortune in the late nineteenth century and went on to donate the well-known Yasuda Auditorium to the University of Tokyo at the end of his life.

The donor set three requirements: The new hall was to be large enough to hold a full class of students for matriculation and graduation ceremonies, but at the same time would have to also serve the university's daily needs and be suitable for classical music concerts. There were some three thousand students in each intake class at the university. It would be a tremendous challenge to achieve the desired acoustics in a hall of that size. At the same time, in order for the building to serve daily needs, the university requested that the space be divisible into one larger hall with a capacity of about a thousand people and five smaller lecture halls with stadium seating. Both large and small configurations would need to be suitable for classical music performances.

Offering a sense of unity for a large crowd gathered in one space and at the same time providing for a sound field that can carry the delicate strains of classical music – two largely incompatible demands – has long been one of architecture's most daunting problems. I was now being asked to make it work on both large and small scales. I found an occasion to explain the difficulty to the donor, but he remained firm in his classical music requirement. Why was he so fixated on classical music? As I was nearing completion of my conceptual drawings, I asked him about it once again.

In his youth, the man had fallen seriously ill with tuberculosis and was on the verge of death in the hospital. Tuberculosis was still among the most dreaded diseases at the time. One day, when he doubted he could hold on for more than another day or two, he heard music coming from somewhere. He didn't know the work at the time, but apparently someone was playing Beethoven's Fifth Symphony in a nearby room. As he listened, the strains of music boosted his spirits and rekindled his will to live. Because of that experience, classical music had become more than mere music to him; it had become a vital sustenance for his heart throughout his life. Beethoven's music is overwhelmingly constructive. It can, at times, have the power to shift the border between life and death.

Since listening to classical music is essentially my one and only hobby, I have a collection of several hundred CDs lining a section of my bookshelves. For some reason, however, there are relatively few Beethoven CDs among them. Why is it that I don't listen to Beethoven so often? Setting aside differences of scale, I suspect it's because there are too many similarities between his music and what I face on a daily basis in my work as an architect.

Building is an act of architectural intention. Giving life to the spaces that emerge requires a measure of fervour that will make the structure pulse. Any encroachment of human desires and whims, functionality, and economic or other social concerns into this architectural intention prevents the true realization of the structure.

Beethoven's music embodies a powerful architectural intention, and it also holds an enormous measure of passion that makes his structures pulse. These structures of sound simply bear too close a resemblance to the structures of architecture. And that, I think, is why I've come to prefer listening to other music – music that is different, more lyrical.

The new auditorium was packed when it was opened to the sounds of the university orchestra performing Beethoven's Ninth Symphony before the donor as guest of honour. The hall became a single, unified space, the building harmonized with the music, and I felt the entire structure become a musical instrument. For a moment, the music and my architectural mind appeared to have melded into one. For the two to reach true consonance, however, both my personal way of life and the buildings I create will need to go through a period of further maturation.

1 [… welche eiserne Ruhe und Klarheit, welch unerbittlicher Wille nach Beherrschung, Gestaltung alles Stofflichen bis ins Letzte!] Wilhelm Furtwängler, *Ton und Wort. Aufsätze und Vorträge 1918 bis 1954* (Wiesbaden, 1982), 9. Translation from German original by Nadezda Kinsky Müngersdorff.

CymaScope makes music visible by imprinting sound vibrations onto the surface of water. The result is an intricate network of interlacing patterns that can reveal the complexity of an individual music note, or that of an entire musical piece. In this way, people can see the nuances of a sound, which would otherwise not be sensed by the human ear alone.

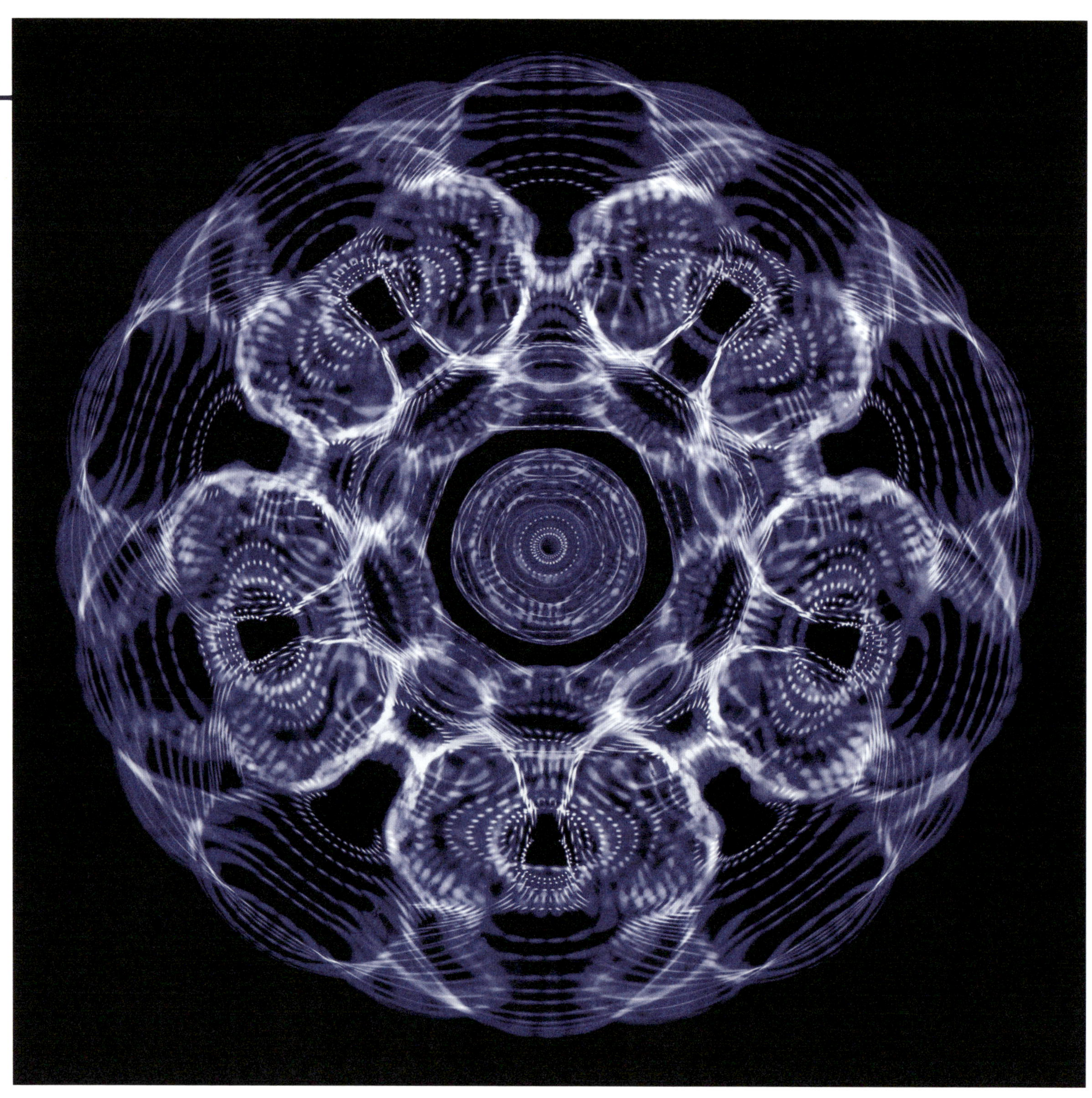

CYMATICS RESEARCH

12 Piano Notes (C1)
2013

川野里子

テンペスト2019

2019 年夏。東京の電車は清潔でとても静かだ。誰も話さない。誰も電話をしない。満員の車内にぎっしりと人は立ち、互いの体に触れぬよう気づかいながら、運ばれてゆく。まるで棺桶のように。

ヒロシマ。ナガサキ。フクシマ。そののちの静寂に黒きピアノ一台

なぜ泣かぬなぜ怒らない語らない夏の欅は焦げながら立つ

感情をもたぬがごとく闇なかにいまだ弾かれぬピアノがありぬ

なぜ?といふ問ひのやうなるニ短調芽吹きのやうにピアノは鳴りぬ

イヤホンからベートーヴェンのピアノソナタ17番が鳴り始め、私は目を閉じる。
初老の Wilhelm Kempff が追いかけるしなやかで強靱な光のような音。

静寂の中に待つときにわたしは震へる小枝となりぬ

pp
オクターブ駆け抜けてゆく指先が鍵盤の果てに触れたり光に

落雷として　燃えあがる欅　わたしはここだ

sf　*fz*
急いで、急いで、もつと急いで　滅亡が追ひかけてくる蔓草のやうに

フクシマでは今、人が住めなくなった町や田畑を蔓草が覆ってゆく。草はとめどもなく氾濫し、
人の気配も記憶も消してゆく。草が人間を消してゆく。

黒鍵は夜、白鍵は昼　くりかへしくりかへし呼ぶ人間はどこだ

ここに　嵐がありぬ　わたしのなかに

fz　*rf*
躓きの石。躓きの炎。人間をやりなほすために吾は生まれて

電車が鉄橋にさしかかる。橋梁の音が体に響くとき、音のない世界に生きた音楽家を思う。
微かな振動としてあったベートーヴェンにとっての音。ああそうか。音は鼓動か。

あさがほの蔓先のやうなあなたの孤独がわたしに触れた

pp
それでも人間であるほかなくてピアノは鳴りぬ

fff
ルートヴィッヒ・ヴァン・ベートーヴェンここにピアノはありぬ心臓として

車窓から隅田川が見える。夏の川面が強く光る。私は一本の嵐となったまま林立する人間の間に、
すなわち嵐の最中に立っている。

SATOKO KAWANO

The Tempest 2019

It is the summer of 2019. The trains in Tokyo are clean and very quiet. No talking. No telephoning.
People are standing on a crowded train, taking special care not to touch. Everybody is carried away, as if in a coffin.

Hiroshima. Nagasaki. Fukushima. A black piano for the silence afterwards.

Why don't you cry, scold, talk? The keyaki trees stand scorched.

Devoid of emotion, there is a piano in the darkness that has not yet been played.

The piano sounds like a bud. As if it's asking 'WHY?' in D minor.

Beethoven's Piano Sonata No. 17 starts to sound from my headphones, and I close my eyes.
A sound as constant as strong light and yet elegant, like that favoured by the older Wilhelm Kempff.

As I waited in silence, I became a twig that trembles.

pp The fingertips run through the octaves and at the end of the keyboard, touch light.

Like a thunderbolt. A keyaki tree flames up. I am here.

sf Hurry, hurry, hurry *fz* up. Just like the weeds that are chased by decay.

In Fukushima, climbing plants cover fields and towns where people can no longer live.
The grass has flooded everywhere, erasing both signs of life and memories of people. The grass is deleting humans.

Black keys at night, white keys for the day. I am calling again and again. Not a single body.

There is a storm. Inside my body.

fz Stumbling *rf* blocks. Stumbling flames. We were born to start all over again.

The train approaches a bridge. My body resonates with the sound of the structure, and I think about the musician who lived in a silent world. Music for Beethoven must have been mere slight vibrations. Oh, I see. Sounds are heartbeats.

Like a recent vine of Japanese morning glory your loneliness touched me.

Still without a human, a piano doesn't *pp* sound.

fff Ludwig van Beethoven, the piano is here, like a heart.

I see the Sumida River from the train window. The river surface shimmers starkly in the summer light.
I had become a storm within a crowd of people. I am virtually standing up in the midst of a huge hurricane.

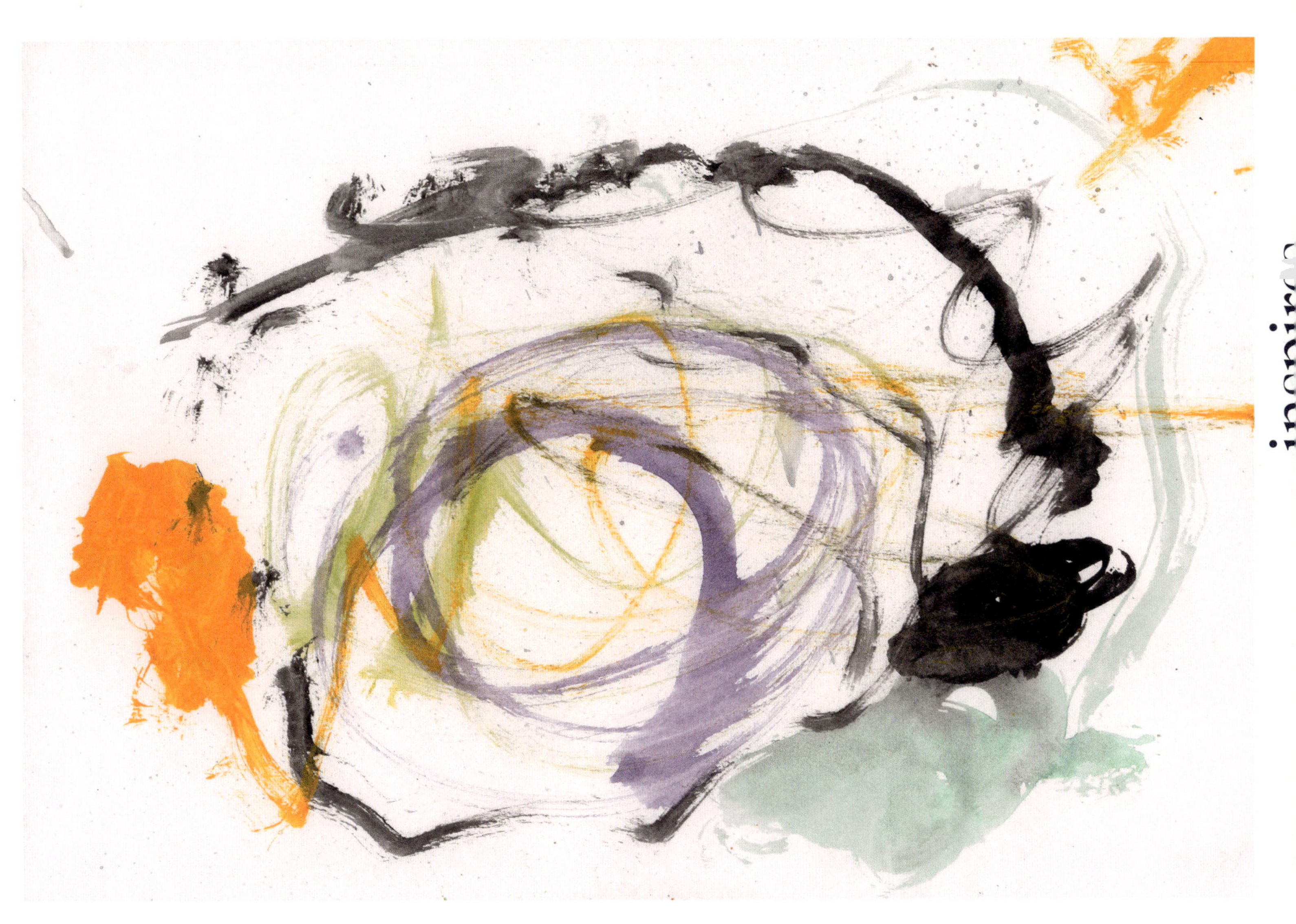

PAULA NOLL
Piano Sonata No. 16 in G major, op. 31, no. 1
2019

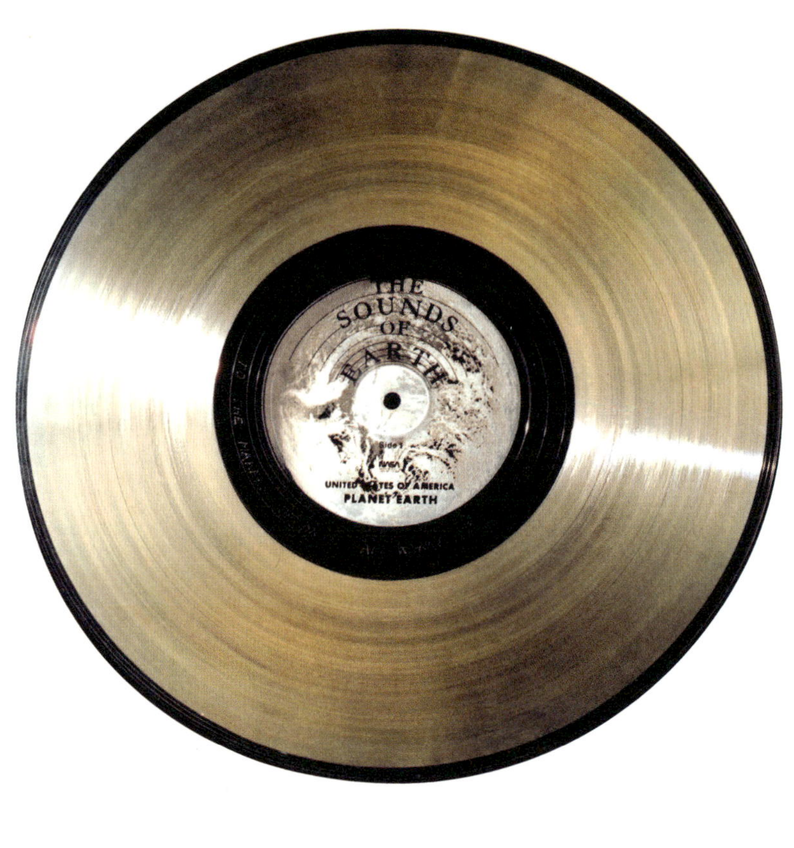

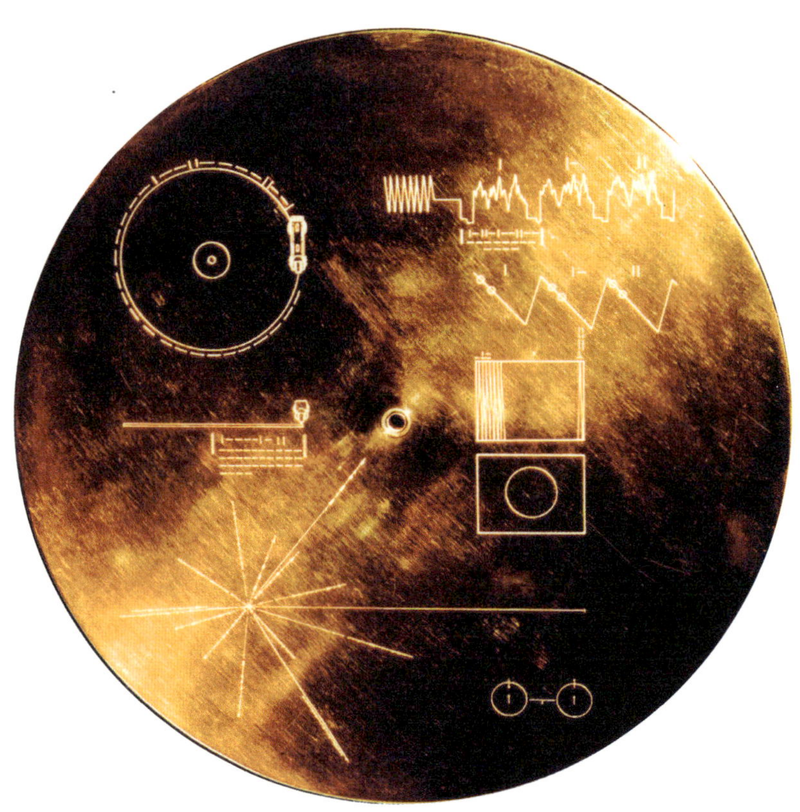

In 1977, NASA released two probes – Voyager 1 and 2 – to study the solar system. They each carry a golden record, which is to communicate the story of humankind to extra-terrestrials. Tellingly, Beethoven's Fifth Symphony and String Quartet No. 13 are both featured on the record. *Pale Blue Dot* is a photograph of planet Earth taken by Voyager 1 from the record distance of six billion kilometres.

NASA

Voyager 1, Voyager Golden Record
1977

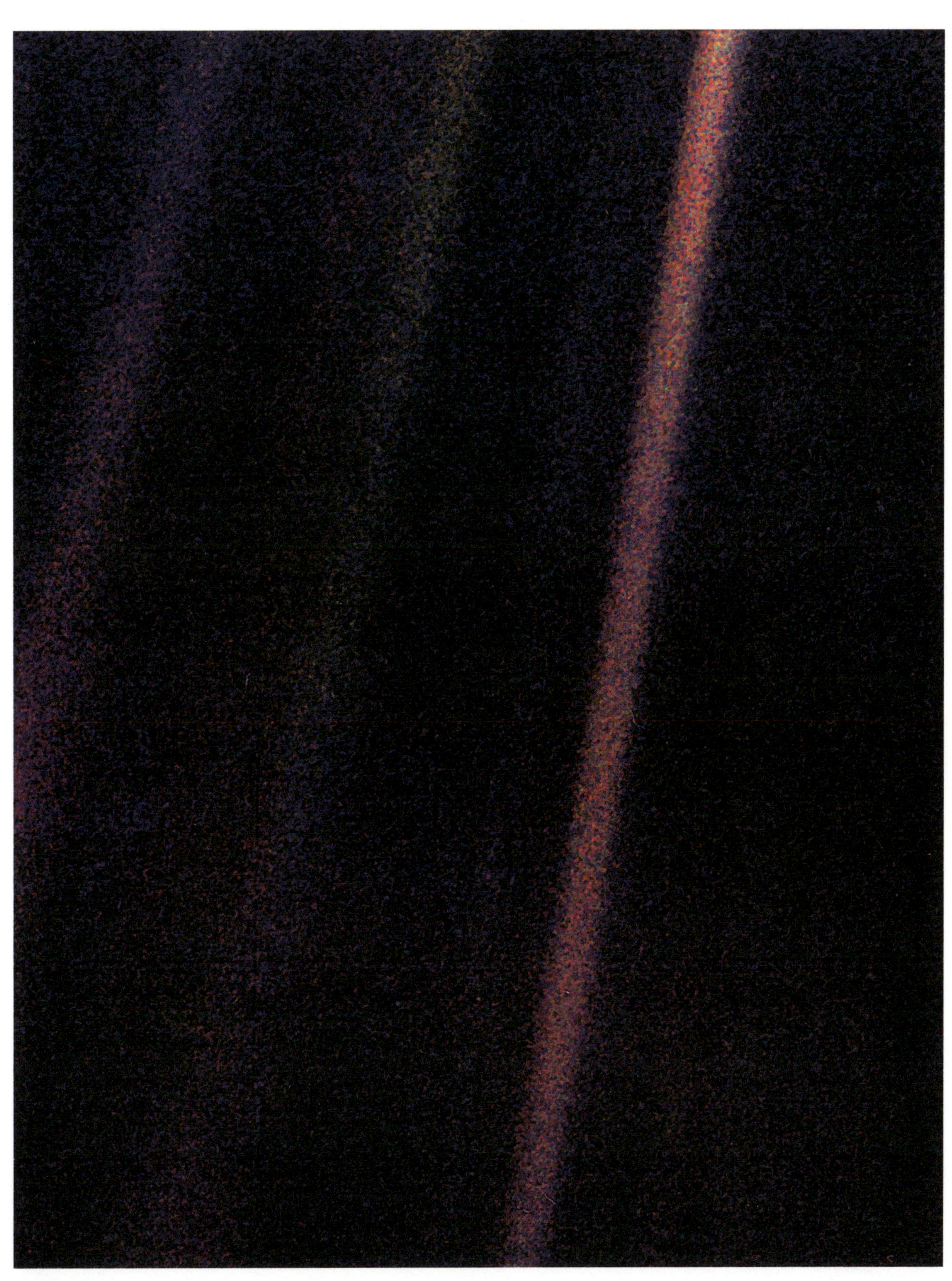

NASA

Voyager 1, Pale Blue Dot
1990

KATIE PATERSON

Earth-Moon-Earth
2007

For this work, Beethoven's *Moonlight Sonata* was translated into Morse code and transmitted to the surface of the Moon using Earth-Moon-Earth (E.M.E.) radio transmission. Fragmented by the Moon's surface, the returning code was converted into a new score, the gaps and absences becoming intervals and rests.

JULIA RONGE

The ‘Waldstein’ Sonata

Beethoven composed his Piano Sonata in C major, op. 53, known as the ‘Waldstein’ Sonata, around the turn of the years 1803 and 1804. It was first published in the *Wiener Kunst- und Industriekontor* in the spring of 1805. The date of the first performance is unknown.

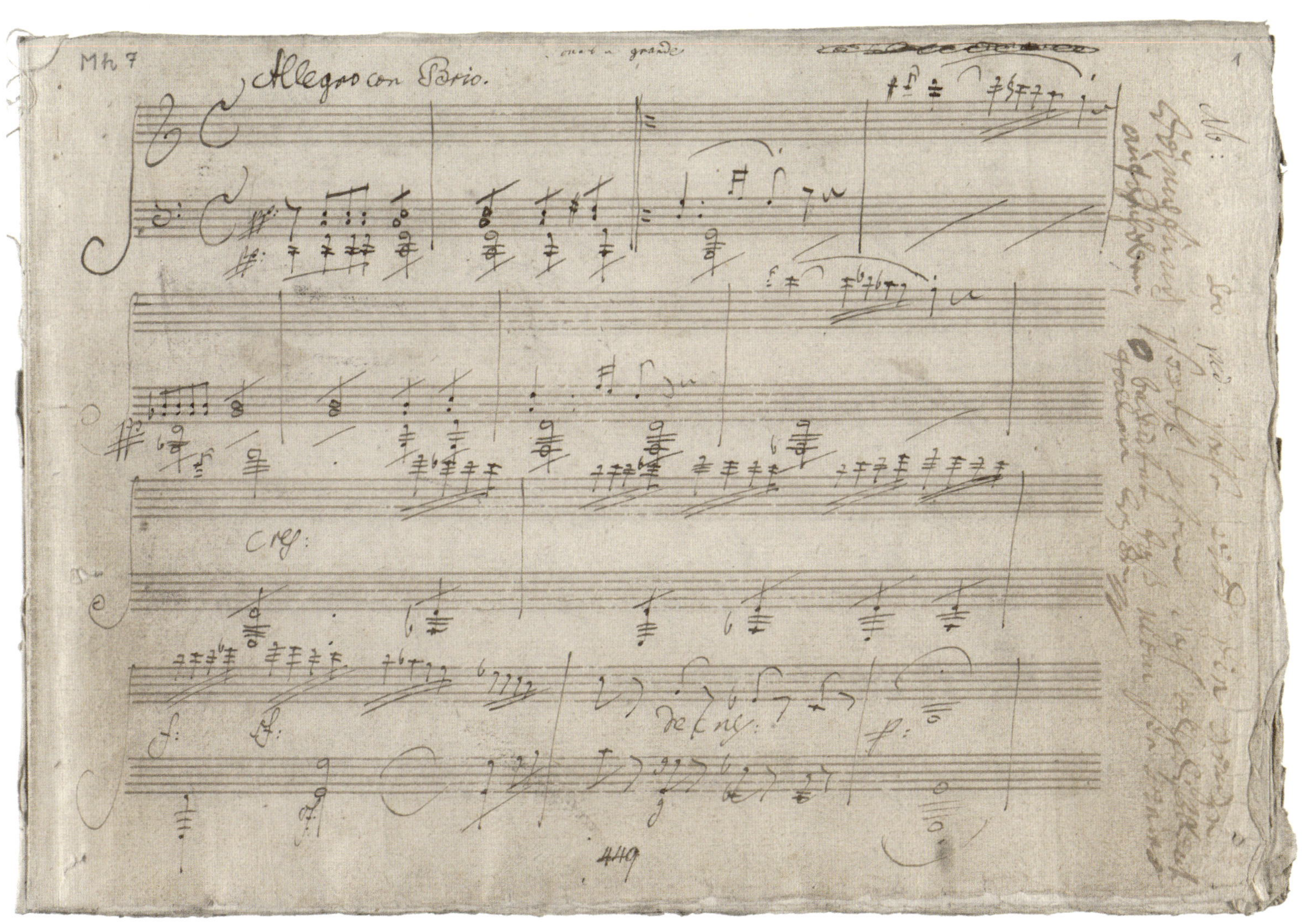

However, Beethoven apparently performed the work to a circle of friends or in a semi-public concert in a salon, as Ferdinand Ries reports: 'The Sonata (in C major, opus 53), which is dedicated to his first patron, the Count of Waldstein, initially contained a large Andante. A friend expressed his opinion to Beethoven that the sonata was too long, upon which the latter lashed out at him. After calm consideration, however, my teacher was soon convinced that the comment was justified. He subsequently published the large Andante in F major in 3/8 time on its own and later composed the interesting introduction to the Rondo that is now part of the sonata.'[1] Beethoven published the Andante he had dropped from the sonata separately, also in 1805 in the *Industriekontor*, where, from the second edition in 1806 onwards, it was given the subtitle *Andante favori*. Nothing in the title of the publication, nor indeed in any other source, indicates that the piece had once been the central movement of the 'Waldstein' Sonata. However, the autograph manuscript verifies Ries' report. The slow introduction to the last movement (*Introduzione. Adagio*) that was composed to replace the long middle movement appears on sheets 14 and 15, which were evidently added later. Both inserted sheets are secured to two pages of the original autograph. At the edge of sheet 14 with the beginning of the introduction are clearly the remnants of the left page of what must previously have been a double sheet. This stub was glued down beyond the binding so it can still be seen on sheet 9r. Sheet 15 has not been glued in but stitched onto the half-sheet behind it (it was not removed completely as the third movement begins on this page). The ink on the two inserted sheets is also somewhat lighter than in the rest of the manuscript.

Removing the original middle movement was not the only decisive change Beethoven made to the proportions of the sonata. After he had in effect made a two-movement sonata out of a work in three movements – the introduction leads into the Rondo and cannot really be considered an independent movement – Beethoven made a further major change in the balance of the work with a simple cut. He had initially envisaged a repeat of the development section and the recapitulation of the first movement. The indication prima volta can be clearly seen on sheet 11v, followed immediately by a coda marked seconda volta. Beethoven crossed out the two bars of the prima volta and the brackets of the seconda volta with decisive pencil strokes, thus dispensing with the lengthy prolongation of the first movement. As the indication vide, which confirms the cut, is written in the same reddish ink as the newly composed *Introduzione*, we can assume that this shortening of the movement was made at the same time as the central movement was replaced.

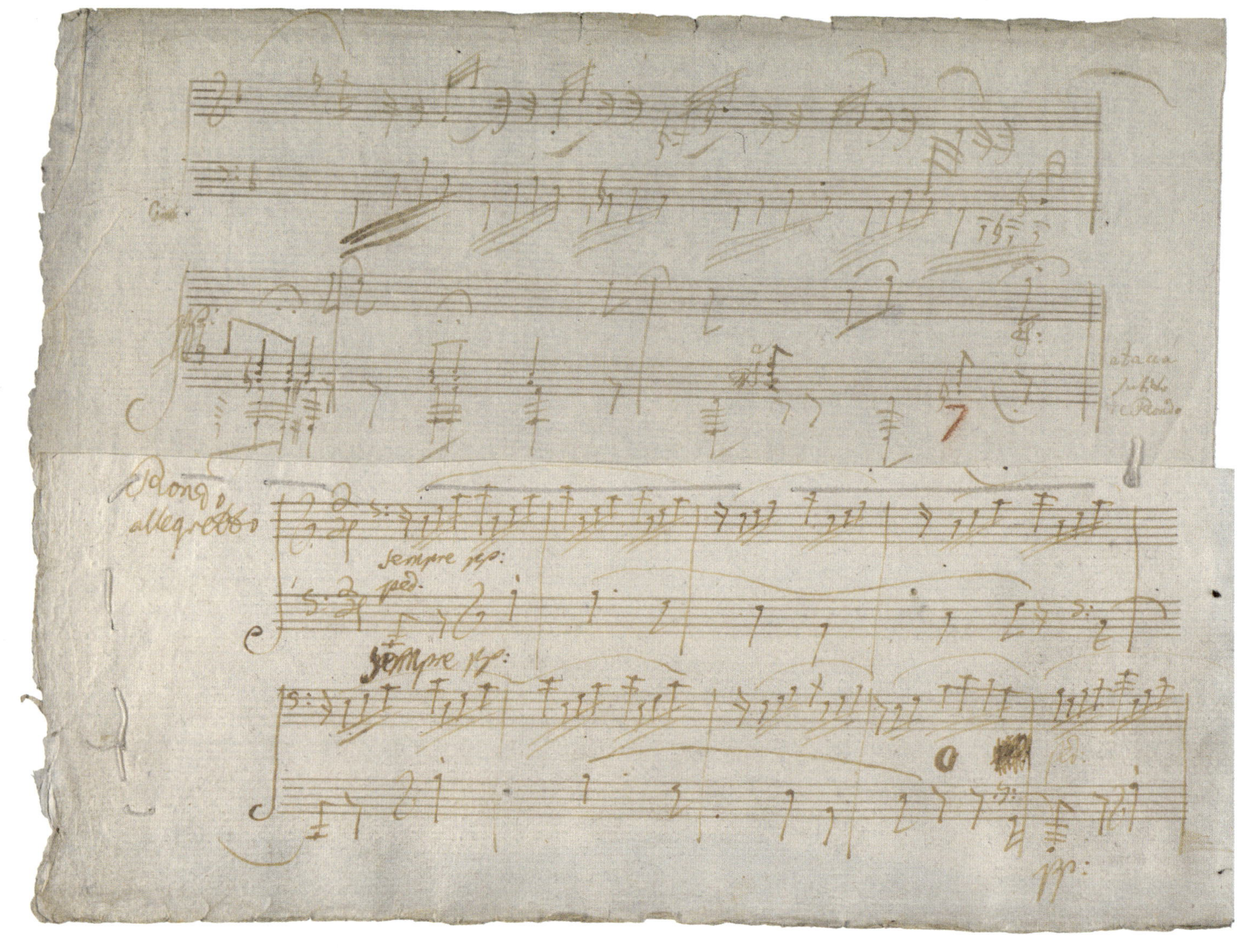

Beethoven would have liked to have sold his twenty-first piano sonata to the publishers Breitkopf & Härtel in Leipzig with whom he had already tried to establish business relations in the summer of 1804. The reason for this lay primarily in his hope for a prompt publication date from Breitkopf & Härtel. 'Another concern of mine is that previous publishers have often delayed terribly before my compositions could reach the light of day, with each publisher blaming this or that for the hold-up. I remember distinctly that you once wrote to me that you could deliver a very large number of copies in just a few weeks. I now have several works, and as I intend to entrust all of these to you, perhaps my wish that these works should soon see the light of day may the more readily be acknowledged,'[2] Beethoven wrote to Leipzig on 26 August 1804, offering the 'Waldstein' Sonata together with other works. After Breitkopf & Härtel confirmed that the works would be printed without delay,[3] Beethoven and the publishers came to an agreement and the composer sent an engraver's copy of the sonata to Leipzig.

The agreement stipulated a greater number of works than Beethoven finally delivered. After repeated warnings from Leipzig had gone unheeded, the publishers withdrew from the agreement on 21 June 1805 and returned the manuscripts they had already received.[4] However, Beethoven had evidently already had a change of heart in the spring of that year, as he was not happy with the conditions of the Leipzig publishers ('All in all, the whole business is far too humiliating for me to waste another word about it.'[5]) and the fee wasn't high enough ('the fee is far below what I normally receive'[6]). By May 1805, the 'Waldstein' Sonata had already appeared in the *Wiener Industriekontor.*

Beethoven had to give his own autograph to the *Industriekontor* in lieu of an engraver's copy, probably as there was no suitable copyist to be found in Vienna for the professional copy of the sonata – Beethoven had complained of the 'lack of a reliable copyist'[7] in April 1805.[8] Luckily this was exceptionally cleanly written and contained only a few corrections, all of which had been clearly executed to avoid any possible misreading. In the few ambiguous places Beethoven further clarified matters by adding letter names to the corrected passages,[9] making it doubly certain what notes he intended. Cuts were made precisely and unmistakeably, often with the added indication vide, which showed where a passage was to be omitted or replaced. At the bottom of sheet 22r and the top of sheet 22v an incorrect passage was to be completely omitted and was covered with two paper strips that contained the corrected bars. The new paper was stitched onto the original sheet. How the first edition nonetheless came to contain various

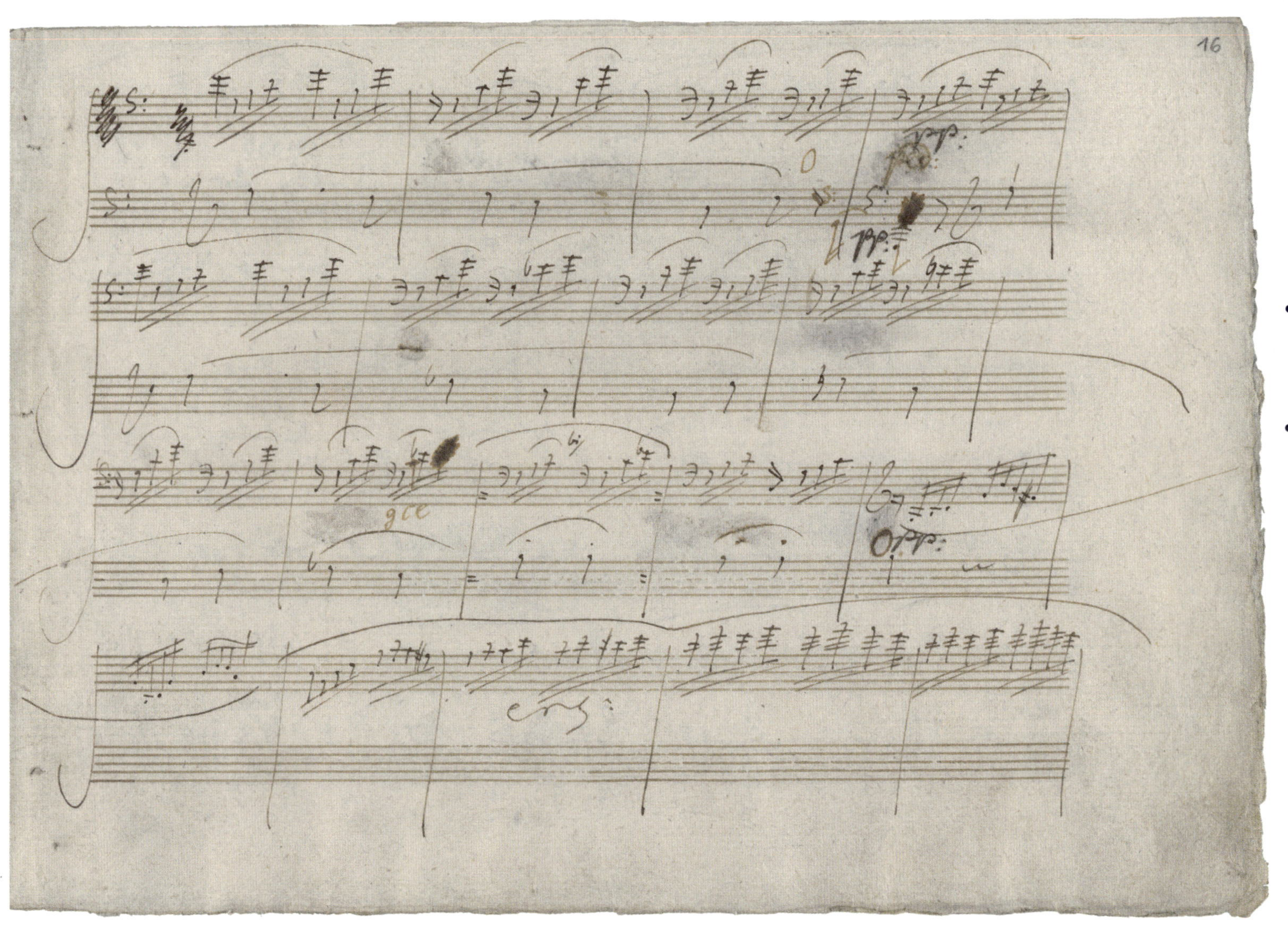

deviations from the original autograph, particularly in dynamic markings, remains a publisher's secret. Are these mistakes of the engraver (identified as a certain 'Herr Fischer' by a note in a hand other than Beethoven's across the last page of the manuscript)? Or did Beethoven perhaps pay the publisher a visit to correct the proofs and add changes, as was his custom?

The fact that the autograph was used as an engraver's copy also led to particular directions for the publisher: in small and discrete letters, as if as an afterthought, Beethoven wrote the title of the work along the top edge of the first page, marking it *sonata grande.* Indeed, none of the twenty sonatas he had already written were as extensive as this one, not even the *Grande Sonate pathétique.* In the letter to Breitkopf & Härtel from August 1804 quoted above, Beethoven had promised 'three new solo sonatas'. This, too, may have referred to the character of the work as a *sonata grande*: a solo sonata ('quasi come d'un concerto', as Beethoven had described the 'Kreutzer' Sonata*),* in contrast to the previously published three sonatas op. 31 or the two shorter sonatas op. 49. Furthermore, of course, the technical demands of the 'Waldstein' Sonata far exceeded what had gone before.

In addition, the composer added an important indication to the engraver across the right-hand edge of the first page: 'Nb: where ped. is written, all dampers both of bass and descant should be lifted, o means that they should be released again.'[10] He had already indicated the lifting of the dampers in earlier works. The indications senza sordino and con sordino (or sordini) occur as early as 1800/01 in the piano sonatas op. 26, op. 27 No. 2 and op. 33 as well as in the first two piano concertos op. 15 and op. 19. If Carl Czerny is to be believed, the indication senza sordino 'was only used as long as the damper-release mechanism was operated with the knee'.[11] Beethoven already mentions the use of the knee-lever for the lifting of the dampers in notes from his time in Bonn. His indication 'with the knee' is found in the 'Kafka Sketchbook'.[12] The new instrumental feature of a pedal instead of a knee-lever first becomes apparent in Beethoven's manuscripts in 1803. In this year, Beethoven bought a piano fitted with pedals from the firm Frères Érard in Paris. However, the pedal indications appear before the instrument arrived. Beethoven first wrote 'ped.' for the lifting of the dampers and 'o' to revoke the indication in the first movement of the piano sonata op. 31 No. 2. Beethoven was well informed about technical innovations of pianos on the market and could try them out at the rooms of other musicians or aristocrats even if his own instruments were not always up to the latest technical developments. In 1804, however, these directions were so new that he felt he had to explain them to the engraver. Retaining such an explanation for potential interpreters of the sonata does not seem to have been an option for the publisher – the directions do not appear in the first edition.

There is another remarkable direction on the last page of the 'Waldstein' Sonata. Beethoven, who was not particularly bothered whether passages were playable or unidiomatic for the instrument, offered alternative solutions for trills that might prove too difficult in the final movement. 'Nb: players who find the trill that appears with the theme too difficult may either play it in the following simplified manner: [musical ex.], or, according to their ability, doubled: [musical ex.]. Of these groups of six-notes, two are played on each quarter in the bass. It is not of paramount importance if this trill forfeits some of its usual speed.'[13] Only on one future occasion was Beethoven to offer such a simplification – in a letter to Eleonore von Breuning, sent with the twelve variations on the cavatina 'Se vuol ballare' from the opera *Le nozze di Figaro* by Wolfgang Amadeus Mozart for piano and violin, WoO 40, which he had dedicated to her: 'the variations will be rather difficult to play, particularly the trill in the coda. This should not put you off you as it is written in such a way that you need only play the trill, leaving out the other notes, as these also appear in the violin part. I would never have written something like this if I had not often observed that in v.[ienna] there is always someone or other who boasts how he has written down many of the idiosyncrasies of my playing the day after I had been improvising. Now that I anticipate something of this sort, I have decided to be one step ahead of them. There is another reason, namely to embarrass the local piano *maestros,* some of whom are my sworn enemies. In this way I wanted to take my revenge, as I can foresee that somebody will no doubt put these v.[ariations] in front of them and the said gentlemen will be sure to make a bad showing of themselves.' [14] Eleonore von Breuning was a close friend to whom Beethoven had given piano lessons as a child, so it doesn't seem unusual that he should offer her an easier version – particularly as he could be sure that she would keep it to herself. Beethoven eventually withdrew the directions for technical simplification in the 'Waldstein' Sonata and they do not appear in the first edition.

Even without these simplifications the Piano Sonata op. 53 was a success. It was so popular that the Berlin publishers Laue decided in 1825 to publish an arrangement by Franz Succo for four hands. The critic 'v. d. O. r', who attested 'original power, grandeur and charm' to the first movement of the sonata and 'the breath of spring' to the finale, criticized this arrangement that was intended to make the sonata more technically approachable for less skilled players: 'Whoever knows it [i.e. the work] for two hands (and what music-lover does not know it) will not allow half of the work to be stolen from him when he can take the whole to his heart.'[15] The 'Waldstein' Sonata had become part of the standard piano repertoire even during Beethoven's lifetime and is today one of the composer's most frequently played sonatas.

1 [In der Sonate (in C dur, Opus 53), die seinem ersten Gönner, dem Grafen von Waldstein gewidmet ist, war anfänglich ein großes Andante. Ein Freund Beethoven's äußerte ihm, die Sonate sei zu lang, worauf dieser von ihm fürchterlich hergenommen wurde. Allein ruhigere Ueberlegung überzeugte meinen Lehrer bald von der Richtigkeit der Bemerkung. Er gab nun das große Andante in F dur, 3/8 Tact, allein heraus und componirte die interessante Introduction zum Rondo, die sich jetzt darin findet, später hinzu.] Franz Gerhard Wegeler and Ferdinand Ries, *Biographische Notizen über Ludwig van Beethoven* (Koblenz, 1838), 101.

2 [Eine andere Sache, die mir am Herzen liegt, ist, daß mehrere Verleger mit Kompositionen von mir so erschrecklich lang zögern, bis dieselben ans Tageslicht kommen, die Ursache davon gibt jeder bald dieser bald jener Veranlassung schuld – ich errinnere mich recht wohl, daß sie mir einmal schrieben, daß sie im stande wären eine ungeheure Menge Exemplar[e] in wenigen Wochen zu liefern – ich habe jezt mehrere werke, und eben des wegen, weil ich gesonnen bin, Alle ihnen diese[l]ben zu überlassen, würde mein Wunsch, dieselben bald ans Tages licht kommen zu sehen, vieleicht um desto eher erfüllt können werden.] *Ludwig van Beethoven: Briefwechsel. Gesamtausgabe,* ed. Sieghard Brandenburg (i-vi: Munich 1996, vii (Register): Munich, 1998), no. 188 [henceforth: BGA [number]].

3 'Our music engraving and printing house is so organized that we can print even extensive works quickly and in large numbers.' 30 August 1804, BGA 189.

4 BGA 226.

5 [so ist das ganze Verfahren zusammengenommen viel zu erniedrigend für mich, als daß ich nur ein Wort drum verliehren sollte.] May 1805, to Breitkopf & Härtel, BGA 223.

6 [das honorar ist weit geringer als ich es gewöhnlich nehme.] ibid.

7 To Breitkopf & Härtel, BGA 218.

8 The autograph was verifiably with the publisher. It remains unclear whether this was used directly as the engraver's copy or was used to make a further copy.

9 Sheets 10v, 16r, 21v, 22r.

10 [Nb: Wo ped. steht wird die ganze Dämpfung sowohl vom Bass als Dißkant aufgehoben, o bedeutet, daß man sie weder falle laße.]

11 Carl Czerny, *Die Kunst des Vortrags der ältern und neuen Claviercompositionen oder: Die Fortschritte bis zur neuesten Zeit. Supplement oder 4ter Theil zur großen Pianofort-Schule, op. 500* (Vienna, 1846), 59.

12 British Library, Add MS. 29801, fol. 96r. The sheet dates from 1790–1792.

13 [Nb: für diejenigen denen der Triller, da wo das Thema mit demselben verbunden, zu schwer vorkömmt, können sich denselben auf folgende Art erleichtern: [musical ex.] oder nach Maßgabe ihrer Kräfte auch verdoppeln [musical ex.] Von diesen 6ser Werden auf jedes Viertel im Baß zwei angeschlagen. überhaupt kömmt es nicht drauf an, ob dieser Triller auch etwas von seiner gewöhnlichen geschwindigkeit verliehrt.]

14 [die V.[ariationen] werden etwas schwer zum spielen seyn, besonders die Triller in der Coda, das darf sie aber nicht abschrecken, es ist so veranstaltet, das sie nichts als den Triller zu machen brauchen, die übrige[n] Noten lassen sie aus, weil sie in der Violin Stimme auch vorkommen. nie würde ich so etwas gesezt haben, aber ich hatte schon öfter bemerkt, daß hier und da einer in v.[ien] war, welcher meistens, wenn ich des Abends fantasirt hatte, des andern Tages viele von meinen Eigenheiten aufschrieb, und sich damit Brüstete; weil ich nun voraus sahe, daß bald solche Sachen erscheinen würden, so nahm ich mir vor ihnen zu vor zu kommen. eine andere Ursache war noch dabey, nemlich: die hiesigen Klaviermeister in verlegenheit zu sezen, ma[n]che davon sind meine Todtfeinde, und so wollte ich mich auf diese Art an ihnen rächen, weil ich voraus wußte, daß man ihnen die V. hier und da vorlegen würde, wo die Herren sich den[n] übel dabey produciren würden.] 2 November, 1793, BGA 11.

15 Berliner allgemeine musikalische Zeitung 3 (1826), no. 20 (17 May), 155.

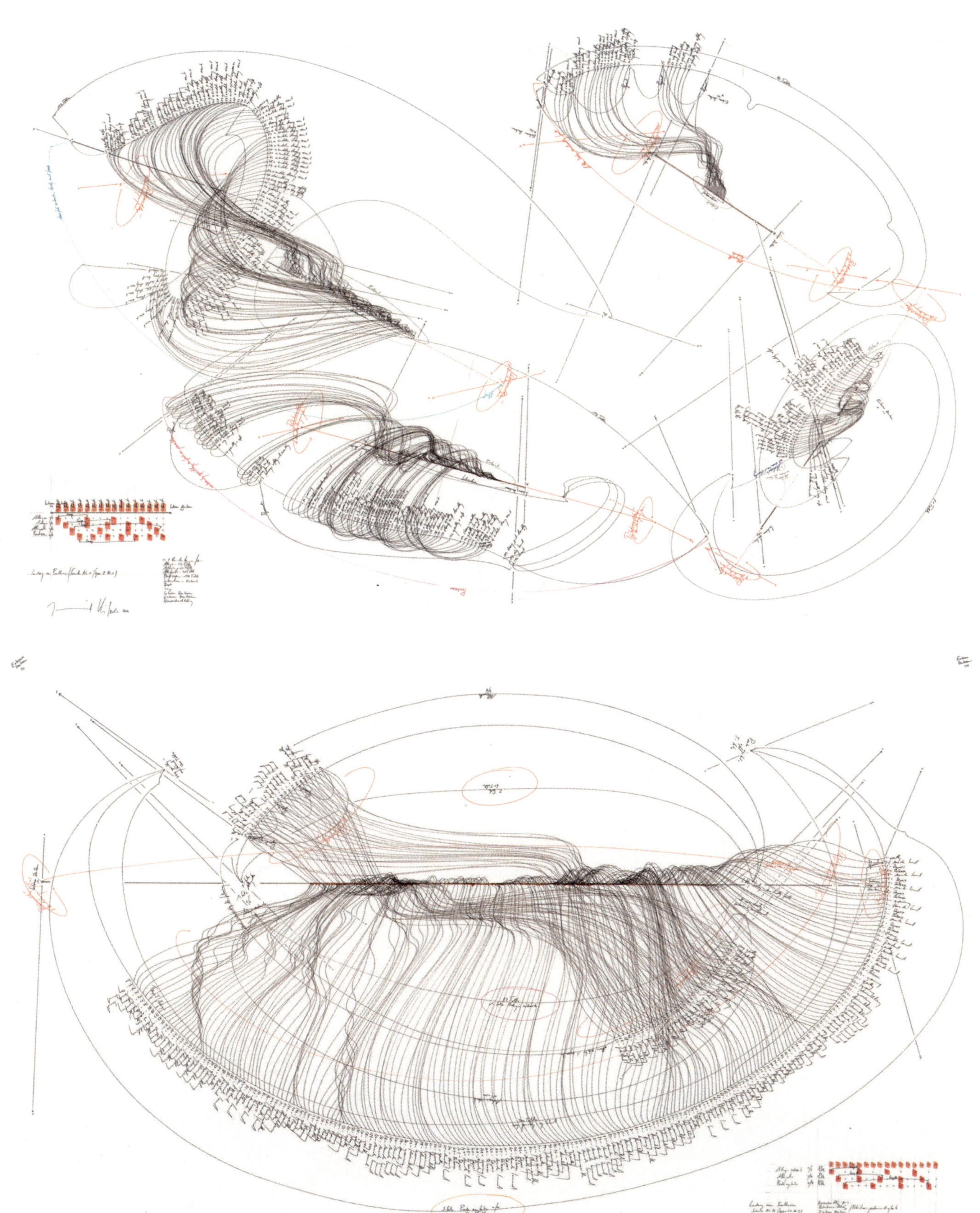

JORINDE VOIGT

Ludwig van Beethoven Sonata 1, 14, 17, 21
2012

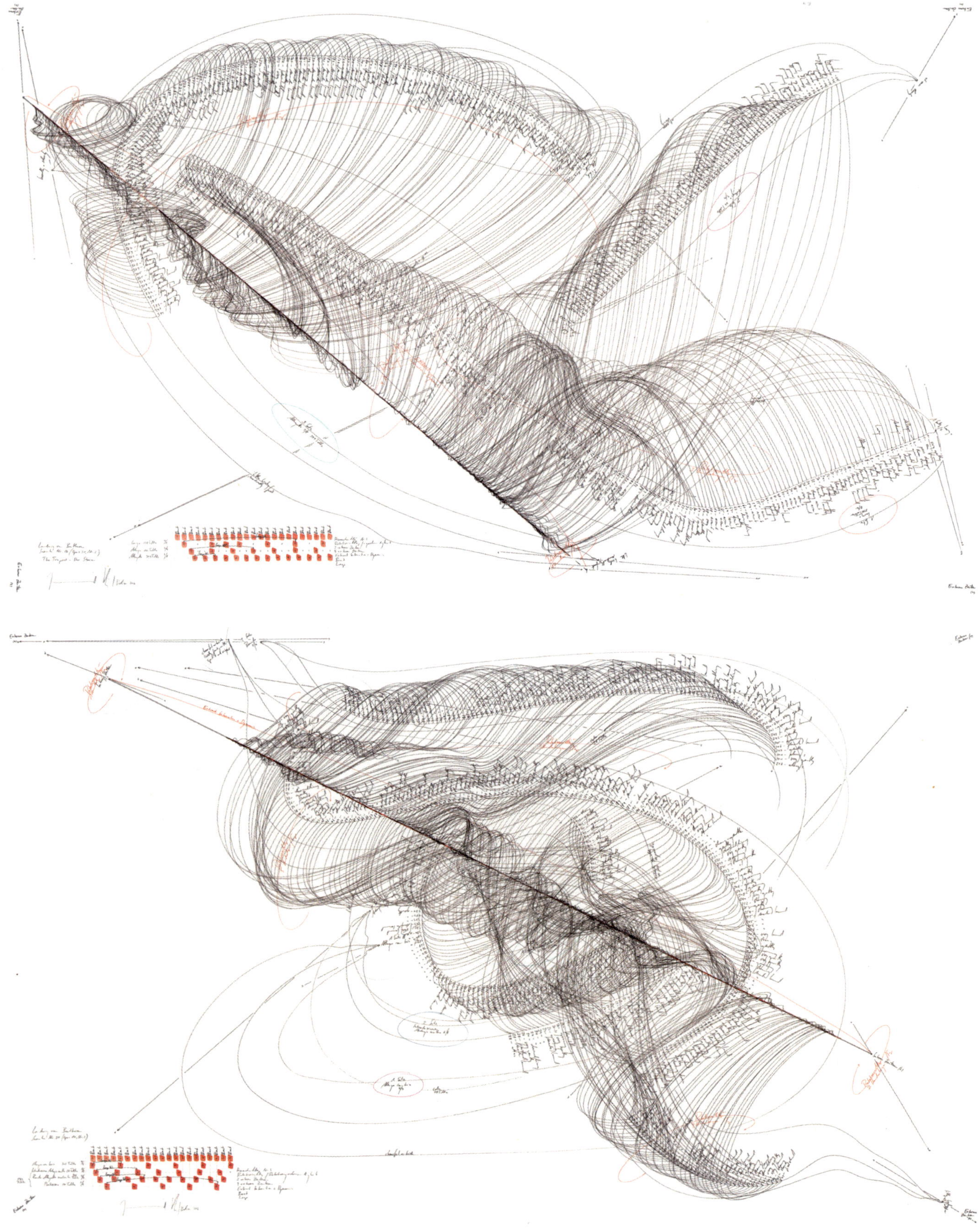

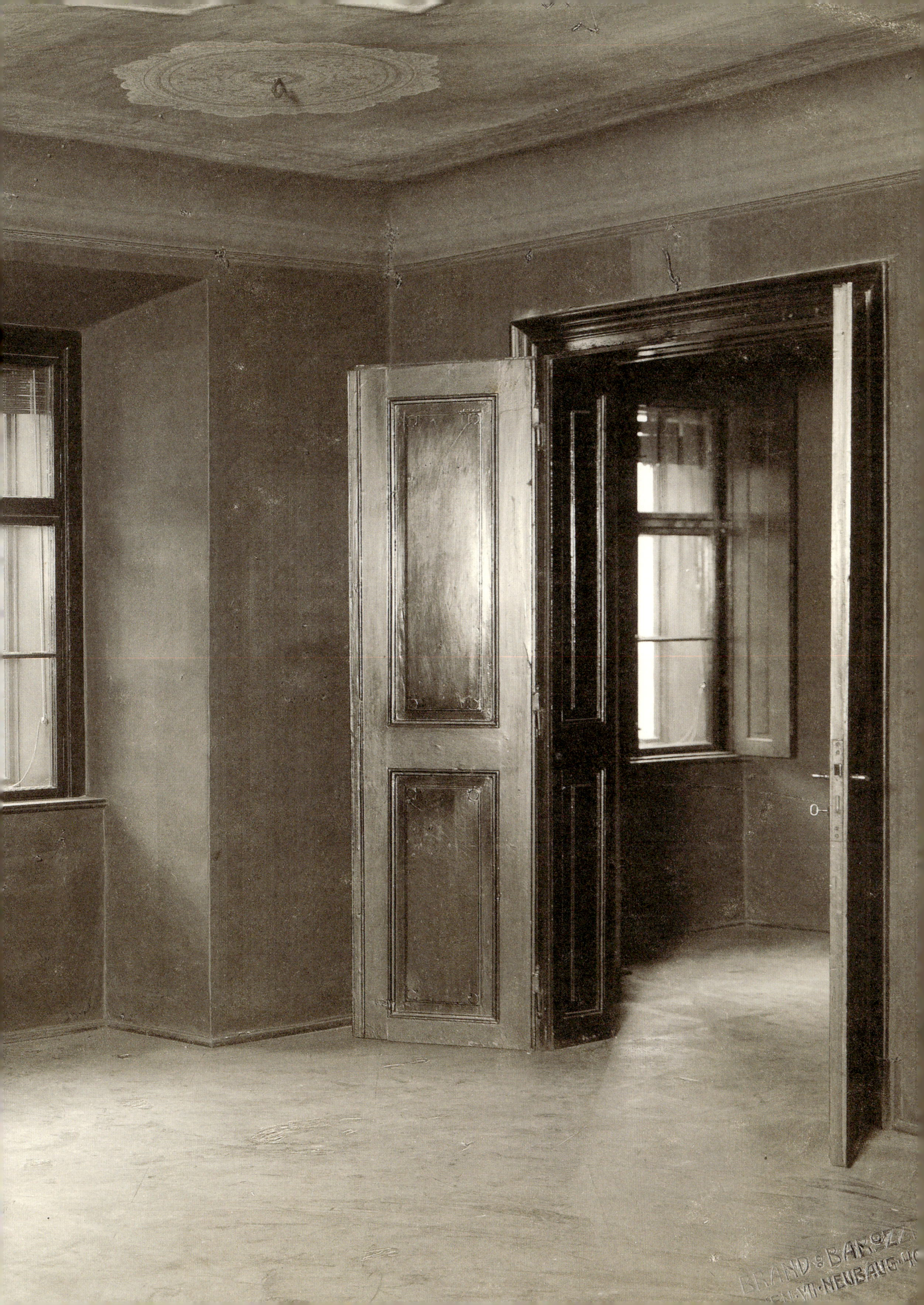
VII·NEUBAUG·40

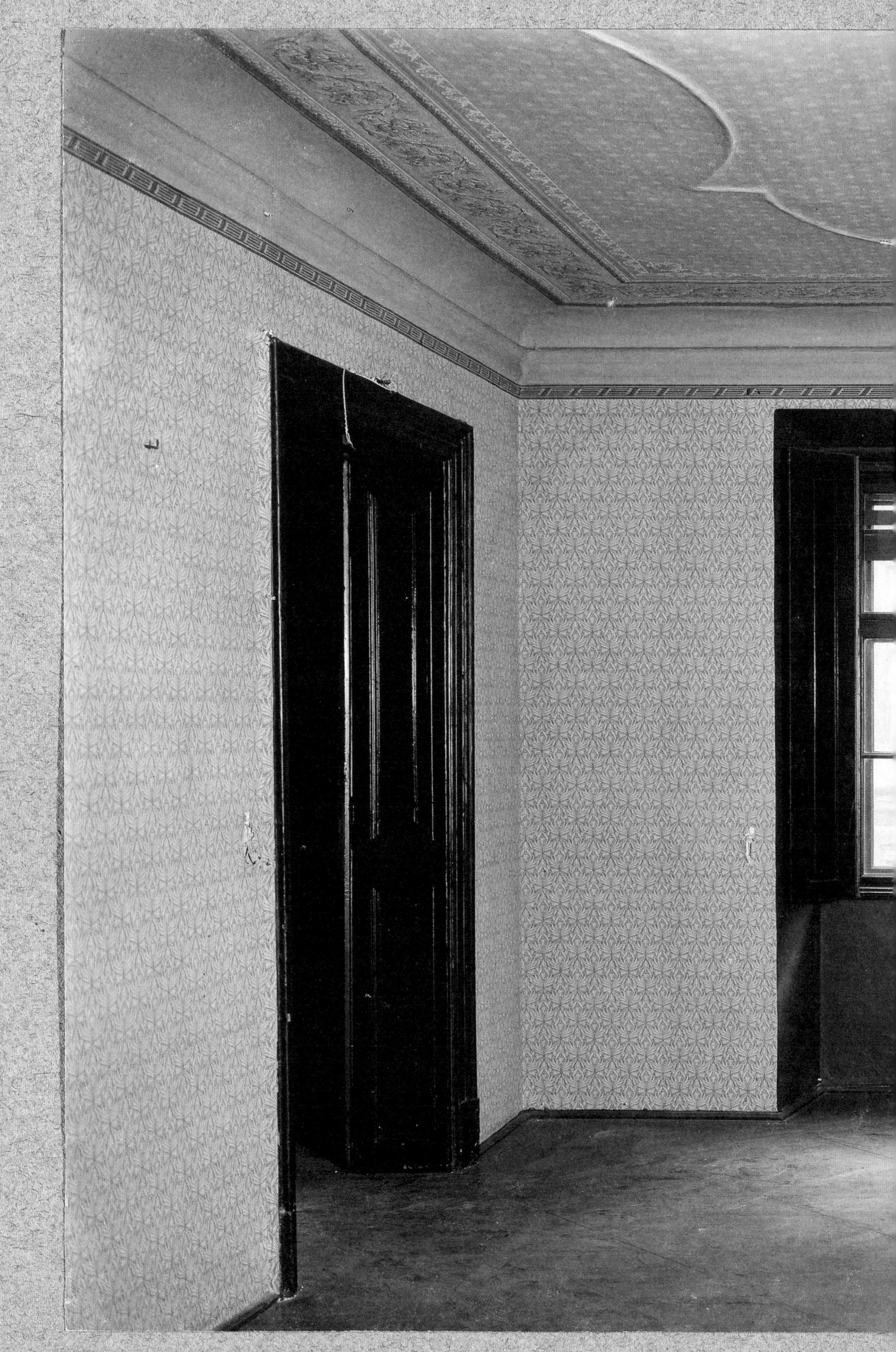

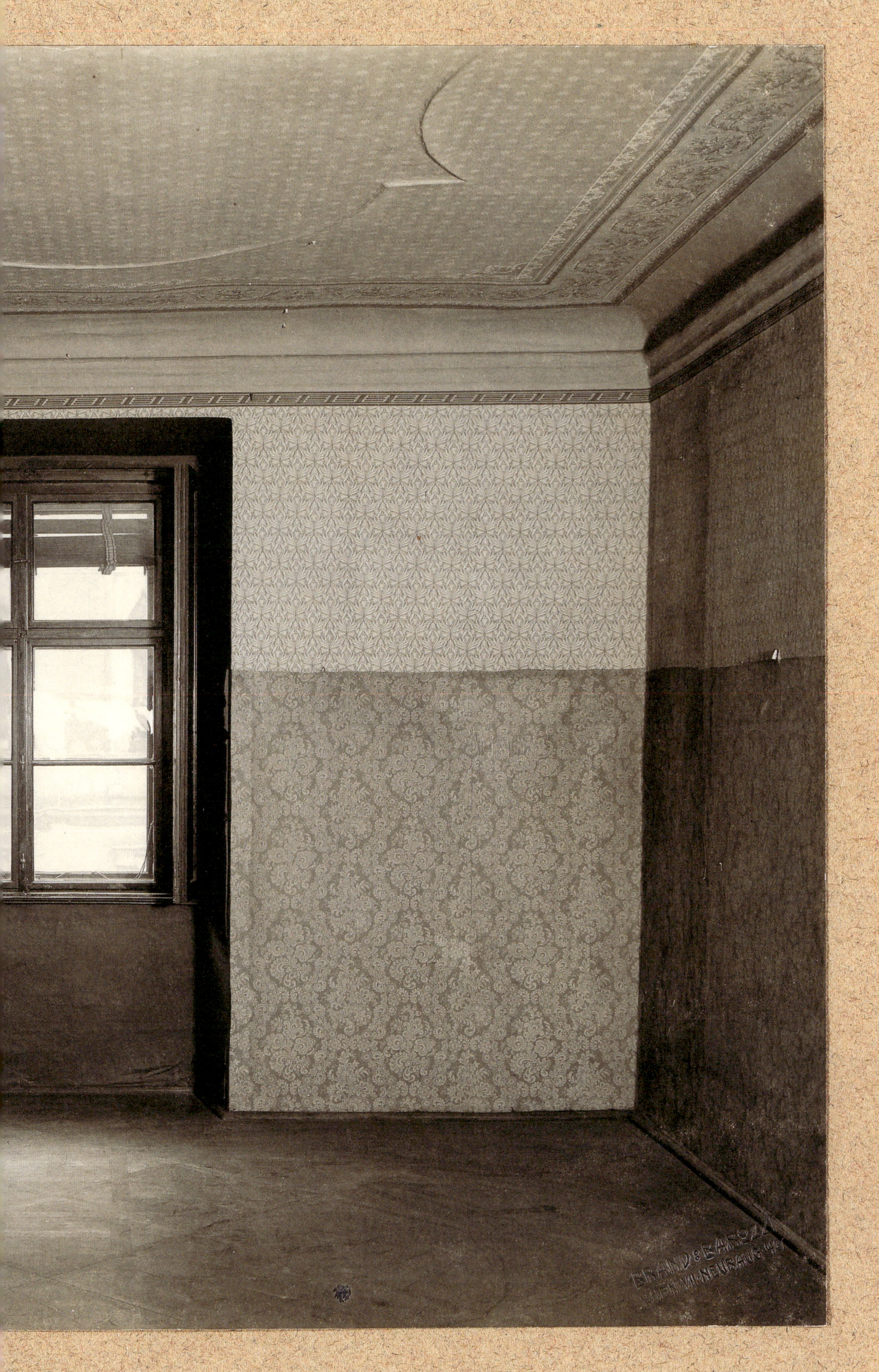

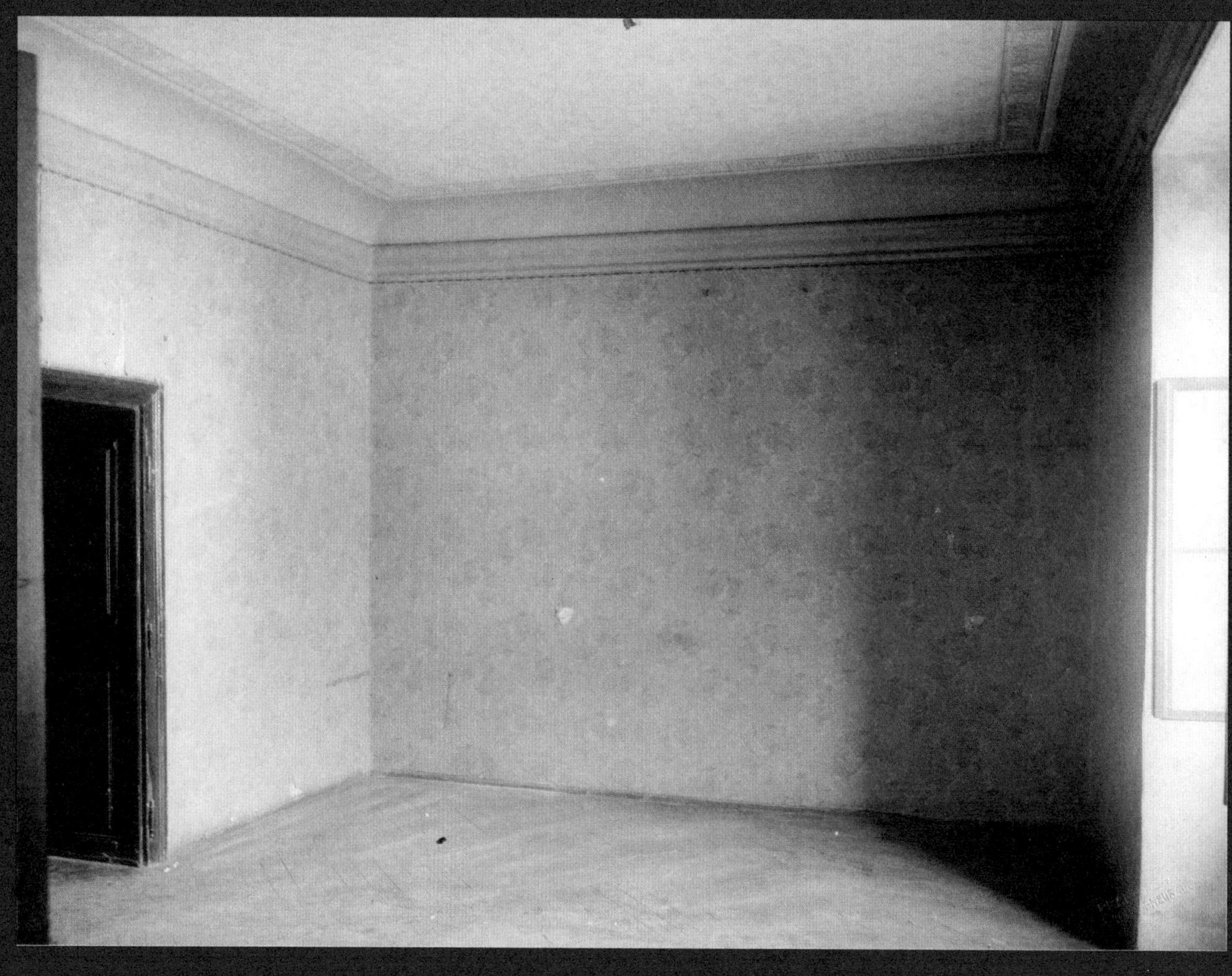

BRAND & BAROZZI, PHOTOGRAPHS OF BEETHOVEN'S LAST APARTMENT, 1903

EDMUND DE WAAL

Late

Beethoven's Great Fugue in B flat major, op. 133 of 1826 was 'incomprehensible, like Chinese' according to the critics. It was 'a confusion of Babel'. There were passages that could be understood but there was no structure, no development. It was genius in ruins. It was chaotic, angry, complex.

In her late poem of 1965 *Little Fugue* Sylvia Plath writes on her father and death of 'The yew hedge of the Grosse Fugue', a deep and dark and forbidding barrier:

'He could hear Beethoven:
Black yew, white cloud,
The horrific complications.
Finger-traps – a tumult of keys.'

It was *late*.

Reading the responses I think of the moment of revelation of the great painter's masterpiece in Balzac's *Le Chef-d'oeuvre inconnu*;

'In a corner of the canvas, as they came nearer, they distinguished a bare foot emerging from the chaos of colours. Half-tints and vague shadows that made up a dim, formless fog. Its living delicate beauty held them spellbound. This fragment that had escaped an incomprehensible, slow, and gradual destruction seemed to them like the Parian marble torso of some Venus emerging from the ashes of a ruined town.'

Lateness needs a response, an understanding of how much is left to achieve, a weariness with making things fit together.

As I listen to the Great Fugue I remember Rainer Maria Rilke's last poem, written in 1926, about ten days before his death.

This is lateness. It sits in the mind near Beethoven.

Komm du, du letzter, den ich anerkenne,
heilloser Schmerz im leiblichen Geweb:
wie ich im Geiste brannte, sieh, ich brenne
in dir; das Holz hat lange widerstrebt,
der Flamme, die du loderst, zuzustimmen,
nun aber nähr' ich dich und brenn in dir.
Mein hiesig Mildsein wird in deinem Grimmen
ein Grimm der Hölle nicht von hier.
Ganz rein, ganz planlos frei von Zukunft stieg
ich auf des Leidens wirren Scheiterhaufen,
so sicher nirgend Künftiges zu kaufen
um dieses Herz, darin der Vorrat schwieg.
Bin ich es noch, der da unkenntlich brennt?
Erinnerungen reiß ich nicht herein.
O Leben, Leben: Draußensein.
Und ich in Lohe. Niemand der mich kennt.

You, the last I recognize; return,
pain beyond help that sears the body's cells:
as I burnt in the spirit, see, I burn
in you; the wood, that for so long rebels
against the flame you kindle, comes of age;
behold, I nourish you and burn in you.
My earthly mildness changes in your rage
into a rage of hell I never knew.
Quite pure, quite planless, of all future free,
I climbed the stake of suffering, resolute
not to acquire what is still to be
to clad this heart whose stores had become mute.
Is it still I that burns there all alone?
Unrecognizable? memories denied?
O life, o life: being outside.
And I in flames – no one is left – unknown.[1]

1 Rainer Maria Rilke, *Komm Du. . .* in *Sämtliche Werke*, vol. 2, 1956, p. 511. Adapted by Scott Horton from a transl. by Walter Kaufmann [presumed], *Times Literary Supplement*, Dec. 1975. URL: https://harpers.org/blog/2007/10/rilkes-komm-du/ [last accessed: 11.02.2020].

DORIT MARGREITER

Experimental Noise 2016 – 2019

Though seemingly abstract at first, a closer inspection of *Experimental Noise* reveals traces of dust particles, scratches and chemical streaks. In photography, image noise is any undesirable by-product that visually obscures a photograph; Margreiter isolates these imperfections instead. Just as image noise obscures sight, Beethoven's hearing was obscured by his enduring struggle with tinnitus. In this sense, Margreiter's work can be interpreted as a visual parallel to Beethoven's own affliction.

In *Desert*, Celmins fills the picture plane by painstakingly drawing the desert ground undisturbed by any sign of life. From afar, her drawings convey a sense of emptiness and loneliness; the scene shows the freedom of vast space, while at the same time being potentially oppressive and overwhelming.

VIJA CELMINS

Desert
1971

WERNER BUSCH

Beethoven and Goya: Two Rank Outsiders

I

Does it make any sense to compare Beethoven with Goya and look for parallels between them? Neither is likely to have been aware of the other's existence. Beethoven almost certainly never saw any of Goya's works, not even his prints, and Goya almost certainly never heard any of Beethoven's music – indeed, he would physically not have been able to.

Although Goya, born in 1746, was somewhat older than Beethoven, he was a late developer. He went to Madrid in 1775 to work as a designer for the Royal Tapestry Manufactory, but thanks to his success as a portrait painter in the early 1780s he secured a foothold at the court, becoming Painter to the King in 1786, Court Painter in 1789 and First Court Painter in 1799. Beethoven, born in 1770, was a musical wunderkind. This means that the decisive creative period of both men began in the 1780s; it lasted as long in both cases, since Beethoven died in 1827 and Goya in 1828. Both their lives were marked by the French Revolution, the Napoleonic Wars and the ensuing years of reaction. Since both were social outsiders who lived almost exclusively for their art and broke with established norms in their works, a comparison certainly seems worthwhile.[1] We have ventured such a comparison in a series of ten brief points in the first part of this essay; in the second part, we take a closer look at a number of Goya's works.

FIRST Both Beethoven and Goya were deaf, which greatly impaired their interaction with society. Goya's deafness was the result of a severe illness in 1792–93. Beethoven's hearing loss, on the other hand, was a gradual process which began around 1798. Its symptoms became worse in 1801, but then remained stable until 1813, when further deterioration occurred. From 1817 onwards he could no longer hear music and was forced to abandon his public performances as a pianist and conductor; by 1818–19 he was completely deaf. Their deafness notwithstanding, Goya continued to paint and Beethoven to compose. Both tried shock treatments for their condition, but in neither case were these of any avail.

SECOND Both artists succumbed to misanthropy. They increasingly lost faith in man's positive qualities; Goya, in particular, lost the Enlightenment-inspired belief in the ability to change human nature for the better. Beethoven could be gruffly dismissive, mistrustful and liable to heap reproaches even on those who had been close to him for many years. In Beethoven's case, growing estrangement from the world went hand in hand with great personal suffering, especially since he was often afflicted by illness. Goya's health took another sharp turn for the worse in 1819, and his circumstances made him more and more pessimistic.

THIRD With Beethoven in particular, growing isolation was inseparably tied to a Promethean attitude. *The Creatures of Prometheus* is an early work, testifying to the composer's identification with Prometheus as someone who had brought light and hope to mankind, but at the price of trespassing against the gods and, as a result, being condemned to suffer ever thereafter. Not only the Third Symphony, 'Eroica' (1803–04) but also the Fifth – the so-called 'Symphony of Fate', premiered in 1808 – clearly displays Promethean features. Isolation and a sense of being at the mercy of fate fed into an idealized conception of the artist of genius – a conception that was very much fostered by society. With Goya it was not so much a case of self-stylization as of extreme scepticism. There is a distinct literary tradition of scepticism in Spain, but in Goya it acquired a strongly individualistic character.

FOURTH Both men were – and remained – committed to the French Revolution's notion of liberty. Moreover, they both put their trust in Napoleon as the hero who would forcibly realize the ideals of *liberté, égalité, fraternité*. Beethoven originally intended to dedicate the 'Eroica' to Napoleon, but was profoundly disappointed when the latter crowned himself Emperor in 1804. He would thenceforth regard Napoleon as a traitor to those ideals. The Napoleonic Wars of 1808–14 saw Beethoven now siding with the allies fighting France. One of his greatest successes came with the first performances of *Wellington's Victory*, op. 91, in 1813–14. Significantly, in 1820, after the onset of the dispiriting Restoration era under Metternich, he recognized the futility of the struggle for freedom, while retrospectively praising Napoleon, whose downfall, in his view, had been caused solely by hubris: 'Yet, he overthrew the feudal system everywhere and was a protector of justice and laws.'[2] With Goya it was much the same. He welcomed the liberal Constitution of Cádiz of 1812, which, modelled on the French constitution, set out to abolish aristocratic privileges and put a stop to the Inquisition. Goya belonged to the *afrancesados*, that is, to those who sympathized with France. When Napoleon's troops under the command of Marshal Murat entered Spain at the end of 1807, it seemed as if many liberal reforms would be instituted in their wake. However, the French soon forfeited their popularity as a result of their extreme brutality and cruelty towards the Spanish population. After Murat's army occupied Madrid in early 1808 and Napoleon shortly thereafter had the Spanish royal family removed to Bayonne, an uprising broke out in the capital in May which rapidly turned into a guerrilla war across the whole country. Goya, too, was now torn by divided loyalties. While he did not want to renounce the liberal ideas, the popular revolt, despite being steered by the ancient nobility and the Church, seemed justified to him, all the more so since he had witnessed the people's suffering at first hand. Like Beethoven, he transferred his allegiance to Wellington, who managed to end French rule in Spain. Goya at once set about painting his portrait. Wellington, however, distrusted the liberal currents and restored the reactionary Ferdinand VII to the Spanish throne. One of the king's first acts was to reinstate the Inquisition, from which Goya himself was to receive a summons. Tossed back and forth by the vicissitudes of his times, Goya became utterly disillusioned.

FIFTH For a long time, Beethoven extolled Napoleon as a hero and projected a similar image of himself. However, the Congress of Vienna of 1814–15 shattered his notions and by the time of the Carlsbad Decrees of 1819, if not earlier, he had resigned himself completely. Even so, already in the Piano Sonatas, op. 31 (1802–05) there is no longer unalloyed celebration of the heroic. Goya, on the other hand, openly denounced war. The first large group of etchings from his series *Desastres de la guerra*, nos. 2–64, was produced between 1810 and 1814. After Ferdinand's return in 1814, publishing the prints became out of the question. It was not until 1820, when a series of uprisings and revolts forced the king to swear to uphold the Constitution of Cádiz, that Goya could continue his work on the series. The liberal period, however, came to a close already in 1823, when Ferdinand was restored to absolute power with the help of a foreign coalition. Spain was plunged into misery yet again, and it ultimately proved too much for Goya to bear.

SIXTH Both Beethoven and Goya were faced with an irreconcilable dilemma arising from the tension between the growing democratization of art and a strong dependence on courtly patronage. Beethoven was supported mainly by aristocratic patrons. Goya could not make ends meet without membership of the Royal Academy and the associated privileges, and in order to safeguard these, along with his pension, he repeatedly had to pay homage to Ferdinand, despite his loathing for the king. Neither artist was able to rely on the free market as a source of income, however much they wanted to.

SEVENTH They both tried to devise economic arrangements that would enable them to make a living as freelance artists. They negotiated contracts with publishers and also occasionally tried self-publishing. They offered their works through subscription, adopting the principles that had evolved in the literary market in the 18th century. Moreover, they sought to secure patrons through dedications and set their own prices.

EIGHTH The years from 1800 to 1812 are referred to as Beethoven's 'heroic period'. Even if in the works from this period one already finds instances of the mould of the classical forms being broken, the fact is that, all such 'fractures' and turbulent passages notwithstanding, the musical content is ultimately tamed and channelled into an orderly structure. This has rightly been described as a classicizing style. The same is true of Goya, though it has often escaped the attention of scholars. Not for nothing did our painter allow himself to be guided by the Neoclassical outline style of John Flaxman, whose engravings to the *Odyssey* and the *Iliad* he studied, along with the stylized Dante illustrations. Such an outline style may, too, violate traditional norms – the rules of perspective and anatomy – if the subject is thereby rendered more effectively. In Goya's case, we see this notably in the print series *Los Caprichos* of 1799, but also in a number of oil paintings executed under the influence of Anton Raphael Mengs.

NINTH The disintegration of classical structures begins to manifest itself in Beethoven's works after 1812; with Goya, it is heralded by the *Desastres* starting in 1810. For both men, political events have by then made any rosy view of the world untenable. The fractures in their works, now openly flaunted, are a way of expressing what they have seen and experienced. They both set their own rules: in that sense, their works have become autonomous. It is quite legitimate to speak of Beethoven's 'absolute' music, which seeks to convey experiences without regard for classical laws of form. The music develops a rhetoric of its own: deliberately form-destroying elements come to the fore, expectations are deceived and the familiar is foiled. Instead of structure, what we get is emotional, vigorous demonstration. The late works are not driven by a striving to fathom the outer world but, rather, by a desire to reproduce inner life. The violence of the present crystallizes into artistic language. No detached analysis of the contemporary situation is offered: rather, its distressing effect is conveyed through expressive means. The extent to which the above observations apply to both artists is truly astonishing.

TENTH To use the terminology of aesthetics, the heroic undoubtedly falls into the category of the sublime, for the hero explodes the bounds of convention. However, the sublime also encompasses terrifying, cruel, incomprehensible and destructive aspects. Burke's 1757 treatise *On the Sublime and Beautiful* declared the sublime in its terrifying guise to be endurable and indeed to be a special manifestation of the beautiful, since it may be observed from a safe distance. This sense of safety is questioned by Beethoven and Goya. In their works, we are exposed to terror as something that is very much part of real life.

II

Using some examples from the *Caprichos* and the *Desastres*, we shall now demonstrate the extent to which the qualities described in the above ten points are reflected in Goya's prints. The famous Capricho no. 43, *El sueño de la razón produce monstruos* ('The sleep of reason begets monsters'), was originally intended to be the frontispiece of the *Caprichos*, as suggested by a preparatory drawing with the caption 'Sueño 1' ('Dream no. 1'). Goya thus had a sequence of dreams in mind. It is generally agreed that the original title *Sueños* was prompted by the Spanish poet Quevedo's widely read eponymous treatise of 1627, in which a number of dreams, often rich in allegorical content, are used to describe the ills of human society. This work clearly exerted a strong thematic influence on Goya's series.[3] Like Quevedo, Goya knew that his critique of reason was likely to attract

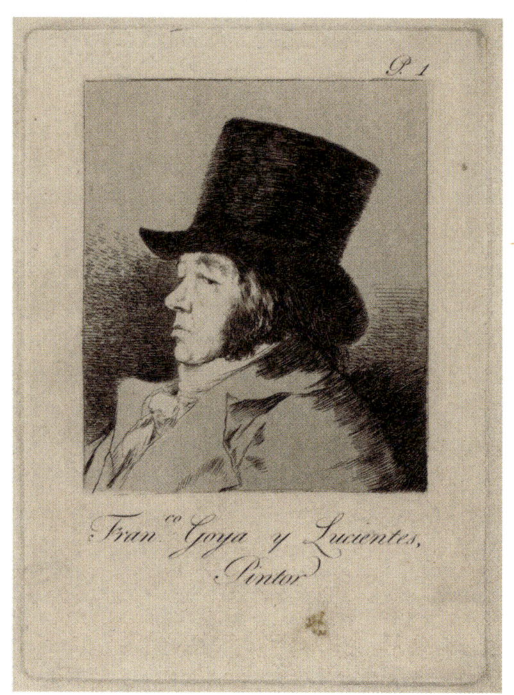

Fig. 1 Francisco de Goya, frontispiece of the *Caprichos*, 1799. Etching, aquatint. Vienna, Albertina, inv. no. DG1935/14

the attention of the Inquisition. By changing the title to *Los Caprichos*, he evidently sought to tone down or veil the purport of his series: 'fancies' or 'fantasies' sounds more light-hearted than sinister dreams of reality. It was, alas, to no avail, for Goya was soon forbidden from publishing the *Caprichos*.

A self-portrait of Goya in profile facing left (fig. 1) was eventually used as a seemingly 'neutral' frontispiece. Yet, as a matter of fact, this picture serves as an eloquent commentary on the whole series. The face is turned away from us, making direct contact impossible. Even so, the portrait's subject keeps us in check: from the angle of his eye he seems to be able to see any movement we may make. Moreover, the corners of the mouth are turned down in surly fashion. In the preparatory drawing, the position of the eyes still matches that of the final profile, but on the back of the sheet Goya's head is sketched out twice in front view, which has something spell-binding about it. In this portrayal, the right corner of the mouth is drawn down sharply and the eyebrows are knitted disdainfully (fig. 2). It has long been recognized that, in creating this frontispiece, Goya was influenced by Charles Le Brun's posthumous treatise on physiognomy *Expressions des passions de l'âme* (1727), compiled from drawings made by Le Brun in the 1660s, specifically by the facial expression for 'Mépris', into which one may read disdain, contempt or scorn. That may also reflect Goya's attitude towards his audience. If we think back to Quevedo again, it soon becomes clear that what we are dealing with is the general air of contempt for the world that marks a sceptic. For in the eyes of a sceptic, mankind as such is bad and not really amenable to improvement.

There is further evidence for conscious intent in all this. The address at which Goya lived and worked was 1 Calle del Desengaño, or 'Disillusionment Street'. According to the advertisement for the *Caprichos* in the *Diario de Madrid*, they were officially published on 6 February 1799, which was Ash Wednesday. The series was offered for sale in the perfume shop (which also served as a pharmacy) situated below his lodgings. None of this is likely to have been coincidence.[4] In Quevedo's *Sueños*, there is a constant play on the juxtaposition of *engaño* and *desengaño*, or 'deceit' and 'undeception, disillusion'. In the fourth dream we even find *desengaño* personified in the shabby figure of a beggar who tells the world the truth it does not want to hear. This personification plays on the double meaning of *desengaño*: what the beggar seeks to achieve is 'un-deception' (with a Heideggerian hyphen!), that is, to hold a mirror up to the deceived world by confronting it with the truth. Yet, this agent of *desengaño* cannot but realize that all his efforts are in vain, that mankind will not be reformed. All that is left to him at the end is disillusionment – the most he can hope for after his death is salvation. Goya was denied even that hope, as the *Caprichos* in particular make abundantly clear. For in the series we find many a scene alluding to contemporary events that is in fact based on Christian iconography (Christ being taken down from the cross, for example, being mourned, or laid to rest).[5] The viewer who recognizes the iconography is startled upon realizing how much it jars with the dreadful present. Incidentally, it is worth noting that Goya did indeed paint religious works on commission, just as Beethoven composed, for example, his *Missa Solemnis*. However, they both approach their religious subjects not out of piety as such, but as an opportunity to explore unique facets of their respective artistic media. Nor did Ash Wednesday as the official date of publication of the *Caprichos* have the same symbolism for Goya as it did for the Church. Once the carnival is over, it is Ash Wednesday that marks the beginning of the fast. The liberties that were allowed during carnival, the reversal of status – all that is taken back and rechannelled into the established order.

In publishing the *Caprichos* on Ash Wednesday, Goya seems – in the ideological tradition of Quevedo – to be saying that Lent by no means restores the order dictated by Church and State.

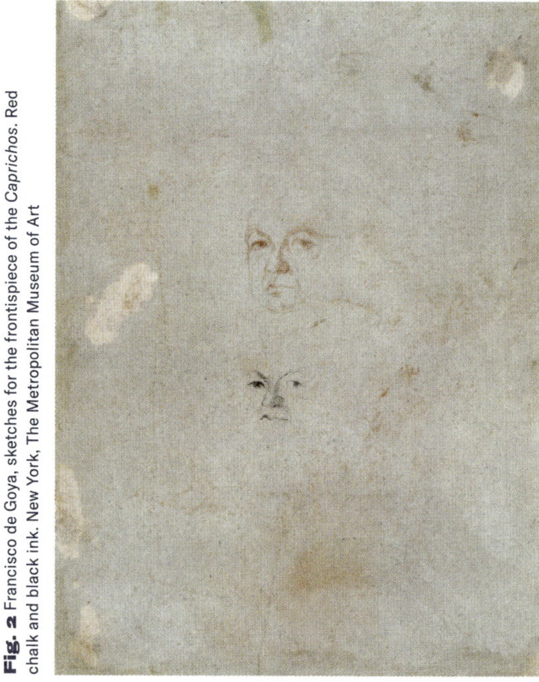

Fig. 2 Francisco de Goya, sketches for the frontispiece of the *Caprichos*. Red chalk and black ink. New York, The Metropolitan Museum of Art

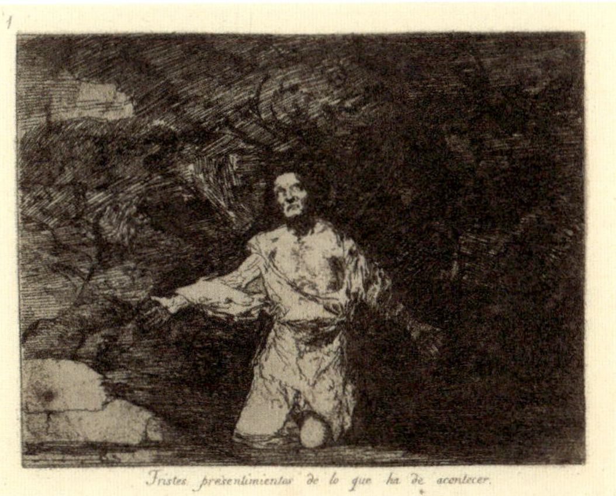

Fig. 3 Francisco de Goya, frontispiece of the Desastres: Tristes presentimientos de lo que ha de acontecer – *Sad presentiments of what is to come*, 1820–23. Etching, aquatint. Vienna, Albertina, inv. no. DG2005/10833/1

Rather, mankind, ever unteachable, behaves as if it were carnival the whole year round and permits anything, barring murder and manslaughter. However, the blame is laid not on the people but on the Church, the aristocracy and the State. Quevedo, in his *Sueños*, treats the reader to a parade of professions whose conduct he regards as reprehensible because they involve duping the people: doctors, pharmacists and, above all, law enforcement officials such as judges, police and their henchmen. All these turn up in Goya's series, even furnished with the same attributes that Quevedo had described. Both poet and painter had lost their faith in justice and civilized behaviour.

The frontispiece of the *Desastres* (fig. 3) was designed by Goya towards the end of his work on that series, namely between 1820 and 1823, that is, during a precarious liberal interlude in Spain. Even so, it is utterly pessimistic, though now no longer solely in the spirit of the *Caprichos*, which, taking their cue from Quevedo, had criticized the follies and aberrations caused by misguided human passions: rather, it makes direct reference to contemporary historical events – to war, depravity, famine and other calamities, which infuse the individual with panic, fears and hallucinations. Unlike the eighty or so other plates in the series, the frontispiece does not portray a specific scene: its function is, instead, emblematic. The lone subject is a kneeling figure, haunted by visions of horror, his arms outstretched in despair. The war of 1808–14 inflicted by Napoleon on Spain has dissolved the whole fabric of civilization, seemingly justifying any atrocity. The country has been thrust into a meandering course between short liberal phases and the most benighted reaction. Moreover, the battle lines are blurred and it is the population that will pay the price. The desperate, lamenting figure is at his wits' end. The gigantic faces grimacing in the darkness overhead, whose features can hardly be made out, represent the fears pursuing him. At the same time, we are reminded of the iconography of Jesus on the Mount of Olives who beseeches God the Father to let the cup of suffering pass from him but finally accepts the Passion and is strengthened by an angel. In Goya's work, such an angel is quite unthinkable. Death is tantamount to annihilation and even the dead are still subject to mutilation. The fact that the haunted figure has raised his eyes heavenward, yet is met with nothing but terrifying darkness, makes clear the futility of hoping for heavenly succour.

Capricho no. 3, *Que viene el Coco* ('Here comes the Bogeyman'; fig. 4), is a good example of the way in which Goya uses form to create meaning. A cowering woman with two terrified children huddled against her gazes up inquiringly at a large cloaked figure which neither we nor, it seems, the children are able to identify. Most of the plate is steeped in darkness because of the use of aquatint. The only exceptions are the back of the cloaked figure and the children – especially their faces, which look as if a spotlight has been shone on them. However, no source of light that would account for such extreme illumination is to be found in the scene. Light and darkness are used purely as expressive means. This becomes clear from the white cone of light emanating from the Bogeyman, which has no justification whatsoever in the spatial composition (if one may call it thus), and whose tip touches one of the children. This cone, the area of which has simply been stopped out in the aquatint plate, encapsulates the inscrutable figure's potential to inspire terror. What we have here is the use of abstract means to achieve heightened expressivity. That Goya was seeking, with the aid of formal elements, to fill the beholder, too,

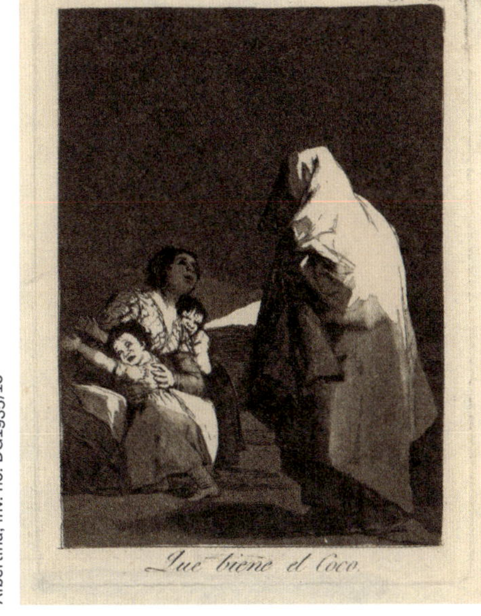

Fig. 4 Francisco de Goya, Los Caprichos: Que viene el Coco – *Here comes the Bogeyman*, 1799. Etching, aquatint. Vienna, Albertina, inv. no. DG1935/16

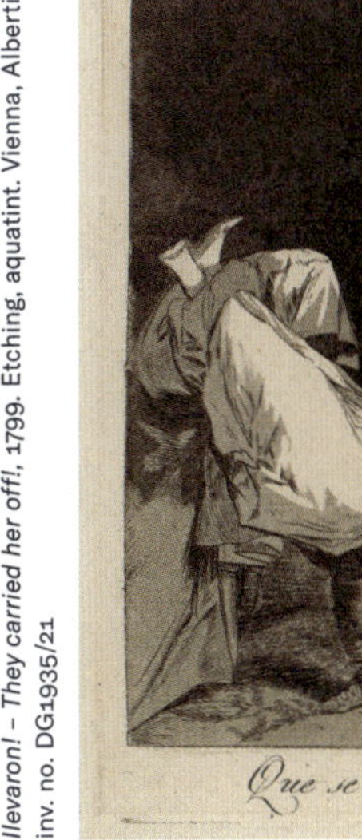

Fig. 5 Francisco de Goya, Los Caprichos: *Los Caprichos: Que se la llevaron! – They carried her off!*, 1799. Etching, aquatint. Vienna, Albertina, inv. no. DG1935/21

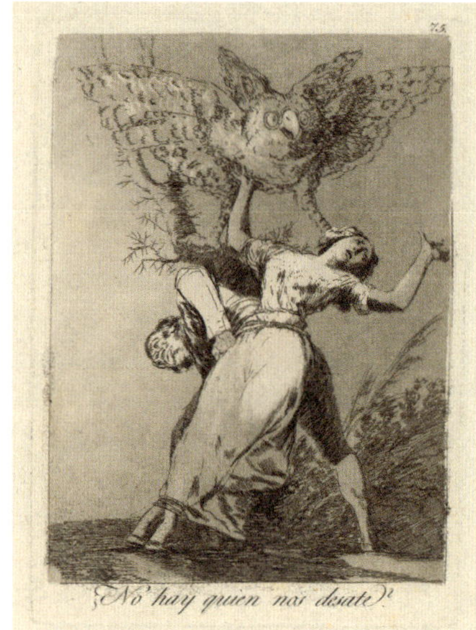

Fig. 6 Francisco de Goya, *Los Caprichos: No hay quien nos desate?* – *Can't anyone untie us?*, 1799. Etching, aquatint. Vienna, Albertina, inv. no. DG1935/88

with a troubling sense of uncanniness, is suggested by Capricho no. 8 (fig. 5). *Que se la llevaron!* ('They carried her off!') is an abduction and rape scene. Two figures, yet again wearing hoods – might the one farther back be a priest? – are carrying away a struggling woman who screams in despair. We should in theory be able to make out the face of the one standing, straddle-legged, in the foreground, but it is in fact pitch-black, as if it had been blotted out. Against a background darkened by the nocturnal aquatint, this man has seized the woman by her waist. Following the curve of his arm around her body, the aquatint cuts, knife-like, through the hapless victim. Once again, pure form becomes, in an abstract way, evocative – in this case of rape.

A quick glance at Capricho no. 75 (fig. 6) shows how Goya unsettles the viewer by suspending the logic of space. *¿No hay quien nos desate?* ('Can't anyone untie us?') is devoted to the theme of divorce, which, in contrast to France, was forbidden in Spain. Although this theme was clearly Goya's starting point, it is transcended by the drama portrayed. A man and a woman are tied together at the waist; the woman, who seems almost like a dummy, even has her legs bound together at the ankles. She faces us head on, while the man, turned away from her, is struggling to tear the rope asunder, but to no avail. Perched above the couple, one of its talons resting on the woman's head, is a huge owl, which is depicted only schematically. The two human figures are propping each other up as in a cross: the woman inclined obliquely to the right, the man obliquely to the left. Yet, what parts are actually his? Bewilderingly, his right leg merges with the trunk of a tree whose branches lean far into the picture. The owl's other talon rests, in a markedly straddling pose, on that trunk. As becomes clear if one looks at its left leg, such a pose is quite impossible according to spatial logic. The owl, a nocturnal bird, is shown wearing a pince-nez (*quevedos* in Spanish!). However, the schematic depiction suggests that this creature is merely imaginary: an expression of the interlocked couple's desperate situation. The trunk and the owl seem to embody power structures in Spain and their fixation on the past.

Desastre no. 39 (fig. 7) is one of the most horrifying scenes in that series. Its title admits of nothing but a cynical interpretation: *Grande hazaña! Con muertos!* ('A heroic feat! With dead men!'). Mutilated and profaned corpses are shown tied to a decrepit tree, which is 'crowned' by an impaled head. Castration and decapitation have been inflicted as the ultimate forms of humiliation. This depiction of cruelty is so disgusting that one can hardly bear to look at it. And yet the scene did become a picture, even one that was transferred on to the etching plate with a sense of artistic measure. Does it therefore fall into the category of the sublime, one possible dimension of which is, after all, the terrifying? Yes and no. On the one hand, the plate does possess aesthetic form; but, on the other, it is utterly devoid of that heightened pathos arising from the beholder's self-assertion that makes for experience of the sublime. We must conclude that, in its awfulness, this plate transcends *ex negativo* the boundaries of the sublime, conveying as it does an unbearable experience of contemporary reality.

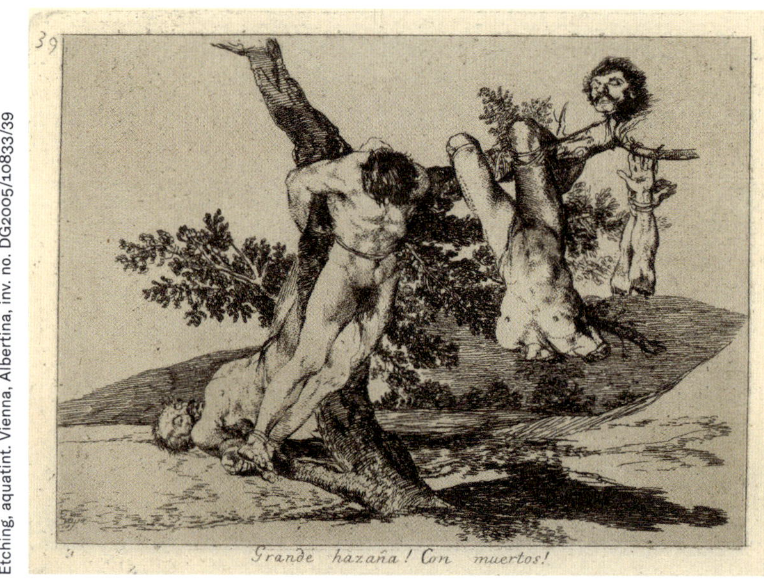

Fig. 7 Francisco de Goya, *Los Desastres de la Guerra: Grande hazana! Con muertos!* – *A heroic feat! With dead men!*, 1810–14. Etching, aquatint. Vienna, Albertina, inv. no. DG2005/10833/39

1 The following exposition is based on Martin Geck, *Ludwig van Beethoven* (8th edn., Hamburg-Reinbek, 2017), and Werner Busch, *Goya* (Munich, 2018).

2 Karl-Heinz Köhler, Grita Herre and Dagmar Beck (eds.), *Ludwig van Beethovens Konversationshefte*, 10 vols. (Leipzig, 1972–93), i, 210; cited in Geck, *Beethoven*, 128.

3 On Quevedo, see Francisco de Quevedo, *Die Träume. Die Fortuna mit Hirn oder die Stunde aller*, with a foreword by Jorge Luis Borges, ed. and trans. Wilhelm Meister (Frankfurt, 1966); Ilse Nolting-Hauff, *Vision, Satire und Pointe in Quevedos 'Sueños'* (Beihefte zu Poetica, 3; Munich, 1968); Joachim Küpper, *Die entfesselte Signifikanz. Quevedos 'Sueños', eine Satire auf den Diskurs der Spät-Renaissance* (Deutsche Hochschulschriften, 419; Egelsbach/Cologne/New York, 1992). On Quevedo and Goya, see Werner Busch, *Goyas 'Caprichos'. Der Zweifel an der Wirksamkeit aufklärerischer Moral* (Hamburg, 2019; in press).

4 As first noted in Victor I. Stoichita and Anna Maria Coderch, *Goya: The Last Carnival* (London, 1999).

5 Werner Busch, 'Goya und die Tradition des "capriccio"', in Max Imdahl (ed.), *Wie eindeutig ist ein Kunstwerk?* (Cologne, 1986), 41–73, 172–74.

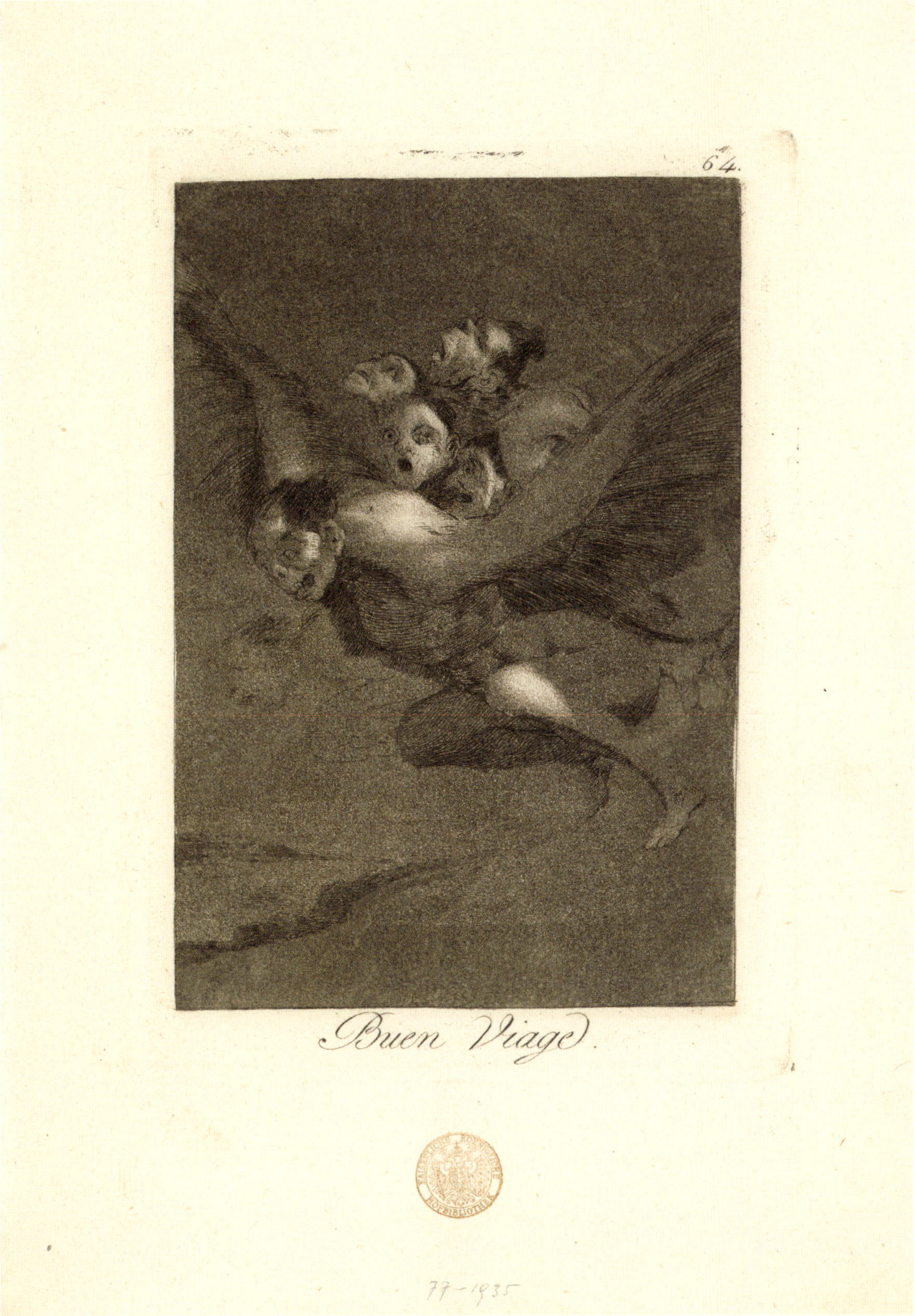

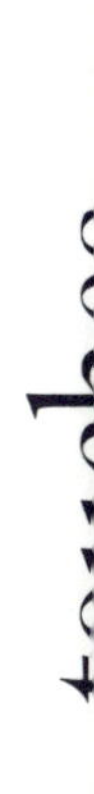

FRANCISCO DE GOYA

Los Caprichos
1799

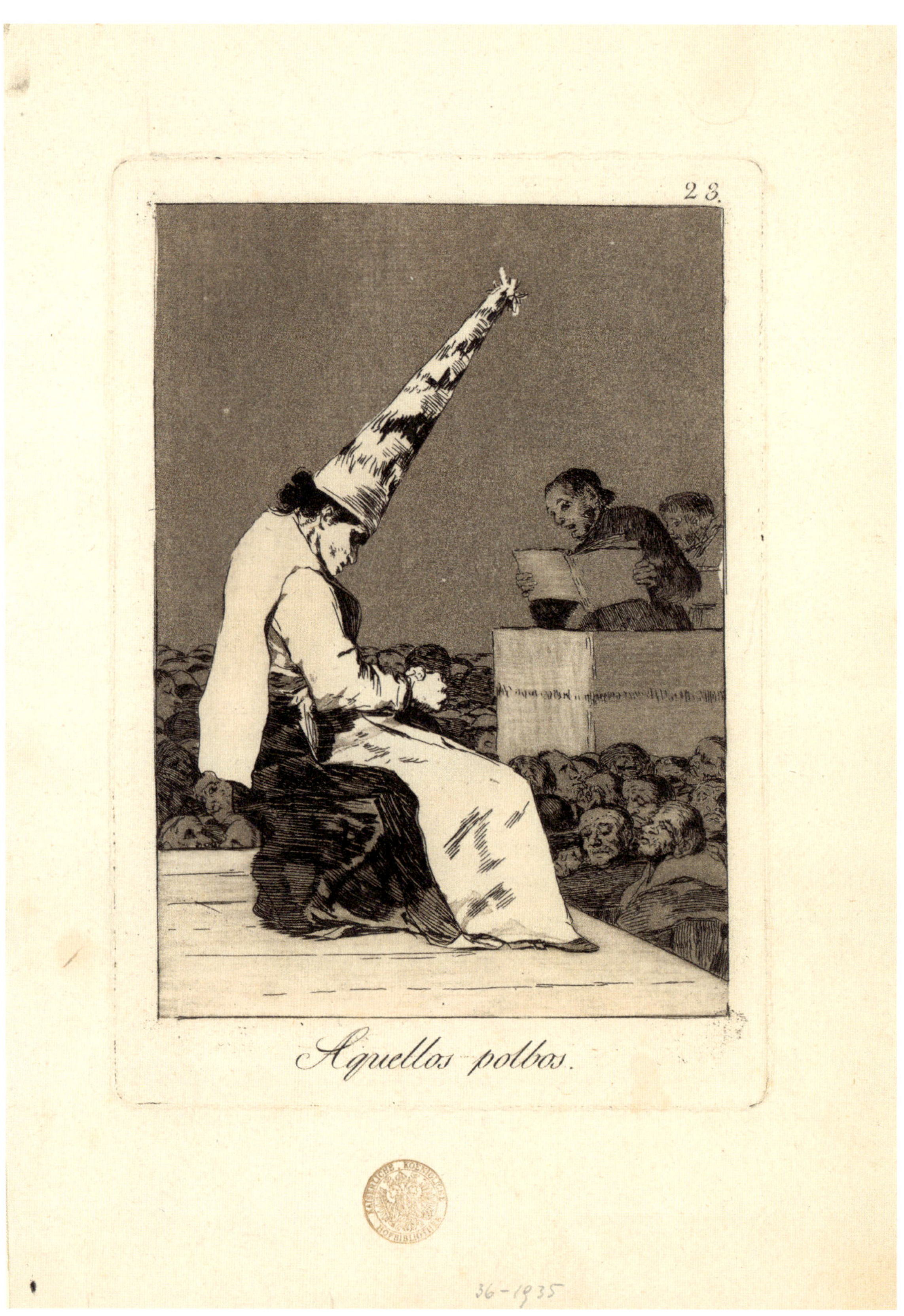
23.
Aquellos polbos.
36-1935

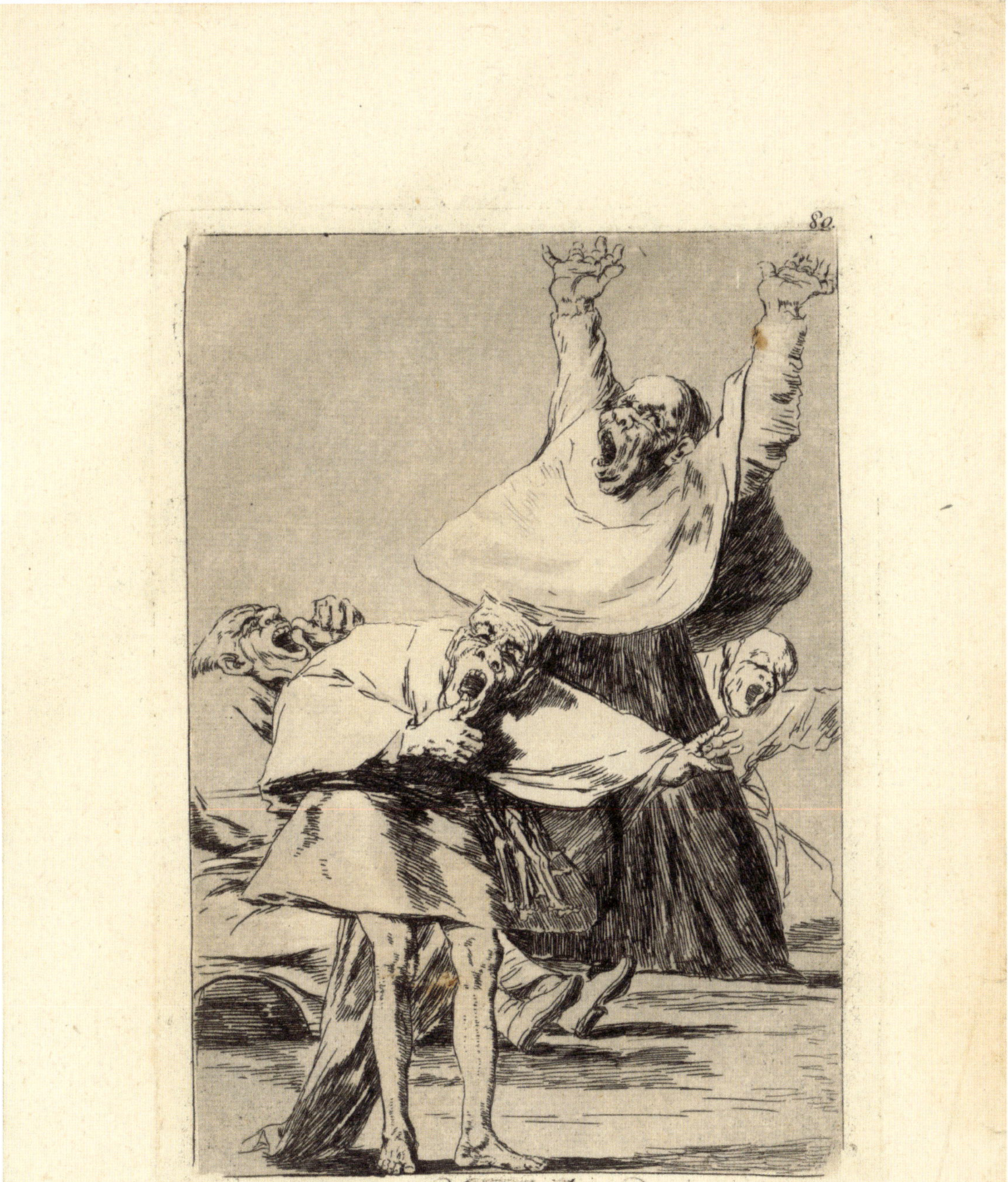

80.

Ya es hora.

93 - 1935

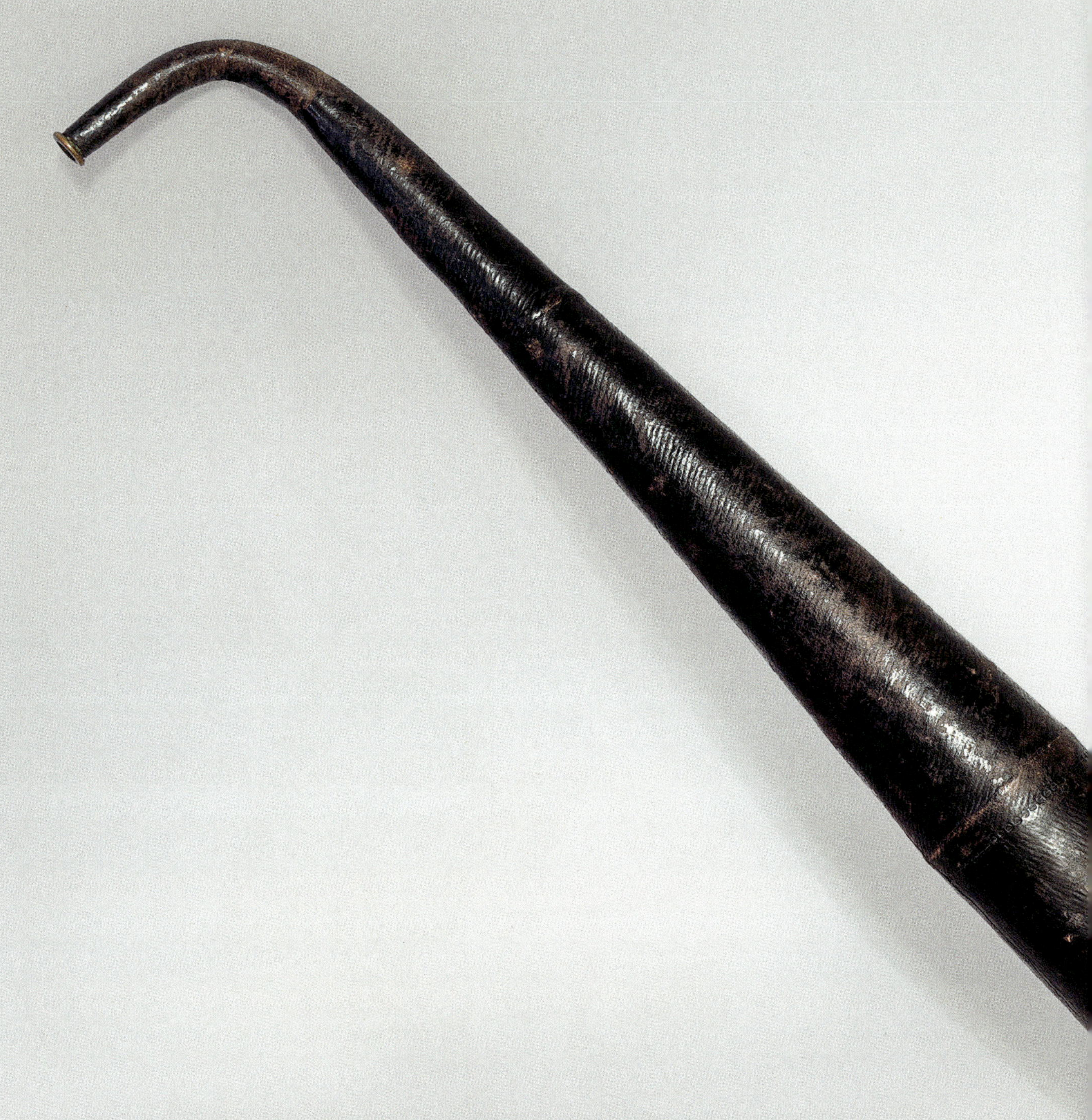

EAR TRUMPET

owned by Ludwig van Beethoven
After 1812

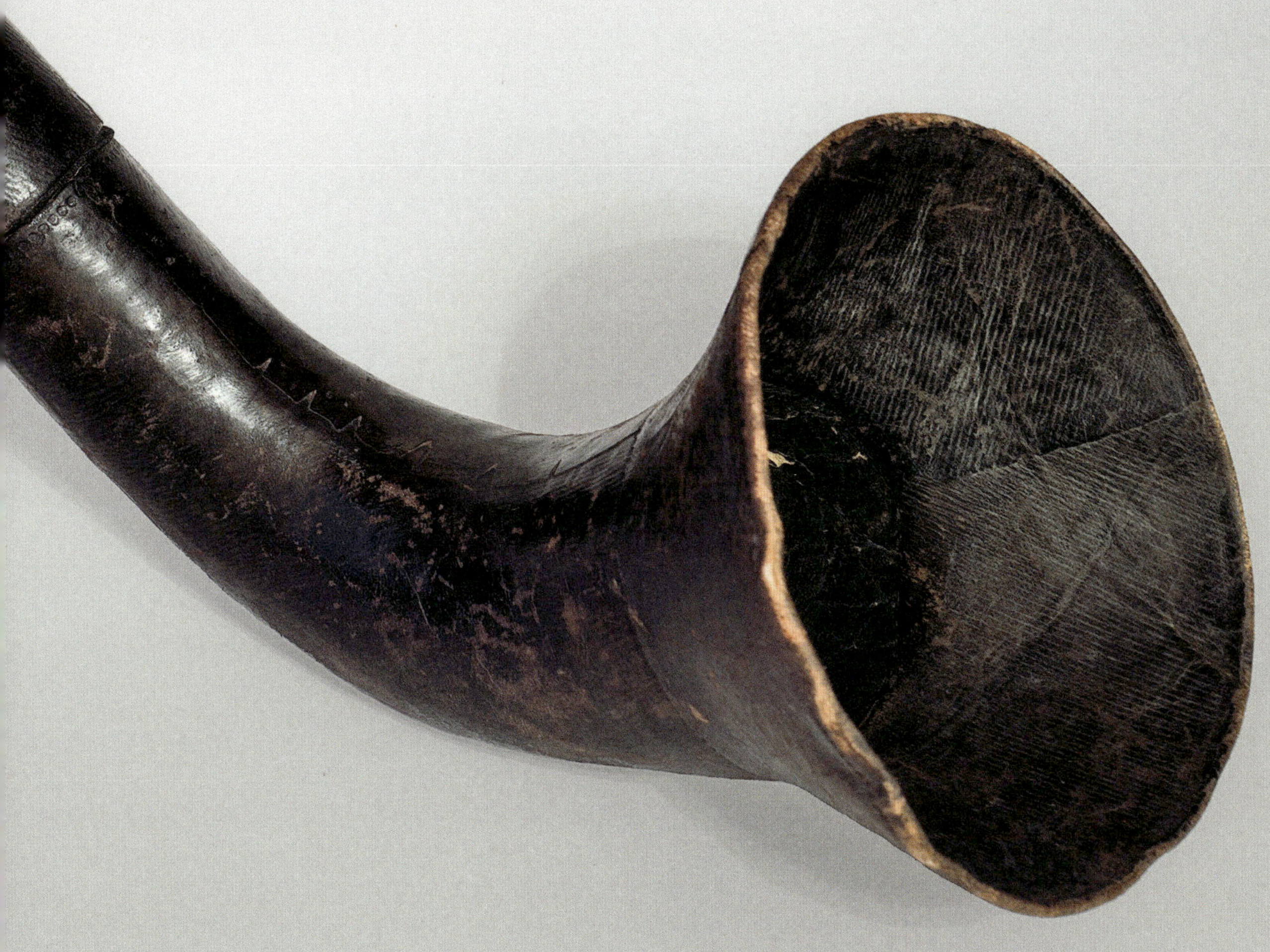

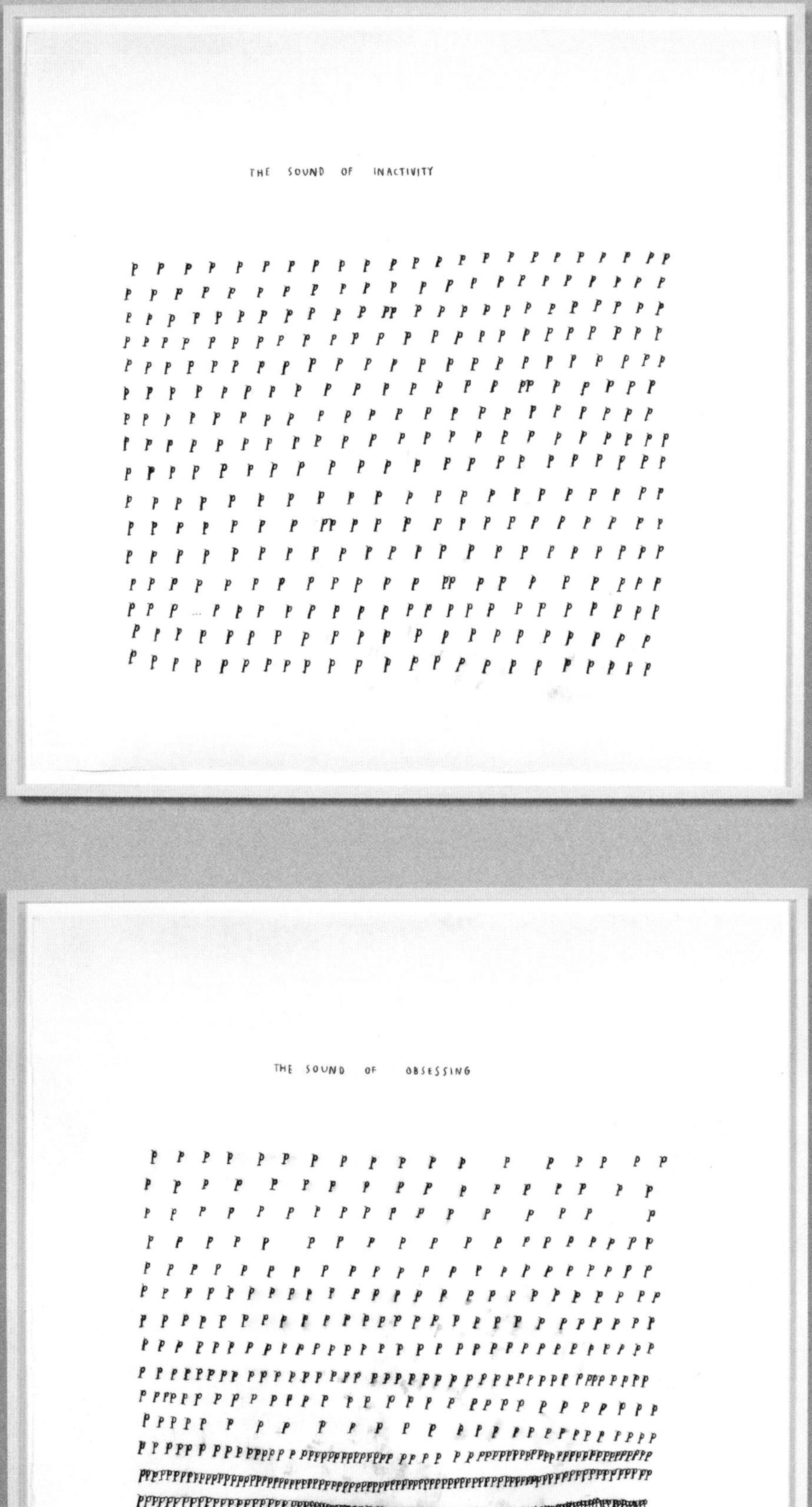

THE SOUND OF INACTIVITY

THE SOUND OF OBSESSING

CHRISTINE SUN KIM

The Sound of ... 2017

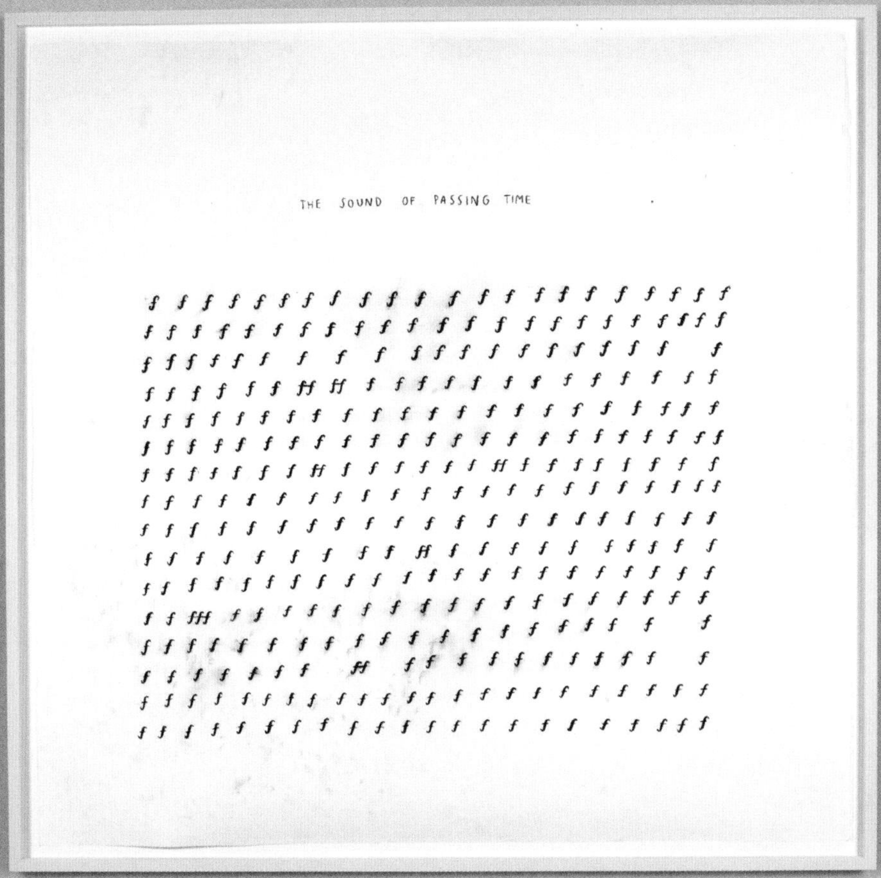

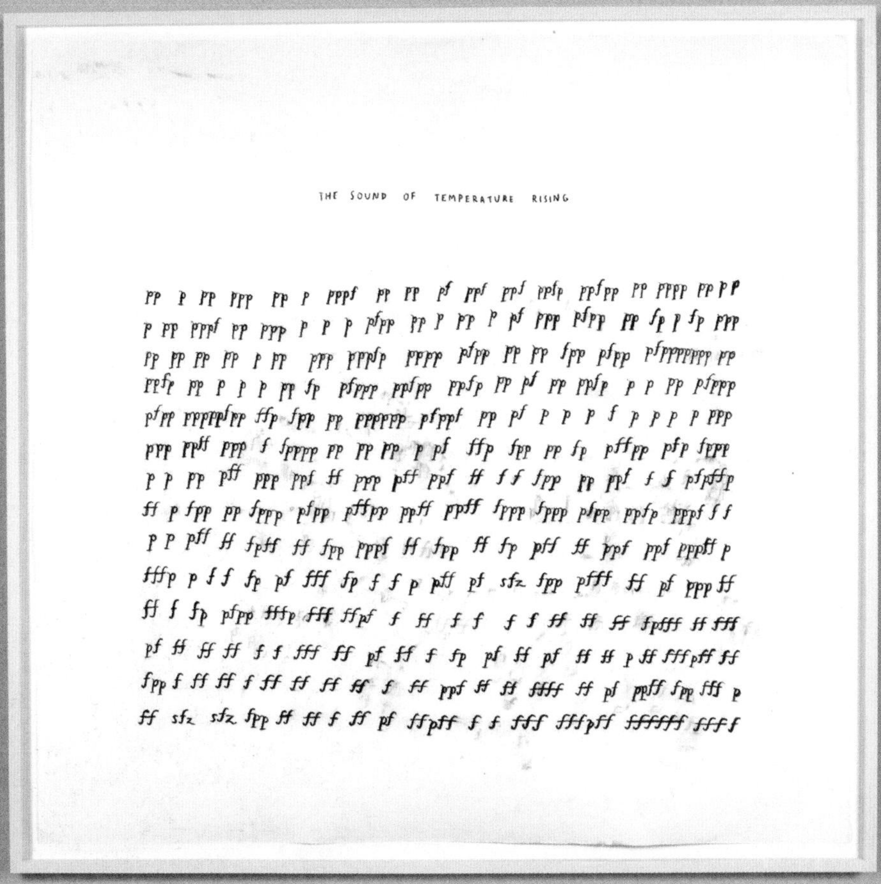

I was thinking about sound captioning in movies and television and how non-sounds such as emotions or concepts might be captioned. Each drawing uses the musical notations for forte (louder), piano (quieter) and sforzando (strong, sudden emphasis) to narrate the feelings of an experience over a period of time.

This predominantly white painting represents what we cannot perceive; like a space before a voice, a question awaiting an answer or the pause in a piece of music. Where I attempt to depict silence, Beethoven imagined the music that he was no longer able to hear through his deafness. It is in this imagined space, where sound is about to appear, that infinite patterns are possible.

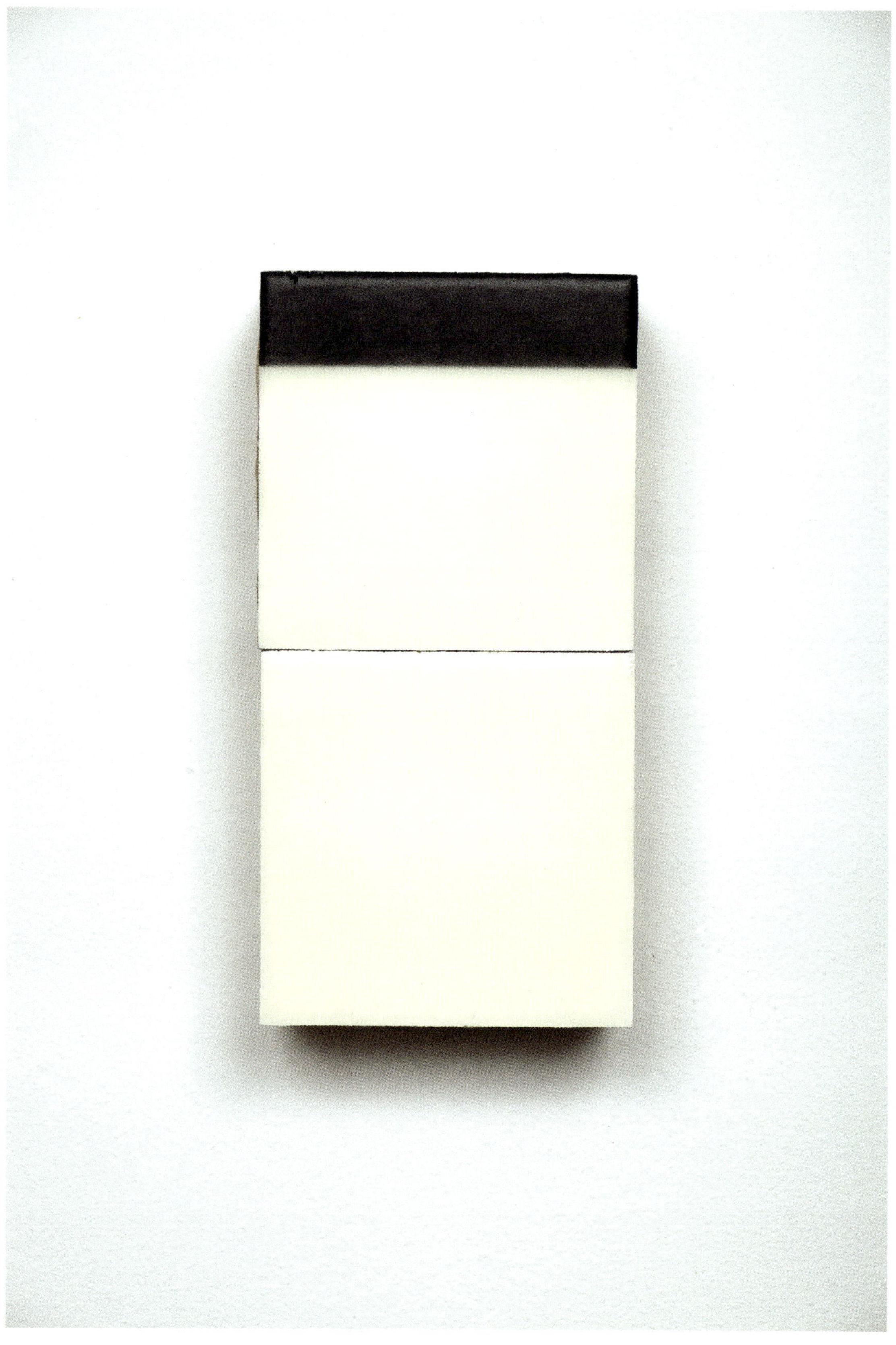

ISHA BØHLING

Silence
2002

BARBARA ZEMAN

The Maid

White, all white. All the ground and the roofs and the sky as well. The flakes that fell in the night were the size of handkerchiefs. It has been snowing for days, the footprints on the Glacis are covered over and over, a flat stretch of land that no one has ever walked upon even though it is quite bustling with people.

The maid's feet are wet already, she could use new boots, or at least a pair with fewer holes, but she is happy to stamp through the snow which comes up above her knees at its deepest points, she holds her long skirt gathered, and moves so quickly because she has things to do, almost running because she is happy to be out of the Schwarzspanierhaus where she is employed. The black-robed Spaniards the house is named for were monks, they built it many centuries ago. They went about in black, like death, but they hated it, they wanted to wear white collars like the white-robed Spaniards only a few houses on.

From its windows you can see a long way off, trees on the courtyard side, the suburbs, and the hilly woods beyond, but inside it is grim, always gloomy and everything is crooked, nothing fits from the back to the front, the passageways are endless, without doors or windows. The ceiling of one room is low, the next one has walls that are twice as high, and next door there is the façade of a church, but with no church behind it. Yesterday, before going to sleep, she lay down and ran her hand over the parquet floor, which seemed quite rough to her, like the scabby skin of an animal, it seemed to be alive, in a bad way, lurking. In her next post, she swears to herself, the first thing she will do is pay attention to the floor, perhaps it's only because of the floor that she finds the house uncanny. You can get lost in the building, more easily than in the big city that rises right in front of the maid above the vast, flat Glacis, the houses loom tightly packed beyond the walls, Vienna, every house seven houses high, the maid has been here for a year already, but she never ceases to be astonished. She takes recklessly big paces, she almost throws herself against the snow, but it doesn't matter, you don't feel a fall into deep snow, she shakes herself, the crows flap above her, they try and shake the snow off all the branches, and from here the maid can go no further, it's a snowdrift, and the coaches can go no further and a man has got stuck in his coat, just imagine, if it's like this here, *what must it be like for the people in the mountains.*[1] Switzerland, the whole of the *Tyrol*, it must all be a *horrific nest of snow, where the snow is deepest, they had to dig tunnels into it* so that they can get out again, imagine that, whole villages, closed off all around, such *a terrible quantity of snow. Avalanches!* A joy.

And how easy it is to breathe out here, all that stench of nitric acid and the smell from the printing press has been swallowed up, the air is icy and so clear, not like inside in the apartment, right at the top of the Schwarzspanierhaus, where her Herr Beethoven lies dying, but no one is allowed to say so, and if anyone does it doesn't matter, because he can't hear anything anyway, but they still give you reproachful looks, particularly his visitors, often including a child.

There is a dull smell in the apartment, the smell of old damp, mildewed dust and wine and beer; Malfatti, the doctor, *originally wanted to give him juniper beer, but then he opted for Horner Beer.* He says: *It must be not too cold and not too warm*, he should drink it *when he is thirsty, and one large jug will suffice for the whole day*.

Beethoven has a liver condition, and fluid on the abdomen, and to treat it he bathes in hay. The maid *was in the bath-house, where she was given a big tub, admittedly not quite new, for 14 fr*. It is fine and even if it had holes, nothing would happen, nothing can leak from it. Hay goes in the tub first, followed by *large jugs of hot water*, then with the help of the cook she lifts Beethoven – he can hardly stand by now – into the tub, *covered only by a linen cloth*, with flowers on top of him to make it smell nice. The first time *not for longer than h a l f a n h o u r*, Malfatti said, stretching the words out, and he wrote it in big capital letters in Beethoven's notebook, the one he reads his conversations out of. He isn't blind, he's deaf, she wanted to tell the doctor, Malfatti doesn't trust them in the slightest, he sneers at everything, *the smell of coal is not good*, the dust, but how is she to get rid of the dust if everything here is in complete confusion, she has a keen sense for practical matters, one or two changes would strike her instantly, for example the pianos in the middle of the room, how much time they could save if they could push them to the side and didn't have to spend an age walking around them, but no one listens to her, even the cook scolded her, she's supposed to do the heating with the soft wood, the hard wood is only for cooking, but they haven't got any soft wood and the house needs heating, the windows are misting up on the inside, the damp won't go away however much wood she puts on the fire. After the bath the hay was very wet and nothing will make it dry, you can't put it too close to the stove, and then it mustn't catch fire either. How pale Herr Beethoven was after the flower-bath, *water flowed from every one of his pores, he was very overheated*, his head was feverishly hot.

Even at the thought of it the maid has to pull the scarf tied around her neck a little looser, she has got quite warm from stamping through the snow, she took a detour through the trees, and she doesn't care that the cook might see her on the big white patch between the city and Alservorstadt, the Glacis is sprinkled with young people in dark coats, but if the cook looks closely she can see the maid even from a distance, because her scarf is red and fabulously bright.

She turns around to face the Schwarzspanierhaus; the snow has covered the corners of the window-panes, the cook would be better off keeping an eye on Beethoven, he's so poorly, and at the same time the maid envies him the frozen sherbet that he is served every day. Twice!

That's why she's outside, she has to get across the Glacis, through the cold and the snow, to fetch the frozen punch from the cake shop on Graben. Just think of the colour and the fragrance! So sweet and so cold! Now the maid is running again, she crosses the avenue and there is the pretzel boy with his panier, rods in it with the pretzels threaded on to them. The maid exhales small white clouds, the snow throws up dust, it is so silent and everything is soft and muted and perhaps also slower than usual, but she wouldn't swear to it, because the armed sentries are already there, *marching on the spot* so that their feet don't freeze to the ground, *one would feel sorry for them,* the way their sabres clatter, someone laughs, a bell rings somewhere, and already she is in the cake shop. The door slams shut far too loudly behind her and everyone looks, it's unpleasant, but it's good in a way too, it means the lady has seen her, the one who knows that the maid always comes for frozen sherbet to take to the immortal composer, but unfortunately she still has to wait, *the confectioner doesn't make it in portions,* but always in one large mass. The ice is made of cream, she doesn't know much more than that, it's *supposed to be made fresh every day,* it *melts if it stands for a day, then it turns to poison.* Beethoven has to take it *in the afternoon and in the evening after dinner,* it *soothes his stomach, also encourages urine* and *makes the organs smaller,* but at the moment it gives him nothing but *a sore throat, but he is still supposed to eat frozen sherbet so that the sore throat does not get even worse.* The maid would love to switch places. The smell of it here, of cinnamon and juicy dough and pears and plums, as if it were summer. Two other housemaids are chattering right in front of her: *The day before yesterday there was a glittering ball at Geymüller, the asparagus alone cost 6000 Viennese francs,* the maid takes a step back, she feels far too hot, *all the notables of the Reich were there, even Metternich.* Behind the glass the pastries shine, they look like jewels to her, gleaming with glacé icing and caramel and chocolate, there are candied cherries here too. She waits and her feet start prickling in the heat, her shoes are too small, her cheeks glow, her hands sting, where do they keep the fruit and the asparagus here, in this *extraordinarily thick snow.* She goes and stands at the edge and yet she's still in everyone's way, she thinks of Herr Beethoven's nephew, of course this would never happen to him, Karl, how lovely the sound of it, he wrote in his uncle's conversation book: *I have sometimes taken raspberry juice with water in the coffee-house. You usually pour a small liqueur glass-full into a glass of water.* She would like to try that, she'd even like to try two glasses. The nephew is very dashing, except he's with the army in Iglau now, but he's bound to be back soon, for the funeral if not before. The prickling in her feet is terrible, *the nephew lost his watch, it isn't good enough for him any more, even though it keeps time with St Stephan's to the minute,* one of the visitors said. Beethoven misses Karl too, *I'm taking a knife, fork and spoon away with me,* he said, then he was gone. The maid shifts from foot to foot, she'll have to buy herself new boots, the old ones really won't do any more, her feet really hurt, she's sore and hungry, later she will ask the cook for an apple or a pear, she's bound to be out of plums.

The maid carries the package, it dangles from her arm on a string, nothing's going to melt on her, the cold is freezing the sherbet rock solid. She would like to rest, but it's already very late and *extraordinarily hard to walk,* very smooth where the snow has been trodden down, and far too deep where it has not yet been walked upon. Dusk has made it *ferociously cold, today is the coldest day,* the pretzel boy has gone and the other maids have gone, only the crows sit in the bare branches, a trickling sound comes from the trees, the maid must hurry, it's dangerous on the Glacis at night, the snow crunches loudly, there's hardly anyone here any more, men are coming from the wood market, she wishes she could walk faster. She can see the Schwarzspanierhaus from a distance, to its left the church that isn't a church, and on the other side the gun factory, with guns in it, for God's sake don't wander about on the Glacis in the dark, the cook had impressed on her on the first day, all the things that go on there as soon as it's dark, but she refused to talk about it.

The maid has to wait in front of the house until the porter comes and opens the door to her; she darts into the house and greets him fleetingly, otherwise he might feel her up again. What a *winter's day, an enormous mass of snow lies there,* hard to imagine when it all melts, you'd drown on the Glacis, isn't that right, he says to the maid, who nods and runs to the main staircase, up the two storeys to Beethoven's apartment on the top floor. The house is dark and stony and as forbidding as ever, but today she is glad to be back, although she feels that the house doesn't want anyone to live in it. Its shadows are so heavy, the air is bitter. The maid can still see her breath, as she could outside.

There's broth with sliced pancakes. The cook stands in the huge kitchen doing things with *celery and parsley,* she's a good cook, particularly soups. The maid hangs up her coat and struggles to pull her shoes off her feet, it's not easy to keep from putting her left foot, bare and bright red and prickly, in the puddle that formed immediately, and she almost loses her balance.

A visitor stands irresolutely by the two pianos, saying goodbye in a lot of languages, *gute Nacht, bona note, bon soir, good neight, dobrou noc!* How she wishes she could lock the visitors out. Not all of them, but some come in, look curiously around like thieves and take something away, a figurine, a sheet of paper that Beethoven has written his notes on. *You could give me the sketches, because they get lost over time, like everything else.*

Whenever she comes into the apartment she has made a habit of first looking around to see if anything's missing, she's becoming more and more suspicious, almost angry. Once someone bit off a lock of his hair, that was what it looked like, it had stuck up quite irregularly from his head. The gentlemen look educated, but they have funny ideas, *You must bless a little boy, like Voltaire blessed Franklin's son,* and they assure him: *Maybe after a second flood people would forget that a Beethoven had existed,* and Beethoven *breathes heavily* at that, he becomes anxious, somebody said to him: *you should put yourself in a better humour, because sadness will inhibit your recovery.* Sometimes she would prefer it if they just let him sleep. Often over the past few days he has not woken up at all, it seems to the maid as if he is already dreaming himself into his death. Even when he's awake he isn't really there, it's probably because of the wine, Malfatti said: *Put some of the old Gumpoldskirchner wine in the water. You need not fear that this will do harm, since there are over 600 bottles in the cellar. But only in small doses, by the spoonful.* When he is awake he says things that are very confused, the Turks are coming, he can already see black smoke in the east, another time he was terribly shocked, there is lightning in the golden dome, then he sees the plaster falling from the walls to reveal beneath it paintings that show the celestial arch, of quite exceptional horrible frightfulness.

It is warmer in Beethoven's bedroom, a big stove, a clothes horse next to it, but it has smelled bad since the wounds have continued to suppurate. The bed is pushed into the corner, its legs are bent as if there is something very heavy lying in it and pushing downwards on the frame. The black money-box is still on the bedside table. The maid sits down on the chair; she likes to keep him company in the evening until the cook comes and chases her away. She whispers, *I can barely see her, so small.* Beethoven sleeps. His face has sunk in on itself. His body is quite bloated, his belly under the blanket distended as if he were about to give birth, even though it is tightly bound with a bandage – this is done *so that the extended parts may contract once more.* His feet are swollen too, and the maid is tempted to advise Malfatti to lay Beethoven briefly in the snow; that might help with the swelling.

Yesterday they tapped him again. The doctor makes an incision in the belly, on the right-hand side, where there are already three other similar wounds, a small tube is inserted, normally the water flows slowly, but yesterday it came flooding out at random, all the way to the clothes horse, Beethoven a spring and everything wet, even the doctor's glasses, and the maid can't help it, she laughs. *Someone had the witty idea of suggesting that the water thus released should be injected into all other composers in a suitable dose that they might have good thoughts.* But she quickly remembers herself and places a *wooden vessel under the bed so that the water cannot flow into the room.* They measure *15 pints,* afterwards *the belly and the feet are smaller and softer.* Later she carries the water that is in the bowl, carefully, without spilling it on herself, into the courtyard, *it looks better than last time, much clearer;* the maid pours it into the snow, the Beethoven-water is clear, but as soon as it freezes she can see it's much darker than the snow. *When you are well again, I will request snow waltzes,* someone has written in his notebook. Except that it will not be like that, his eyes are quite remarkably fogged when they are open. The maid wishes she could wipe them with her scarf to make them gleam again.

The water has stopped flowing so powerfully out of Beethoven, and a wax cloth is spread out underneath him, but the mattress is still drenched in water, *the straw is already quite rotten,* you can smell it.

After the first operation, he was told to *get up 2wice a day for ½ hr* so as not to get bed sores. Except that now he can't get up any more, and it would be better if he could turn on to his back, but he is not allowed to do that because then the water wouldn't flow from the wound and the water must flow, so he always has to lie on his right side. The *life flows from the wound,* a friend of his said, and everything smells and everything is turning grey, his face a pile of shadows. The only beneficiary of all the water is the floor. The maid doesn't like it, it shines under the water, it creaks often and loudly, as if with contentment, tickled by the many droplets. Its colour has grown lighter and more immaculate, that floor, she is sure of it, is a sleeping animal that wakes every time they tap the old man.

She looks at her feet, standing in slippers on the floor, only last night she dreamt of the floor, a face was enclosed in it and she can't remember whether there was a mouth in the middle of the face or perhaps a beak. The floor was some kind of bird, it consisted of countless wings, they were all numbered with lots of figures, except it could hardly move because it was nailed to the spot at all corners and ends. She taps the floor with the tip of her slipper, if it was not held firmly in place by the nails she is sure it would take a fluttering bath in Beethoven's murky water, splashing it like a huge baby bird, and having bathed in it sufficiently, it would rise on all its wings and perhaps fly through the window, into a terrifying land.

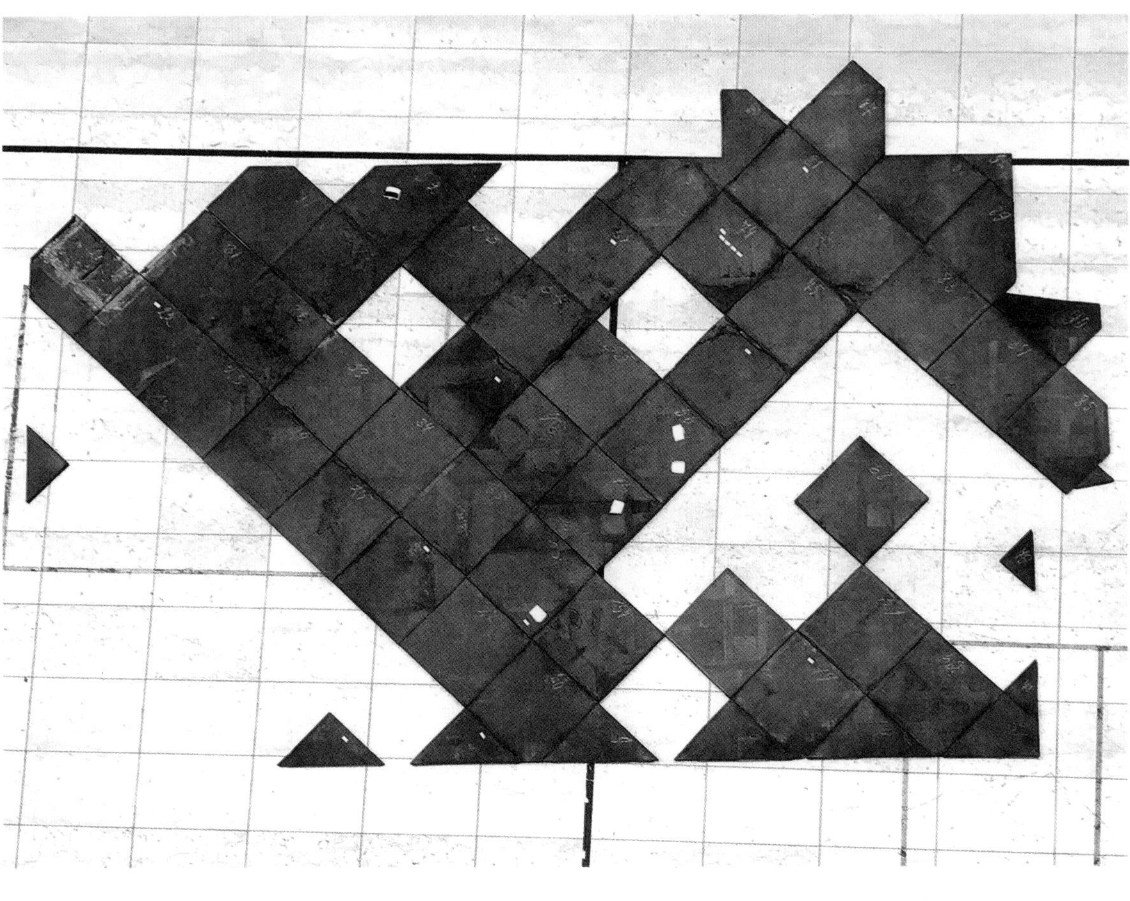

THE FLOOR

Vienna, 1903, in December. There was much talk of saving the Schwarzspanierhaus on the Alsergrund. There were plans to set up the *Schubert room from the Museum of the City of Vienna*[2] right next to the room in which Beethoven died, and the possibility was also considered of *transferring the Brahms room from Karlsgasse to here. There is talk of a Bruckner room.* All of it came to nothing.

They demolished the house in which Beethoven, for the last time and before witnesses, raised his fist to the heavens. On 26 March 1827. Between five and six in the evening. A winter storm. Hail, lightning and thunder. A musician kept watch over him, and a woman whose identity has never been established.

Left to the City of Vienna were:
In the bedroom 152 pieces of parquet. Made of *walnut and cherry wood. Pattern: 4 tiles, 4 points.*

And also *the false floors beneath the parquetry, including baseboards and mouldings.* The doors with door-frames and lining.

The walls were left behind. They mourn themselves with flowers that fall motionlessly, silently on the wallpaper of the last tenant.

Also victims of the demolition: the windows. The city of Vienna translates the relics of Beethoven, each piece numbered with stickers, to no. 339 Stadtbahnviadukt. They rest there beneath the vaulted ceiling.

1 All quotations in italics in The Maid from: *Ludwig van Beethovens Konversationshefte,* xi: Hefte 128–139 mit Registern zu den Bänden 1, 4, 5 und 6, ed. Grita Herre and Günter Brosche (Leipzig, 2001).

2 All quotations in italics in The Floor from: Peter Pötschner, *Das Schwarzspanierhaus. Beethovens letzte Wohnstätte* [vol. ii of Wiener Geschichtsbücher] (Vienna, 1970).

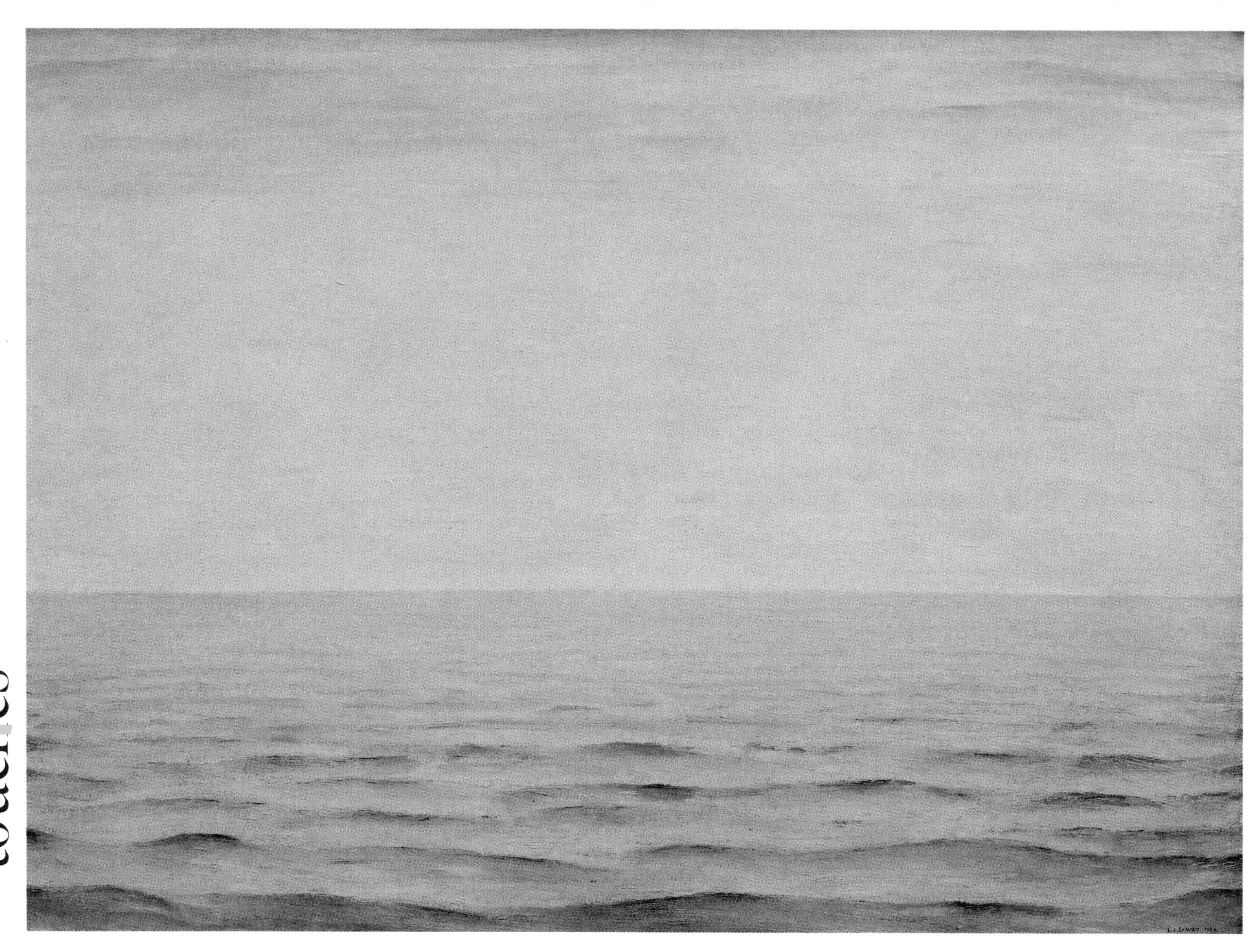

People are noticeably absent in Lowry's painting of land- and seascapes. The painter himself admitted: 'I'm by nature a person who's spent a lot of time by himself.' It was only painting and his devotion to certain composers – Bellini, Bach and Beethoven – that remained with him as a solace all of his life.

L.S. LOWRY

The Grey Sea 1964

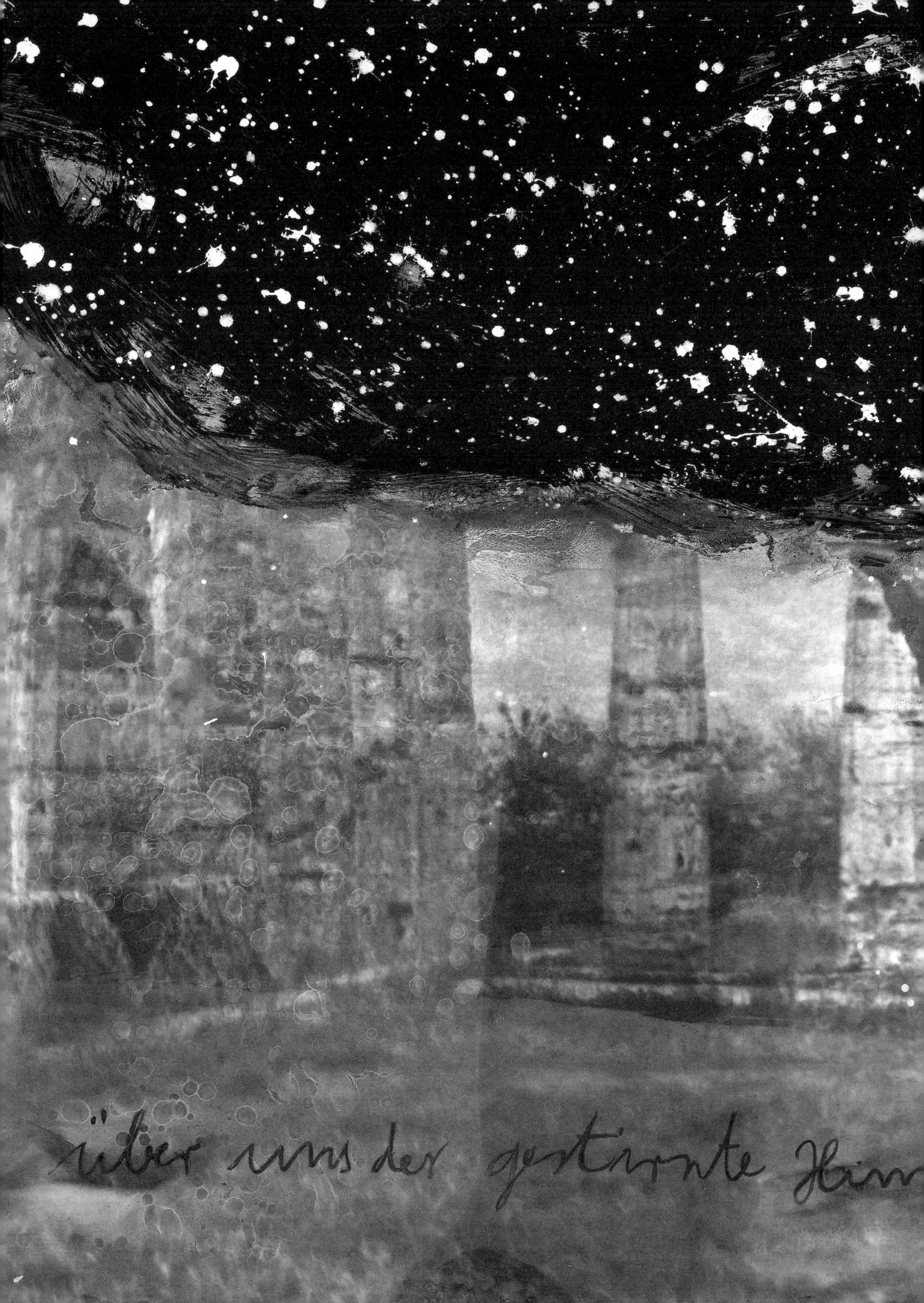
über uns der gestirnte Him

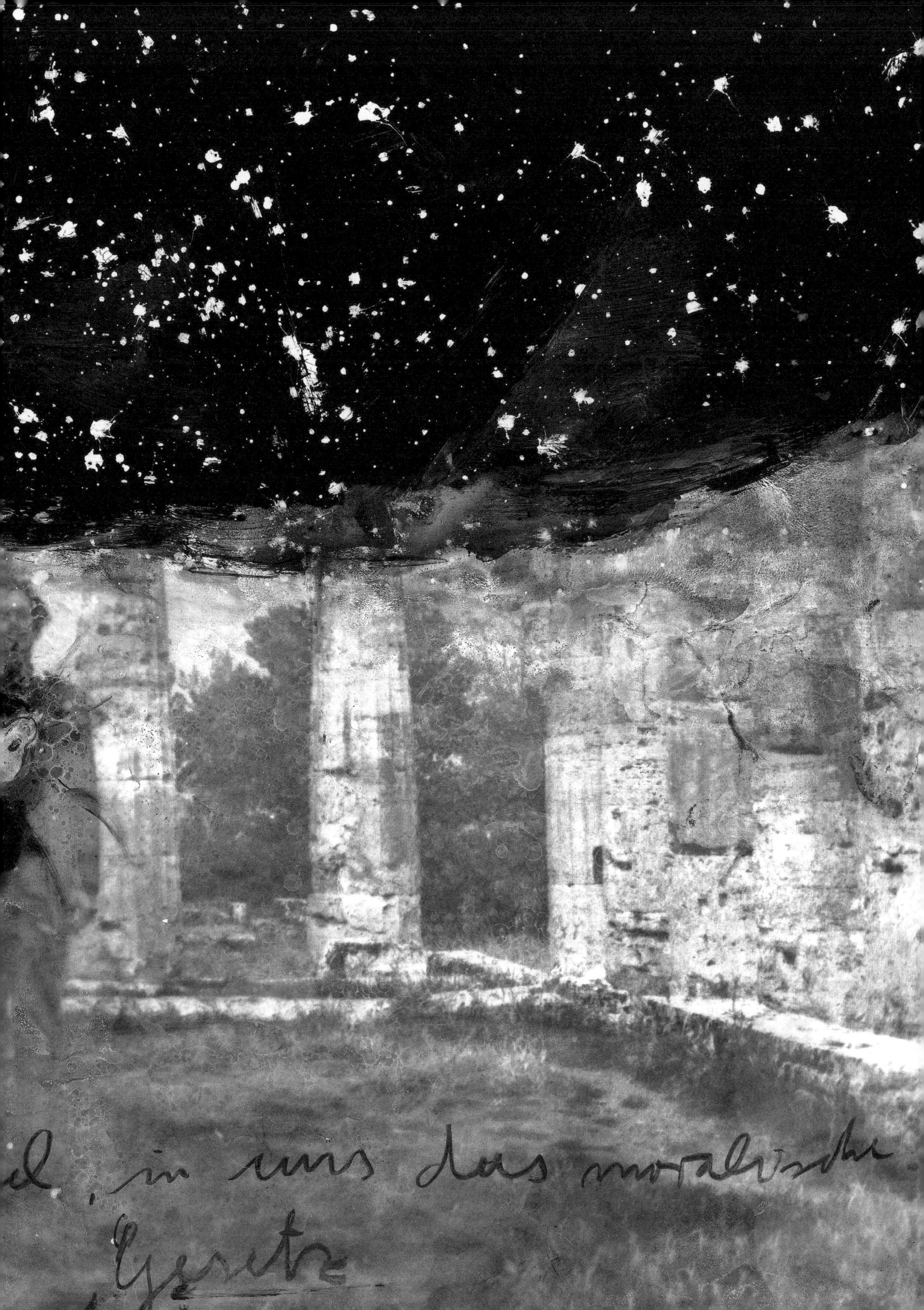
d, in uns das moralische
Gesetz

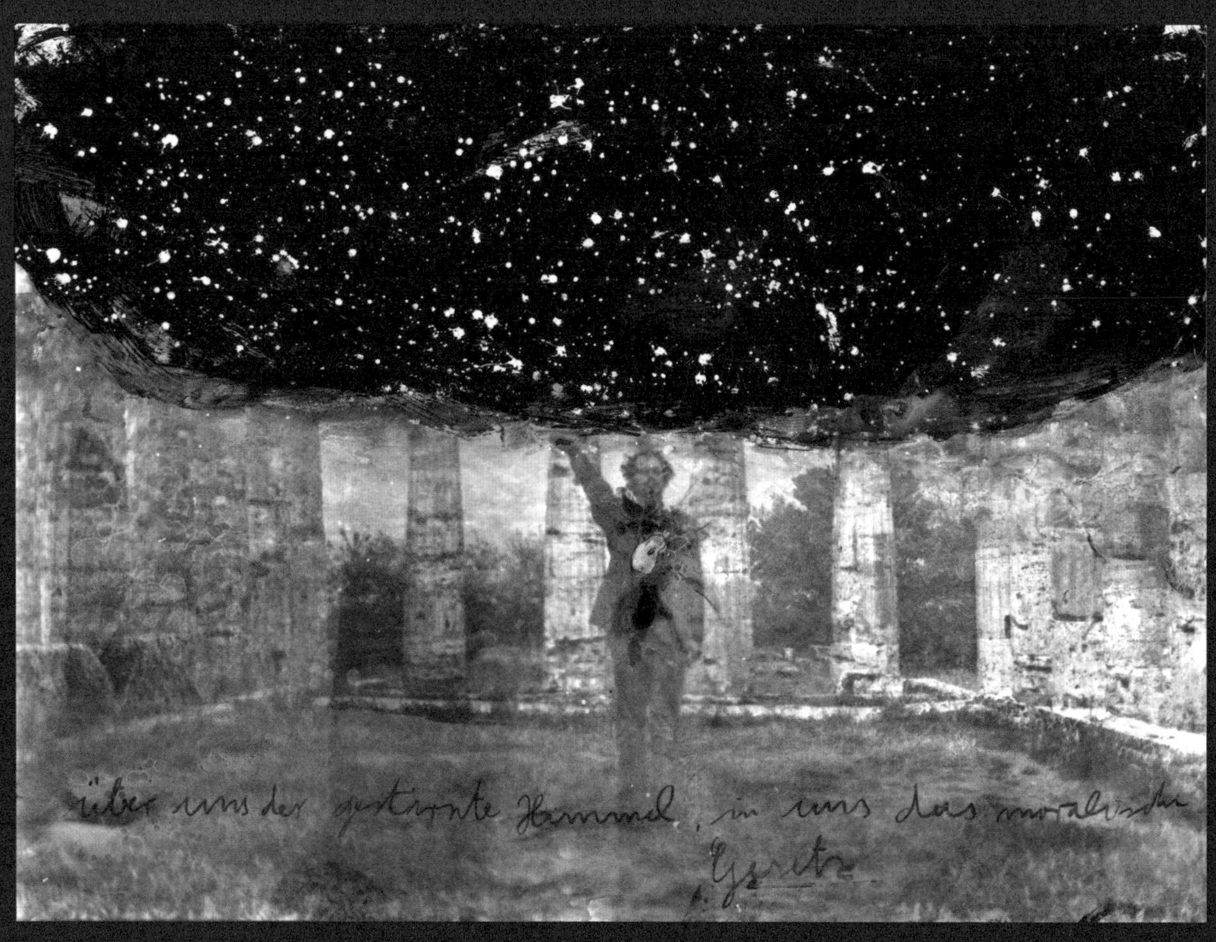

ANSELM KIEFER, THE STARRY HEAVENS ABOVE US, AND THE MORAL LAW WITHIN, 1969–2010

JÜRGEN MÜLLER

The Power of Music: Stanley Kubrick's *A Clockwork Orange* and Ludwig van Beethoven

One would be hard put to find a film with more laconic opening credits than Stanley Kubrick's *A Clockwork Orange* from 1971. The first shot shows no more than a rectangular red surface, with eerie music from a synthesizer as the soundtrack.

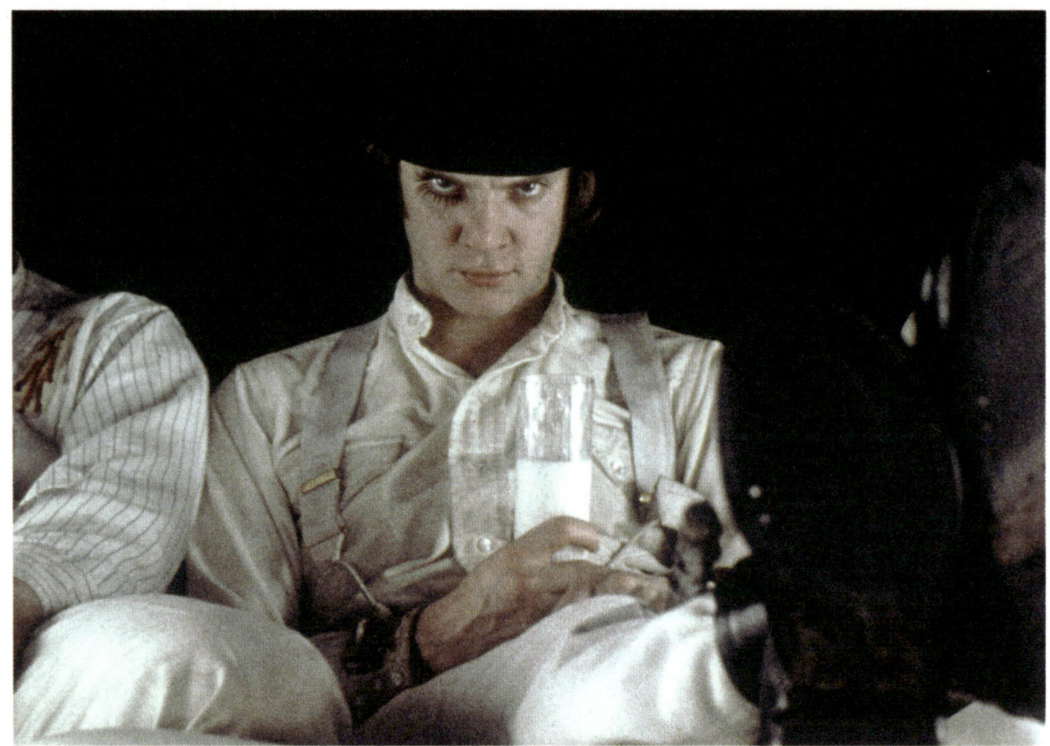

After twenty seconds, that sparse information is added to as the name of the film distributors fades in: 'Warner Bros. Presents'. The background colour then changes to blue and we read: 'A Stanley Kubrick Production'. Finally, the screen becomes steeped in red again and the title of the film fades in. This sequence of shots lasts barely forty seconds and is followed immediately by a frontal closeup of the protagonist, his right eye accentuated with false eyelashes. He is wearing a bowler hat and looks us straight in the face.

A Clockwork Orange is one of the most controversial films made in the 1970s and enjoys cult status as an icon of pop culture. One could describe the film as a hinge, as it were, that joins the 1960s and the 1970s because it may plausibly be interpreted as a questioning or, rather, a critique of the student movement's appeals for a society free of violence and authority. While Kubrick's work constantly alludes to the 1960s and that decade's optimistic belief in progress, it does in fact encompass the entire twentieth century with all its inhuman utopias and mankind-despising ideals.

Kubrick's film deals with the power of music, which is presented to us as an intoxicating experience and repeatedly associated with scenes of physical aggression. Indeed, the director of *A Clockwork Orange* stages a veritable *theatrum mundi* of violence for us. The film tells the story of the young gang leader Alex DeLarge, a fanatical admirer of Beethoven who makes the streets of London unsafe. After a robbery that leaves a woman dead, Alex is arrested and sentenced to fourteen years in prison. While behind bars he is offered the opportunity to take part in a therapy programme authorized by the Minister of the Interior, which is meant to rid Alex of his violent instincts as quickly as possible – an urgent necessity because of overcrowding in the country's penal institutions. He is bound into a straitjacket and strapped to a chair in a cinema. This coercive therapy, known as the 'Ludovico treatment', involves Alex being injected with drugs and forced – his eyes are clamped open – to watch one brutal scene after another until he is nauseated by the violence being shown to him and has turned into a supposedly peaceful young man. The images of Nazi terror and war atrocities that the 'patient' is exposed to ultimately even take possession of the music of the 'lovely Ludwig van' that, quite unintended by the doctors, is played together with the film footage. Like all forms of violence, Beethoven's music, too, becomes unbearable for the young music lover from now on. The technique used to treat Alex resembles the experiments conducted by the famous Russian behavioural scientist Ivan Pavlov, who in the early twentieth century succeeded in conditioning dogs to the extent that the sound of a bell was sufficient to make them salivate. Such an interpretation is indeed suggested by the film, given that the tests carried out upon conclusion of the therapy show Alex, like one of Pavlov's dogs, confusing the trappings of an event with the event itself.

Kubrick constructs the cinematic narrative in a highly didactic manner. For after his release, Alex re-encounters all the people who had crossed his path in the first part of the film and on whom he had inflicted violence. Now, though, it is the aggressor's turn to see things from the victim's perspective. The aggression that he had once practised rebounds on him. After a botched suicide attempt, provoked by a former victim forcing him to listen to Beethoven's Ninth Symphony, Alex finds himself in the hospital again. Since the government is afraid that its dubious conditioning experiments on criminals may spoil its chances of reelection, Alex is subjected to a second therapy programme, at the end of which he is again primed for violence.

Being the adventures of a young man
whose principal interests are rape,
ultra-violence and Beethoven.

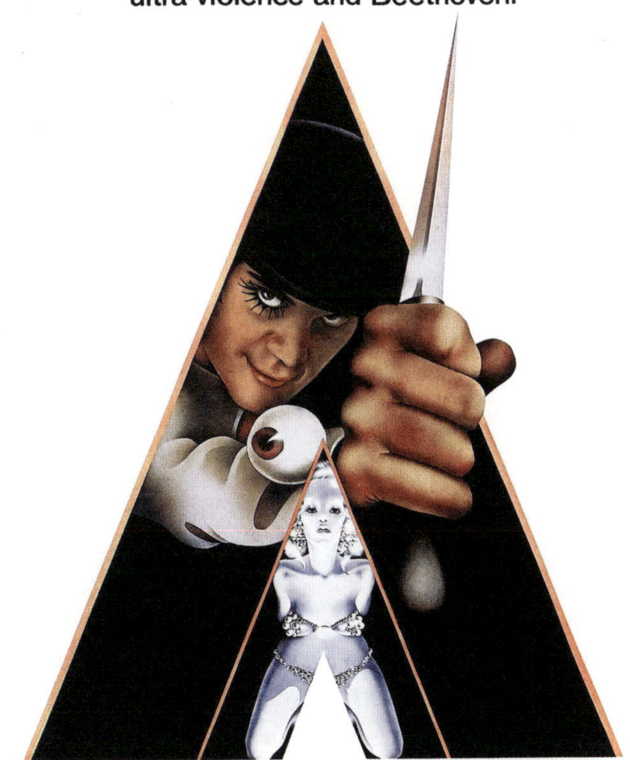

STANLEY KUBRICK'S

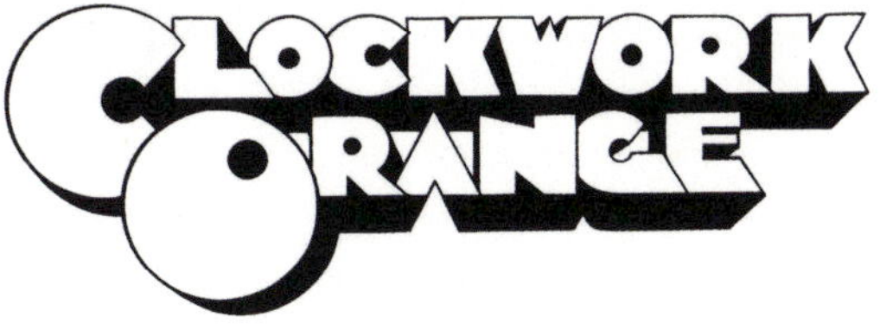

A Stanley Kubrick Production "A CLOCKWORK ORANGE" Starring Malcolm McDowell • Patrick Magee • Adrienne Corri and Miriam Karlin • Screenplay by Stanley Kubrick • Based on the novel by Anthony Burgess • Produced and Directed by Stanley Kubrick • Executive Producers Max L. Raab and Si Litvinoff • From Warner Bros. A Kinney Company

Exciting original soundtrack available on Warner Bros. Records

72/30

In the course of the film, those scenes that are fundamental to the protagonist's development are time and again accompanied by allusions to Beethoven: the music of the German composer is used in leitmotif fashion, as are portraits of him. This is already evident in the film's first scene, in which Alex, his head slightly inclined, fixes his eyes upon us. It is almost as if he wanted then and there to show us those features that we shall later on encounter in his bedroom, where the window-blind is decorated with Beethoven's face. The reproduction is based on the statue of Beethoven designed by Ernst Hähnel, which was cast in bronze by Jacob Daniel Burgschmiet and unveiled in Bonn in 1845. In Alex's room, moreover, we find a reproduction of a drawing of Beethoven on his deathbed that was made by Joseph Danhauser after the composer's death. A further example of the Beethoven leitmotif is the raid by the 'droogs' on Mr Alexander's house, the doorbell of which plays the first few notes of the Fifth Symphony. Before invading the house with his gang, beating the writer up and raping his wife, Alex causes the opening motif of the so-called Symphony of Fate to ring out five times in succession. Alex's veneration of the German composer is finally visualized for us unequivocally when he returns to his parents' flat in a drab London suburb. Seeking to crown a 'wonderful evening', the protagonist inserts a Deutsche Grammophon recording into the mini-cassette player in his bedroom so that he can at last listen to his beloved 'Ludwig van'. By showing us this diminutive sound carrier, Kubrick seems to be trying to convey visually the overwhelming impact of music, which can by no means be explained in terms of the material process of its production.

We are further alerted to the significance of Beethoven's music by the way in which the opening notes are accompanied by the camera zooming in on the above-mentioned iconic likeness of the composer. In a voice-over, Alex gives eloquent expression to the joy he derives from the music: 'Oh, bliss! Bliss and heaven! Oh, it was gorgeousness and gorgeosity made flesh. It was like a bird of rarest spun heaven metal. Or like silvery wine flowing in a spaceship, gravity all nonsense now. As I slushied [listened], I knew such lovely pictures.'[1] With the second movement *(Molto vivace!)* of Beethoven's Ninth Symphony playing in the background, an associative montage is used to present us with an extravagant train of pictures that does not shy even from mocking Jesus as a naked cancan dancer. The holiest of all holy phenomena – in this case, Beethoven of course – and blasphemy are no longer mutually contradictory.

Kubrick attempts no less than to demonstrate, with ironic detachment, the state of ecstasy of a person whose individuality disintegrates while listening to music and is subsumed into its lofty sounds. Shots of Beethoven's portrait and Alex's face are repeatedly cross-cut, the effect being to suggest that the two have merged. This is one of the most absurd sequences in film history. And yet we are overwhelmed – by the pop-art goddess lasciviously stretched out, by the porcelain figure of a naked Jesus in quadruplicate who throws his arms in the air to the music of the Ninth, by the nightmarish decor of the parental home – and succumb, whether we like it or not, to the charm of this voluble thug. As far as Alex is concerned, the German composer is the ideal of a creative genius, of an *Übermensch* – but, above all, Beethoven's music is the source from which he draws his inspiration to violence. When listening to Beethoven he is quite at one with himself. It is not surprising, therefore, that the Ninth Symphony was variously deployed by the director in the course of the film, where we hear not just the aforementioned scherzo movement but also part of the Ode to Joy. Why, though, was Beethoven's music selected in the first place?

The few shots described above make it sufficiently clear that the act of seeing in *A Clockwork Orange* is represented as a craving, even as a drive. As its agents we are like blithe voyeurs and accomplices who take pleasure in the gratuitous display of brutality, just as it is a matter of course for us to keep looking even when Alex is casually peeing into the toilet bowl.

Kubrick demonstrates in different ways how seeing is a kind of action – most obviously perhaps by having Alex wear cufflinks styled like severed eyeballs: these symbolic eyes are inextricably linked to every criminal act perpetrated by his hands. Not for nothing does just such an eyeball occupy a central place in the original poster of the film. The eloquent narrator Alex, who regales us with his life-story in a series of voice-overs, takes our collusion entirely for granted. And he is right, too, for we do see the world through Alex's eyes. The director uses all the cinematic means available to present Alex's world to us as authentic. That is why we not only see through his eyes but are also meant to listen through his ears and, thanks to the musical backgrounds that accompany his infamies, to experience vicariously the thrill he gets out of abusing others. When we watch a brutal fight inside a derelict theatre and listen at the same time to the overture to Rossini's *La gazza ladra*, the enjoyment of everyone involved becomes palpable. Kubrick seeks to enable us to savour violence 'from the inside out'.

Violence here is an artistic principle. It denotes joy and frenzy in the sense of Friedrich Nietzsche's study *Die Geburt der Tragödie aus dem Geiste der Musik* (The Birth of Tragedy Out of the Spirit of Music), first published in 1872, the programmatic text of which may be cited in explanation of the enthusiasm for Beethoven we are shown in Kubrick's film. In this study, the philosopher invokes the Dionysian nature of Beethoven's music, observing already in the first chapter: 'To gain an approximate idea of the Dionysian, all one has to do is to transform Beethoven's exultant song of joy into a painting without holding back one's imagination at the moment when the "millions" [from Schiller's ode] sink shuddering into the dust.'[2]

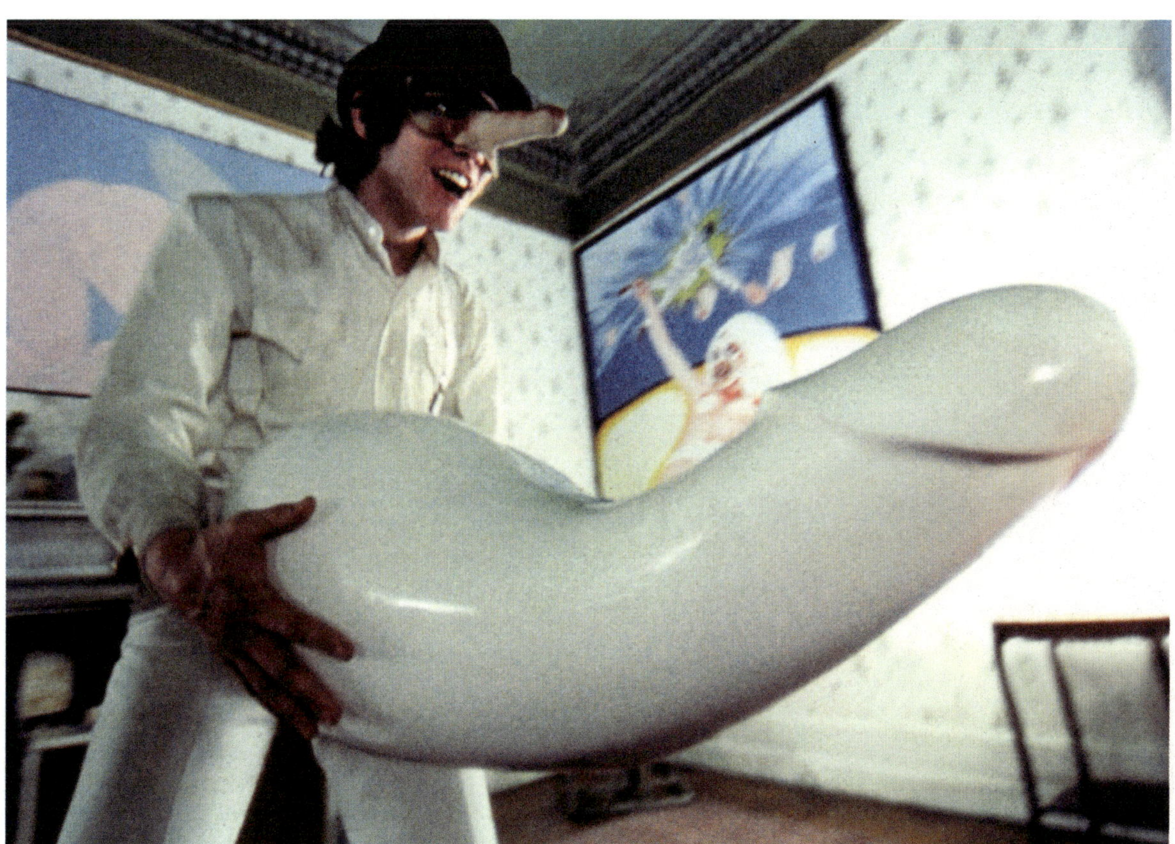

As is well known, Nietzsche's book is a major transformative text of the modern era. Proceeding from Schiller's distinction between naive and sentimental poetry, Nietzsche drew up the programme for a reform of culture that was meant to lead to a realm of sensual immediacy. In Richard Wagner's operas and in the Wagnerian concept of the *Gesamtkunstwerk* the philosopher duly saw a step in the right direction, namely a step towards reversing the growing fragmentation of the arts. His treatise holds out the prospect of returning to a golden age. Music and lyric poetry are deemed to belong to the Dionysian aspect of art, while sculpture and epic poetry symbolize the Apollonian aspect. In accordance with the old adage 'nomen est omen', the interior minister in Kubrick's film is called Friedrich. A further allusion to Nietzsche lies in the fact that the minister shares Alex's passion for Beethoven. Curiously, it is the minister's political programme that is put into practice with the implementation of the 'Ludovico treatment'. Later in the film, he will visit Alex in his prison cell, where he notices a small bust of Beethoven and a portrait of the composer.

The antithetical pair of the Apollonian and Dionysian presented in Nietzsche's treatise together make up a striking juxtaposition that, despite its origins in antiquity, seems to be universally valid from an anthropological perspective. Analytical, or dissecting, thought is juxtaposed with the wholeness of feeling, or, to put it using Alex's words before he brutally disciplines the members of his own gang: 'But suddenly I viddied [saw, realized] that thinking is for the gloopy [stupid] ones and that the oomny [clever] ones used, like, inspiration and what Bog [God] sends.' The Dionysian power invoked by Nietzsche manifests itself most memorably when Alex, readying himself for yet another fight, takes hold of a frozen artwork – the sculpture of a phallus – and awakens it to life during a grotesque ballet. Wielding the phallic object, he turns it into a weapon against his latest victim, the 'Cat Lady', who threatens to hit him with a bust of Ludwig van Beethoven. The scene is instructive also in the sense that Kubrick, following Nietzsche, has Alex play the part of a satyr. As in ancient depictions, Alex carries a gigantic phallus in front of him and becomes a Dionysian reveller. At the end of the fight he kills the woman with the huge penis sculpture. The act of killing is experienced by us as a parallelism of camera and phallus: seeing becomes slaying. For when Alex lifts up his arms in order to deliver the final blow, we look down on the victim lying on the floor from the viewpoint of the ceramic penis, the camera being located inside its head.

The Dionysian triumphs over the Apollonian. It is the moment at which things and concepts disintegrate, and we as spectators are confronted with a series of subliminal images, the singularity of each of which we are unable to comprehend. Even for Nietzsche, the realization of the Dionysian implied the dissolution of the social world, made up as that world is of interrelated actions and images that

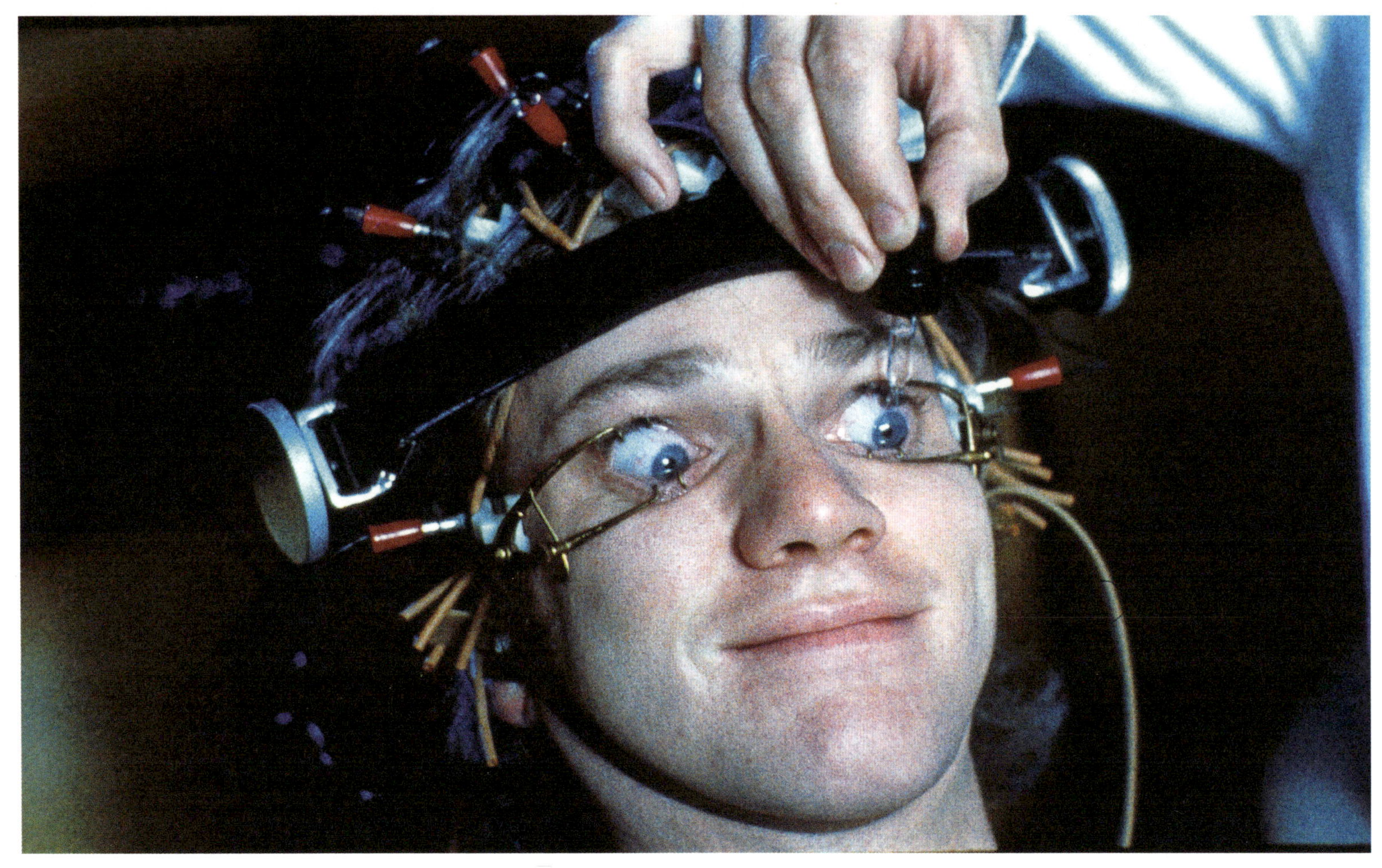

causally succeed one another. Returning to Kubrick's film and its context, we even come across an ironic manifesto of subliminal visual aesthetics, namely the trailer for *A Clockwork Orange* that was intended for US audiences. The trailer runs for less than a minute and consists of a riotous montage of shots from the film that are held together by an accelerated version of the overture to Rossini's *William Tell*. Various intercut captions flash on the screen – 'WITTY', 'FUNNY', 'SATIRIC', 'MUSICAL', 'EXCITING', 'BIZARRE', 'POLITICAL', 'FRIGHTENING', 'METAPHYSICAL', 'METAPHORICAL', 'SARDONIC', 'COMIC' and 'THRILLING' – advertising ironically the film's entertainment value. In aesthetic terms, the predominant impression is one of speed. It is as if a record meant to be played at 33 1/3 revolutions per minute (rpm) were made to turn at 45 rpm, resulting in a kind of visual 'Mickey Mouse effect'.

Even though the shots shown in the trailer are part of a serious, to some extent even gruesome narrative, we register them with amusement. After just a few seconds, the sequence of images has overpowered us and we surrender to the flow of apparently unrelated visual impressions which the music invests with a comical dimension. The extreme tempo leads to the triumph of form over content. The title of the film, styled in pop-art lettering, is inserted repeatedly, while the background colours change. There is no intelligible meaning in the world that flashes, lightning-like, before us in the various scene fragments, yet it is precisely for that reason that the shots take on an emotional quality. They emanate an atmosphere that is playful and ominous at the same time, leaving us with the irritating feeling that something essential is being withheld from us. That emotional quality is in fact their content: we are both amused and unsettled. In just 58 seconds, the trailer evokes the above-mentioned coercive therapy. As spectators we are exposed to all that violence in a similar way to Stanley Kubrick's protagonist Alex when he is strapped to a chair in a cinema. The outwardly funny effect of super-fast motion, which makes it almost impossible to tell all the images apart, has a serious connotation in that speed is the key to the subconscious. It is obvious that this montage is meant to adumbrate the 'Ludovico treatment' which Alex will undergo later in the film. By means of visual brainwashing, the brutal hoodlum is to be turned into a good, conformist citizen. In tongue-in-cheek fashion, the trailer applies that very same method to 'force' the spectator to watch the film in the cinema.

Kubrick also plays with the physiology of visual perception by repeatedly using afterimage effects in the trailer: the changing colours have a lingering aftereffect on the human eye so that the visual impression lasts beyond the original stimulus. This is surely a hint at how easily cinematic images can overwhelm our faculty of perception. Kubrick makes it clear that what we are dealing with is an anti-humanistic aesthetic, since subliminal images very much rely on the physiological 'apparatus' of human perception. In the technocratic world of *A Clockwork Orange*, man is defined as a being who is not meant to perceive, let alone understand things: he is, rather, to be 'treated'. In that sense, the trailer may be interpreted on two levels: on the one hand, on a comical and parodic level because the director flouts the conventional cinematic idiom and pokes fun at any aspirations to seriousness; on the other, on a political level because the trailer alludes to the use of images for the deliberate conditioning of people. The advertising for the film is alone sufficient to turn us into accomplices of the protagonist; throughout the film itself we are constantly pushed into such an accessory role. Like Alex DeLarge, whom mechanical devices prevent from shutting his eyes during his treatment, we are unable to turn our eyes away from Kubrick's masterfully staged displays of subversion. For *A Clockwork Orange* demonstrates how the projection of a film can be a most effective means of inculcating political conformity; it turns us into victims of a sophisticated aesthetic manipulation.

To conclude, if we may once again refer to *The Birth of Tragedy Out of the Spirit of Music*, the alternation of red and blue in the colours of the titles at the start of the film may be said to represent the Dionysian and Apollonian. It is precisely in the scenes of violence, dominated by the colour red, that the youthful protagonist is wholly self-possessed. In connection with Alex, the following passage from Nietzsche's treatise springs to mind – a passage in which the transformation of man into satyr is described: 'His very gestures bespeak enchantment. ... Man is no longer an artist, he has himself become a work of art – and the artistic force of all Nature ... manifests itself here amid the shuddering of ecstasy.'[3]

The director of *A Clockwork Orange* calls into question the possibility of a world free of violence. The utopia of a conflict-free society is to be discarded, since oppression and opportunism are also rife in the 'future' that he projects for us. Sadism and ignorance are not exclusive to any one epoch. The film reminds us that culture is never innocent. Few artists have been instrumentalized to the same extent as Beethoven has in order to create communal experiences and manufacture national or ethnic identity. His music was not just heard in concert halls but was also used as the soundtrack for newsreels of war. In letters sent home from the Russian front, soldiers wrote about how thrilling it was to drive through the Soviet Union in tanks while listening to Beethoven. The composer is of course not to blame. For it is evident that music is sometimes used to overcome inhibition thresholds or to turn what is horrible into an 'aesthetic' experience. The film leaves us puzzled, for it ultimately poses more questions than it gives answers. We have been warned. Political utopianists who promise definitive solutions mostly achieve the opposite. We must make choices – all the time. Dionysian or Apollonian, proximity or distance, identity or difference, laughing or crying. But we cannot get rid of the irrational: it is evidently a part of us. By accepting the irrational, we may not only sample the power and the ecstasy of Beethoven's music but also discover something about the mechanisms of violence. The inevitable conclusion is that the price we must pay for the Dionysian experience of music can be very high indeed.

1 In quotations from Alex's voice-over narration, the English equivalents of the more abstruse argot ('Nadsat') words he uses are given inside square brackets. Many of these words were invented by Anthony Burgess, the author of the original novel, by borrowing from the Russian (e.g., 'to slushy' is a calque on the verb slushat', 'to listen', while the name of Alex's gang, the 'droogs', is derived from the Russian noun drug, 'friend').

2 [Man verwandele das Beethoven'sche Jubellied der "Freude" in ein Gemälde und bleibe mit seiner Einbildungskraft nicht zurück, wenn die Millionen schauervoll in den Staub sinken: So kann man sich dem Dionysischen nähern.] Friedrich Nietzsche, *Die Geburt der Tragödie aus dem Geiste der Musik*, in idem, *Sämtliche Werke. Studienausgabe*, 15 vols., ed. Giorgio Colli & Mazzino Montinari (Munich, 1988), i, 29.

3 [Aus seinen Gebärden spricht die Verzauberung ... Der Mensch ist nicht mehr Künstler, er ist Kunstwerk geworden: die Kunstgewalt der ganzen Natur ... offenbart sich hier unter den Schauern des Rausches.] Ibid., 30.

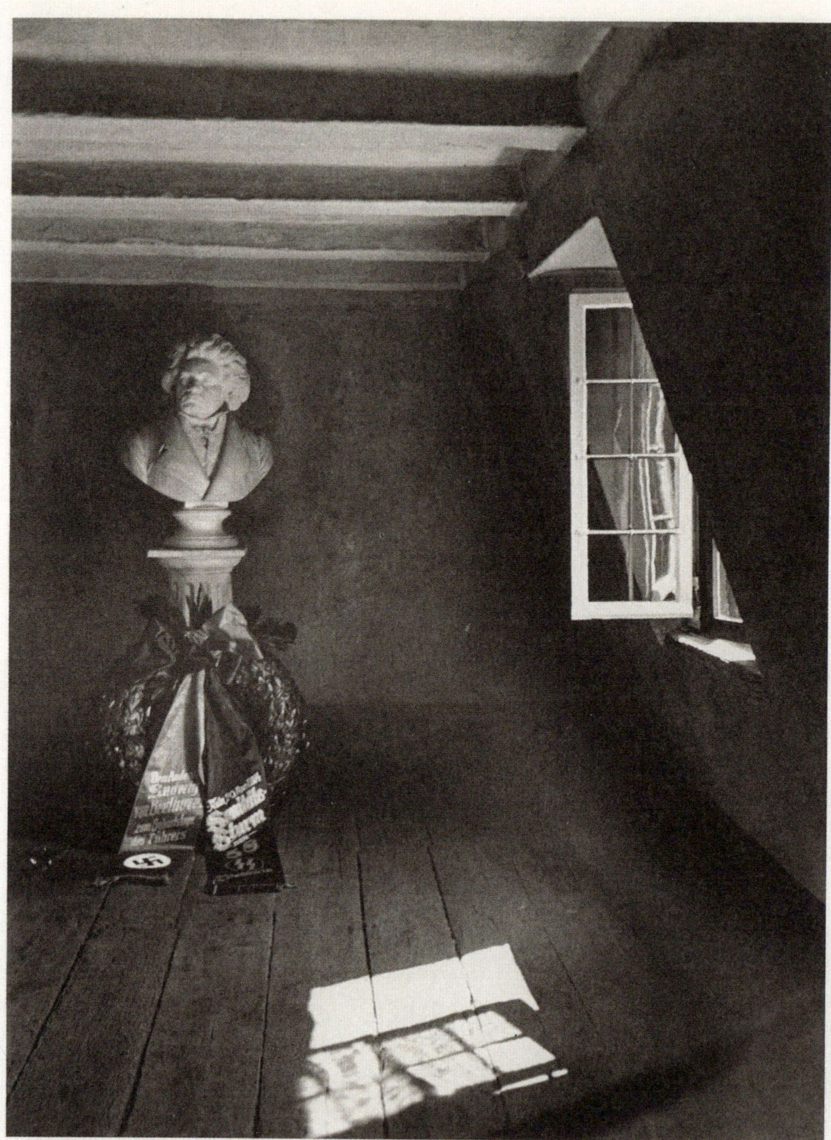

THE ROOM IN WHICH BEETHOVEN WAS BORN, BONN, 1934

In 1979 I went back to Germany to take some additional photographs for a book of mine on Germany. The earlier pictures were taken over a span of many years. Now I was supposed to do a series in a short time. Then there were the memories of the place I'd had to leave. I took this picture of Beethoven's birthplace a year before my departure from Germany. I simply wanted a picture of the famous Beethoven bust, but as I was putting up my tripod some Nazis came in and put a wreath there that read, "On the Führer's birthday—the S.S. Sturmgruppenführer, Bonn."

108

ALFRED EISENSTAEDT

The Room in Which Beethoven Was Born 1934/1979

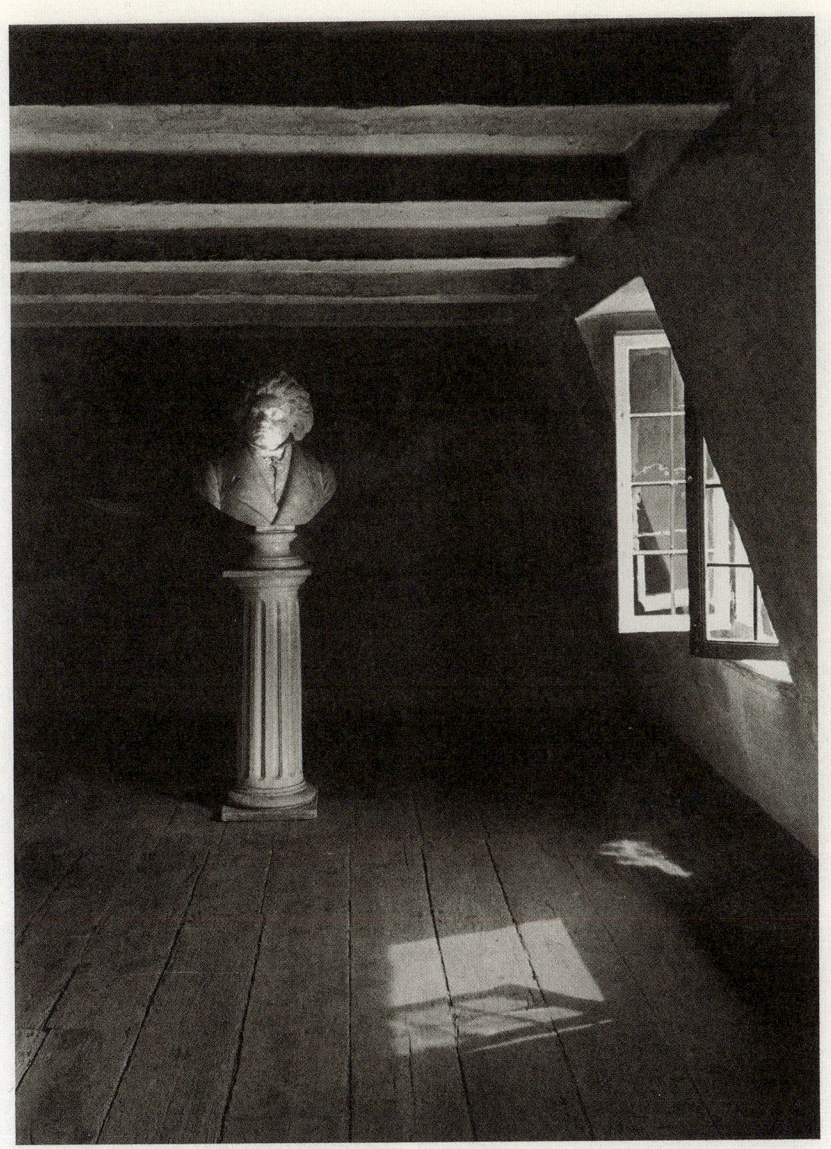

BONN, 1979

Well, I did it without the wreath when they were gone.

109

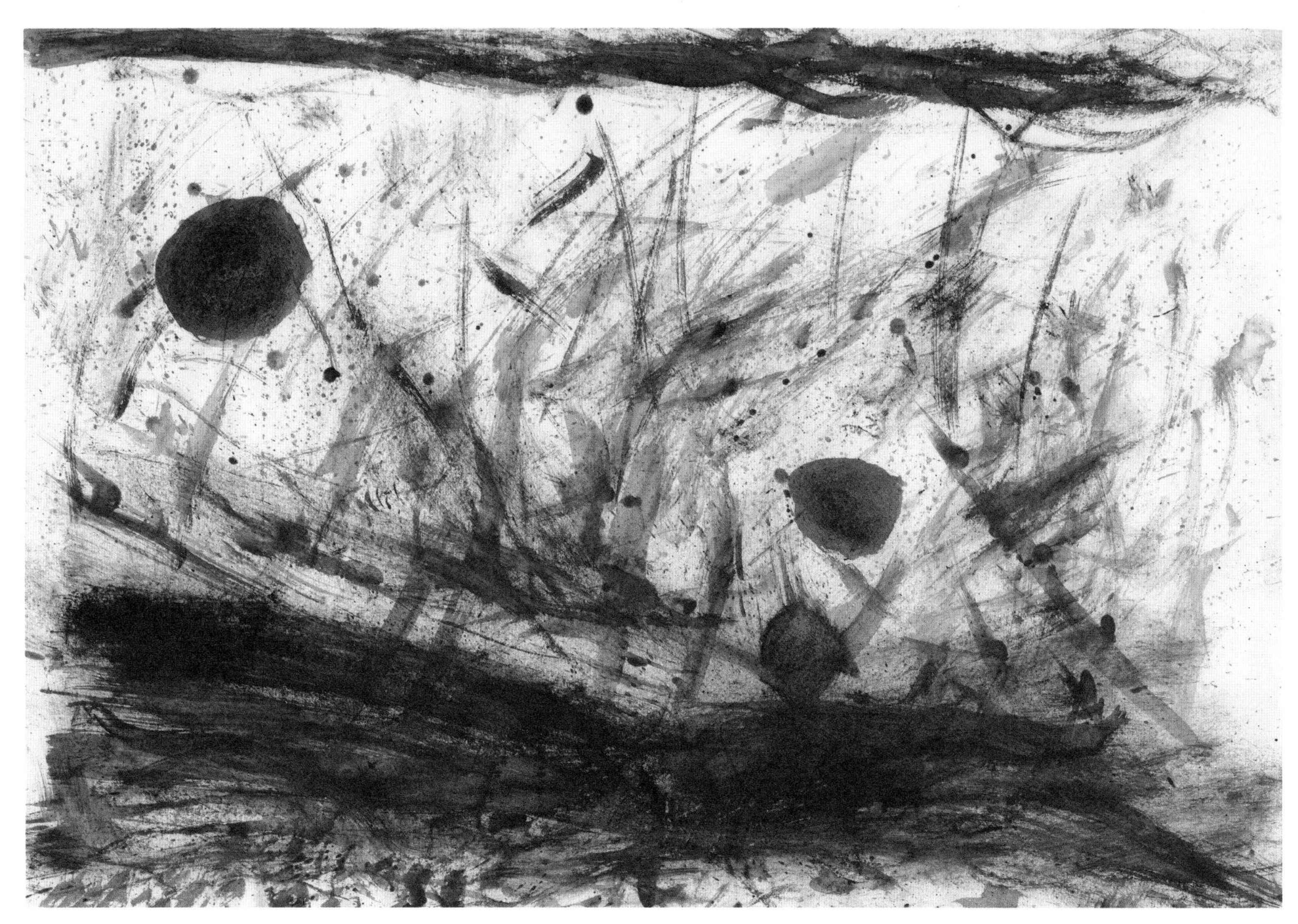

RONJA SPERNEDER

Overture to Egmont, op. 84
2019

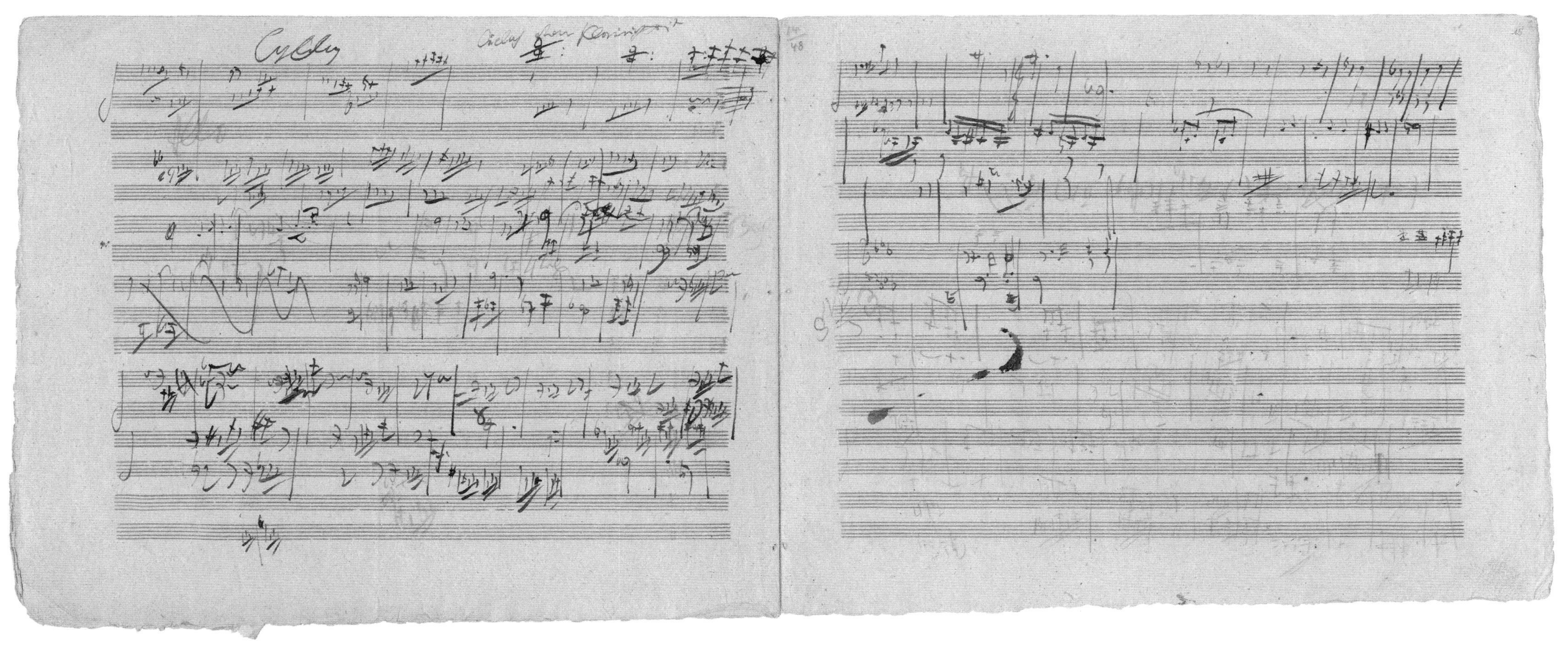

LUDWIG VAN BEETHOVEN

Sketches for Six Bagatelles for Piano, op. 126, nos. 1–3, autograph
1824

MANFRED TROJAHN

Manuscript Pages for the Piece *Ein Brief*, Based on the Text of the Same Name by Hugo von Hofmannsthal

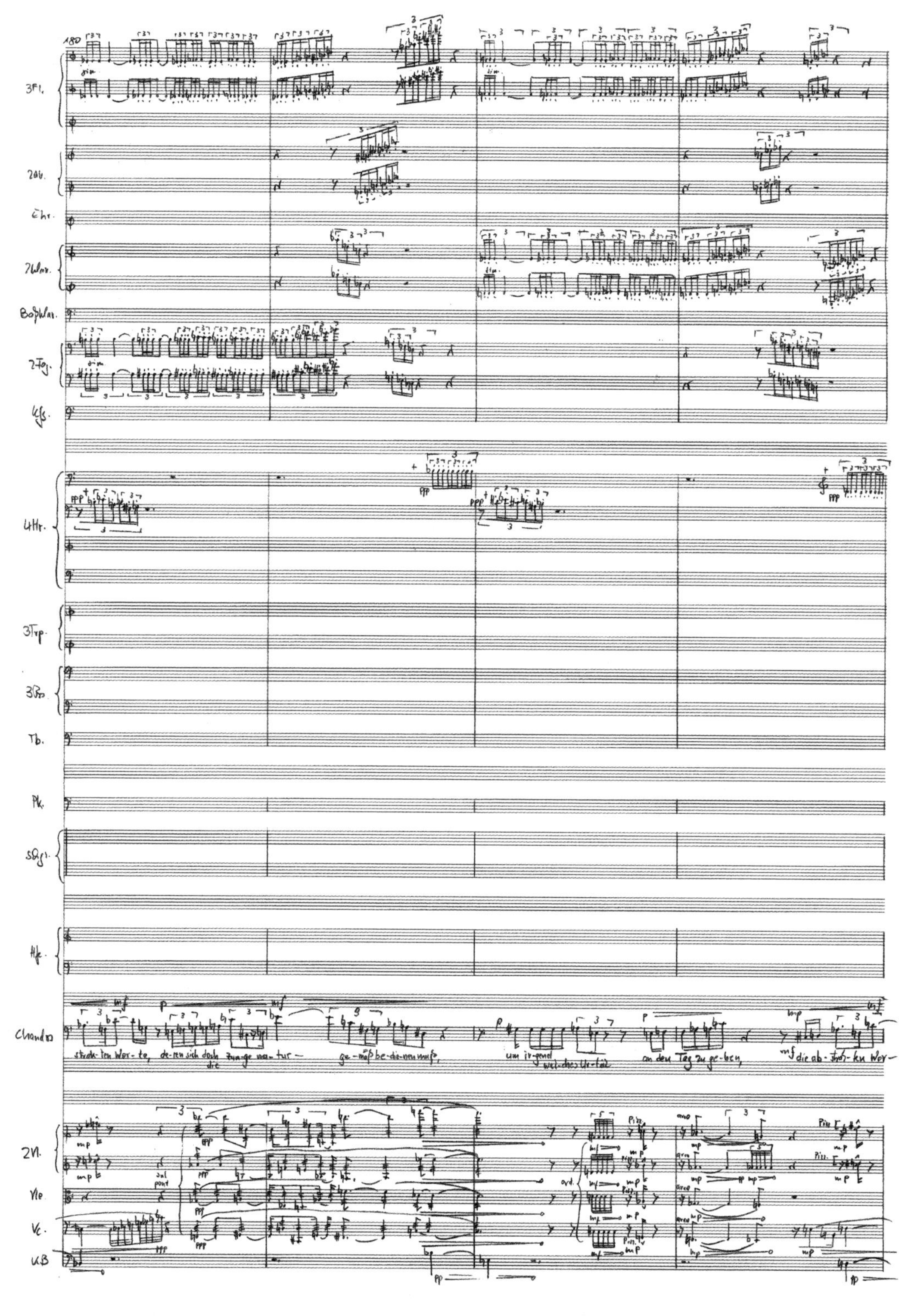

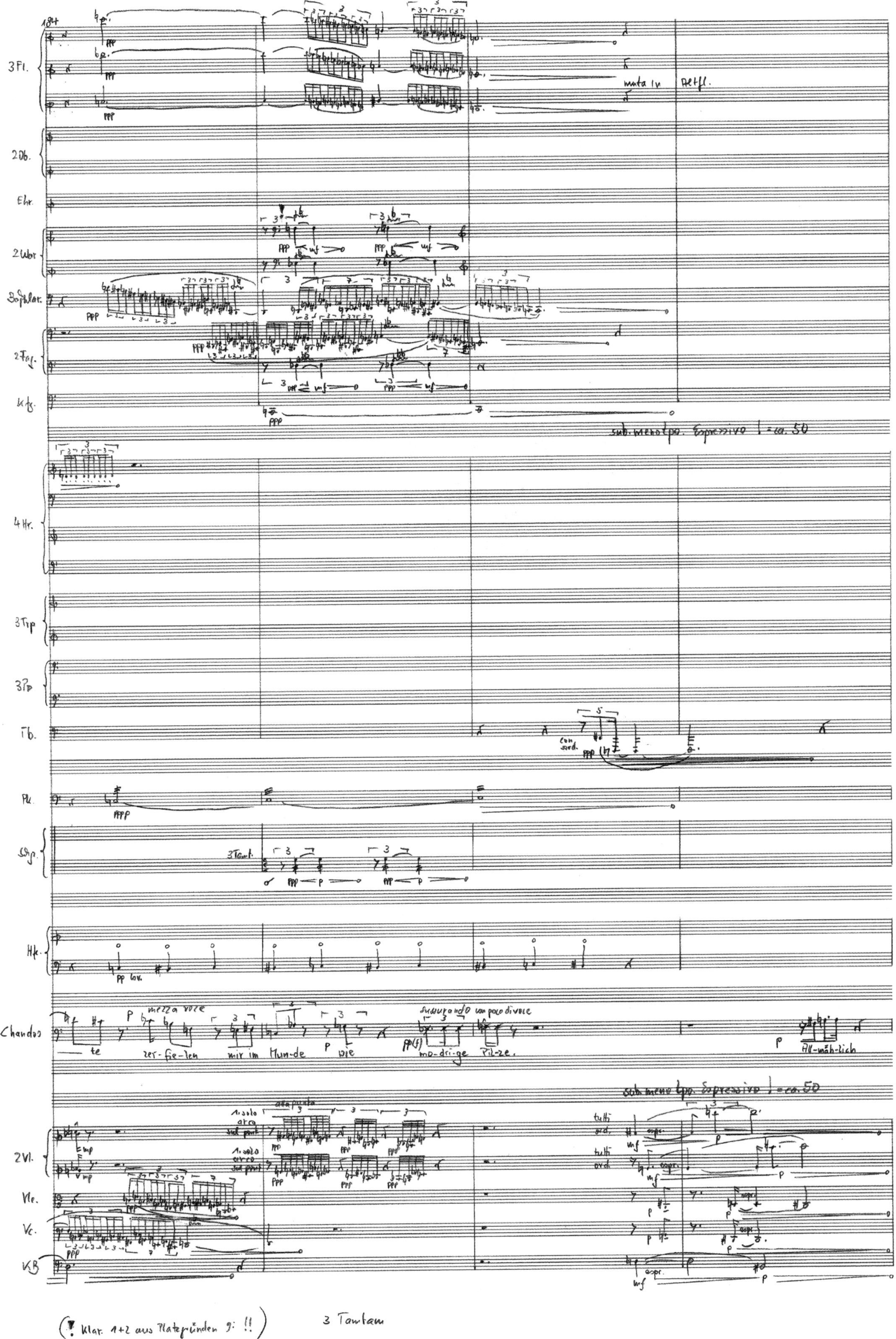
3 Fl.
muta in Altfl.
2 Ob.
Ehr.
2 Klar.
Bassklar.
2 Fag.
Kfg.
sub. meno tpo. Espressivo ♩= ca. 50
4 Hr.
3 Trp
3 Pos
Tb.
con sord.
Pk.
3 Tamt.
Schlg.
Hf.
Chandos
mezza voce
susurrando
con poco di voce
te zer-fie-len mir im Mun-de wie mo-dri-ge Pil-ze.
All-mäh-lich
sub. meno tpo. Espressivo ♩= ca. 50
1. solo arco sul pont.
tutti ord.
espr.
2 Vl.
Va.
Vc.
KB
3 Tamtam

MANFRED TROJAHN

Concept Page Showing an Excerpt from the Work *Ein Brief* by Hugo von Hofmannsthal (above) as well as some Lines from Beethoven's *Heiligenstadt Testament* (below)

Heiglnstadt am 10ten oktober 1802 – so nehme ich den Abschied von dir – und zwar traurig – ja die geliebte Hofnung – die ich mit hierher nahm, wenigstens bis zu einem gewissen Punkte geheilet zu seyn – sie muß mich nun gänzlich verlassen, wie die blätter des Herbstes herabfallen, gewelkt sind, so ist – auch sie für mich dürr geworden, fast wie ich hieher kamm – gehe ich fort – selbst der Hohe Muth – der mich oft in den Schönen sommertägen beseelte – er ist verschwunden – o Vorsehung – laß einmal einen reinen Tag der Freude mir erscheinen . . . . .

geheilet

beseelte

gewelkt

verschwunden

Abschied

Gehör

Zuerst wurde es mir unmöglich, ein höheres oder allgemeineres Thema zu besprechen und dabei jene Worte in den Mund zu nehmen, deren sich doch alle Menschen ohne Bedenken geläufig zu bedienen pflegen. Ich fand ein unerklärliches Unbehagen, die Worte "Geist", "Seele" oder "Körper" nur auszusprechen. Die abstrackten Worte, deren sich ~~doch~~ die Zunge naturgemäß bedienen muß, um irgendwelches Urteil an den Tag zu geben, zerfielen mir im Munde wie modrige Pilze.

unmöglich

auszusprechen

zerfielen

naturgemäß

abstrakt

Sprache

IDRIS KHAN

Struggling to Hear.... After Ludwig van Beethoven Sonatas
2005

NORIO SUDA

Beethoven: Fate

Last autumn, my wife got us tickets for a concert. It was a concert of classical music played by a citizen symphony orchestra, which was to take place in a central Japanese city with a population of 350,000. The centrepiece of the concert was Beethoven's Fifth Symphony, which has by some been nicknamed 'Fate'.

I first came across this symphony when I was in junior high school. Our music teacher brought a vinyl record to the class and played it for us. Listening to this recording, I was overwhelmed by the power and dynamism of the music, which captivated me until the very end. I was only a young Japanese boy who had grown up with Japanese nursery rhymes and children's songs, yet it was grown-up European music that resonated with me. Afterwards, I managed to glimpse the musical score sheet. All I could do was stare blankly at the symbols and notes that I found on the page, but still I tried hard to memorize the very first part. In our high school exams, that is what mattered about the music: we were shown only part of a score in the exam paper and then asked to answer the name of the composer and the title of the work. However, as time passed and I became a high school student – and then a university student –, I drifted away from the world of music, especially from classical music.

The day of the concert arrived. The concert hall was the best in the vicinity and seated two thousand. Since the concert was due to begin at two p.m., we left home early and had our lunch at a pasta shop near the venue. By the time we got there, many people had already been seated in the auditorium. The first half of the concert was followed by an interval and then the second part that I had awaited: Beethoven's Fifth. The music sounded after a moment of silence. I was drawn into the masterpiece once more. From the majestic and powerful opening of the first movement through the second, third and fourth, my emotions were stirred. I felt my body and soul responding to the symphony. The piece of music I had listened to almost six decades ago at high school was still inside me – albeit very faintly. As the performance came to an end, I was utterly entranced. The effect was even greater than it had been when I first heard the piece, as this was the very first time in my life that I had heard Beethoven's work played by a live orchestra. I was truly grateful to my wife, who had brought me to the wonderful performance.

While I basked in the afterglow of the concert, I realized that there was only little more than a month left until the end of the year. The Ode to Joy came to my mind, the fourth choral movement of Beethoven's Ninth Symphony. This piece is traditionally played at the end of every year in Japan, and is therefore closely associated with a sense of the year drawing to a close. Many hobby musicians practice this piece in order to join the choirs singing onstage. As I celebrated my seventieth birthday, I looked back on my life of hard work and felt a desire to try something new. I believe that this fateful symphony brought out what had already been deep inside me: it became my greatest dream and challenge to myself to sing the piece on stage. However, the year was already nearing its end – I had to wait to fulfil my dream.

The new year began. Having so enjoyed the live concert, I started to take an interest in performances by symphony orchestras. I saw that the Symphony Orchestra of the Volksoper Vienna were giving a mid-January performance of their New Year's Concert 2019, in the same concert hall I had visited the previous year with my wife. Again, we went together. It was a wonderful show featuring European classical music accompanied by ballet dancing that gave me a first-hand look at world-class artists of our day. Next, I felt a strong wish to hear Beethoven's Fifth Symphony played by a truly great orchestra. At the same time, I started doing some research to find out what I would need to do to be able to sing the Ode to Joy on stage as part of Beethoven's Ninth Symphony in December. My online research led me to an organization in my local area looking for participants. I wanted to sign up immediately to make my dream come true, but was thwarted. February to early April was the busiest season for my company, which sells and maintains cars, so I chose to wait until this busy period was over. Something unexpected happened, however. I had felt sporadically unwell since the previous summer. I had ignored these signs as I hate visiting doctors. As a result, I was forced to go to hospital in early February and was diagnosed with progressive rectal cancer. After undergoing various tests, I was hospitalized in mid-March and had an operation. It seemed that the cancer was located in a difficult place so the operation would be complicated. Fortunately, I received excellent care at hospital and recovered well from the surgery. It was my first ever time in hospital, and my first operation. Day after day in the hospital, I would wonder why this happened to me. It was difficult to process my emotions. The doctor came by and examined my condition and the nurses checked my body temperature, blood pressure and pulse. I lost weight, physical strength and vigour. In mid-April, when I was somewhat better, my wife gave me good news: 'The Vienna Boys Choir is giving a concert. After you get out of hospital, why don't we go together?'

I had spent forty-five days at hospital before I was able to return home to recuperate there. It was on the third day after leaving hospital that I went to the concert. With hindsight it seems to have been a risky venture. The choir's singing touched my heart; the performance made me feel happy to be alive.

About a month after I left hospital, an old classmate from high school gave me a tablet computer as a present. I was well enough to go back to work at the time. My old classmate kindly delivered the tablet to my office and explained how to use it. When he was finished, he suggested I type something. The very first word that I typed on the new tablet was Beethoven. I don't know why it had to be Beethoven; it was the first word that came to mind. My old classmate, who had known me for more than half a century, was surprised and said 'Beethoven, from you? Really?' I took real pleasure from going on to type 'Symphony No. 5' and 'Symphony No. 9, chorus, fourth movement, Ode to Joy' as he watched.

Since then, I have taken time to listen to the performances of various orchestras on the tablet whenever I could. I began to recognize how differently the same piece of music can sound from different conductors and orchestras. I learned to perceive more keenly. Centuries ago, a composer was born in Europe who was of such distinction that listeners of our day are still impressed by his music. I cannot help but admire this. There are now only four months left of the year and the season of Beethoven's Ninth is fast approaching. It is too late for me after my stint of serious illness and hospitalization to practice the piece and sing it on stage as a part of a choir. I will postpone my project for this year. If there is a concert near me, however, of course I want to attend and listen.

I genuinely believe in fate and destiny. I think it comes from my childhood in a fatherless family. Work hard and do what you have to do; live with sincerity, regardless of the result: I think that is the fate and destiny of each person. Music that was composed a long time ago in Europe, far away from Japan, has stood the test of time and still moves audiences all over the world. This music provides pleasure and delivers a sense of happiness. It is so wonderful. Can it be fate that this invitation to write was so timely?

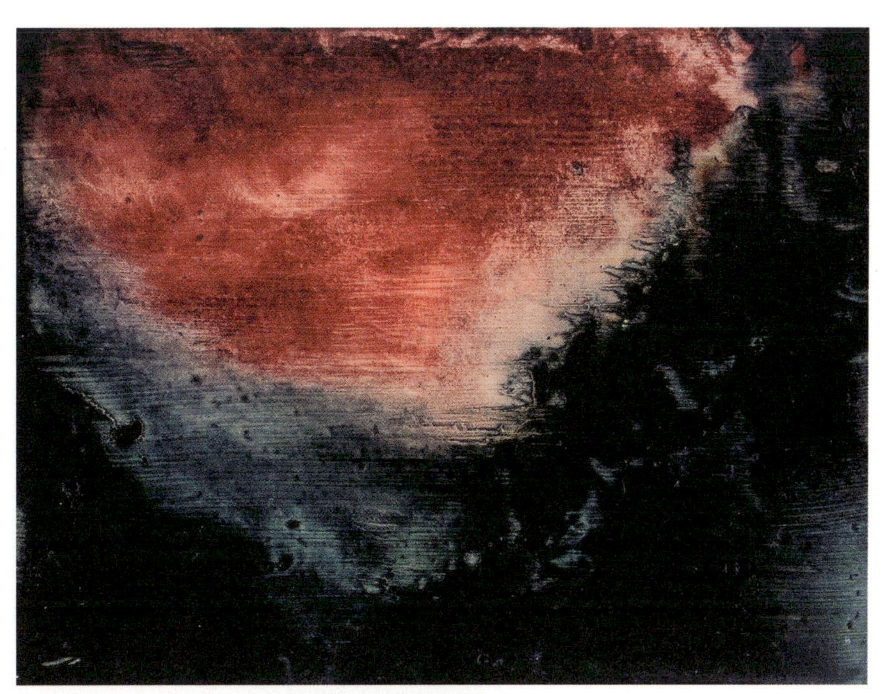

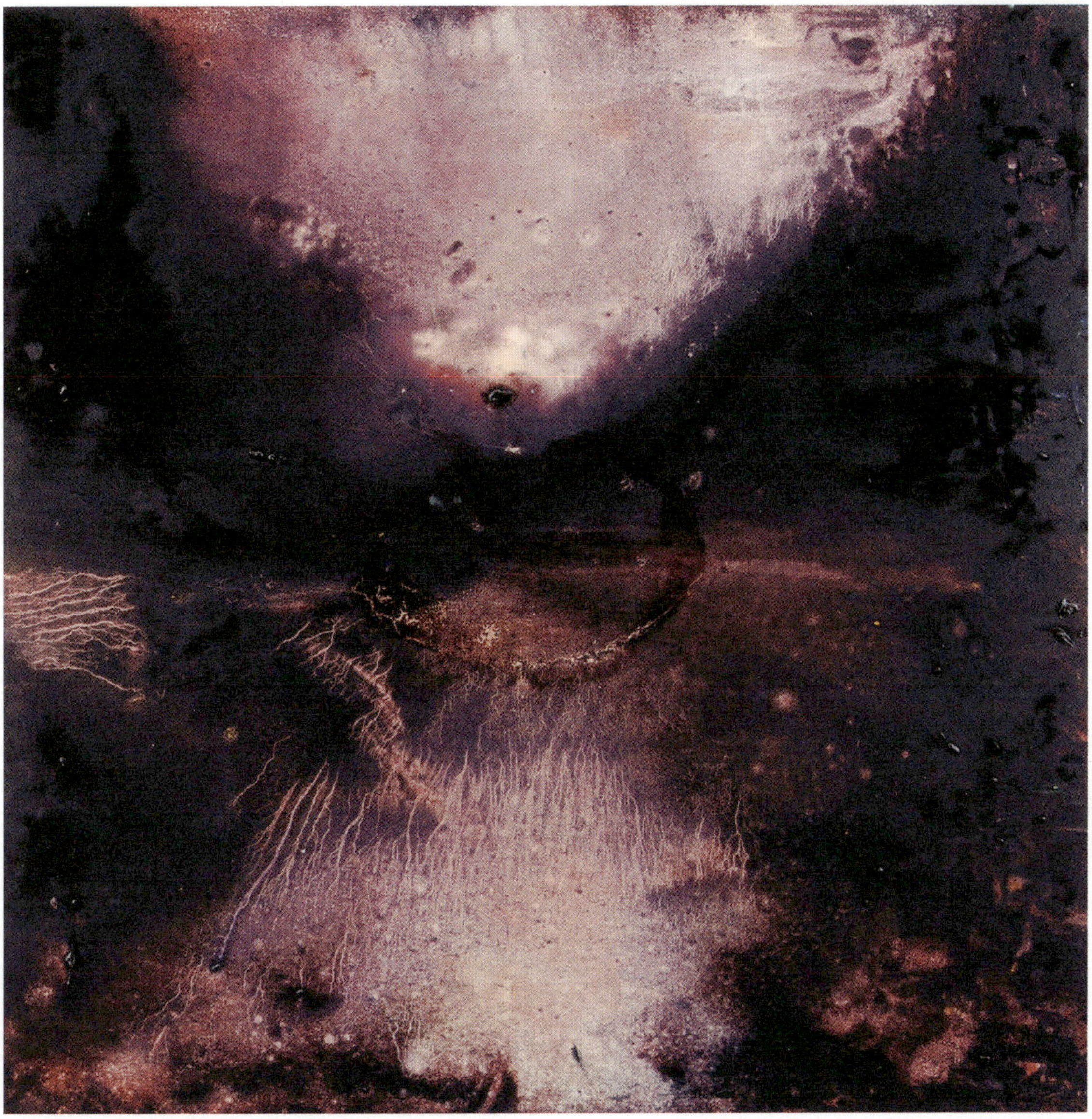

EMMA FRANCIS

Bruiser/Crack/Lost
2004

This series explores the opposition between my longing for and a fear of the wilderness. It references my memories of films; places I have never experienced first-hand. Raised in a city, landscapes made me feel anxious and isolated, but by viewing them in the safety of a film, I am able to explore the unknown and experience the forbidden.

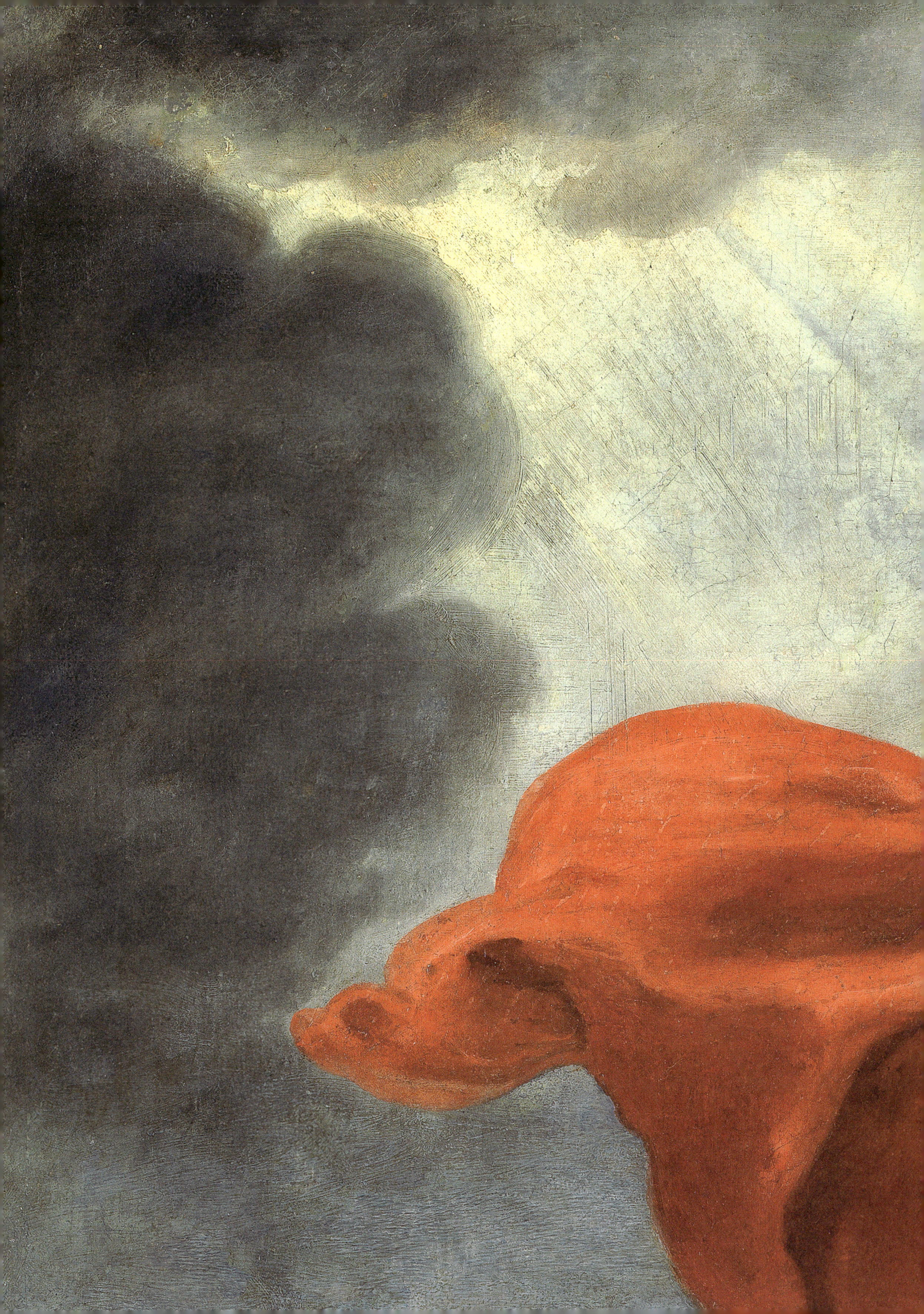

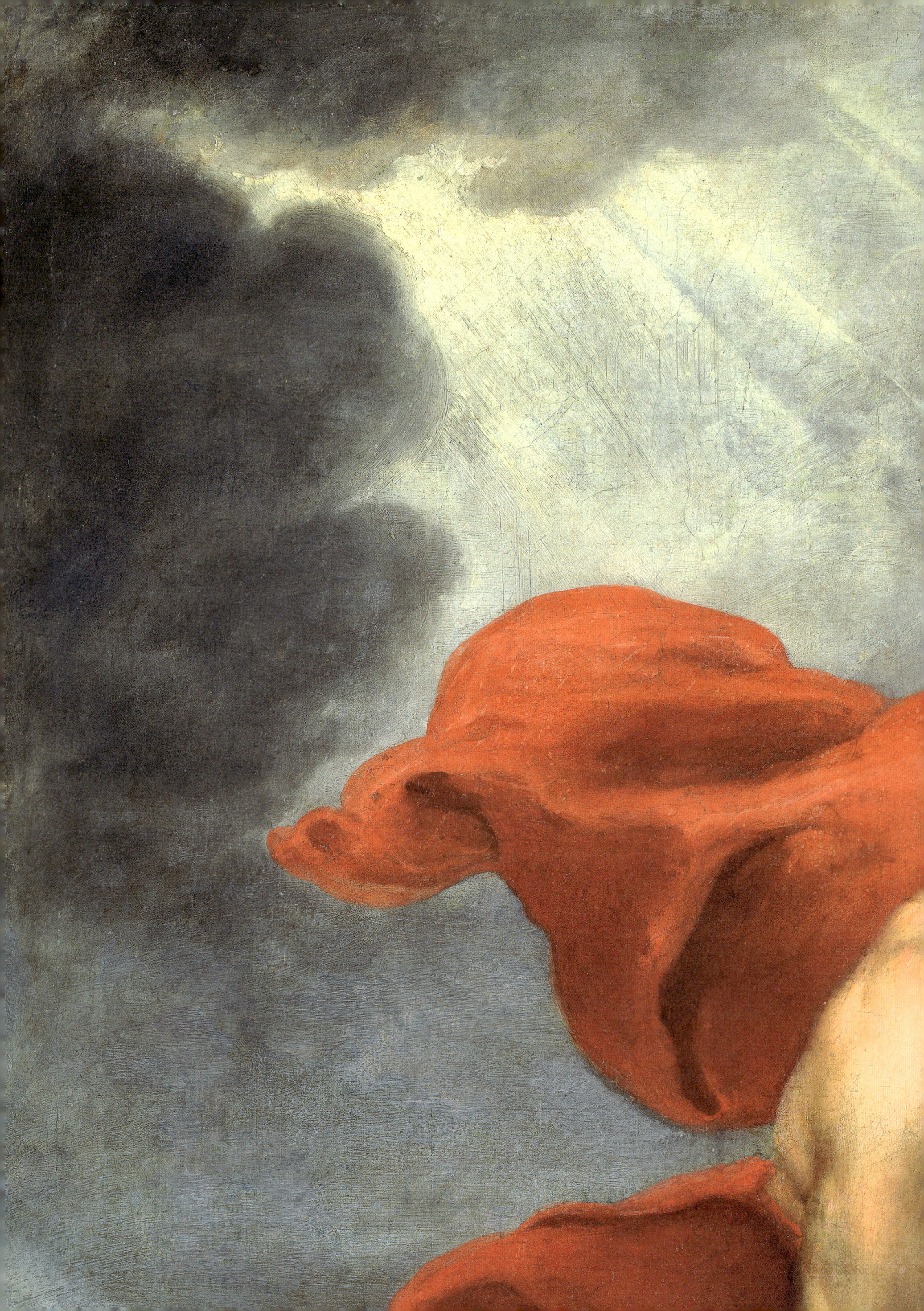

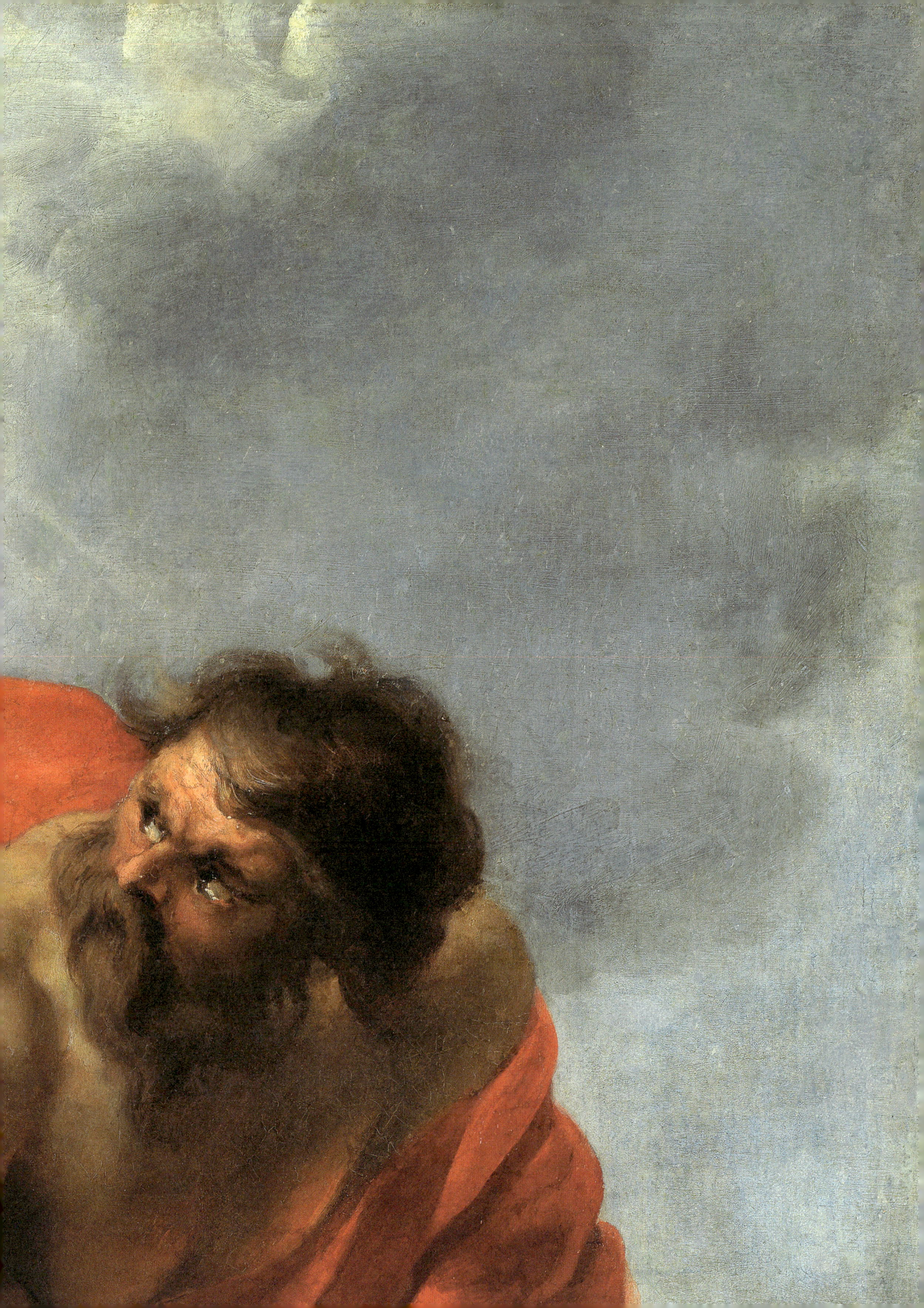

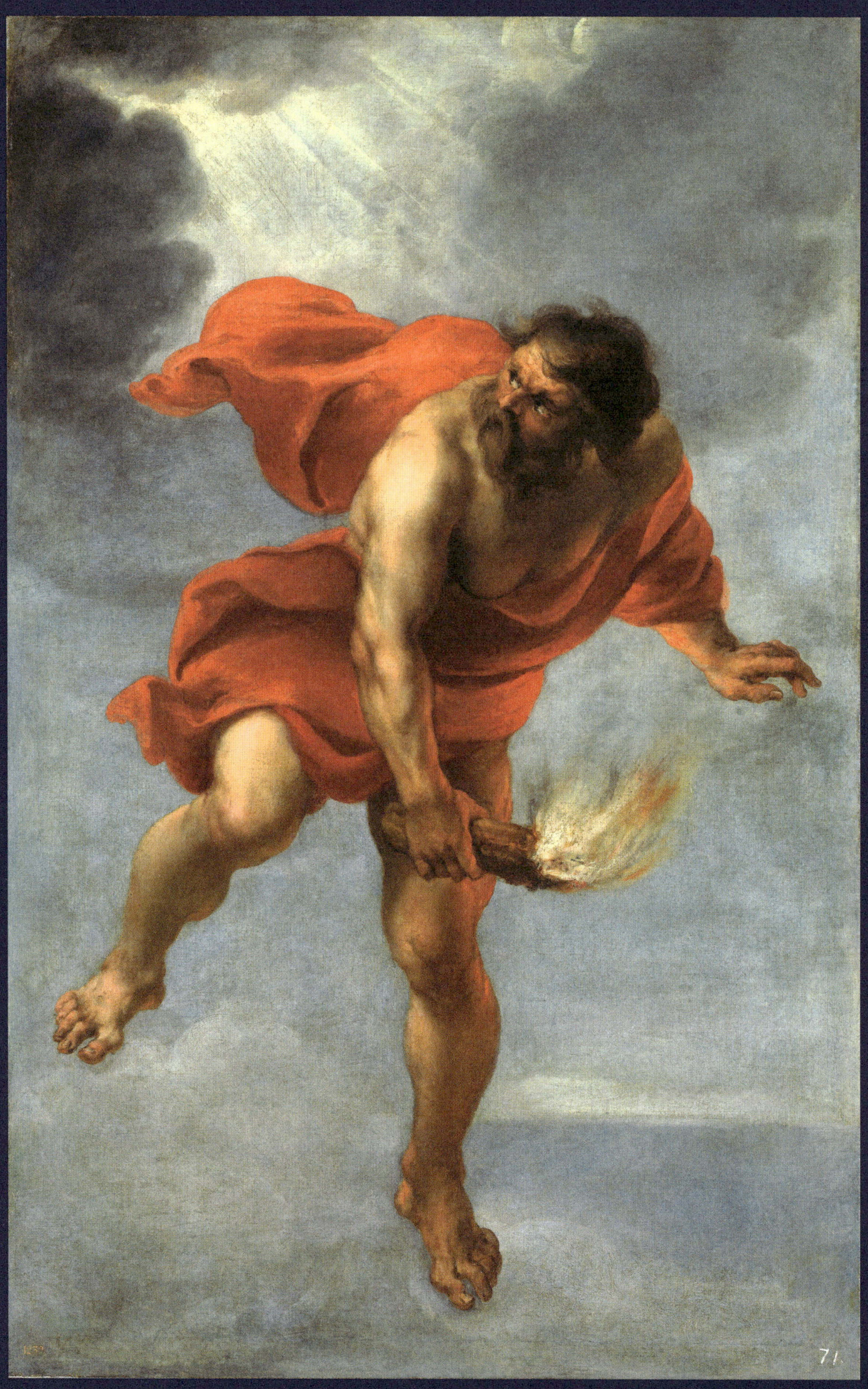

JAN COSSIERS, PROMETHEUS, 1636–1638

THOMAS MACHO

A Secular Messiah: Beethoven as an Icon of the Cult of Genius

One

'Roll over Beethoven and tell Tchaikovsky the news,' sang Chuck Berry on 16 April 1956. His quarrel with Beethoven reportedly went back to his sister's practising on the piano during their childhood.

However, Berry's critique was directed not merely at his sibling rival but also, at least implicitly, at the persistence of a *fin de siècle* para-religious trend that the sociologist of science Edgar Zilsel – later closely connected with the Vienna Circle – had termed the 'cult of genius' ('Geniereligion') in a lucid monograph published in 1918. This late nineteenth-century religion was a faith which blended ardent nature mysticism with national hero-worship and staid burghers' dreams of historic world figures, mainly outstanding artists and scientists. And it also had its dogmas, which Zilsel defined as follows. First, there was the notion of the rarity of geniuses, who stand out from the masses by their 'almost divine creative power' and who 'unlike all other people, form all their thoughts, opinions and value judgements in a completely independent manner'. Second, the notion of an 'eternal league' of all geniuses who, despite the originality of each, sense that they 'belong together' and feel themselves to be 'brethren of an exalted community'. Third, the notion of the transcendent immortality of all geniuses, which stems precisely from their being 'misunderstood' in their lifetime. For, wrote Zilsel, 'their undiscerning contemporaries, who belong after all to the common herd, are unable to understand geniuses. Despite having no way whatsoever of telling genius and superficiality apart, they – guided, as it were, by vague inklings – detest the geniuses of their age and seem to be hellbent on stifling these great men through obtuse indifference or brutal resistance.'[1] It is only posterity that all of a sudden recognizes the resplendent genius, who is henceforth to be praised and worshipped almost ritually.

Geniuses are transformed posthumously into stars, their long-extinguished light illuminating the present. Not for nothing were metaphors from astronomy among the favourite rhetorical devices of the cult of genius: they probably harked back to the traditional identification of rulers with the sun and the sky. Citing an observation from H.S. Chamberlain's monumental treatise on Immanuel Kant (and several other geniuses), namely, that genius is 'a cosmic phenomenon, just like the Sun or Sirius',[2] Zilsel further argued that geniuses were stars that created their imperishable works 'only for posterity' and, therefore, 'they are all musicians of the future [Zukunftsmusiker], painters of the future, poets of the future and philosophers of the future: in short, futurists'.[3] It was in that sense that Nietzsche, in the posthumous fragment 'Among artists of the future', described himself as 'an audacious poet-philosopher', 'refined to excess and "born too late"', yet, even so, capable of speaking the language of the popular moralists and holy men of old – and, moreover, capable of doing so with such naturalness, originality, enthusiasm and straightforward joviality as if he were himself one of the "primitives"'.[4]

Under the spell of such 'artists of the future', everything in the present takes on the form of prophecy. In his *Representative Men* – a veritable bible of the cult of genius, published almost a decade before Darwin's *On the Origin of Species by Means of Natural Selection* – Ralph Waldo Emerson had already written of the future geniuses: 'What indemnification is one great man for populations of pygmies! Every mother wishes one son a genius, though all the rest should be mediocre.' For 'great men exist that there may be greater men. The destiny of organized nature is amelioration, and who can tell its limits?'[5] Geniuses triumph by virtue of being manly wunderkinder who, in contrast to all kings and aristocrats, cannot be defined in terms of their descent or lineage. Since their past is brushed aside, they must always be projected into the future: as precursors of 'even greater men', who will spring forth by means of a 'natural selection' of the 'representative men'. In the same year, 1909, that the chemist Wilhelm Ostwald received the Nobel Prize, there also appeared his anthology of biographies of scientists, fittingly entitled *Große Männer* ('Great Men'). It opened with a question put to Ostwald by a Japanese student as to how great minds could be 'detected', and concluded with a reflection on universities as the 'breeding institutions' of geniuses to come.[6]

TWO

The deities of the cult of genius were selected for adoration from the most varied spheres. Not only painters, poets, composers and virtuosi, but also philosophers, politicians, statesmen, scientists, doctors, inventors, explorers and military leaders could be celebrated as geniuses. From Comte's *Calendrier positiviste* of 1849[7] onwards – in which Beethoven was to be commemorated on the 25th day of the tenth month, named 'Shakespeare' – there is no mistaking the tendency to replace the Christian saints with geniuses and heroes. Indeed, that tendency keeps gathering pace as jubilees and anniversaries follow one another in ever quicker succession. Now, one feature of the dynamics of secularization processes is that they not only replace but also transpose. Thus, the paradigm of the martyr, for example, was transformed into the paradigm of the tragic hero who – like Mozart, Schubert, van Gogh or Rimbaud and, much later, James Dean, Jim Morrison, Janis Joplin, Jimi Hendrix or Kurt Cobain – dies young. The application of Christian metaphors to geniuses is, incidentally, something that already Kierkegaard had noticed and criticized, though in his youth he too had been 'infatuated with Mozart like a young girl'. In *Either/Or* he even wrote of his determination to put Mozart on the highest pedestal:

> And I will go to the deacon and the pastor and the dean and the bishop and the whole church council, and I will beseech and implore them to grant my request, and I will challenge the whole congregation on the same matter, and if my appeal is not heard, my childish wish not fulfilled, then I will secede from the association, then I will divorce myself from its way of thinking, then I will form a sect that not only places Mozart first but has no one but Mozart.[8]

However, precisely this 'childish wish' was subjected in *Either/Or* – that strategic confrontation between ethics and aesthetics – to a fundamental critique, which Kierkegaard amplified in his treatise *The Difference between a Genius and an Apostle* (1847). A genius was not indebted to any authority for his *auctoritas*, Kierkegaard argued there, and, conversely, no true authority had any need for legitimation by genius. 'To ask if a king is a genius, and in that case to be willing to obey him, is basically high treason,' he wrote, 'and to honour one's father because he is exceptionally intelligent is impiety'.[9] For completely different reasons, Nietzsche was to chime in with Kierkegaard's arguments once he had recanted his earlier idolization of Wagner, which itself had borne all the marks of the religion of genius. In *The Antichrist* he thus inveighed against Renan's *La vie de Jésus* (1863):[10] 'To make a *hero* of Jesus! And, moreover, what a misunderstanding is the word "genius"! ... Were one to speak with the rigour of a physiologist, a quite different word would be to the point here, namely "idiot".'[11]

Ludwig van Beethoven prospered – not just in Vienna – as a particularly prominent deity of the cult of genius and greatness. Stories about the suffering composer who had been misunderstood by everyone around him achieved mass circulation by the turn of the twentieth century and were evidently lapped up by readers. For example, in the novella *Beethovens Gang zum Glück* ('Beethoven's path to happiness') by the Styrian writer Rudolf Hans Bartsch, the composer encounters, while out walking, a 'cretinous peasant boy' but takes no notice of him. The boy, however,

> saw that wholly other-worldly figure and, with the intuition of a cruel young beast, recognized at once the sparkle of infinite other-worldliness and ingenuousness. And so, brimming over with malice, he burst out shouting 'dummkopf, dummkopf!' ... The boy stared at him with that ineradicable hatred which the vulgar and malicious, the pragmatic and mundane have always felt at the sight of someone enraptured with the sublime – and which they will continue to feel for as long as this profaned Earth of ours is fated to roam the cold firmament.[12]

The cult of Beethoven culminated with the death of Otto Weininger in Vienna on 4 October 1903. The day before, the author of *Sex and Character* (1903) had taken a room in, of all places, the house in Schwarzspanierstraße 15 where Beethoven had died. That night, at so symbolic a location, after writing farewell letters to his father and brother, he shot himself in the chest. (The house was demolished not long after, in 1904.)

Beethoven as a Messiah who turns his sacrificial death into resurrection to immortal glory? In *Doctor Faustus* (1947), Thomas Mann put such a Christologically tinged interpretation of Beethoven's life into the mouth of the organist Wendell Kretzschmar (perhaps with only partly ironic intent):

> Kretzschmar told us a horrifying story that impressed us with a tremendous and indelible image of the sacred import of that struggle and of the tormented creator's personality. It was in the midsummer of 1819, at the time when Beethoven was working on the *Missa Solemnis* in the Hafner House in Mödling, despairing that each movement was turning out much longer than originally planned, which meant that the deadline for its completion – namely, the First of March of the following year, on which date Archduke Rudolf was to be consecrated as Archbishop of Olomouc – could not possibly be met; it was then that two friends and disciples went to see him one afternoon and on walking into the house discovered that something dreadful had happened. That very morning, both of the Master's maidservants had taken to their heels because the previous night, towards one in the morning, there had been a ferocious row that had woken the whole house. The Master had been toiling away, the whole evening and then deep into the night, on the Credo – the Credo with *that* fugue – and had not cared to think about the supper being kept warm for him on the kitchen stove; and the maidservants, waiting there all the time in vain, had finally succumbed to sleep. So when, between the twelfth hour and the first, the Master had come out to ask for food, he had found the maids asleep next to the charred remnants of the meal. At this he had erupted into the most violent rage, without the least consideration for the sleeping house – not surprisingly, since he could not himself hear his own loudness – and over and over again had roared: 'Could ye not watch with me one hour?'[13]

Readers will have no trouble in recognizing this scene. Every year, it is read out in the liturgy of Holy Week. It is set on the Mount of Olives, shortly before Jesus is arrested.

THREE

In 1970, the German federal capital of Bonn commemorated the bicentenary of the birth of her famous son, who was all too often associated exclusively with the Austrian capital. At that time, the reunification of Germany was as inconceivable as the political and economic integration to be brought by the European Union. Grand anniversary celebrations – on the scale of the Schiller Year of 2005 or the Mozart Year of 2006 – were rarely organized then, and no one fifty years ago could have foreseen the later elevation of cities to the rank of European Capitals of Culture. Indeed, barely two years after the student demonstrations of 1968, any attempt at parading the 'highbrow' culture of the middle classes would almost certainly have met with fierce resistance. And so in 1970 people had to make do with little more than numerous concerts and performances of Beethoven's music. An imaginative, yet also iconoclastic contribution to the Beethoven bicentenary was made by the composer Mauricio Kagel in the form of the film *Ludwig van*, which was shot in Cologne and premiered on 28 May 1970 during the Vienna Festival. Relying on collage and montage, the film takes as its starting point a visit by the composer to his native town. Beethoven, played by the cameraman in historical costume, looks into a music shop in which the latest recordings of his works have been put on display for the bicentenary. He also enters the official Beethoven-Haus, which is soon transformed into an imaginary home done up by mainly German artists from the Fluxus movement. Dieter Roth was responsible for the bathroom, in which busts of Beethoven made of lard were sunk in the bathtub; Ursula Burghardt designed the living room and the garden; Mauricio Kagel, the music room; Stefan Wewerka, the children's room; Robert Filliou, the lumber room; and Joseph Beuys, the kitchen. In the kitchen sequence, flames shoot out of the gully in the yard while Beuys, his face covered by a death mask of Napoleon, prances around in front of the window, emitting grunts. The musical accompaniment to the scene is the first movement of the Ninth Symphony, played by an amateur orchestra.

Napoleon in front of the window of 'Beethoven's kitchen'? It was with Napoleon that the cult of genius surrounding great men had originated. The European intelligentsia had at first eagerly joined in this cult – one has only to think of Goethe, Hegel or Heine. Beethoven was no exception either; as is well known, he had originally named his Third Symphony (composed in 1803–04) after the great Corsican: *Sinfonia grande, titolata Bonaparte*. After Napoleon proclaimed himself Emperor in Paris on 2 December 1804, Beethoven is said to have exclaimed: 'So even he is just like any other ordinary person! Now he will most surely trample underfoot all the rights of man, only indulging his personal ambitions. He will place himself above everyone else and become a tyrant!' Beethoven scratched out the title, but wrote over it, in pencil, the words 'Geschrieben auf Bonaparte' ('Written for Bonaparte'). Ever since the score was first published in 1806, the symphony has borne the title *Sinfonia Eroica ... composta per festeggiare il sovvenire di un grand Uomo* ('Heroic Symphony ... composed to celebrate the memory of a great man'). So all that remained of Beethoven's admiration for Bonaparte was the memory of a great man and a certain ambivalence. This ambivalence also manifested itself subsequently in the composer's work on his only opera, which was to occupy him from 1805 to 1814.

Let us return to Mauricio Kagel's film *Ludwig van*. In contrast to Stanley Kubrick's *A Clockwork Orange* (1971), where the Nazi troops in Alex's fantasy march to the Ode to Joy; to Jean-Luc Godard's *Prénom Carmen* (1983), where the action is interrupted by rehearsals of Beethoven's String Quartet in C sharp minor, op. 131; to Andrei Tarkovsky's *Nostalghia* (also from 1983), in which the old mathematician Domenico immolates himself astride the equestrian statue of Marcus Aurelius in Rome while, again, the Ode to Joy resounds from a portable turntable – in contrast to all these, Kagel concentrates on deconstructing the interior. The 91-minute-long film ends with a glimpse of the chock-full lumber room, the contents of which, as one may read in Kagel's script, 'tumble down, when the door is opened, and land at the feet of Beethoven, the visitors' guide, the cameraman and the viewer'.[14] It is almost as if Kagel – like Chuck Berry fourteen years earlier – wanted to lay to rest the props and imagery of that *fin de siècle* cult of genius by consigning them once and for all to a lumber room, to the stores of archives and museums.

1 Edgar Zilsel, *Die Genierelígion. Ein kritischer Versuch über das moderne Persönlichkeitsideal, mit einer historischen Begründung* [1918], ed. Johann Dvořak (Frankfurt, 1990), 59–61.

2 Ibid., 239. See also Houston Stewart Chamberlain, *Immanuel Kant. Die Persönlichkeit als Einführung in das Werk* (Munich, 1905), 575.

3 Zilsel, *Die Geniereligion*, 60.

4 Friedrich Nietzsche, 'Unter Künstlern der Zukunft', in idem, *Sämtliche Werke – Kritische Studienausgabe*, ed. Giorgio Colli and Mazzino Montinari (Munich/Berlin/New York, 1980), xii, 239–40.

5 Ralph Waldo Emerson, *Essays and Lectures*, ed. Joel Porte (New York, 1983), 627, 632.

6 See Wilhelm Ostwald, *Große Männer* (Leipzig, 1909), 1–20, 412–14.

7 Auguste Comte, *Calendrier positiviste, ou Système général de commémoration publique* (Paris, 1849).

8 Søren Kierkegaard, *Kierkegaard's Writings*, ed. and trans. Howard V. Hong and Edna H. Hong, 26 vols. (Princeton, 1978–98), iii: *Either/Or. Part I*, 48.

9 Søren Kierkegaard, *The Difference between a Genius and an Apostle* [1847], in: *Kierkegaard's Writings*, xviii: *Without Authority*, 101.

10 See Ernest Renan, *Das Leben Jesu* [1863] (Zurich, 1981), 216.

11 Friedrich Nietzsche, *Der Antichrist*, in idem, *Sämtliche Werke*, vi, 165–254 (200).

12 Rudolf Hans Bartsch, *Beethovens Gang zum Glück*, in idem, *Unerfüllte Geschichten* (Leipzig, 1916), 265–96 (283–84).

13 Thomas Mann, *Doktor Faustus. Das Leben des deutschen Tonsetzers Adrian Leverkühn erzählt von einem Freunde*, ed. Peter de Mendelssohn (Frankfurt, 1980), 81–82.

14 Mauricio Kagel: *Ludwig van – Drehbuch*, 1969, quoted after: Stiftung Museum Schloss Moyland, Sammlung van der Grinten, Joseph Beuys Archiv des Landes Nordrhein-Westfalen (ed.), Bedburg-Hau 2004, 57.

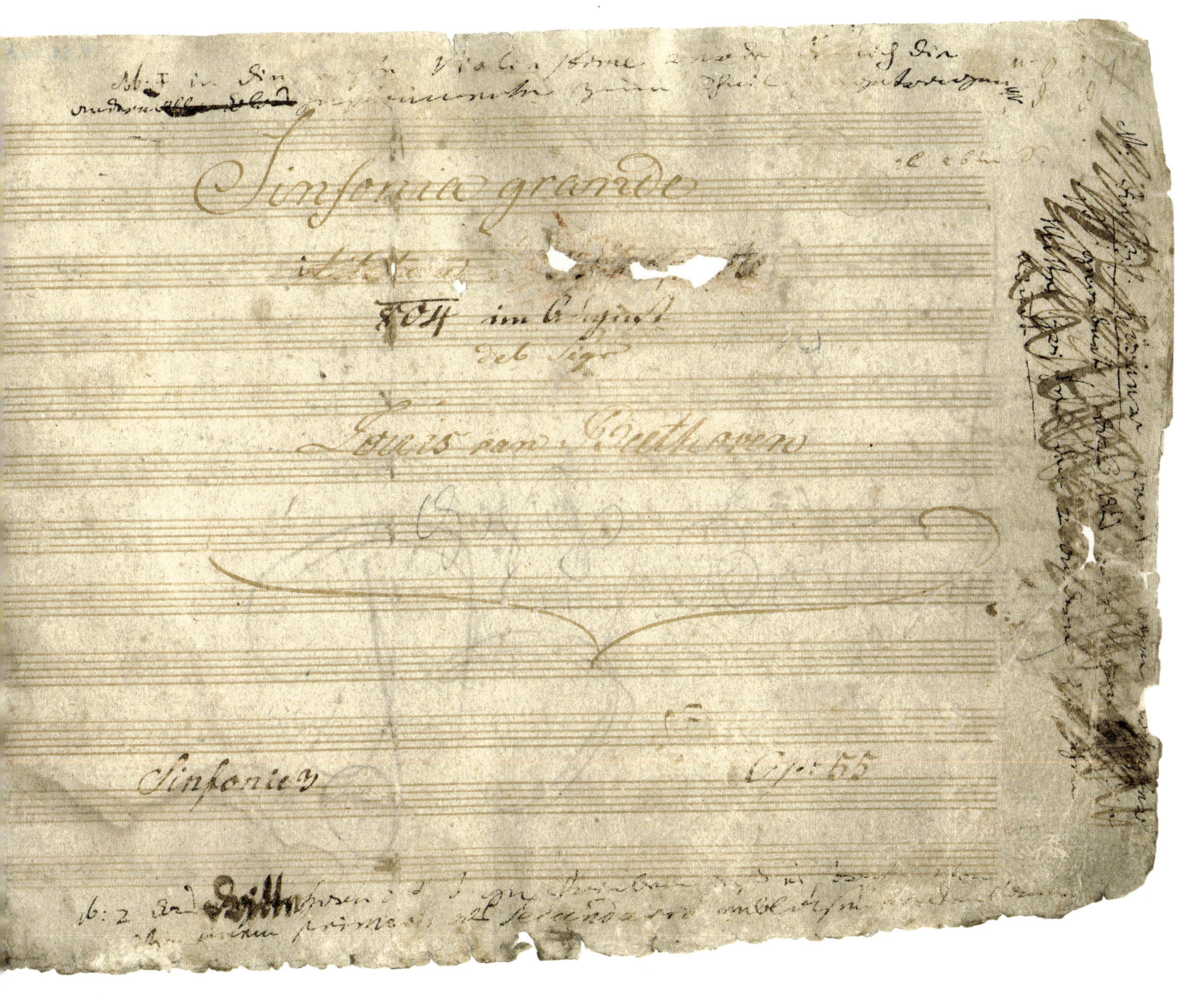

LUDWIG VAN BEETHOVEN

Symphony No. 3 in E flat major, op. 55, 'Eroica', manuscript score
1804

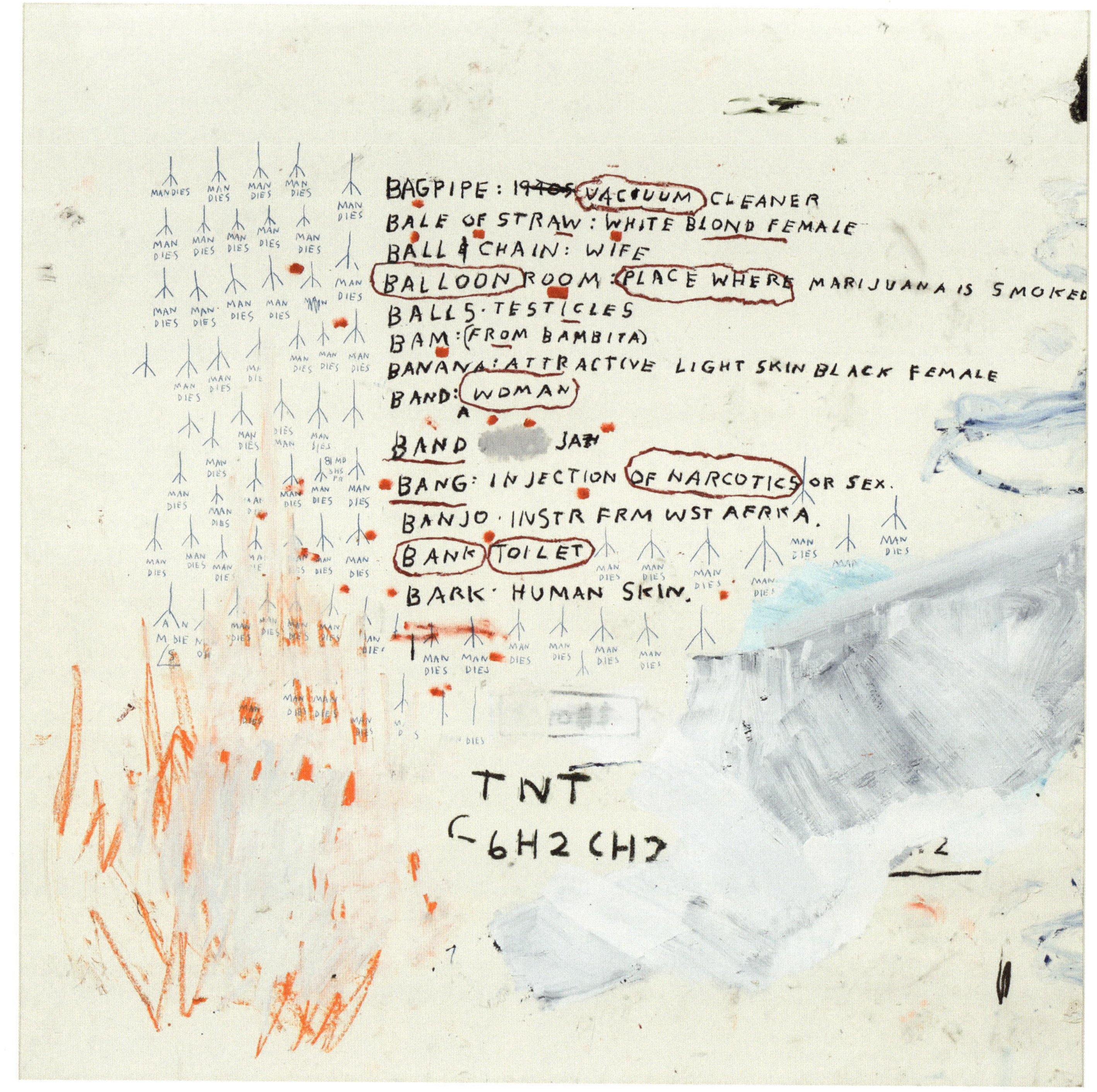

JEAN-MICHEL BASQUIAT

Eroica II / Eroica I / Eroica
1987/88

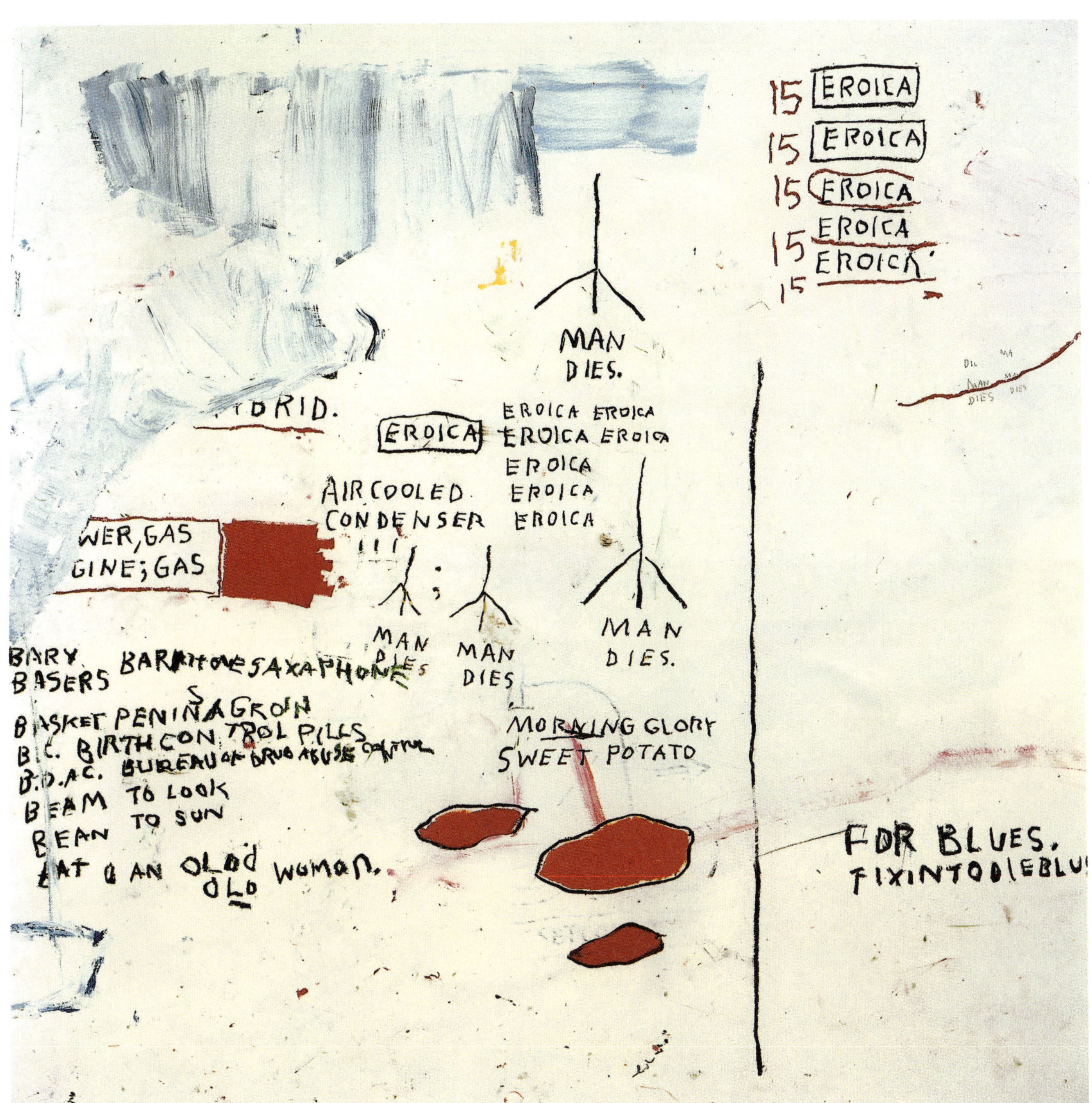
15 EROICA
15 EROICA
15 EROICA
15 EROICA
EROICA
15
MAN
DIES.
EROICA
EROICA EROICA
EROICA EROICA
EROICA
EROICA
EROICA
AIRCOOLED
CONDENSER
WER, GAS
GINE; GAS
MAN
DIES
MAN
DIES
MAN
DIES.
BARY
BASERS
BARITONE SAXAPHONE
BASKET
B.C. BIRTH CONTROL PILLS
BEAM TO LOOK
BEAN TO SUN
MORNING GLORY
SWEET POTATO
FOR BLUES.

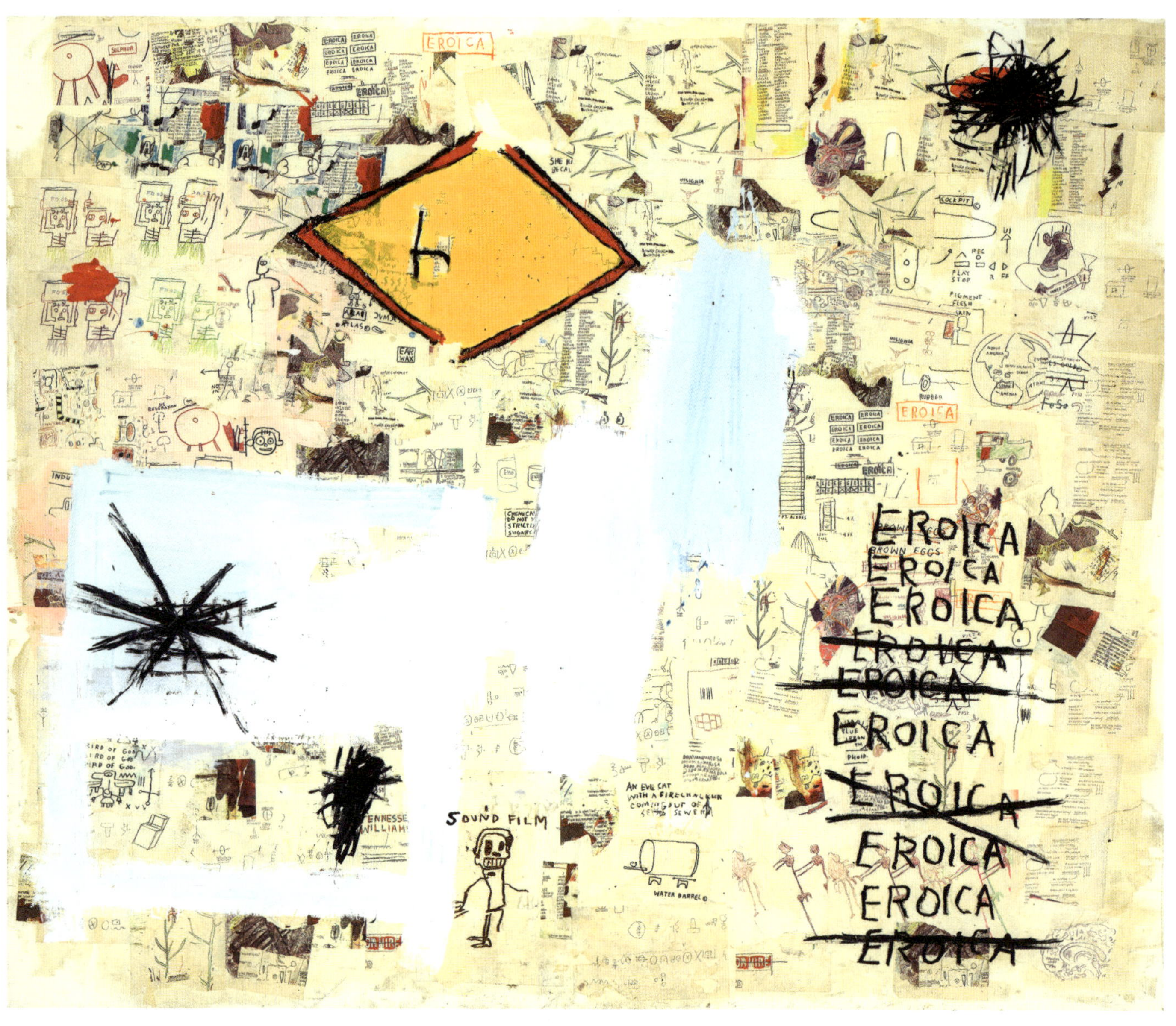

The funeral march of the fallen hero during the second movement of Beethoven's Third Symphony – also entitled 'Eroica' ('Heroic') – speaks directly to Basquiat. The artist struggled profoundly to come to terms with the death of his friend Andy Warhol in 1987. In scrawling 'Eroica' across the canvas and surrounding it with other, more profane, words, Basquiat questions the notion of the hero and shows his own troubled state of mind: MAN DIES.

SHEILA MELVIN AND JINDONG CAI

Beethoven: China's Sage of Music[1]

Ludwig van Beethoven was first introduced to the Chinese public at the dawn of the twentieth century, a tumultuous time of questioning and crisis.

Over the course of the eighteenth century, China had been invaded by European powers in two Opium Wars, devastated by an internal conflict incited by millenarian rebels which left millions dead and soundly defeated by the Japanese in the First Sino-Japanese War in 1895. The foreign nations who triumphed over China created semi-colonial enclaves in coastal cities such as Shanghai in which their expatriate citizens lived according to their own laws rather than China's. In 1900, a secret society, the Boxers, led a bloody anti-foreign uprising that prompted military intervention by eight foreign countries. The Eight Nation Alliance captured Beijing and, in an ultimate act of humiliation, occupied, looted and otherwise desecrated the Forbidden City where the emperor lived.

Desperate to 'save China', tens of thousands of patriotic young Chinese departed for Europe, the United States and Japan, determined to learn from the very same people who were carving their nation up 'like a ripe melon'. Convinced that the culture of the West was the source of its strength (and that of Japan, which had already imported much Western learning), they studied, translated and propagated works by Western intellectuals like Rousseau, Darwin, Dante and Shakespeare. Among these idealistic reformers was a brilliant young artist and polymath named Li

a 'counter-revolutionary'. I do not think any other country in the world has harboured such hatred for Beethoven.

When the Cultural Revolution was over, Beethoven was rehabilitated. It seems that his fate is similar to that of the Chinese people. In the early 1980s, his name and his works spread all over China, reaching even the most remote villages. There was a restaurant by the name of 'Moonlight', our phones played 'For Elise' as the ringtone and many young mothers chose the name Elise for their baby girls. At my university, we called ourselves the 'Beethoven soccer team'.

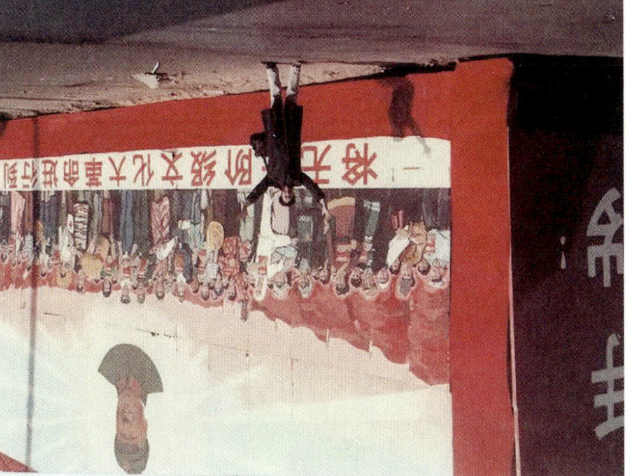

I left China for the first time in 1993, and took a plane to Europe. I do not speak a foreign language and am unfamiliar with the Roman alphabet. Nevertheless, I set out for Beethoven's birthplace Bonn. I was searching for the Beethoven of my dreams and his 'music without titles'. Following his footsteps, I travelled from Bonn to Vienna. I celebrated my god of music with my camera and in numerous poems. In 2009, I brought my son to Vienna, so that he might also visit Beethoven's home and listen to his music. He shall carry on Beethoven's legacy, his love, his joy.

Shutong who left for Japan in 1905 and discovered Beethoven while studying at an art school in Tōkyō.

Li was a strong believer in the importance of moral exemplars and an adherent of the Confucian ideal that man could be 'perfected by music'. In Beethoven he found a perfect role model for a China that needed to triumph over adversity and reinvent itself for a new age. He dubbed Beethoven the Sage of Music and introduced the composer via a small music magazine that was printed in Tōkyō but distributed in Shanghai. For its first (and only) issue, Li drew a charcoal sketch of a wild-haired Beethoven and wrote a short accompanying biography in which he emphasized the many hardships the composer had had to overcome – stormy family relationships, romantic disappointment, the unstoppable onset of deafness – and the honesty, sincerity and profundity with which he approached his music. Li's article was probably only read by a handful of people, but it sufficed to kindle an interest in the composer. Soon such renowned writers as Lu Xun and Xu Zhimo were referencing Beethoven in their essays and poems. Their focus, like Li's, was on Beethoven's life story rather than his music.

In the late 1920s and early 1930s, an artist named Feng Zikai offered the first comprehensive accounts of Beethoven's life. Feng explained that Beethoven was not just a great musician but a 'hero' to all mankind. He explained that the composer ranked with Napoleon in terms of importance – but that while Napoleon would one day be forgotten, Beethoven would be remembered forever. Feng also outlined Beethoven's oeuvre, discussing all nine symphonies and 32 piano sonatas. Around the same time, the Berlin and Bonn-based scholar Wang Guangqi took the interesting step of placing Beethoven in a Chinese context by comparing him to the renowned historian Sima Qian (c.145–86 BCE), one of China's great heroes. Sima was castrated in punishment for 'defaming the emperor' by speaking his mind, but overcame this painful and humiliating emasculation to write a monumental history, just as Beethoven overcame his deafness to write the monumental Ninth Symphony.

Knowledge of, and access to, Beethoven's music followed upon the growing interest in the composer's life. China's first orchestra – now the Shanghai Symphony Orchestra – certainly played Beethoven soon after its founding in 1879. Indeed, the first extant program of the orchestra, which dates to the 1911/12 season, includes the finale from Beethoven's Third Symphony; all told, the orchestra played music by Beethoven eight times in that season alone. However, in the quasi-colonial, often overtly racist foreign settlements of Shanghai, the orchestra was comprised exclusively of foreign musicians and Chinese were not generally permitted to enter the venues where it performed.

This finally changed when a charismatic Italian conductor named Mario Paci took the helm of the orchestra in 1919 and later threatened to quit if Chinese people were not allowed to attend concerts; by the mid-1920s, about a quarter of the audience was Chinese. In March 1927, Paci staged a concert to commemorate the centennial of Beethoven's death that included the first performance of Beethoven's Ninth Symphony in China. Paci permitted a young Chinese violinist named Tan Shuzhen to join the second violins on this special occasion:

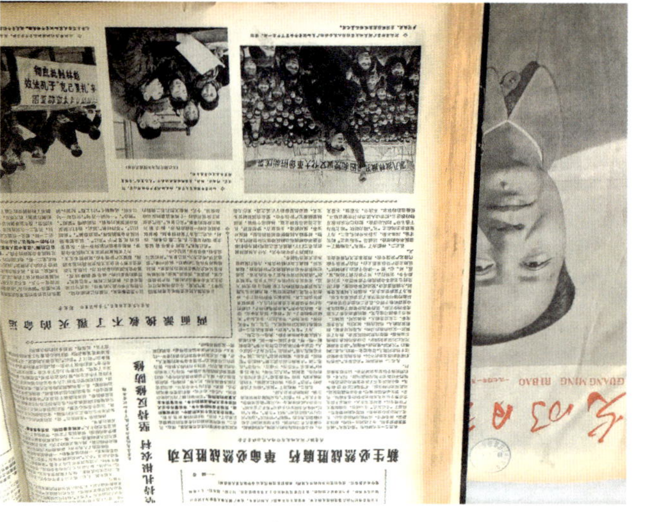

after month, year after year of their youth condemning something. We had nothing, we understood nothing. Our only success was in the development of our voices, which we used to cant phrases and slogans on every occasion. The fact that, to this day, Chinese everywhere speak loudly and vociferously can be traced back to those times.

The campaign against Beethoven and his absolute music spread throughout China and into all levels of society. All over the country, scathing articles were published and 'criticism sessions' held. A concert of Beethoven's music was a crime during the Cultural Revolution. Many symphony orchestras with a classical repertoire disbanded, some re-invented themselves as folk music bands in which the string section performed on the two-stringed Chinese erhu and wind instruments were substituted by the suona.

No one understood the reasons why this extensive campaign against Beethoven and his music had been launched. It was inexplicable – but it did stir our curiosity. Who was this Beethoven, what had he done? And what on earth was 'music without titles'? In spite of all the restrictions, there were clandestine means to investigate these questions. Whoever managed to receive Voice of America and dared to listen to its broadcasts was able to hear Beethoven's music every evening. Others rummaged through secret hiding places in search of old records. The mystery surrounding Beethoven gave our sad, monotonous life a diversion. One evening I arranged with some friends to meet in the apartment of a double-bass player of the then dissolved Central Music Academy. We waited until dark, locked the doors and windows, pulled the curtains, turned the volume of the record player to nearly inaudible and held our breath. That night remains unforgettable to all of us. The night belonged to Beethoven. We played the 'Pastoral' Symphony over and over again, losing ourselves in the lovely melodies, dreaming of open fields, pure springs and the wonders of nature. We did not sleep that night – with Beethoven commenced our hope for a new life.

The chorus of the Ninth Symphony also stands at the beginnings of my Christian faith: the goddess of joy in all her beauty illuminates earth. 'Above the canopy of stars must dwell a loving father'; 'be embraced, you millions!' Friendship and love, and God's mercy to protect us. Like a thin ray of light, joy brightened my dark path and evoked a deeper insight, it gave me a new soul.

How proud I was when I realized my birthday was on the same day as Beethoven's. Together with three friends who also share his birthday, we celebrate every year, the Ode to Joy being our personal birthday song. There was also another side to all of this, however: some of our friends, who, like us, secretly listened to Beethoven's music, were not able to conceal their enthusiasm. They were denounced, interrogated and punished, some by imprisonment or the death penalty. One of my friends was sentenced to death as an event that marked the beginning of the orchestra's integration and the end of the bifurcated understanding of Beethoven in China. Henceforth, many Chinese would seek inspiration not just by reading about Beethoven's life, but also by performing and listening to his music.

Two of the men who helped to make this possible were Cai Yuanpei and Xiao Youmei. Cai, a pioneering educator and philosopher, studied in Leipzig in Germany in 1907 and again in 1913. He had a strong interest in aesthetic education which he saw as free, progressive and universal, and he believed fervently in the transformative power of art; it was his goal that 'any kind of person, at all times, should have the opportunity to come into contact with art'. In Leipzig, Cai studied music, including the piano and the violin, and became a fan of Beethoven, whose music inspired him to write this little poem:

> Our nation's music is too plain,
> Westerners are surprised to hear.
> I love Beethoven's music,
> Which embodies deep and broad aspirations.[2]

In 1916, following his return to China, Cai was appointed president of the newly founded Peking University and began to implement the theories he had developed in Germany. This included creating the Peking University Music Society to train young Chinese in Western music, in part as a means of supplementing what Cai saw as 'deficiencies in Chinese music'. In 1920, Cai invited the German-trained musicologist Xiao Youmei to run the nascent music school. Xiao had spent many years in Germany, studying at Leipzig Conservatory of Music, Berlin University and the Stuttgart Conservatory of Music. He had mingled with prominent European musicians – such as the Hungarian conductor Arthur Nikisch and the composer and conductor Richard Strauss – and had become a fan of the 'dignified and serious' musical sage Beethoven. Xiao oversaw the formation of a small orchestra of teachers and students. Between 1922 and 1927, they gave twenty-nine concerts in which they performed Beethoven's works more than any others: the Second, Third, Fifth and Sixth Symphonies, the Piano Sonata No. 8 and the Egmont Overture. Xiao wrote detailed programme notes for each performance in which he sought to explain Beethoven in a Chinese context; these were then published in the Peking University newspaper as a way of educating more people. For a performance of Beethoven's Third, Xiao wrote that the composer of such a heroic work must have possessed a high moral standard. He further opined that if Beethoven were alive today, he would certainly dedicate this symphony to Sun Yat-sen (the president of the Republic of China) who was upholding democracy in China, rather than to Napoleon, as he had originally done. Xiao suggested that the music of Beethoven's Fifth, portraying the struggle to emerge from a dark world into brightness, could be viewed as depicting China's revolutionary history over the preceding thirty years, thereby localizing the work into the Chinese context.

of the Eight Country Alliance was chiefly responsible for the attack on China and the burning of the Summer Palace: Germany. His name is Beethoven. He is a composer who has written many pieces without a title and is the epitome of opposition to the culture of the proletarian revolution. His putrid music poisons the great proletariat. The so-called "music without titles" which he invented is influencing the whole world. Therefore, according to Chairman Mao's strict instructions, let us criticize the representative of bourgeois arts, Beethoven, and his "music without titles"! We must uphold the doctrines of Marxism-Leninism and Mao Zedong Thought, and based on the eight model revolutionary plays criticize Beethoven and his "music without titles" to the utmost, let him never rise again!' Holding up the red Mao-bible, she proceeded to lead us in chanting: 'Down with Beethoven! Down with decadent bourgeois arts! The proletarian arts shall conquer China and the world!'

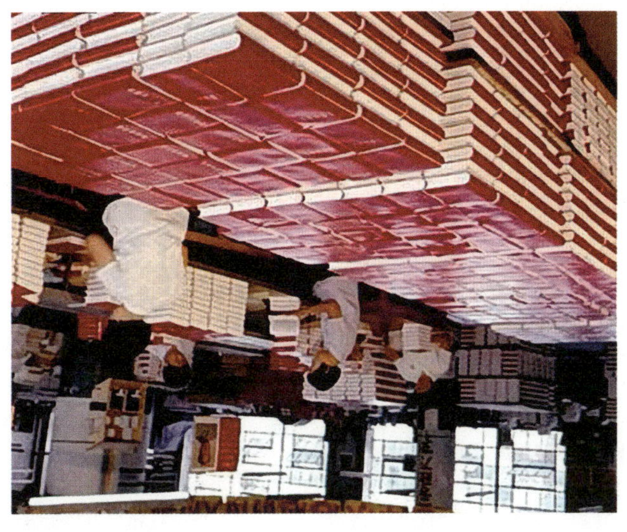

Following the reading of the government paper and the chorus of slogans came the performance of the propaganda team. They sang revolutionary songs and enacted scenes from the eight revolutionary operas. On this evening, they had chosen excerpts from the revolutionary ballet *The White-Haired Girl*. One of the most popular stories in China, this is the tale of a poor girl who flees her cruel landlord into the mountains, enduring such hardships that her hair turns white despite her young age. She is eventually freed by the Communist army and takes revenge. Towards the end of the ballet there is a moving song for mixed chorus entitled *The Sun is Rising*: 'The sun is rising, the sun is rising, the sun is rising. The sun is shining gloriously. After thousands of years of suffering and struggle, today finally the sun is rising. Red Sun is Chairman Mao, Red Sun is the Communist Party. Red Sun is Chairman Mao, Red Sun is the Communist Party.'

This song has been acclaimed as the Chinese Ode to Joy. We used this piece to criticize Beethoven, praising *The Sun is Rising* as a magnificent chorus that expresses lofty ideals with an acoustic colouring that bourgeois music would never be able to achieve. Once the choir performance was finished, this session of criticizing Beethoven was over and so were our tasks for the day. Similar sessions in condemnation of Beethoven were frequently held again during the following month. Their basic message was always the same: the bourgeoisie is using Beethoven to overthrow the rule of the proletariat in China, his 'music without titles' (absolute music) is poisoning the Chinese people's minds. Only the eight revolutionary model operas are truly great and meaningful.

In isolated, autocratic China almost no one in my circle knew who Beethoven was. It even remained unclear whether the composer was male or female. What might 'music without titles' be? We had absolutely no idea. 'Criticism sessions' of this kind were very common at the time. Everyone in my generation wasted day after day, month

Eventually the complicated politics of the era led Cai to leave China again and Xiao to decide that he could not run a successful music school in Beijing, which was ruled by a philistine warlord. Instead, Xiao decided to move to Shanghai to establish a formal conservatory, which he would staff with musicians from the Shanghai Symphony Orchestra. The Shanghai Conservatory of Music opened its doors in 1927 and began training China's first homegrown musicians, many of whom had been drawn to classical music by Beethoven. A young woman named Li Cuizhen, for example, arrived able to play all thirty-two Beethoven piano sonatas from memory. The composition student Xian Xinghai explained how Beethoven had inspired him to write music. 'Beethoven's mother worked for rich people in the kitchen', Xian told Xiao. 'My mother did the same. My goal is to contribute to music just like Beethoven did.'[3] While at the Shanghai Conservatory, Xian, who would go on to become one of China's most renowned composers, wrote an essay in which he praised Beethoven's genius and argued that the composer's greatness sprang from his willingness to confront challenges and accept suffering; only when China's music students cultivated this ability would they achieve any measure of success.

The suffering that Xian saw as essential to the creation of great music was soon forthcoming as China was invaded and occupied by Japan during the 1930s and 1940s. It was during this period that the French-educated intellectual Fu Lei decided to translate Romain Rolland's *Vie de Beethoven* into Chinese. Fu had read Rolland's romantic account of Beethoven's life while he was a student in Paris and been utterly overwhelmed. 'I burst into tears,' Fu later explained, 'and suddenly felt as if I had been enlightened by the divine light and gained the power of rebirth. From that time on, I wonderfully took heart, which was indeed a great event in my whole life.'[4] Back in China, Fu saw parallels between the Japanese occupation of China and the turbulent era in which Beethoven had come of age. His hope, he wrote, was that his translation of Rolland's biography of Beethoven would comfort and inspire his fellow Chinese citizens in their time of trouble. With the same goal in mind, Fu in 1937 began to translate Rolland's ten-volume magnum opus, *Jean-Christophe*, a cradle-to-grave *Bildungsroman* inspired by the life of Beethoven. His translation of the novel would be read by generations of Chinese; the current Chinese president, Xi Jinping, has even gone on record extolling the book.

The 1945 victory over Japan was followed by civil war rather than peace and in 1949 the victorious Communist Party established the People's Republic of China. During the 1950s and early 1960s, many ideological debates ensued over the propriety of performing 'bourgeois' classical music in a newly established socialist country. However, while many left-leaning intellectuals argued against it, there were also many Communist Party members who had been students of classical music and they had the Soviet Union on their side, China's 'dearest elder brother' and 'great teacher'. The USSR was of paramount importance in helping China to rebuild after the war – it sent over ten thousand advisers to assist with infrastructure, industry and the arts – and it was a proponent of much classical music. The USSR's interpretation of Beethoven as 'the musical apotheosis of revolution' was exported to China and the composer's music came to be performed widely by newly-established symphony orchestras.

is Red': 'The east is red, the sun is rising. | China has brought forth Mao Zedong | He strives to bring the Chinese people good fortune | Hooray! He is the people's great saviour.' These songs were played repeatedly all day long, come rain or shine.

Today this seems ludicrous to me. 'The Internationale' clearly states that 'no saviour from on high delivers, no faith have we in prince or peer'. A minute later we were told that Mao Zedong was the 'people's great saviour'! In those days, all five human senses felt numbed. Even if anyone had noticed the contradiction, no one would have dared to mention it. To do so invited the danger of being executed or sent to a labour camp.

Working in the factory was exhausting. The printing presses were running non-stop in order to provide the revolutionaries with their 'spiritual nourishment'. Every one of us had to work at least ten hours a day. The factory was organized like a military unit. We received our daily assignment in the morning and had to report in the evening. There was no free time or entertainment whatsoever. Every morning we were obliged to attend an hour-long study session on Marxism-Leninism and Mao Zedong's works before we started to work. In the evenings, having finished our work, we gathered together to criticize bourgeois thought, to discuss major national and international events, and to confront ourselves with our own mistakes – much like the daily examination of conscience in the Catholic religion.

At the time all Chinese sang 'The Internationale' every day as well as such songs as 'The East is Red', 'Sailing the Seas Depends on the Helmsman', 'Neither Father nor Mother is as Dear as Mao Zedong'. There were eight 'model revolutionary operas' to be watched, all of which had been engineered as such by Mao's wife Jiang Qing: the revolutionary ballets *The Red Detachment of Women* and *The White-Haired Girl* as well as the revolutionary Beijing operas *The Legend of the Red Lantern*, *On the Docks*, *Raid on the White Tiger Regiment*, *Shajiabang*, and the revolutionary symphonies *Shajiabang* and *Taking Tiger Mountain by Strategy*.

February 1974. The main auditorium of the publishing house, which had two thousand seats, was filled (our factory alone hat 1800 workers). In the middle of the auditorium hung a large banner with red characters against a white background: 'Severely criticize the representative of bourgeois culture, Beethoven, and his "music without titles"'. The atmosphere in the room was solemn and austere, with row upon row of lethargic, emotionless Chinese faces looking on. The presenter that evening was a pretty young woman from the publishing house's revolutionary propaganda team (members of this team were exempt from work). Her voice was pleasant and she had a gallant stride. Placing herself in the middle of the stage, she opened the meeting holding a microphone in one hand, and the *Guidelines of Criticism*, a central government publication as well as the newest editions of the *People's Daily*, *Guangming Daily* and the *Red Flag Magazine* in the other. First, the young woman led us in reciting Mao's slogans: 'All reactionaries are paper tigers, but if you do not fight them, they will not be overthrown. The force at the core leading our cause forward is the Chinese Communist Party. The theoretical basis guiding our thinking is Marxism-Leninism.'

Then she pointed to the banner and shouted: 'Today we will criticize the representative of reactionary bourgeois arts. He comes from the country which as a member

In 1957, the 130th anniversary of Beethoven's death was commemorated in Beijing with a concert that included the Fifth Symphony and the violin Romance in F; the East German conductor Werner Gosling also gave an influential talk called *Beethoven's Spirit Has Made All Progressive People Join Together*. Public celebrations of the tenth anniversary of the People's Republic in 1959 included a performance of Beethoven's Ninth Symphony that was the first by an all-Chinese orchestra and sung in Chinese by an all-Chinese chorus. Demand for tickets was so high that a dozen performances were added, enabling over twenty five thousand people to hear the Ninth in Beijing, among them Premier Zhou Enlai. At the official tenth anniversary celebration, attended by Chairman Mao Zedong and Soviet First Secretary Nikita Khrushchev, an orchestra of 300 played Beethoven's Egmont Overture.

By the early 1960s, China's political climate was moving increasingly leftward and in 1966 the Cultural Revolution broke out. During this period, performances of both Western and traditional Chinese music were forbidden, replaced by 'model operas' that had politically correct themes. Artists and intellectuals were humiliated and sometimes tortured; many resorted to suicide, including Fu Lei, the translator who had done so much to popularize Beethoven and Li Cuizhen, the pianist who knew all the Beethoven piano sonatas by heart. Although Beethoven's compositions could not be played in public during this period, many still sought secret refuge in the composer's music. The Shanghai Symphony Orchestra conductor Lu Hongen, for instance, was arrested for his vocal defence of classical music and criticism of the Cultural Revolution. According to an account left by his cellmate, Liu Wenzhong, Lu coped with the beatings and abuse by humming his two favourite Beethoven pieces, the Third Symphony and the *Missa Solemnis*. In a great tragedy of modern China's music history, Lu was sentenced to death. While awaiting execution, he asked his cellmate for a favour: 'If you ever have a chance to escape China, help me do something I have wanted to do my entire life. Visit Austria, the home of music. Go to Beethoven's tomb and lay a bouquet of flowers. And tell Beethoven that his disciple in China, Lu Hongen, was humming the *Missa Solemnis* as he marched to his death.'[5] Lu did indeed hum Beethoven's mass as he was being dragged off to be shot in April of 1968. Many years later, Liu Wenzhong fulfilled his promise and laid flowers on Beethoven's grave on behalf of his Chinese disciple, Lu Hongen.

The Cultural Revolution finally ended in 1976. Just a few months later, Beijing's Central Philharmonic sought permission to commemorate the 150th anniversary of Beethoven's death; their request was deemed so sensitive that it was sent to the standing committee of the Communist Party Politburo, which at last gave permission to proceed. On 26 March 1977, the orchestra played Beethoven's Fifth; the last two movements of the symphony were broadcast nationwide, a signal to many that the Cultural Revolution was really and truly over. The Beethoven broadcast was followed by visits of foreign orchestras like the Toronto Symphony under Andrew Davis, the Boston Symphony under Seiji Ozawa, and the Berlin Philharmonic under Herbert von Karajan in 1979; they all played Beethoven. In the early 1980s, a 'Beethoven Fever' broke out as crowds of people queued to hear orchestras like the Central Philharmonic and Shanghai Symphony play all of the composer's symphonies. An account of Beethoven's life was added to the national curriculum, where it remains to this

YANMING ZHOU

'Music Without Titles'

Half a century has passed. Memories fade. And yet there are some memories that stay with us forever: the critical assault on Beethoven and his music will forever be carved into the minds of my generation.

In 1971, when I had not yet graduated from high school, I was assigned to work in the Xinhua publishing house in Beijing. It specialized in the works of Marx, Engels, Lenin, Stalin and Mao Zedong as well as producing illustrated books and posters. At the time Xinhua publishing house was renowned in China as a model production site, adhering to the principles of Marxism-Leninism and Mao Zedong. It was hailed as a 'red flag of Communism'.

My strongest impression when I first joined the press was the incessant, earsplitting sound of 'The Internationale' blasting out of all the loudspeakers every morning as I entered the factory grounds at 7:30 a.m. 'Arise, ye workers from your slumber, | Arise, ye prisoners of want […] | No saviour from on high delivers, | No faith have we in prince or peer, | Our own right hand the chains must shiver, | Chains of hatred, greed and fear!' There followed the song 'The East day. As China's economy took off in the 1990s and 2000s, spectacular concert halls and opera houses were built across the country. The music of Beethoven resounds in all of these.

China has transformed almost beyond recognition in the century and more since Beethoven was first introduced, but the Chinese people's loyalty to the German composer has never faltered. Indeed, Beethoven and his music have become a part of China's social, cultural and political fabric and, just as Beethoven has been there for China, so China will be there for Beethoven.

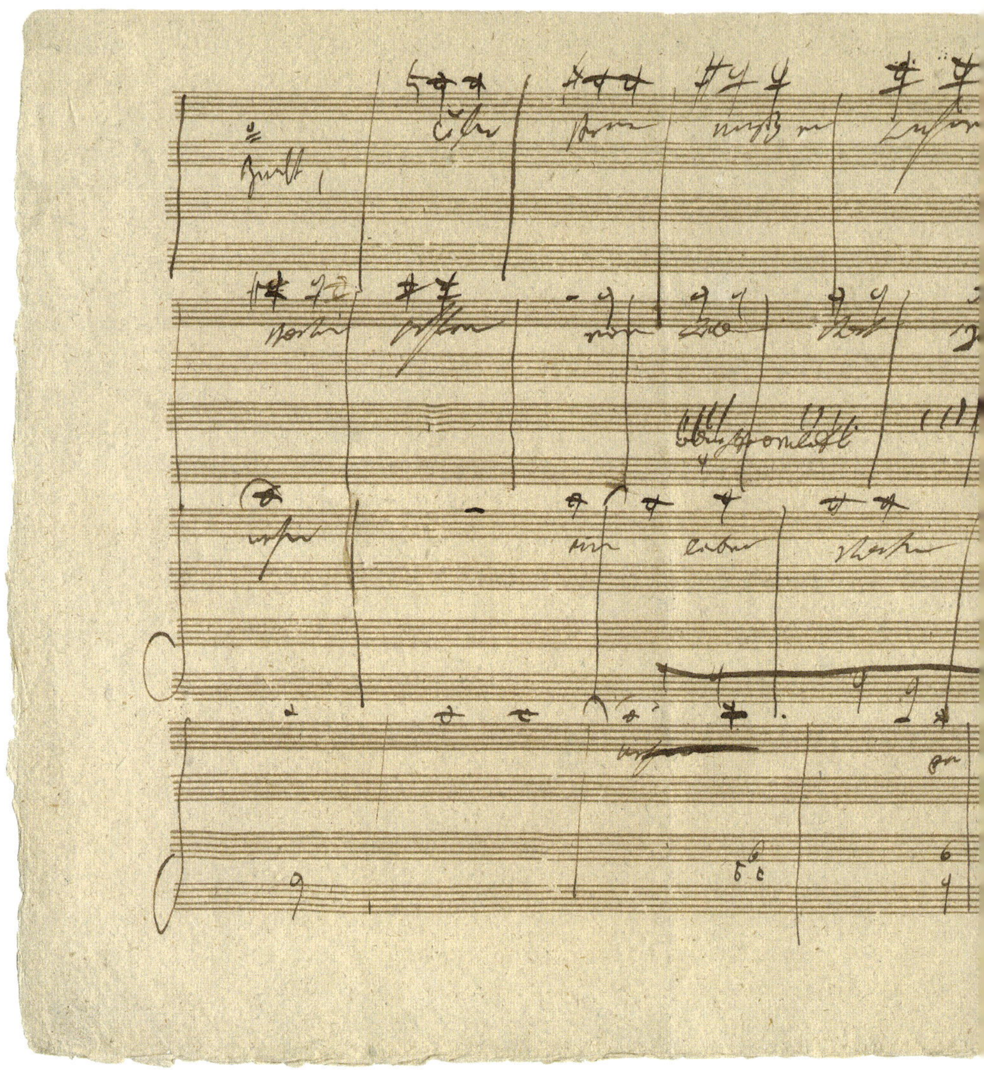

1 This text draws on our two previous books, Sheila Melvin and Jindong Cai, *Rhapsody in Red: How Western Classical Music Became Chinese* (New York, 2004) and Sheila Melvin and Jindong Cai, *Beethoven in China: How the Great Composer Became an Icon in the People's Republic* (London, 2016).

2 See Yik-man Edmond Tsang, 'Beethoven in China: The Reception of Beethoven's Music and its Political Implications, 1949–1959', thesis, University of Hong Kong, 2003, 71.

3 See Xiao Shuxian, 'Huiyi wode Shufu, Xiao Youmei [Remembering my uncle Xiao Youmei]', in: Dai Penghai and Huang Xudong (eds.), *Xiao Youmei Jinian Wenji* [Collected Articles on Xiao Youmei] (Shanghai, 1993), 83-99.

4 See Joys Hoi Yan Cheung, 'Chinese Music and Translated Modernity in Shanghai, 1918–1937', dissertation, University of Michigan, 2008, 209.

5 For Lu Hongen's story, see Liu Wenzhong, 'Austria – Remembering Lu Hongen, my friend in shared suffering', in: *Xinhai Guotuzhi*, July 2009.

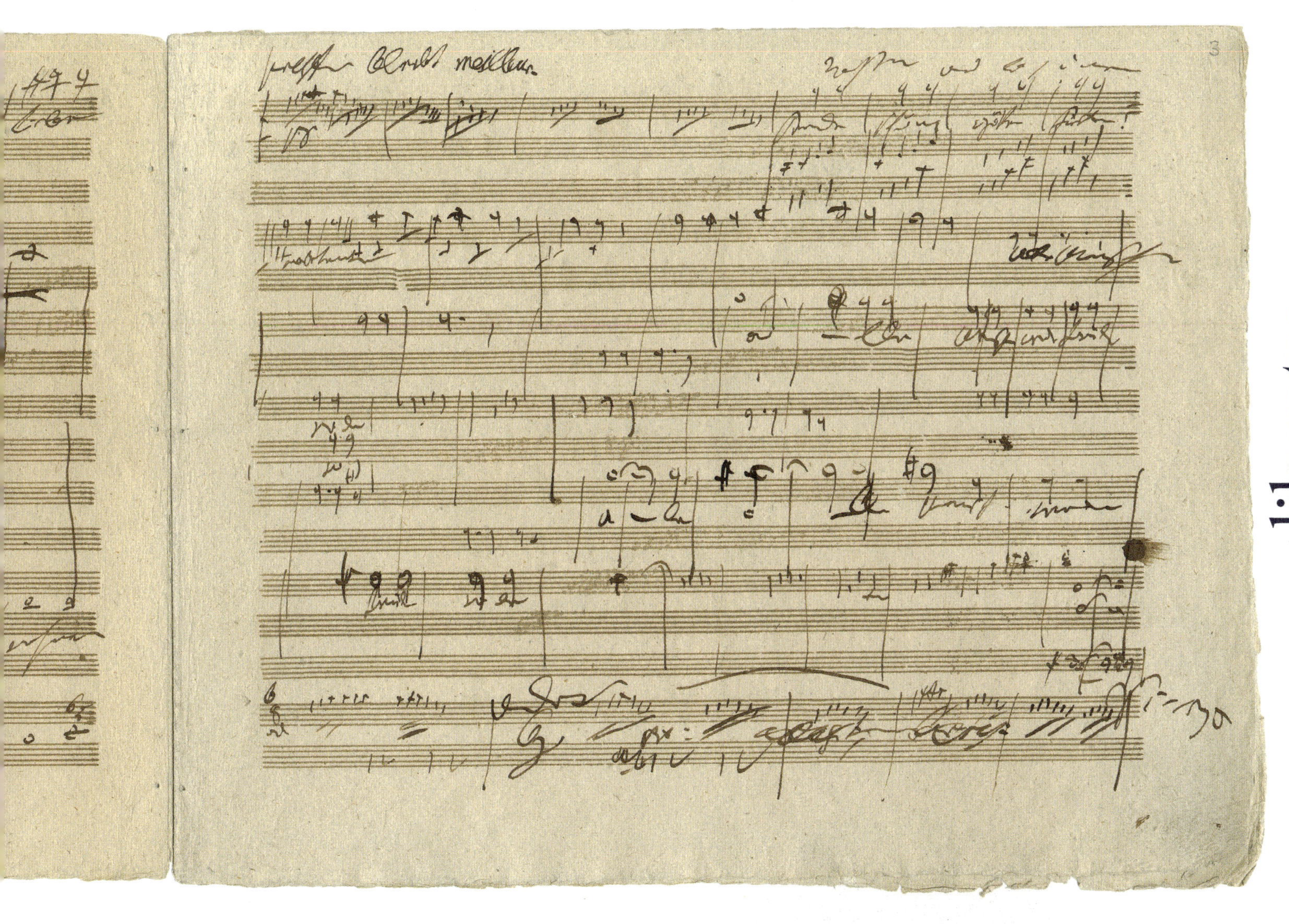

On the right side, the last bars of the first stave are underwritten: 'Freude schöner Götter Funken!', below the fourth, sixth and tenth staves is written: 'a-lle Menschen werden Brüder'.

LUDWIG VAN BEETHOVEN

Sketches for the Choral Finale of Symphony No. 9 in D minor, op. 125, 4th mvt, autograph 1823/24

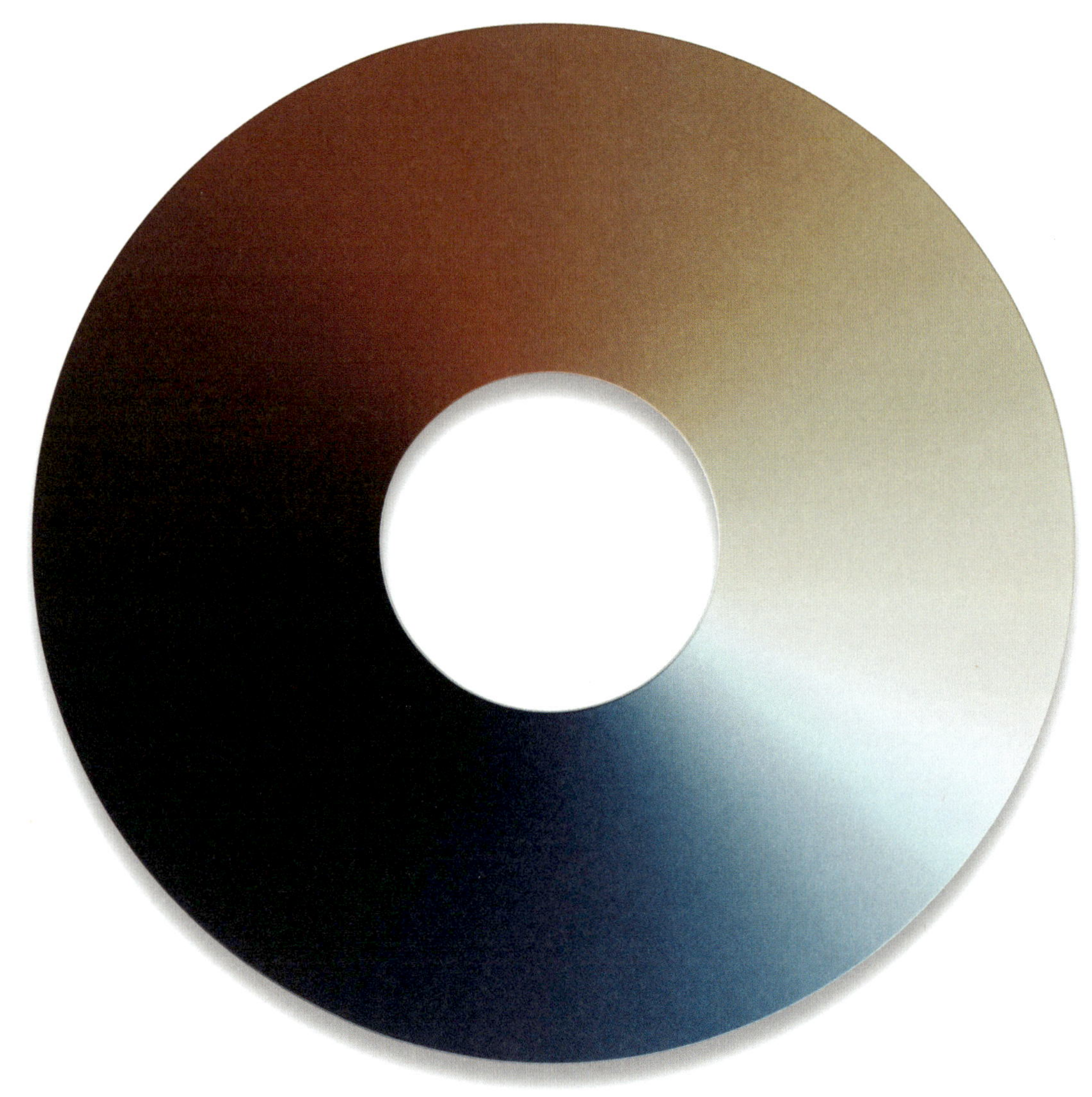

OLAFUR ELIASSON

Colour Experiment no. 58
2014

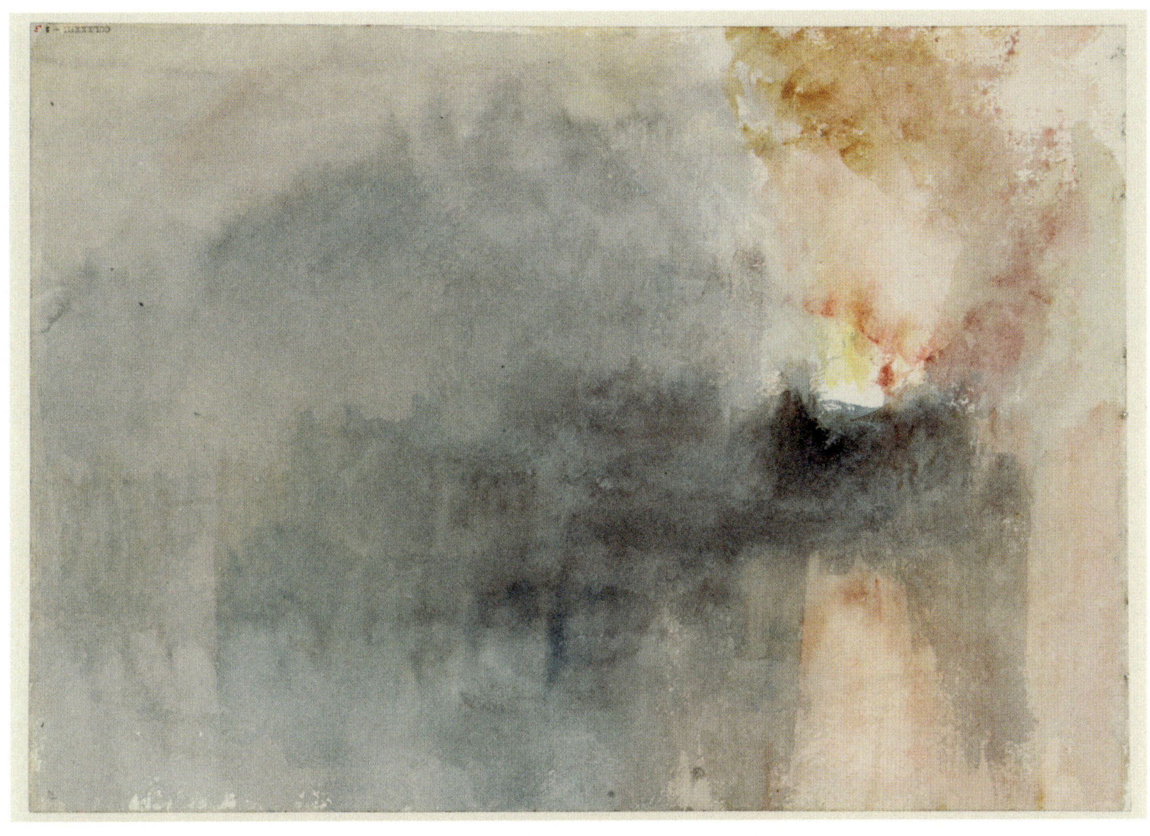

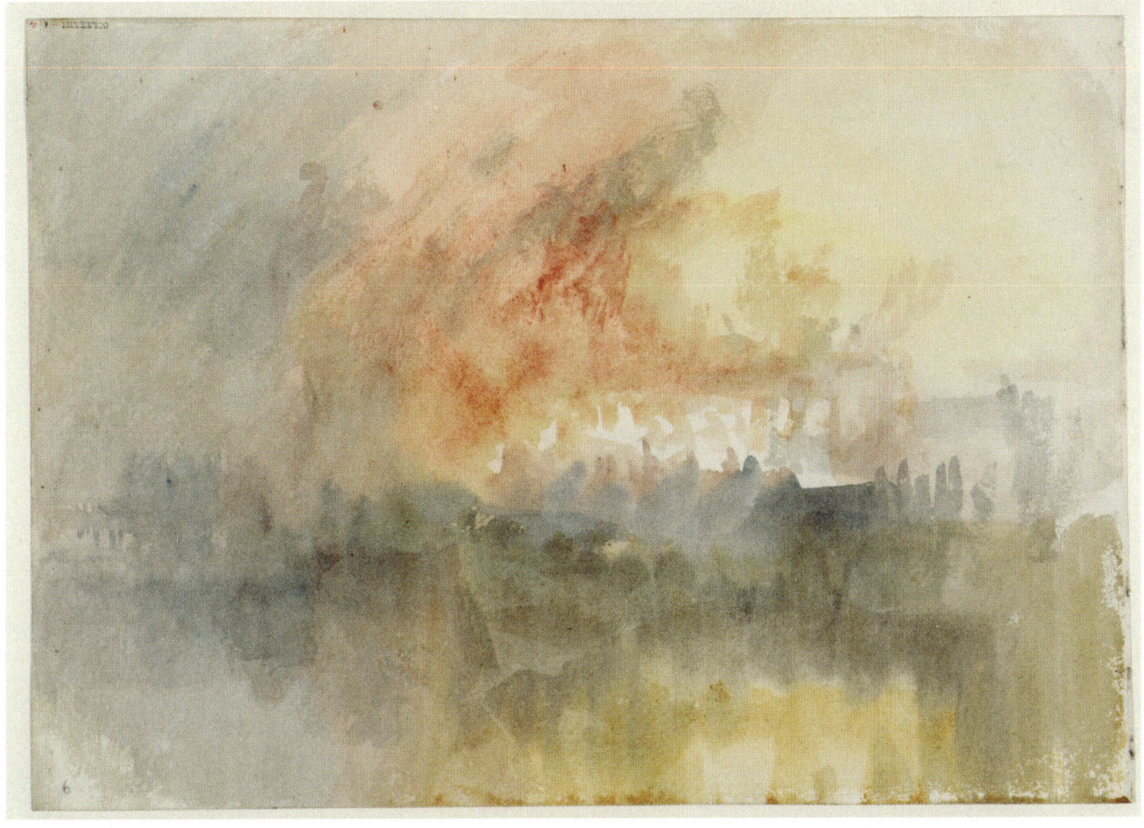

JOSEPH MALLORD WILLIAM TURNER

Fire at the Grand Storehouse of the Tower of London, 1841

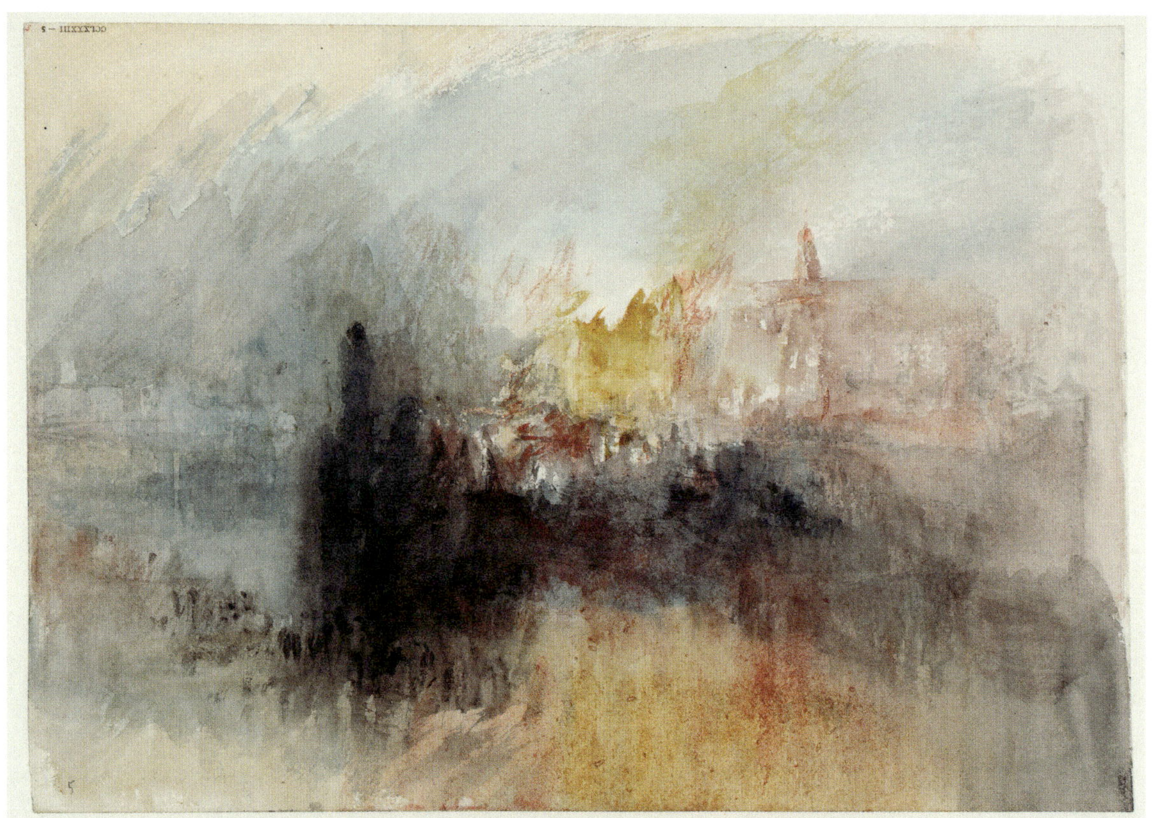

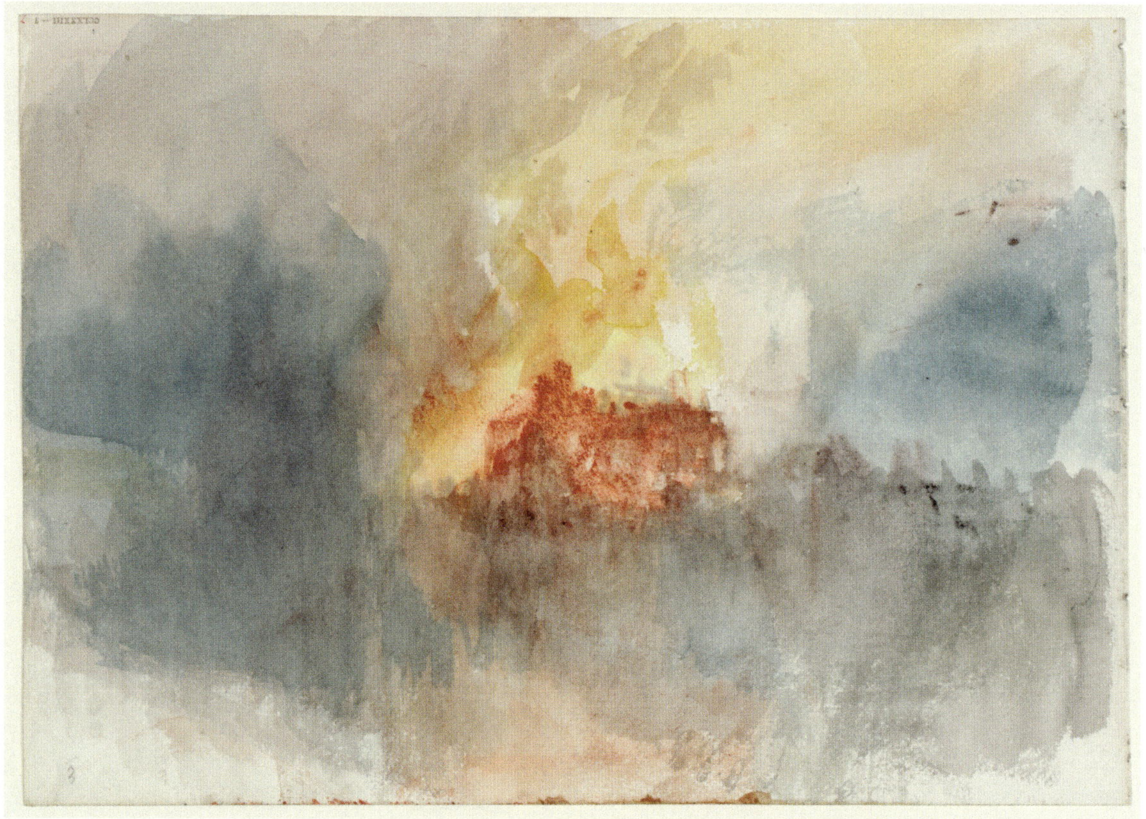

In the Turner colour experiments, I've isolated light and colour in Turner's works in order to extract his sense of ephemera from the objects of desire that his paintings have become. The schematic arrays of colours on round canvases generate a feeling of endlessness and allow the viewer to take in the artwork in a decentralized, meandering way.

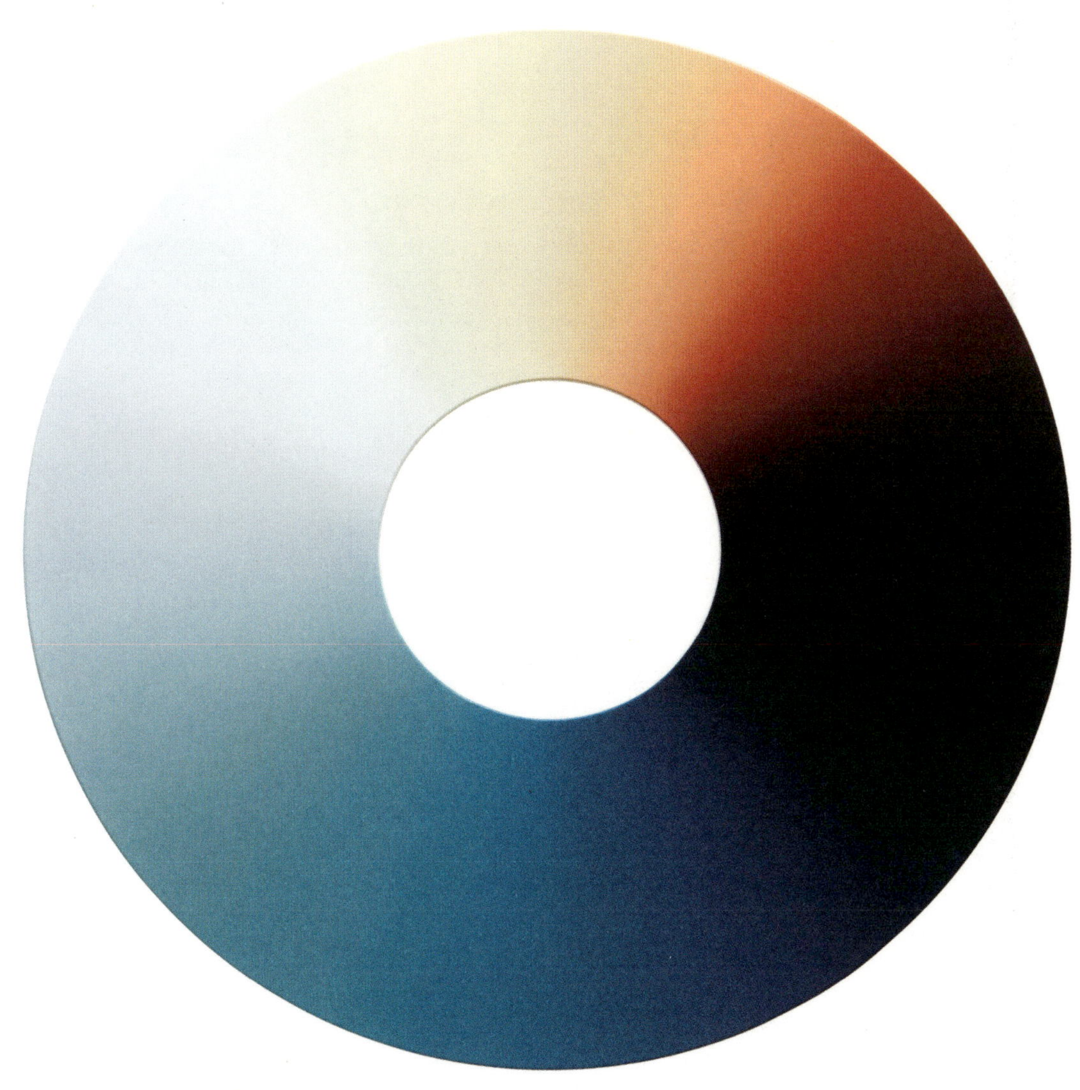

OLAFUR ELIASSON

Colour Experiment no. 61
2014

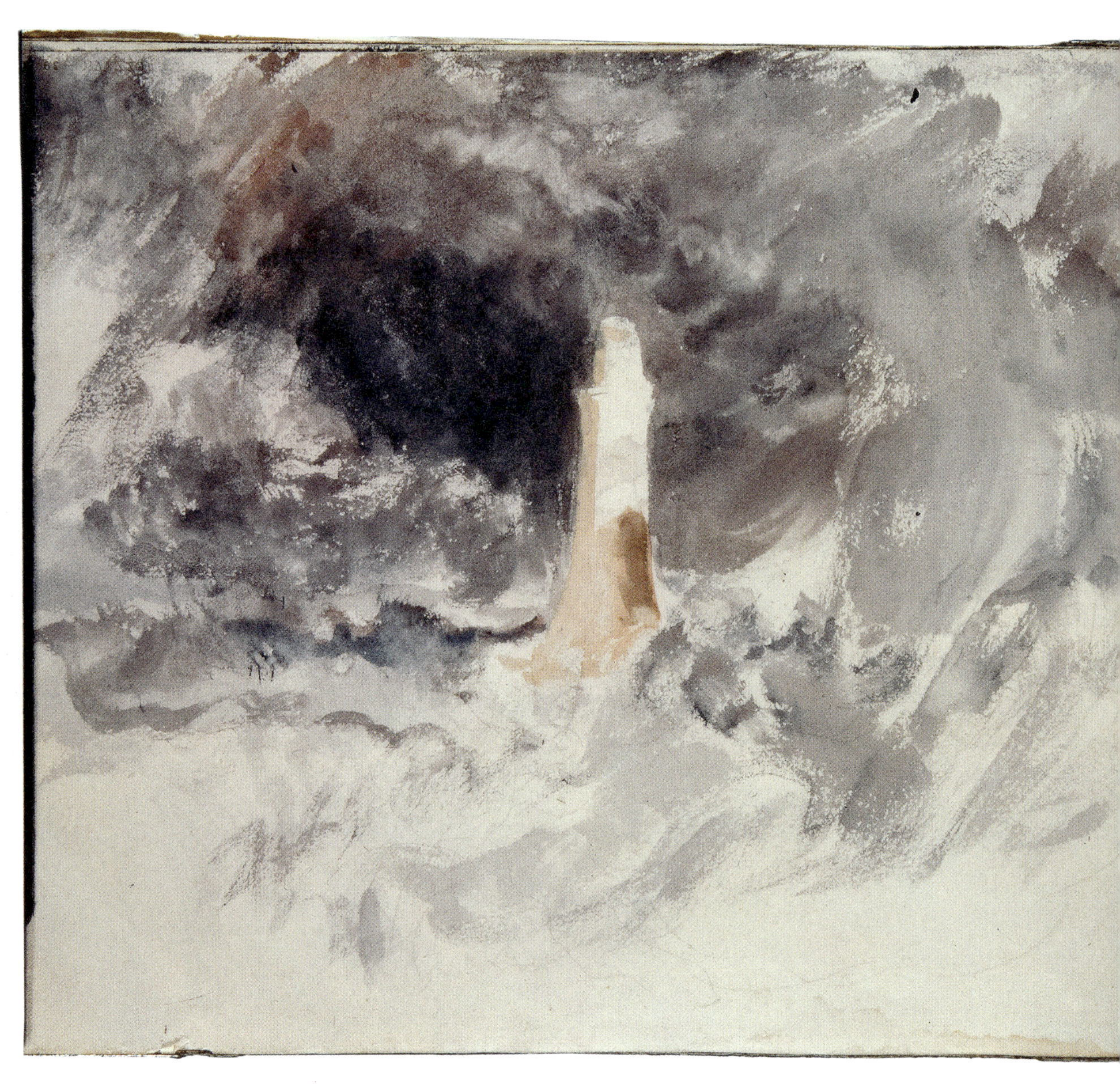

JOSEPH MALLORD WILLIAM TURNER

Skies Sketchbook
1816–1818

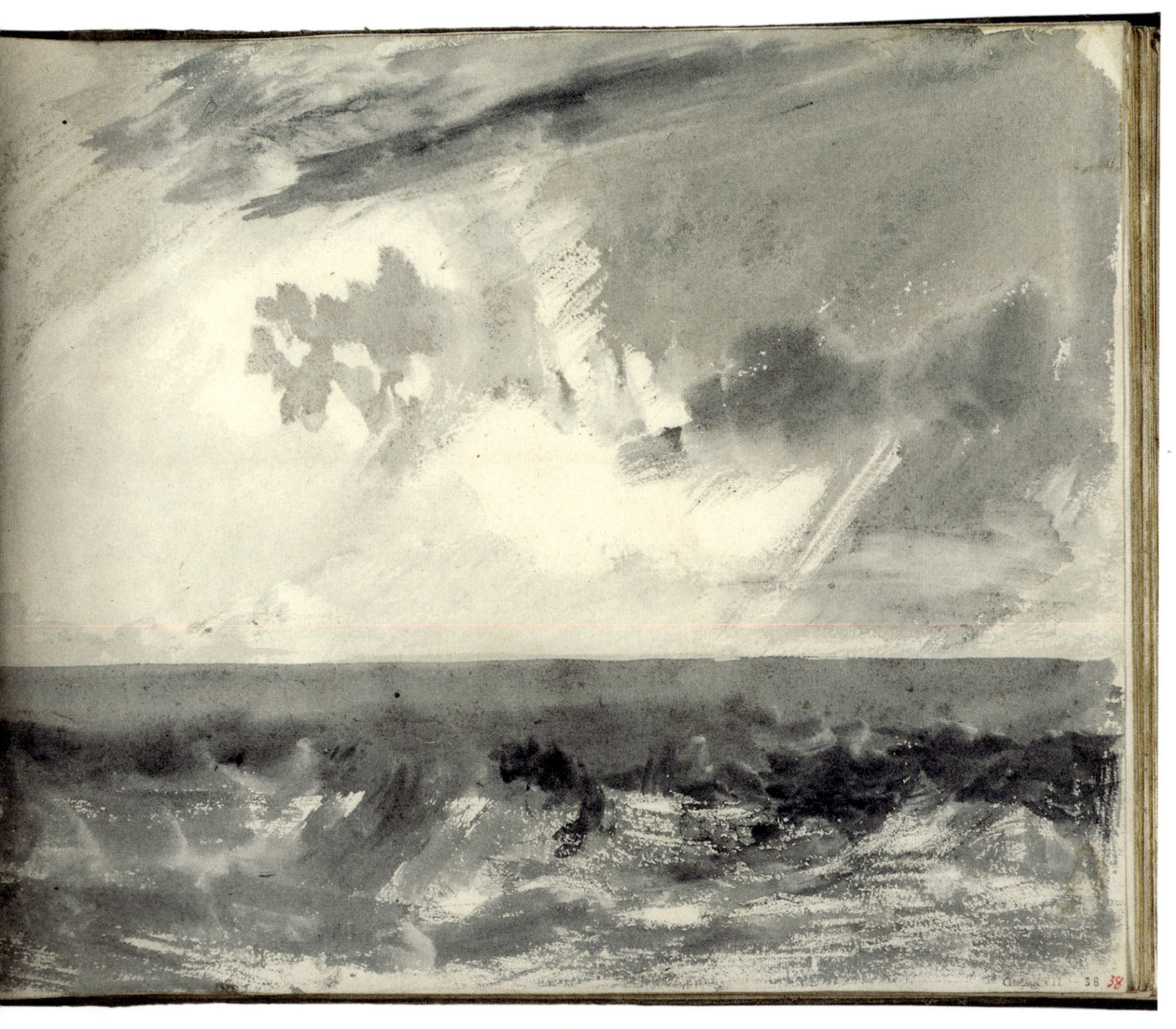

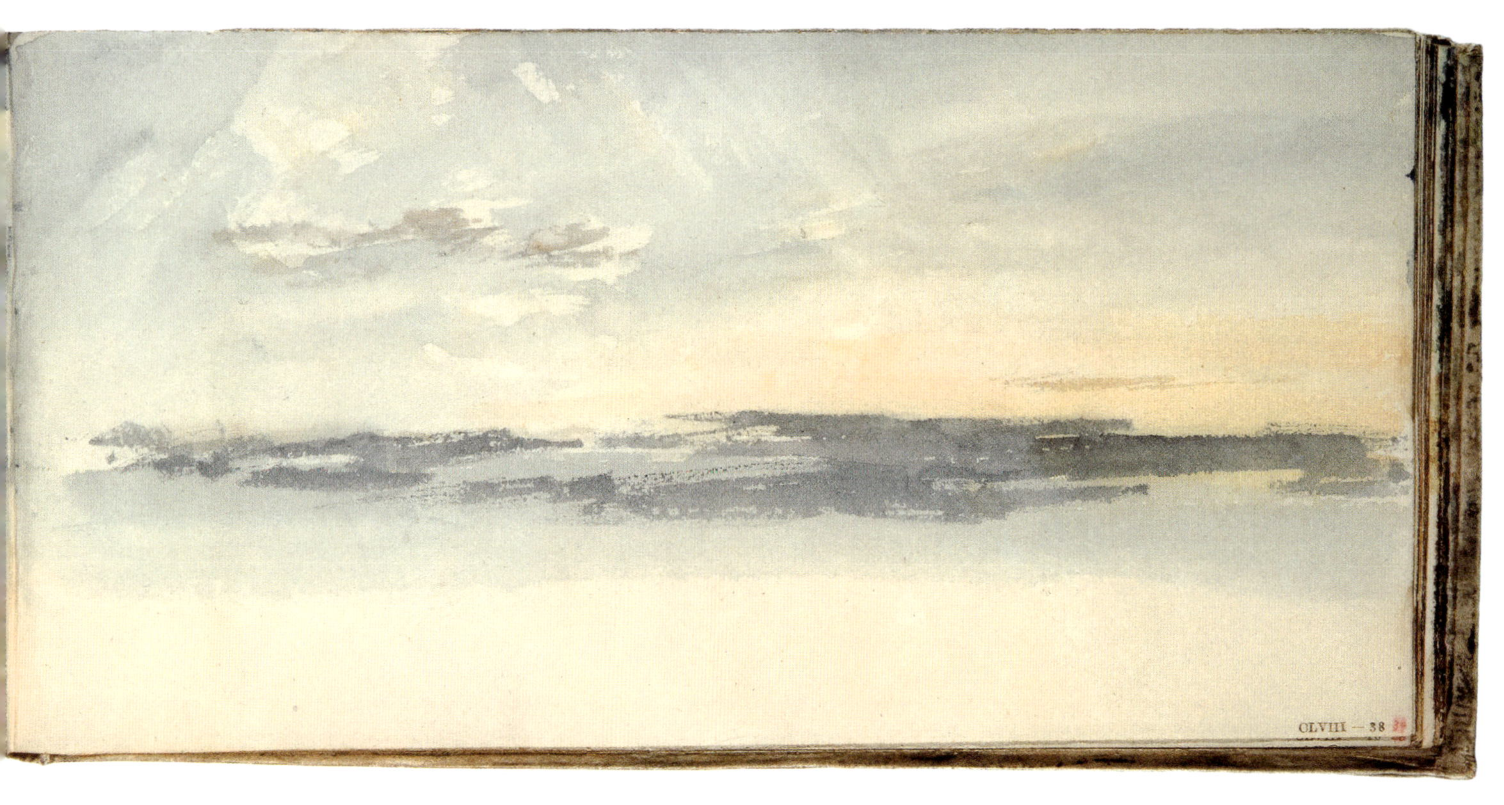

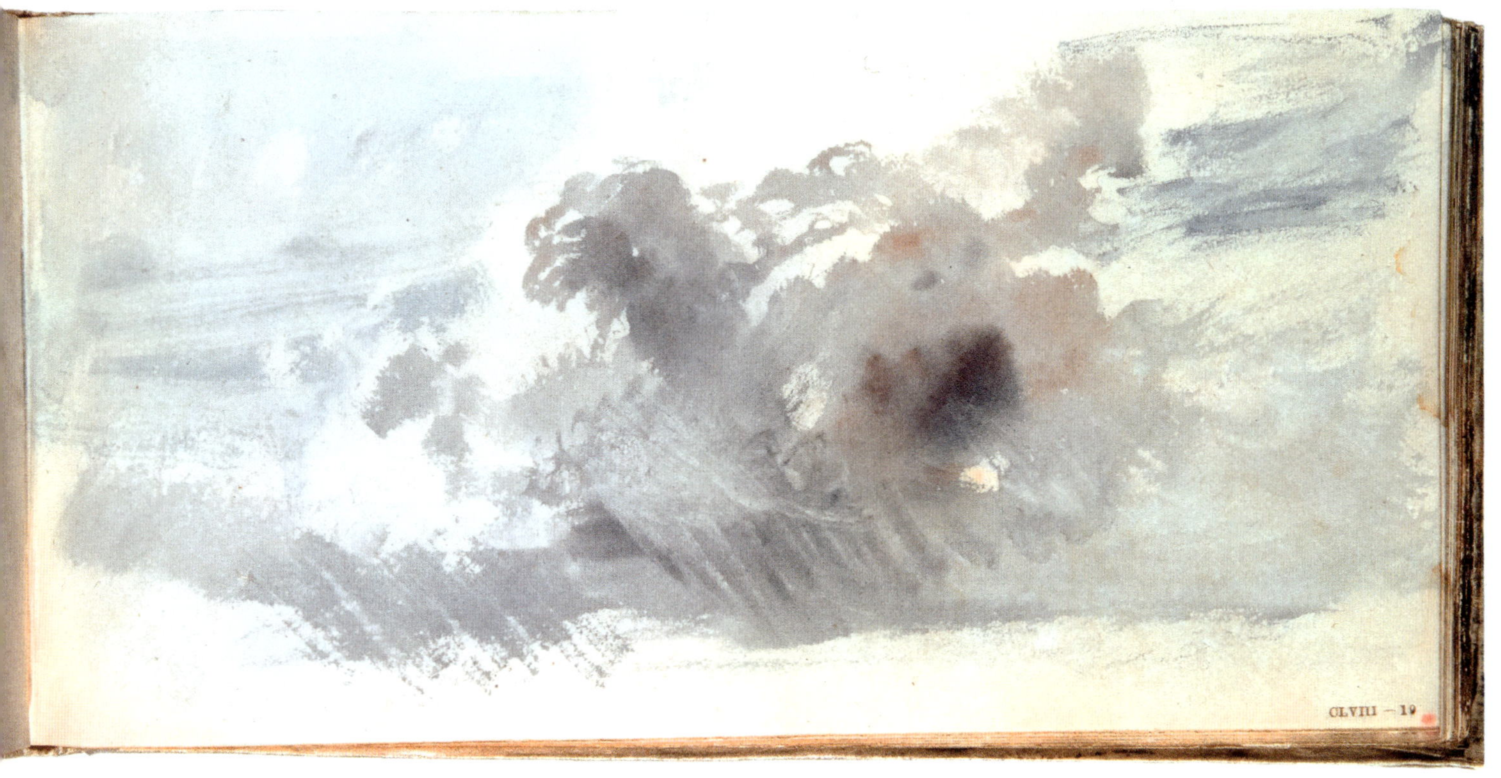

JOSEPH MALLORD WILLIAM TURNER

Vale of Heathfield Sketchbook 1809–1816

LARISSA KIRILLINA

Russia through Beethoven's Eyes

'It would scarcely be right to regard Beethoven as a *German* composer. He belongs to the whole world and, consequently, to us Russians, too,' wrote Sergei Taneyev on 6 April (OS)[1] 1900 to the patron of the arts Mitrofan Belyaev, whom he was trying to persuade to publish a workbook containing musical sketches by Beethoven from the years 1802–03 that had recently been discovered in Moscow.[2]

The topic of Beethoven and Russia encompasses the most varied subtopics, such as the composer's personal contacts with Russian admirers, his use of Russian folk music and the Russian premieres of his works (notably the world premiere of the *Missa Solemnis* in St Petersburg in 1824). Beethoven's persona was a regular presence in Russian literature from Vladimir Odoyevsky's 1830 novella *Poslednii kvartet Betkhovena* ('Beethoven's last quartet') right up to the 20th century, when it was invoked by poets such as Osip Mandelstam. The performance of Beethoven's music in Russia can look back on a rich tradition, and his oeuvre exerted considerable influence on Russian composers from Glinka to Prokofiev, Shostakovich and Schnittke. During the Soviet period, the cult of Beethoven was promoted by the highest state authorities. Although Beethoven is no longer celebrated with such pomp and circumstance in modern Russia, his music continues to be loved with loyal devotion.

We may also approach our topic from another angle, namely, by asking whether that longstanding love was reciprocated – that is, what did Beethoven himself think of Russia, of its people, culture and politics? Very few relevant remarks by Beethoven have actually come down to us, but we can piece together a more complete picture by looking at the historical context and drawing on other sources.

The earliest memorable statement by Beethoven on Russia is to be found in a letter of 17 September 1795 to Heinrich von Struve, a friend of his youth: 'So you are now in the cold country where mankind is still treated with such contempt; I know for certain that you will come across many things there that run counter to your way of thinking, to your heart – indeed, to your whole sensibility.'[3] These words strike a chord uncannily similar to the tone and tenor of Franz Grillparzer's 1839 poem 'Rußland':

> Ich grüße dich, du Land der eisgen Steppen,
> Mit deinen Völkern rauh und starr und roh,
> Wo sie die Unschuld zum Polarkreis schleppen,
> Wo noch Gewalt des Übermaßes froh.[4]

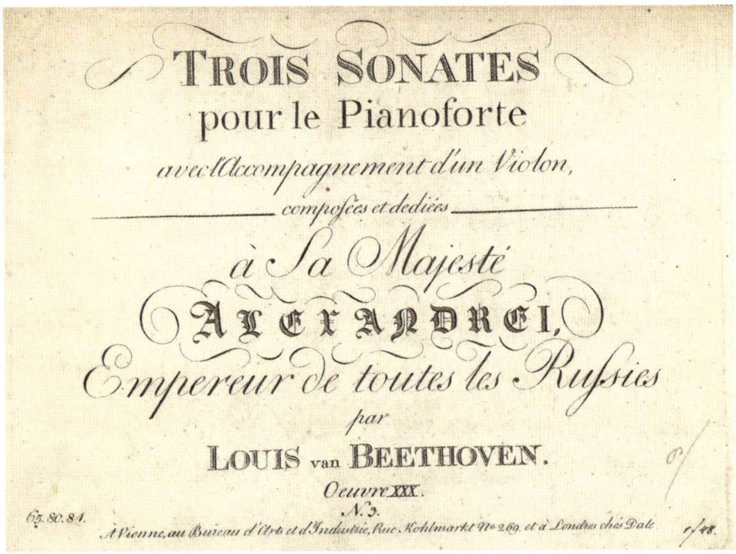

Fig. 1 Ludwig van Beethoven, title page of the Three Sonatas for Piano and Violin, op. 30, with a dedication to Tsar Alexander I. Bonn, Beethoven-Haus, inv. no. C30/17

Hackneyed notions about Russia as the country of grim frosts and boundless expanses, populated by semi-wild peoples and ruled by fierce tyrants and autocrats, were part of the intellectual baggage of even the most enlightened contemporaries of Beethoven's. While these notions undeniably contained more than a grain of truth, they reflected only one side of the extremely complex image of Russia – a country that had burst on to the stage of European politics in the 18th century and was to play a key role in the eventual victory over Napoleon in the wars of 1812–14.

Stereotypes of Russia manifest themselves not just in Beethoven's above-quoted letter to von Struve but also in several more light-hearted remarks of his.

It is interesting that, in the same letter to von Struve, after recording his negative opinion of Russia, Beethoven expressed his desire to tour that country, writing that 'my first trip will be to Italy and then perhaps to Russia.' That desire was, however, expressed at a time when Catherine the Great was still on the throne. The idea of visiting Russia was afterwards never again raised by Beethoven in earnest, though he did try to establish contacts in the very highest circles. For example, in 1802 he dedicated the three opus 30 violin sonatas to Tsar Alexander I (fig. 1); moreover, it is likely that in 1805 he sent some of his songs to the empress dowager, Maria Fyodorovna.[5]

In two letters to Amalie Sebald from September 1812, Beethoven mentioned some Russian acquaintances whom she was seeing at Teplitz. He wrote in the first: 'Enjoy yourself for now gadding about with Russians, Lapps, Samoyeds, etc., but don't sing the song "Long live!" too often.'[6] Of course in those times only wellheeled members of the Russian nobility could afford to stay at the spa town of Teplitz, not members of the numerically small indigenous peoples of northern Russia. The contacts with these Russians probably came about through such mutual friends of Amalie and Beethoven as the poet Christoph August Tiedge and his companion, Countess Elisa von der Recke, herself a poetess and a native of Courland (now a region in Latvia but then part of the Russian Empire). 'Long live!' evidently refers to the Russian celebratory song 'Mnogaya leta' ('Many years'), which to this day is sung as a toast during festive meals in Russia. In his second letter to Amalie, Beethoven expressed the hope that 'your Samoyeds will release you today from your voyage to polar latitudes.'[7]

The 'semi-wild' mode of life of certain indigenous peoples in Russia attracted the attention of many a German writer and journalist, including those writing about musical matters. For example, in Christian Friedrich Daniel Schubart's treatise *Ideen zu einer Ästhetik der Tonkunst* (1784), published posthumously in 1806, we find these observations on Russian music: 'There is much that is wild and rough about Russian folk music, as one may readily appreciate. In most of their folk songs one finds

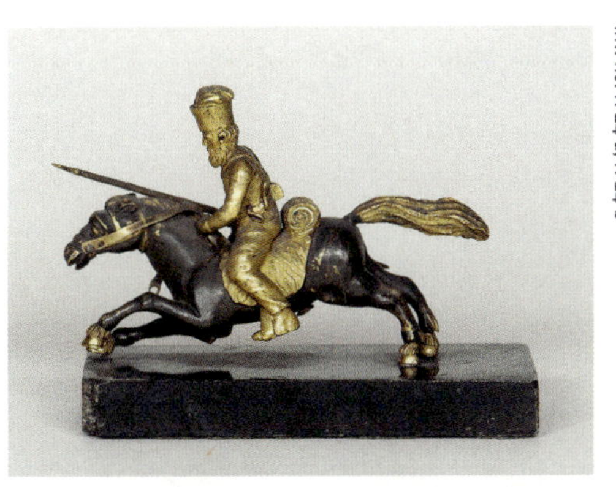

Fig. 2 Statuette of a Cossack on horseback used by Beethoven as a paperweight on his writing desk. Bonn, Beethoven-Haus, inv. no. R 14 a, R 14 b

imitations of the cries of certain birds, which in terms of form and tone greatly resemble those of our wild ducks. A people who in many parts of the country – say, in Kazan, Astrakhan, Kamchatka and Siberia – are still very close to the animal state and are so fond of hunting must easily succumb to such imitation.'[8]

We know that Beethoven read Schubart's book. Moreover, he subscribed to the Leipzig journal *Allgemeine musikalische Zeitung*, which regularly featured essays on musical life in Russia and on the music of her peoples.

To Western Europeans the way of life and music of Russia's 'small peoples' seemed even more exotic than Russian and Ukrainian folk songs proper, which even in the 18th century had found their way into the oeuvre of various composers. Some of those songs became very popular – above all, the 'Kamarinskaya', which was cited by, among others, André Grétry, Ivan Mane Jarnović, Paul Wranitzky and Beethoven himself.

Schubart had observed: 'One may readily imagine the fearsome effect that such music must have when performed by a Cossack regiment.'[9] Beethoven and his contemporaries had plenty of opportunities to set eyes on such Cossack regiments and to hear them sing, for during the Napleonic wars (1799–1815), detachments of Cossacks repeatedly showed up in Vienna and other Austro-German cities. Their outward appearance, conduct and military songs awakened tremendous interest. The Ukrainian song 'Yikhav kozak za Dunai' ('The Cossack rode beyond the Danube'), for instance, became famous across Europe after it was published in 1809 as *Schöne Minka*, in a German translation by Tiedge.[10] Beethoven included an arrangement in his cycle *Lieder verschiedener Völker* (*Songs of Various Nationalities*, WoO 158) and also wrote variations on it for his op. 107 cycle of *Ten National Airs with Variations* (no. 7). The song's tune evidently appealed to him. Indeed, one may detect a certain resemblance between his settings of *Schöne Minka* and the famous Allegretto of the Seventh Symphony. Two statuettes each showing a Cossack on horseback (fig. 2) stood on Beethoven's writing desk, where they served as paperweights; they were most likely a gift from one of his Russian admirers.[11]

Beethoven was a composer not only of the Revolutionary age but also lived in an era of continuous military conflict. Many German and Austrian patriots sympathized with Russia, not least Karl August Varnhagen von Ense, who became friends with Beethoven in the years 1811/12. In a letter from Beethoven to Varnhagen of 14 July 1812 we find the enigmatic phrase: 'Destroy what is bad and keep yourself at the top.'[12] According to Nathan Fishman, this phrase may have been Beethoven's way of signalling his endorsement of Varnhagen's secret plans. Napoleon's invasion of Russia had after all begun on 24 June (NS) and the new war must have been a constant topic of conversation. The words 'Destroy what is bad' can plausibly be interpreted as an allusion to fighting against Napoleon on the side of the Russians.[13] In 1813, Varnhagen duly entered Russian military service and took part in the Wars of Liberation on German territory.

Both professional soldiers and volunteer militiamen found themselves fighting alongside the Russian army. One such volunteer was the poet Theodor Körner, whom Beethoven had asked to write the libretto for an opera to be entitled *Ulysses' Wiederkehr* ('The return of Ulysses'). Körner, however, fell in battle on 26 August 1813 and the *Ulysses* libretto remained unfinished. The collection of Körner's poetry published posthumously in Berlin under the title *Leyer und Schwerdt* ('Lyre and sword', 1814) contains a sonnet, *Moskau*, which deals with the Fire of Moscow.

Despite the censorship in the Viennese newspapers – which did not report on the Fire of Moscow until after a considerable delay and, when they finally did so, drew on French sources and condemned such 'madness'[14] – the sacrificial self-immolation of the ancient Russian capital caught the imagination of contemporaries and became a popular theme for artists. Daniel Steibelt, who was in Moscow at the time, wrote a piano fantasy *Der Brand von Moskau* ('The Fire of Moscow'). At the end of 1812, Karl Friedrich Schinkel presented in Berlin a diorama with moving figures also entitled *Der Brand von Moskau* (fig. 3), while Johann Nepomuk Mälzel set up a similar one in Vienna. It was Mälzel who induced Beethoven to compose a 'battle symphony' in honour of the Duke of Wellington's military triumph in Spain, namely *Wellington's Victory, or the Battle of Vittoria*, op. 91.

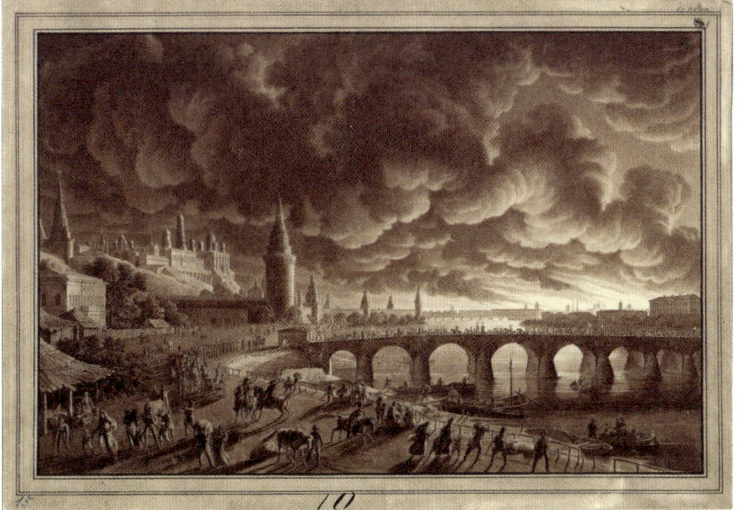

Fig. 3 Karl Friedrich Schinkel, *The Fire of Moscow*, 1812/13. Brush and pen-and-ink drawing in brown and grey, heightened with white, over a pencil sketch, 45 x 64 cm. Berlin, Staatliche Museen zu Berlin, Kupferstichkabinett, inv. no. SM lb.32

The above events formed the backdrop not only for *Wellington's Victory*, but also for the Seventh Symphony – a true 'Symphony of the Year 1812', anticipating in a sense Tchaikovsky's *1812 Overture*, though Beethoven's music is pervaded not so much by images of warfare as by the spirit of unity infusing the European nations in their struggle against Napoleon.

The fact that Beethoven made use of Russian and Ukrainian folk themes on so many occasions testifies to his growing interest in Russian music. Thanks to Count Andrei Razumovsky he was able to acquaint himself with the famous folk song anthology compiled by Nikolai Lvov and the St Petersburg-based Czech composer Jan Bohumír Práč, which was first published in 1790.[15] As is well known, Beethoven used two songs from that collection in the first two string quartets from the opus 59 set, both of which, like the third, were dedicated to Razumovsky. The sensitive treatment of these songs in the 'Razumovsky' Quartets does not square with notions of Russia as a country of barbarians and 'wild' music. This is especially true of the song 'Slava' ('Glory'), which is used in the third movement of the String Quartet in E minor, op. 59, no. 2, as a theme for sophisticated polyphonic variations.

Melodies from the Lvov–Práč anthology crop up in other works by Beethoven, notably in the *Songs of Various Nationalities*, WoO 158 (1816–18), and the *Ten National Airs with Variations*, op. 107 (1817–18). However, the song on which the variations in op. 107, no. 3, are based does not appear in the Lvov–Práč collection, and Beethoven's exact source has to this day not been identified. It was not until 1983 that Nathan Fishman was able, with the help of Boleslav Rabinovich, to establish the song's title – 'Pozhaluĭte, sudarȳnya, syad'te so mnoĭ ryadom' ('I beg you, Madam, pray be seated next to me') – and to track down its first appearances in print in Russia, which date from 1811.[16]

Beethoven's idea of using themes from such collections of folk songs to represent post-war Europe as a 'chorus of nationalities' may well have been influenced by the Congress of Vienna (1814/15), during which all musical genres were in great demand – from the most serious to purely light music. In the latter group were, for example, Joseph Huglmann's potpourri for piano *Polymelos, oder Musikalischer Congress* (1814) and the numerous sets of variations (e.g., by Friedrich Starke, Ignaz Moscheles and Joseph Wilde) on the theme of what was supposed to be the favourite march tune of Tsar Alexander I. Beethoven could not stay aloof from all this, if only because the Tsarina Elisabeth Alekseyevna (fig. 4) and Grand Duchess Maria Pavlovna had shown such munificence in thanking him for the gala concert of his works that he had conducted at the Hofburg palace on 29 November 1814. That concert featured the premiere of the cantata *Der glorreiche Augenblick* (The glorious moment), op. 136, in which one may recognize a distant predecessor of the Ninth Symphony's utopian finale. Beethoven was rewarded

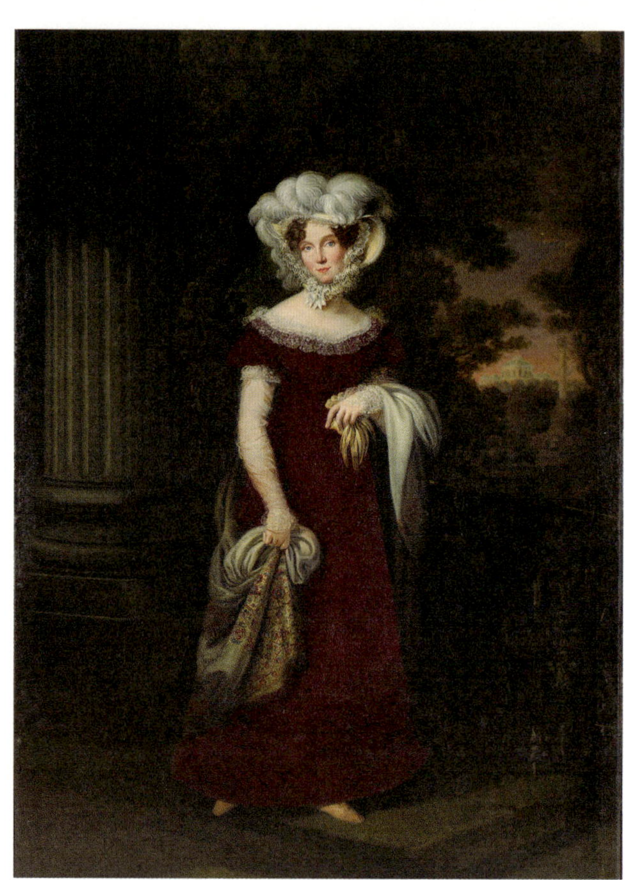

Fig. 4 Ernst-Gotthilf Bosse, *Portrait of the Tsarina Elisabeth Alekseyevna*, 1821. Canvas, 244 x 164.5 cm. St Petersburg, State Hermitage Museum, inv. no. ГЭ-10631

by Maria Pavlovna with 300 florins and by Elisabeth Alekseyevna with around 900 florins. While the grand duchess's gift came to light only relatively recently,[17] that of the tsarina was reported at the time by various Russian newspapers.[18]

It is difficult to overestimate Elisabeth Alekseyevna's gesture. For Beethoven had gone to great personal expense in organizing that concert, and as he wrote to Johann Nepomuk Kaňka in Prague, 'had it not been for the Empress's generous present, I should have been left with almost nothing'.[19] Beethoven's dedication of the Polonaise for piano, op. 89, to the tsarina was meant as a disinterested offering, for which he expected to receive 'no present etc.'[20] in return.

After Razumovsky left Vienna in 1816, Beethoven's contacts with Russian patrons tailed off for a while. However, in the 1820s the 'Russian theme' again came to the fore in both his correspondence and his conversation books. At the end of 1822, Prince Nikolai Golitsyn commissioned three string quartets from Beethoven, initiating a most interesting exchange of letters.

In April 1823, the violinist Ignaz Schuppanzigh returned to Vienna after a stay of several years in Russia; he was often to share his impressions of the country with Beethoven. Although Schuppanzigh told Beethoven in 1824 that 'boozing, stuffing themselves and playing cards' were the 'favourite pastimes of the Russians', he mentioned that preparations for the premiere of the *Missa Solemnis* were under way in St Petersburg and referred to such true connoisseurs of music as Prince Dmitri Saltykov and Golitsyn.[21]

Like many visitors to Russia, Schuppanzigh was fascinated by the church choirs: 'In Russian churches they sing without any instrument and, what is more, they do so with great precision.'[22] At Schuppanzigh's suggestion, Beethoven tried to approach the St Petersburg-based music publisher Carl Lissner.[23] When all was said and done, a country that possessed a quite well-developed concert life, native and foreign-born musicians of a high calibre, and discerning patrons and music publishers could no longer be written off by Beethoven as some sort of 'barbarian fringe' of Europe.

In his letter of 21 June 1823 to the St Petersburg Philharmonic Society, Beethoven spoke of 'la nation Russienne, si noble et si éclairée' and of the 'noblesse Russienne si illustre'.[24] Two years later, in a letter to Prince Golitsyn written around 6 July 1825, he emphasized: 'Believe me when I say that what matters the most to me is that my art should find favour with the noblest and most cultivated people.'[25]

In view of all these statements by Beethoven, it is by no means surprising that he should have intended to dedicate two of his greatest works, the Ninth Symphony and the *Missa Solemnis*, to Tsar Alexander I and the Tsarina Elisabeth Alekseyevna, respectively.[26] Beethoven even contemplated becoming court composer to the tsar if the latter were to assign him an annual pension, 'in return for which,' as he wrote to Prince Golitsyn on 26 May 1824, 'I would send all major works of mine to His Majesty so that he should see them first, and I would also fulfil His Majesty's commissions quickly.'[27]

The Viennese music publisher Tobias Haslinger confirmed the tsar's love of serious music: 'Alexander is very partial to great works.'[28]

The idea of dedicating the Ninth Symphony to Alexander came to naught at the end of 1825, following the tsar's death and the brutal suppression of the Decembrist revolt by his successor, Nicholas I. In early March 1826, the composer's younger brother, Nikolaus Johann, asked him: 'Could one not dedicate the new symphony to the new Emperor of Russia?' However, Beethoven seems to have emphatically rejected that suggestion.[29]

As for the planned dedication of the *Missa Solemnis*, Golitsyn was either unable or unwilling to act as an intermediary in that matter, while the tsarina was evidently unaware of the composer's straitened financial circumstances. Indeed, she led a very reclusive life and did not even attend the premiere of the *Missa Solemnis* in St Petersburg on 26 March (OS) 1824. On that day, she wrote to her mother from Tsarskoye Selo, complaining about her 'impuissance de vivre'.[30]

Beethoven's attitude to Russia was not uniform; his interest in the country's politics and culture fluctuated depending on specific circumstances. However, the trite clichés (Russia as a barbarous country in the grip of eternal cold and sinister despotism) that had at first shaped the composer's mental image of Russia evidently gave way to a growing interest in Russian folk music and in Russia's enlightened patrons of the arts.

1 The Julian calendar was in use in Russia until February 1918. In the 19th century, dates in the Julian calendar, i.e., Old Style (OS) dates, were 12 days behind the Gregorian calendar used in the West. The discrepancy increased to 13 days after 1900, so the New Style (NS) date of Taneyev's above letter would be 19 April 1900.

2 Quoted in N. L. Fishman, *Kniga éskizov Betkhovena za 1802–1803 godÿ. Issledovanie* (Moscow, 1962), 21.

3 [du bist also jetzt in dem Kalten Lande, wo die Menscheit noch so sehr unter ihrer Würde behandelt wird, ich weiß gewiß, daß dir da manches begegnen wird, was wider deine Denkungs-Art, dein Herz, und überhaupt wider dein ganzes Gefühl ist.] J. A. Stargardt, *Autographen aus allen Gebieten. 5. und 6. Juni 2012*, iv: *Musik* (Berlin, 2012), no. 589, 320. The autograph is now held at the Beethoven-Haus in Bonn (inv. no. NE 375).

4 [I greet thee, o land of the icy steppes, | With thy rough, torpid and rude peoples, | Where the innocent are dragged to Arctic climes | And violence still revels unchecked.] Franz Grillparzer, *Sämtliche Werke* (Munich, 1960–65), i, 262.

5 Ludwig van Beethoven, *Briefwechsel. Gesamtausgabe*, ed. Sieghard Brandenburg, 8 vols. (Munich, 1996–98), i, no. 221.

6 Ibid., ii, no. 595.

7 Ibid., ii, no. 596.

8 Christian Friedrich Daniel Schubart, *Ideen zu einer Ästhetik der Tonkunst* (Leipzig, 1977), 193.

9 Ibid., 194.

10 *Schauenburgs allgemeines Deutsches Kommersbuch* (Lahr, 1809), 471, no. 525.

11 They are now in the Beethoven-Haus in Bonn (inv. nos. R 14 a/b).

12 [Zertrümmern sie das Üble und halten sie sich top.] Brandenburg 1996–98 (see note 6), ii, no. 583.

13 L. van Betkhoven, *Pis'ma*, ed. N. L. Fishman & L. V. Kirillina, 4 vols. (Moscow, 2013), ii, 112 (note 8 to letter no. 396).

14 *Österreichischer Beobachter*, 8 Nov. 1812, 1413; *Wiener Zeitung*, 10 Nov. 1812, 405.

15 Ivan Prach, *Sobranie narodnÿkh pesen s ikh golosami* ('Collection of folk songs with their tunes') (St Petersburg, 1790).

16 Fishman & Kirillina 2013 (see note 14), iii, 31–32.

17 Klaus Martin Kopitz, 'Beethoven und die Zarenfamilie: Bekanntes und Unbekanntes zur Akademie vom 29. November 1814 sowie zur Polonaise op. 89', *Bonner Beethoven-Studien*, 5 (1986), 143–49 (145).

18 *Rigasche Zeitung*, 23 Dec. 1814, no. 102; *Moskovskie vedomosti*, 6 Jan. 1815.

19 [wäre das großmüthige Geschenk der Kaiserin nicht – ich hätte beynah nichts übrig behalten] Brandenburg 1996–98 (see note 5), iii, no. 778.

20 Ibid., iii, no. 766.

21 [In Petersburg wird erst jetzt seine Messe einstudiert. ... Saufen fressen und Kartenspielen sind die Lieblingsunterhalt[ungen] der Russen. In Petersburg ist ein einziger Fürst Soltikof welcher für die Künstler etwas thuet] Karl-Heinz Köhler, Grita Herre, Dagmar Beck, Günter Brosche et al. (eds.), *Ludwig van Beethovens Konversationshefte*, 11 vols. (Leipzig, 1968–2001), vi, 260.

22 [In russischen Kirchen singen sie ohne Instrument, und sehr richtig] Ibid., v, 70.

23 Brandenburg 1996–98, v, no. 1647.

24 Ibid., v, no. 1676.

25 [Glauben Sie mir daß mir das Höchste ist, daß meine Kunst bey den edelsten u. gebildesten Menschen Eingang findet] Ibid, vi, no. 2003.

26 In the conversation books from 1824–25 we find frequent references to the idea of dedicating the Ninth Symphony to the tsar, while the plan for dedicating the *Missa Solemnis* to the tsarina was mooted by Beethoven in a letter of 26 May 1824 to Prince Golitsyn (ibid., v, no. 1841) and in conversation book no. 92, which covers August 1825 (*Beethovens Konversationshefte*, viii, 45).

27 [wofür ich alle Großen werke von mir Sr. Majestät zuerst übersenden würde, u. auch aufträge Sr. Majestät schnell erfüllen würde] Brandenburg 1996–98 (see note 5), v, no. 1841.

28 *Beethovens Konversationshefte*, viii, 80.

29 Ibid, ix, 77.

30 State Archive of the Russian Federation, fond 658, list 1, file 10, sheet no. 78.

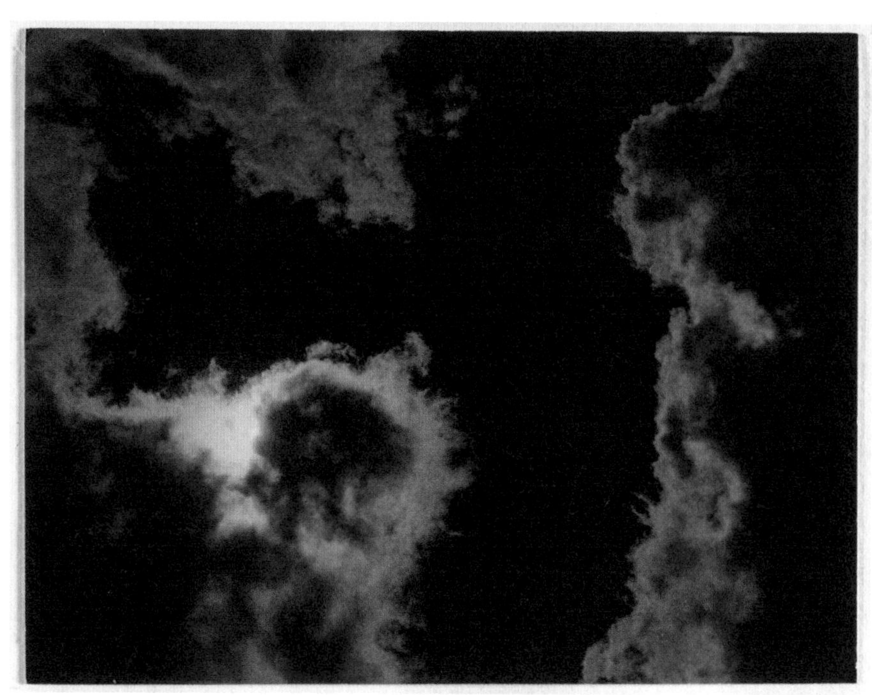

ALFRED STIEGLITZ

Songs of the Sky in Five Pictures 1923

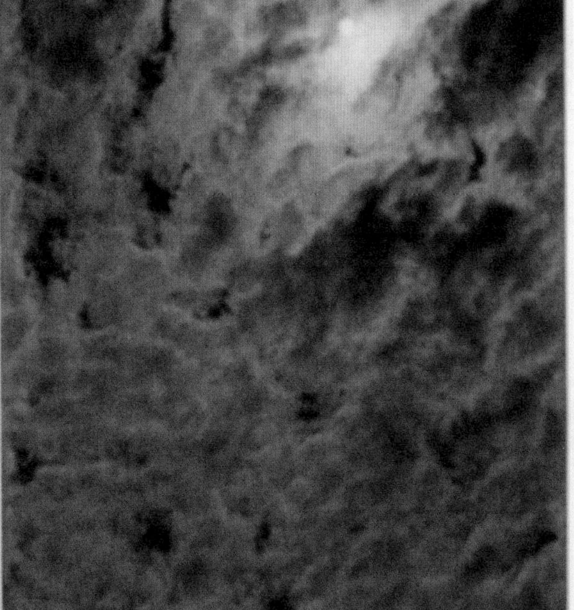

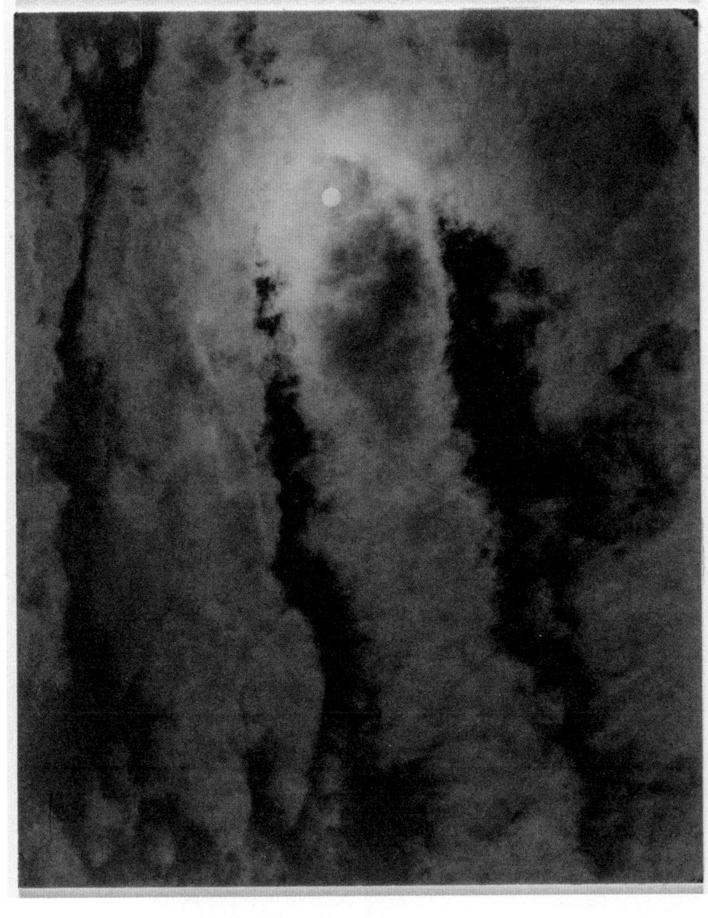

Beginning in 1922, Stieglitz started to point his camera towards the sky. In these abstract images, he sought to evoke in the viewer his own state of mind at the time of taking the picture. The series traces Stieglitz's changeable response to nature, which varies from moments of ecstasy, to infatuation and periods of darkness.

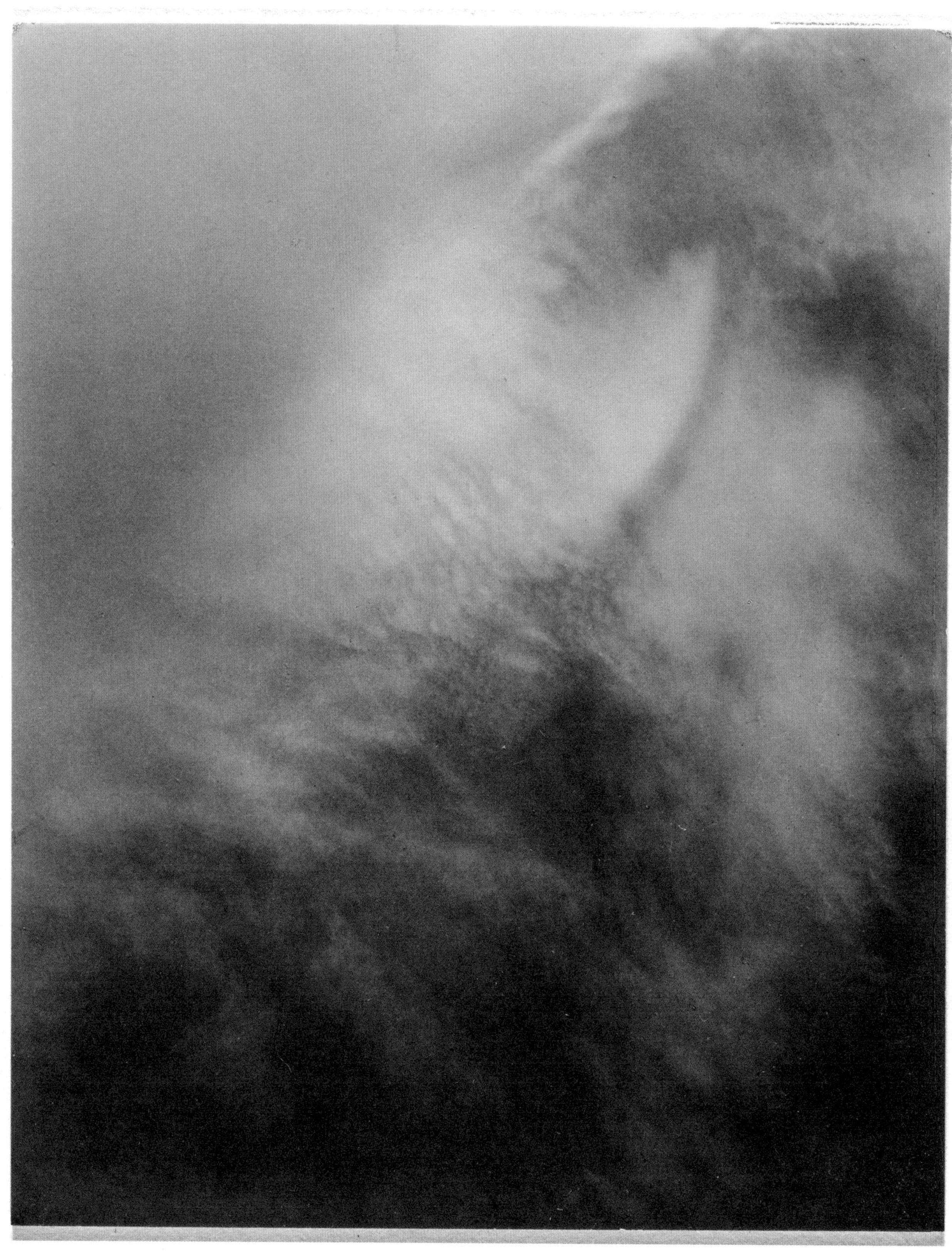

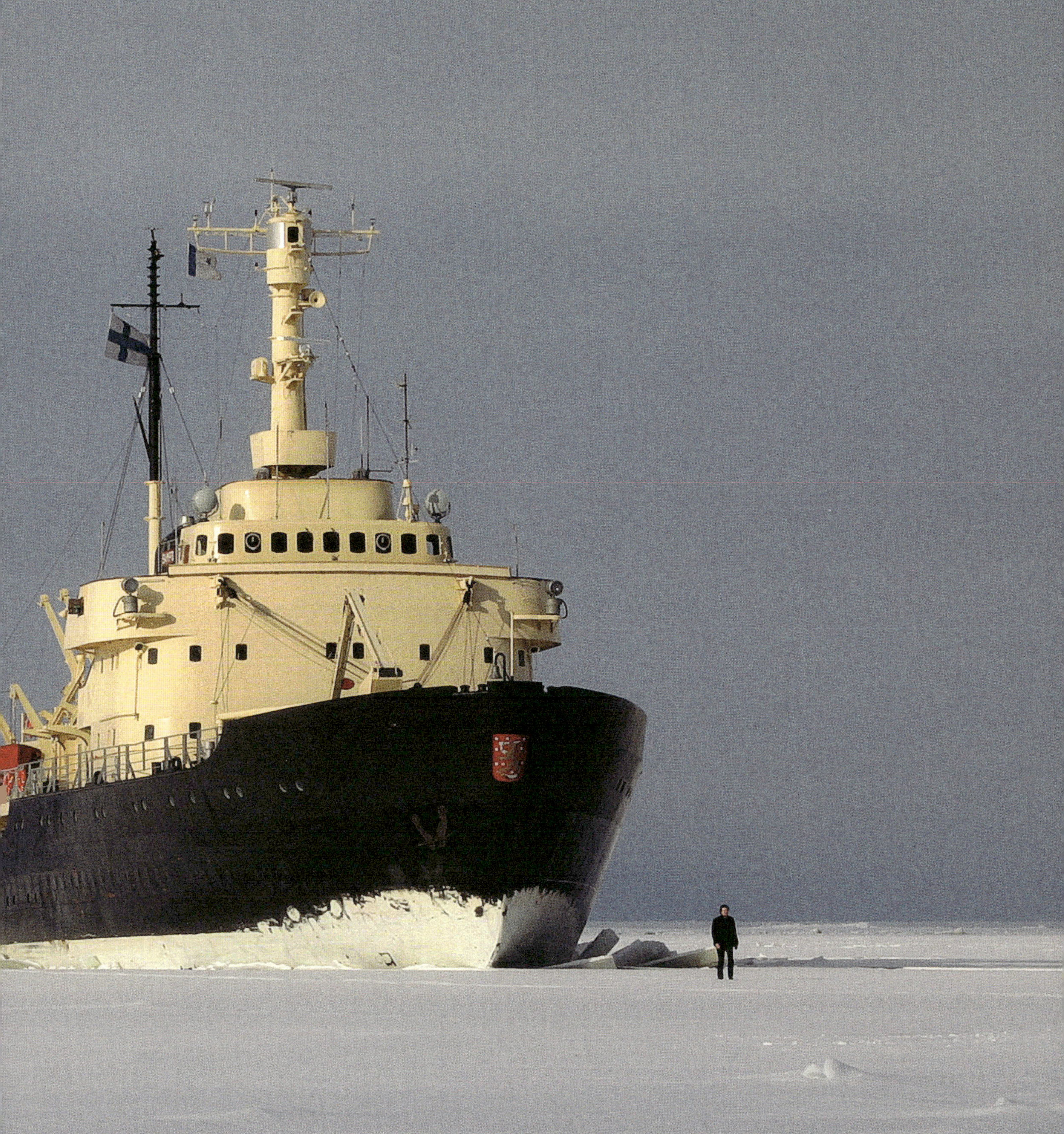

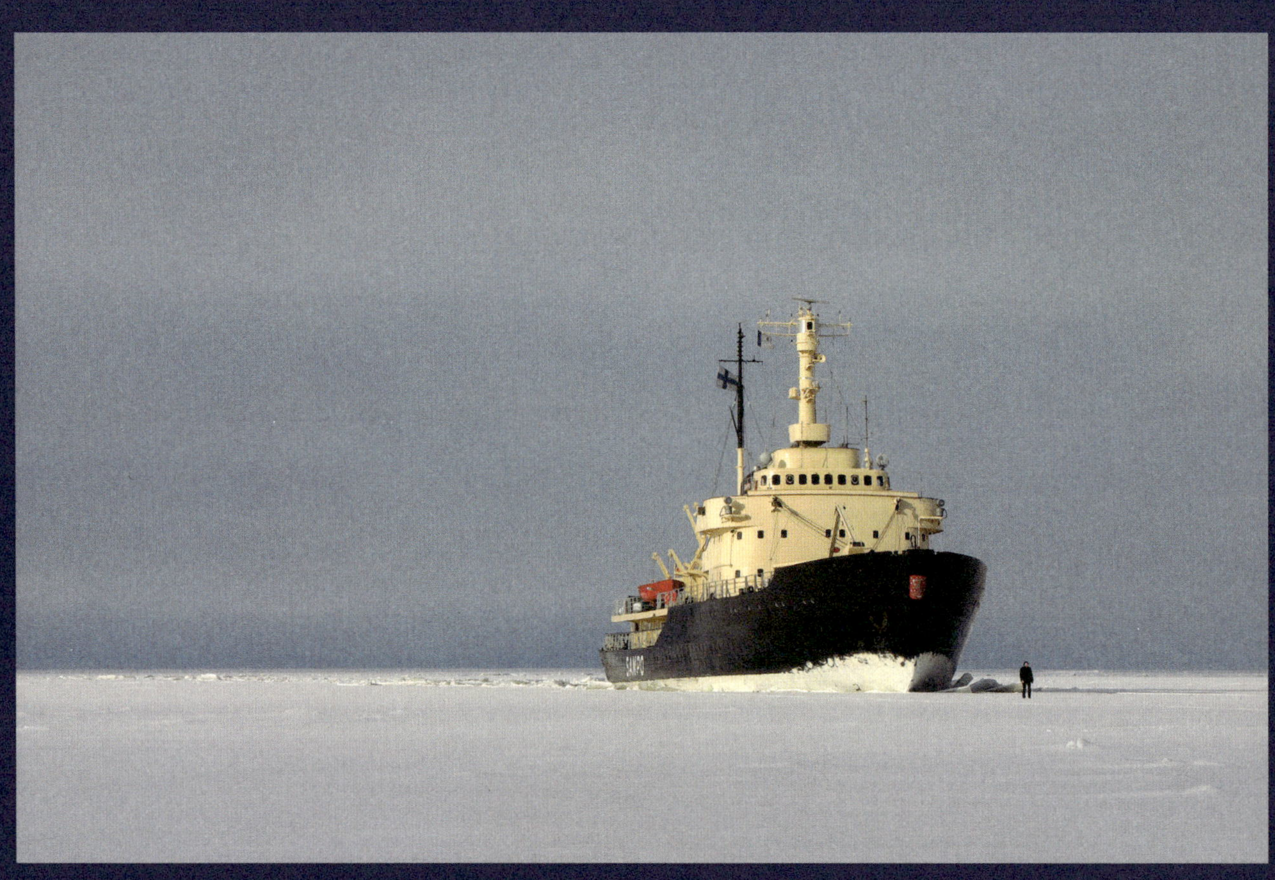

GUIDO VAN DER WERVE, NUMMER ACHT, EVERYTHING IS GOING TO BE ALRIGHT, 2007

ALEIDA ASSMANN

The Heart Is a Lonely Hunter

Today we can hardly imagine a time when music could not be recorded. Those who wanted to listen to music in those times had to ask or have someone around them who was capable of making music. Whether lieder or instrumental works, whether band or orchestra, the only way of experiencing music was through live performance.

When Marcel Proust wished to hear César Franck's String Quartet, he could not simply put on a record: instead, he had to invite the four musicians to his apartment so that they could play it to him. A worldwide market did not emerge for that truly groundbreaking invention, the gramophone record, until the early twentieth century. The new technology had remarkable consequences: the act of listening to music was separated from the musical performance and henceforth developed a life of its own, extending into completely new dimensions and cultural practices.

I should like here to recall a novel from the early years of the broadcasting era, when the world had not yet become fully interconnected. The novel in question is a masterpiece of twentieth-century American literature, *The Heart Is a Lonely Hunter* (1940) by Carson McCullers. In this work, the author, aged just twenty-three when she wrote it, presents to us the complex social make-up of a small town in the southern states during the 1930s, shining a light into the depths of sadness, frustration and violence prevailing there. We are introduced to eccentrics and failures, to people who have been hurt – even crushed – by life, who are violent and yet themselves are the victims of a violence that often erupts by mere chance or unwittingly. In this desolate microcosm, black people aspire to live in dignity alongside their white fellow citizens, but are prevented from doing so by rigid racial segregation. Yet, what unites all the characters in this novel is their impenetrable loneliness. Each chapter has a different protagonist and we are shown one and the same world from their various perspectives. In this way, there unfolds before us a vast narrative panorama which is distinguished by great precision and empathy in the portrayal of human beings.

At the centre of the novel is a thirteen-year-old girl called Mick Kelly who resists being pigeonholed in any way. Her name is deliberately gender-neutral; instead of a skirt, she wears shorts, which was perceived as rebellious in those days. It is her job to look after her younger siblings, but she yearns for something more elevated – above all, for music. Playing the piano enables Mick to escape from the oppressive surroundings; while listening to music she gains a momentary respite from the constraints of her day-to-day life. The name of Mozart she knows only by hearsay, that of Beethoven she has come across once when reading in the library, though she is not familiar with any of his works. Carson McCullers, who was a pianist herself, did not, however, write a typical teen novel about a budding artist, for Mick does not end up studying at a conservatoire, like her creator, but working at the checkout till of a supermarket.

The Kellys have no radio set at home: that was then a luxury which only well-heeled families could afford. Mick, however, knows precisely where such magic devices are to be found and when is the best time to go stalking. In the evening, she leaves her area of town and, as twilight descends, makes her way to the wealthy villa quarter, where she finds a hiding place in one of the spacious gardens, as close as possible to an open window. Under cover of a tree or bush, she then waits patiently for the evening programme to start with its music broadcasts; quite often she dozes off until she is awoken by the sounds she so longs for.

One such musical experience is described at length. In this case it is the strains of Beethoven's 'Eroica' Symphony that stir her from her sleep. She is bewildered by this music because what she is hearing is something utterly unheard of and unique. The sounds sweep past her impetuously. She surrenders herself not only to this music's power and novelty but also to its transience, for it would be folly to hope that this experience might ever be repeated. She is completely overwhelmed and overtaxed as she attempts not just to follow the music emotionally while listening to it but simultaneously also to absorb and retain it in her mind.

> She could not listen good enough to hear it all. The music boiled inside her. Which? To hang on to certain wonderful parts and think them over so that later she would not forget – or should she let go and listen to each part that came without thinking or trying to remember? Golly! The whole world was this music and she could not listen hard enough. Then at last the opening music came again, with all the different instruments bunched together for each note like a hard, tight fist that socked at her heart. And the first part was over. [...] But maybe the last part of the symphony was the music she loved the best – glad and like the greatest people in the world running and springing up in a hard, free way. Wonderful music like this was the worst hurt there could be. The whole world was this symphony, and there was not enough of her to listen.[1]

In his influential essay, Walter Benjamin argued that, in the age of mechanical reproduction, works of graphic art forfeited their 'aura' and turned into merchandise. The example of Mick Kelly demonstrates that this hypothesis cannot simply be applied to music. Although her encounter with Beethoven is facilitated by a device for mechanical reproduction (i.e., a radio), that encounter has the overwhelming effect of a revelation on her. The radio has in no way made her musical experience banal or shallow; rather, it has conveyed to her the music's aura as well as its sounds.

1 Carson McCullers, *The Heart Is a Lonely Hunter* (Boston/New York, 2000), 118–19.

Nineteenth-century critic Walter Pater's famous statement that 'all art constantly aspires towards the condition of music' greatly influenced Whistler's work as a young artist. The parallels between art and music underpin many of his artworks, which he often called 'arrangements' or 'nocturnes' in order to emphasize their tonal harmony.

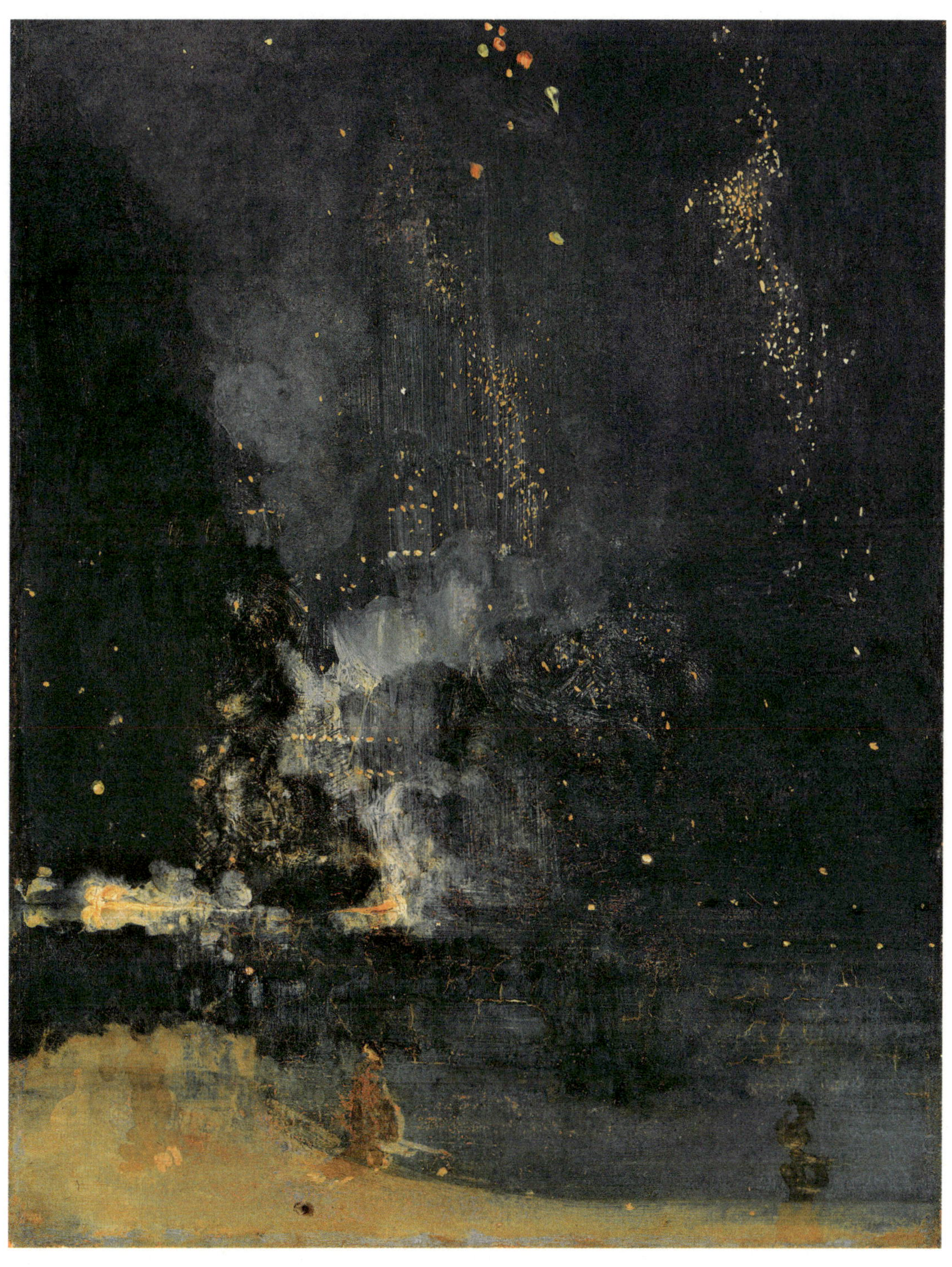

JAMES A.M. WHISTLER

Nocturne in Black and Gold: The Falling Rocket 1875

OLGA FLOR

Death Mask

When I was very young a death mask hung above the piano. That was around the time when the great-aunt who went with it was still sleeping in the small study because the marital bedroom of her long-dead parents was sacrosanct. She knew her place in the world; even her name was a magnificent fit. But she was still a nice aunt who made jam with a certain passion.

Music was sacred too, hence the altar to Beethoven: a pale, grey portrait with closed eyes and a slight sheen. It was a devotional image in its secular variant below which music was to be played with appropriate devotion. I wondered why the facial expression of a corpse should be admired as the cast of the mortal remains of a person, when the very term itself implied that it was the mortal – the deceased, in fact – that was being revered in this way, instead of the immortal. Somewhat later, I came to understand that at the same time the structure of the artistic achievement, that which was considered immortal, had entered conceptual awareness quite unconsciously and naturally; in particular its apogee, the symphony – the form of thesis-antithesis-conflict-resolution –, a path that could be followed, certainly at a preconscious level. And if so, I probably left that path, as I did most paths, somewhere along the way and returned to it only here and there as happens to those who let their writing lead the way. Strange too that music, unlike written language, has such an immediate effect on the emotions, regardless of what the listener does or does not want. It seems to contradict the rigid formal language and construction at its heart in that very act: unconscious sensation formed by what has been consciously formed? True, one can imagine the sound of language while writing and give the language a rhythm and impose motifs upon it and then pick them up again or even negate them – but it will inevitably trip over the conscious thought which is attempting to decipher it; a hurdle that music skirts all by itself.

And that also expresses the problem that I have with music: that it makes you so helpless. The fact for example that I will be sitting in the audience listening to choral music and the tears will come almost unbidden – just because of the voices, and I'm sure also because of their quantity, and at any rate entirely independent of what they are actually singing, so that reading the lyrics afterwards will make you wonder, surprised at yourself. At the fact that the overwhelming power of music lies deep within it, and every attempt at reflection is doomed to fail. Hardly any other medium achieves such immediacy, and that makes music great and sacrosanct and opulent. Only spoken language can come close to such opulence, if at all, and even then it does so at the risk of pathos. Language isn't supposed to seek pathos, it gives it a hollow, rattling sound. But I was attracted by the transformation of language through rhythm, alliteration, figures of speech, which I encountered in the Latin classes that everybody so loves to hate, even though I seldom dared to admit it. And after all: hexameters can drone on endlessly too.

The miracle of the sound originating from drily jotted notes also always seemed stranger to me the longer I thought about it; I didn't actually understand the process, even though I had lived through the whole petit bourgeois flute-and-piano kerfuffle – and it only became clear to me in retrospect that something so extremely irritating had in fact granted me privileged access to music. Nevertheless: in a quite fundamental way music escaped its written form. Because what I understood least of all was how separate scores could be freed from the idea of orchestral sound. How it was even possible to hear the harmony in your head in advance. Beethoven going deaf seemed only logical in this respect, at least not as a significant obstacle in the path of composition. Not that I would ever have got any closer to solving the riddle of how to get from the sound in one's head to the picture on the music stand. The converse, picture to sound, was more easily imaginable, at least theoretically. And there was something truly seductive about the possibility of becoming part of a music ensemble as an individual. For children's choir, it seemed to be required to roll my 'r', so I learned it specially: BADLED BADLED BDLED BREAD. Once again, a riddle before you got the hang of it, and afterwards internalized for ever, even if you couldn't say exactly how.

I saw another problem in the fact that music seemed to go hand in hand with the corresponding emotions; I wondered if I had the right emotions – because it seemed obvious that they must exist – and was sometimes disappointed that I couldn't make that apparently obvious connection, and was less able to do so the more I thought about it. Beethoven's music was overwhelming, however, even its pathos was, and he therefore claimed an absoluteness from within the music itself that could be highly unsettling.

It seemed to me that there was music the experience of which induced an almost inescapable sense of community, music made for big spaces with big emotions for a big audience. On the other hand there was also the experience of music that is best listened to alone, music that is quieter, which also has its charms when played before a big audience, but is almost engulfed by the sheer mass of breathing, living bodies, music which requires silent concentration from everyone. Beethoven has always overtaxed me: the power, the force, the breadth, the work, the *genius* – a concept that is for the first time properly constituted in his person. Music whose dramatic element and its development are inescapable, and which has for that very reason been instrumentalized and also abused.

My aunt died and the flat was cleared. The libretto for *Fidelio* – and as a girl I took libretti very seriously, and was frequently confronted with them, since my mother loved pretty much everything about operas which were played in a historicizing environment – was by a long way the only thing that seemed to me to promise an interesting woman's part, albeit in men's clothing. I read the libretti because I wanted to understand what was happening; the lyrics mostly seemed incomprehensible to me when sung, particularly those of Wagner operas – and after all such a libretto could be read quickly, and even more quickly the synopses in a so-called *Opera Guide* which I read time and again. The heroine who struggles through the hierarchy of the prison and eventually holds the murderous tyrant in check with a pistol – I was enthralled. At last something other than all those Traviatas and Aidas and Carmens perishing beautifully for ever, the mad Lucias, the self-sacrificing Marschallins and Mozart's modestly marriageable heroines. Yes, I liked this opera, and only grasped much later that it should be read as a reaction to the French Revolution. In this realization I also suddenly liked steadfast love. The man I was going to rescue one day would be like that. Admittedly he was a bit passive, but I was confident that we could sort that out and in any case Leonore could stand up to evil itself. What a gain! But the mask had disappeared along with my great aunt, even though the two of them never left the world of my imagination.

This series seems to evoke a walk in the woods, the whiteness resembling the Mediterranean sea that was visible from Twombly's studio in Italy. Discussing his inspiration, Twombly stated 'I spend more and more time sitting in the window looking at the sea. With certain works … it's interesting because it's more like music.' Nicholas Serota (ed.), *Cy Twombly: Cycles and Seasons* (London, 2008), p. 49.

CY TWOMBLY

Untitled I (Green Paintings) [A Painting in Six Parts] 2002/03

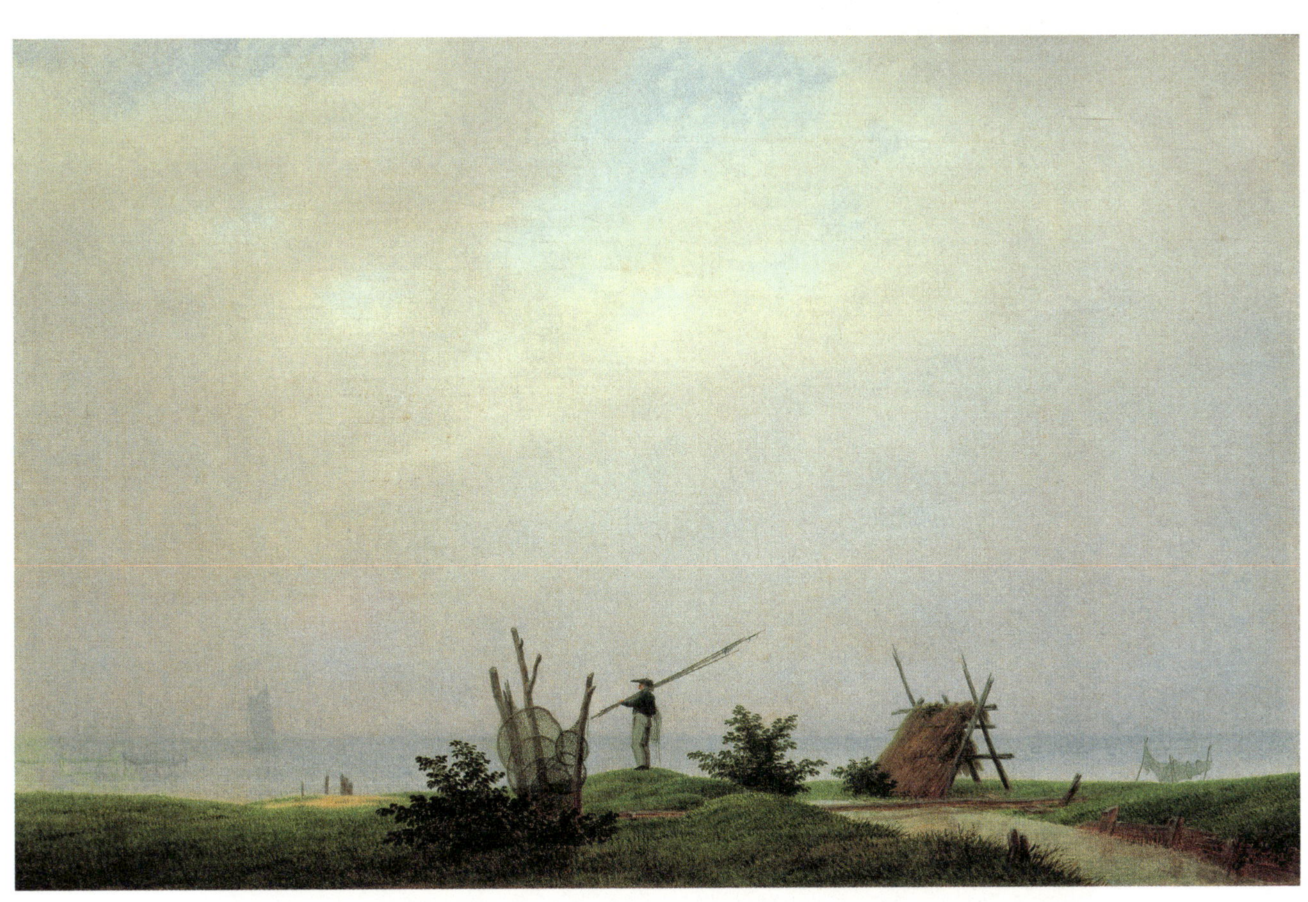

CASPAR DAVID FRIEDRICH

Seashore with Fisherman
c.1807

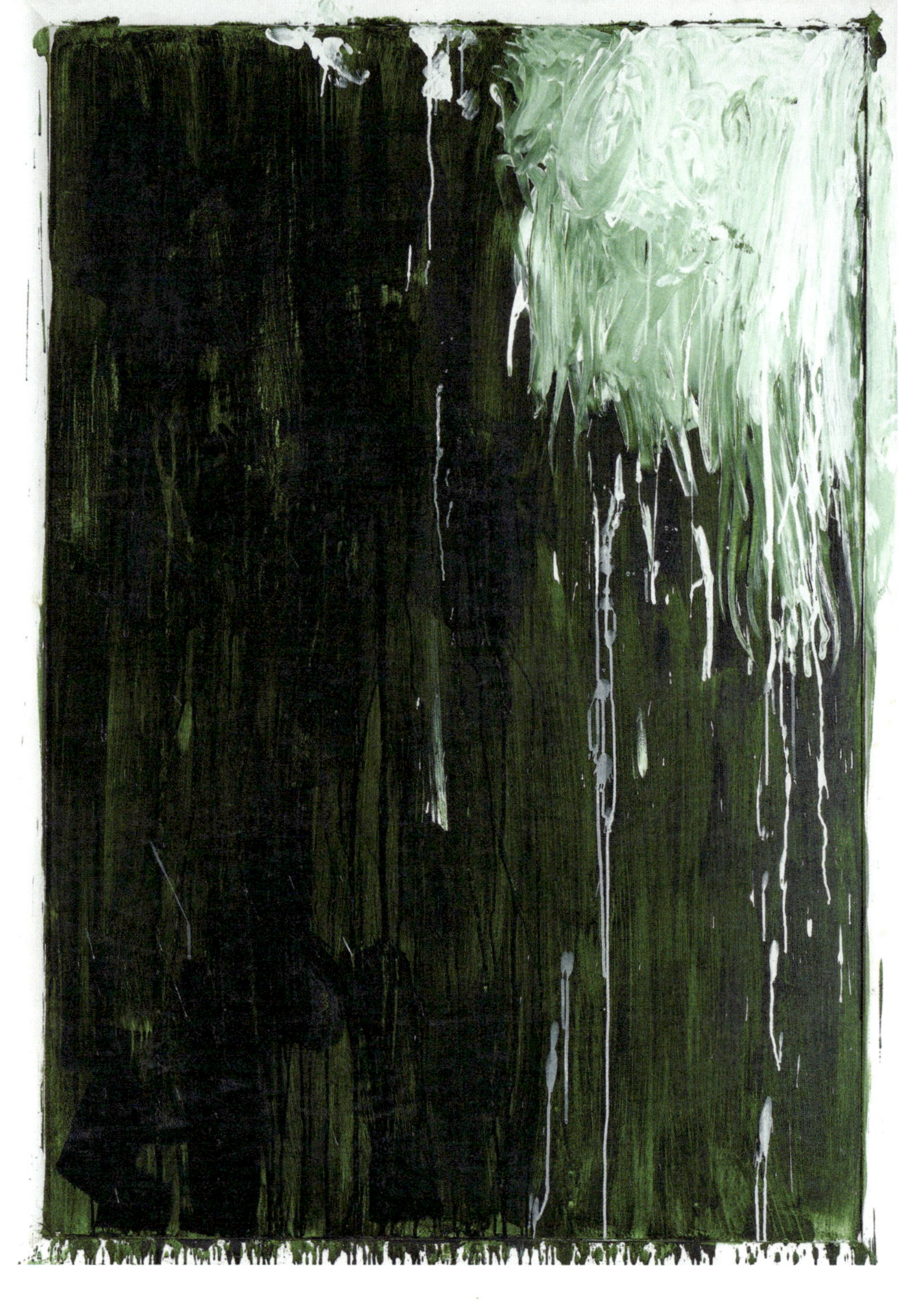

CY TWOMBLY

Untitled II (Green Paintings)
[A Painting in Six Parts]
2002/03

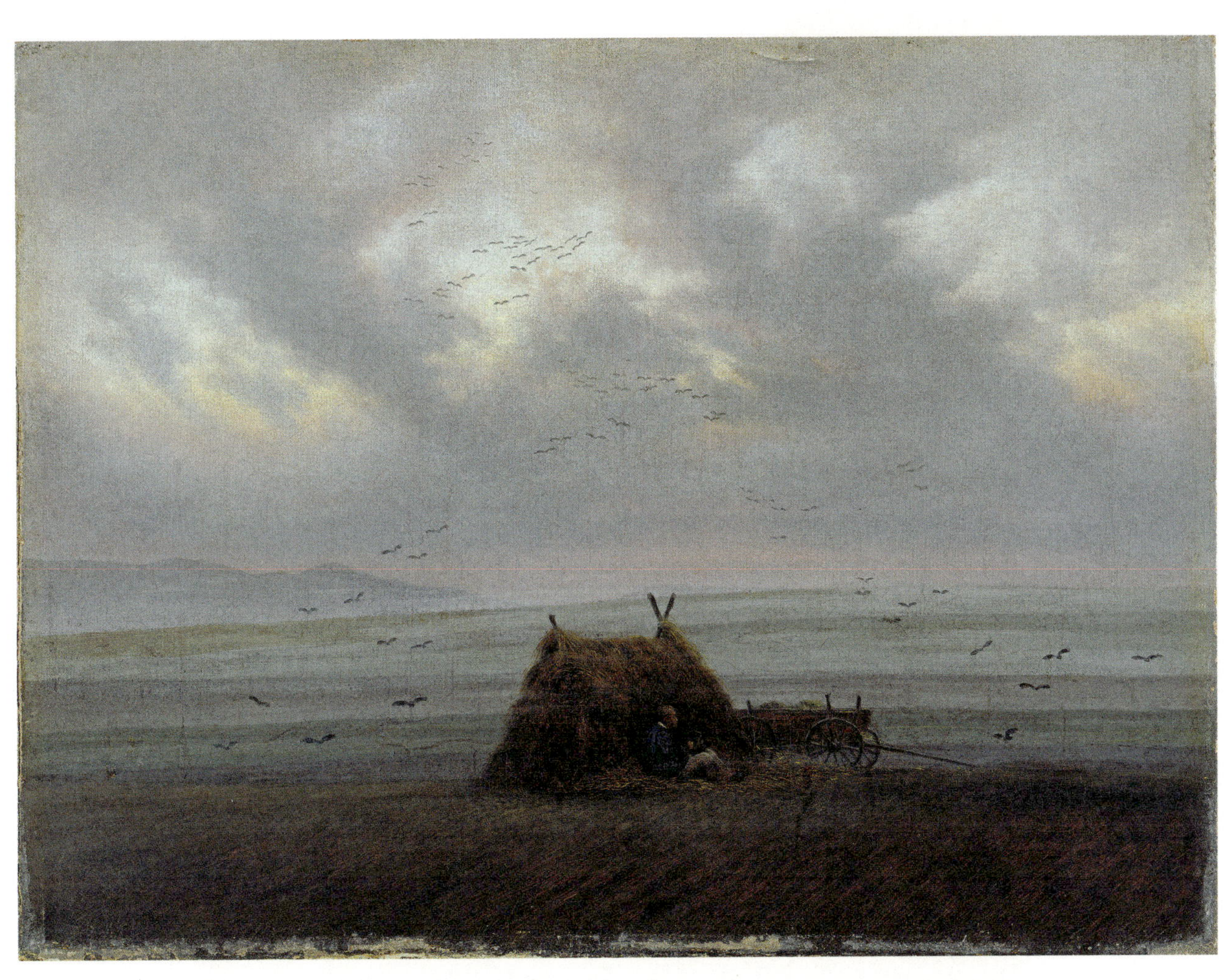

CASPAR DAVID FRIEDRICH

Billowing Clouds
c.1820

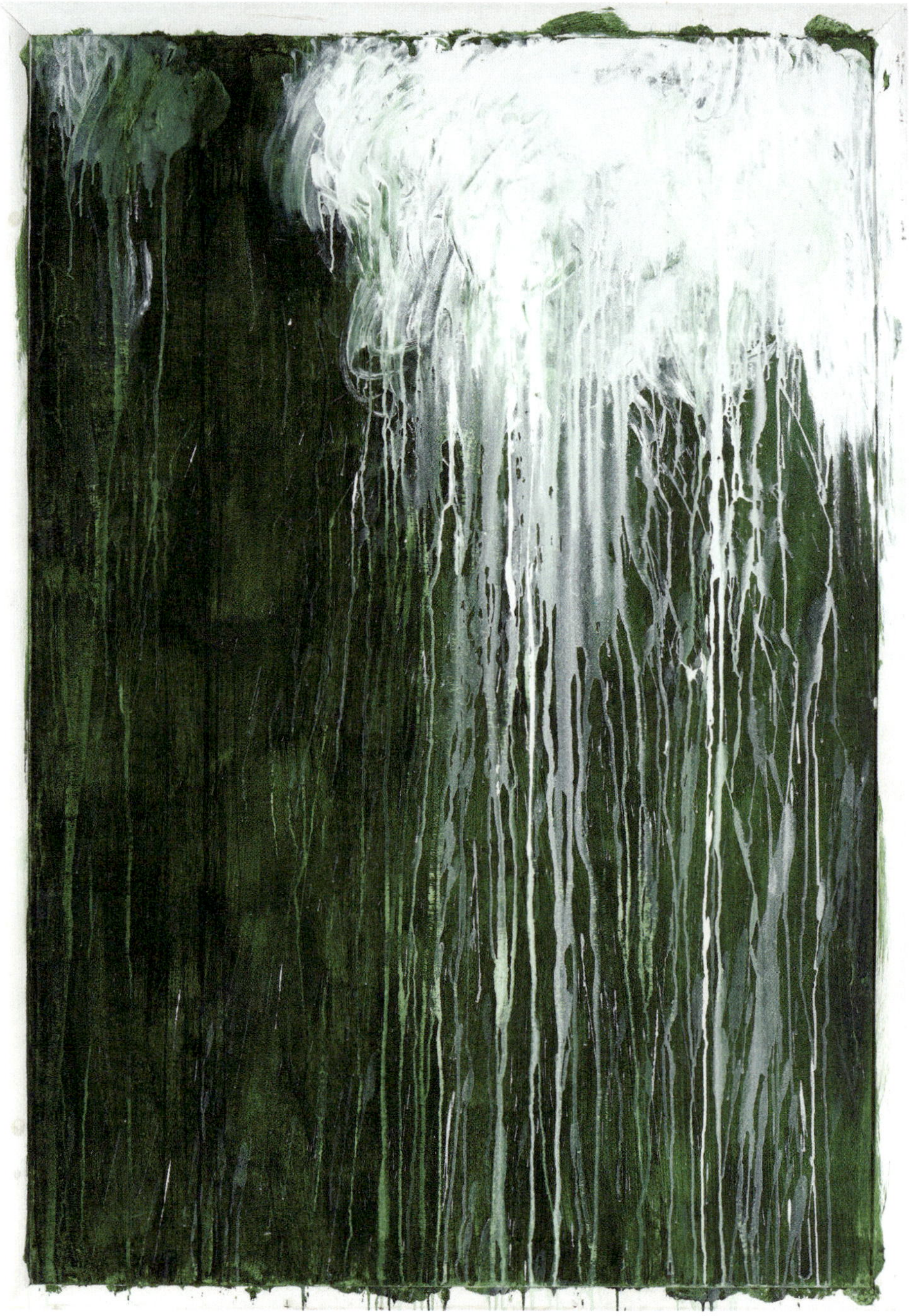

CY TWOMBLY

Untitled III (Green Paintings) [A Painting in Six Parts] 2002/03

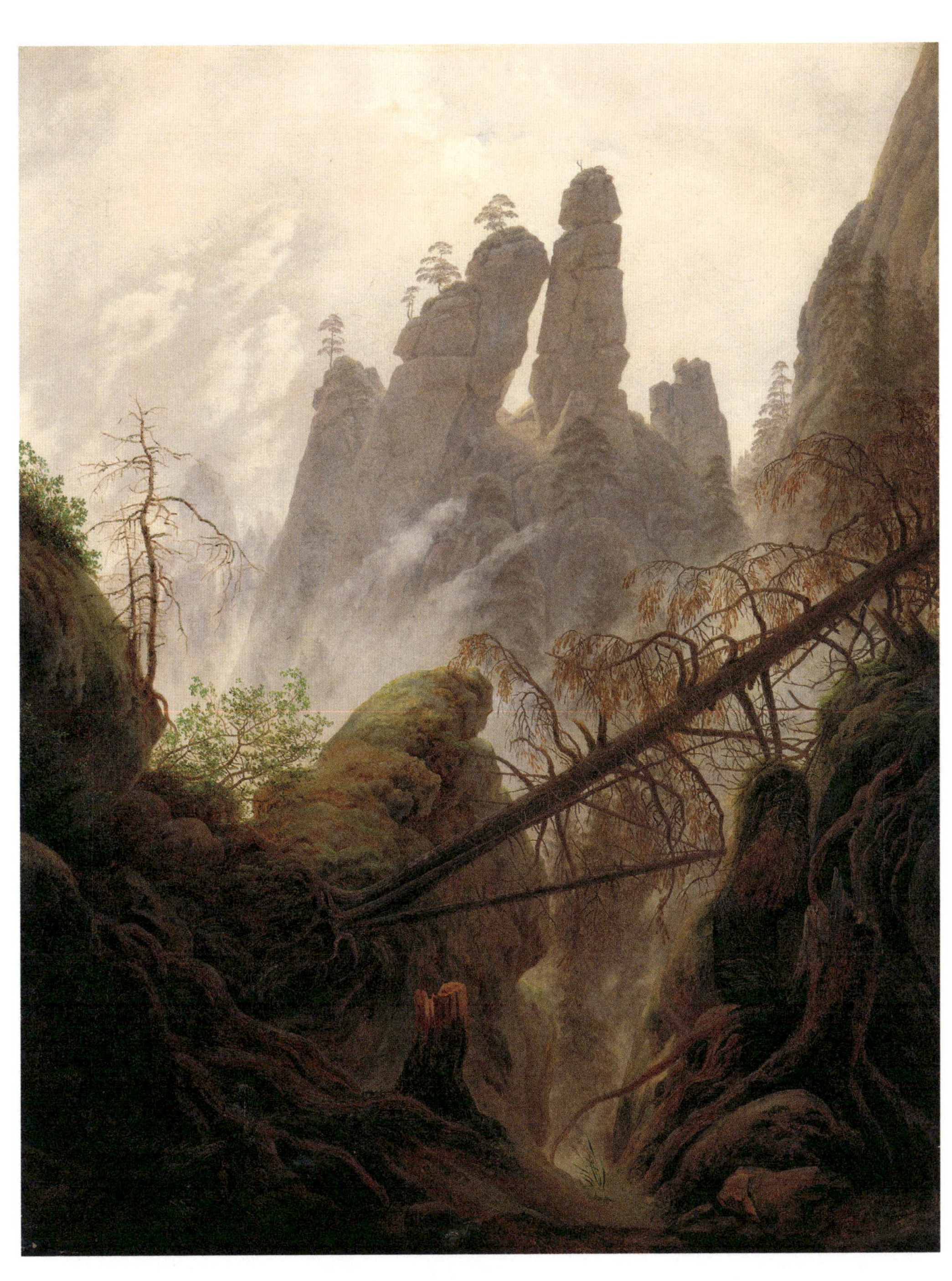

CASPAR DAVID FRIEDRICH

Rocky Landscape in the Elbe Sandstone Mountains 1822/23

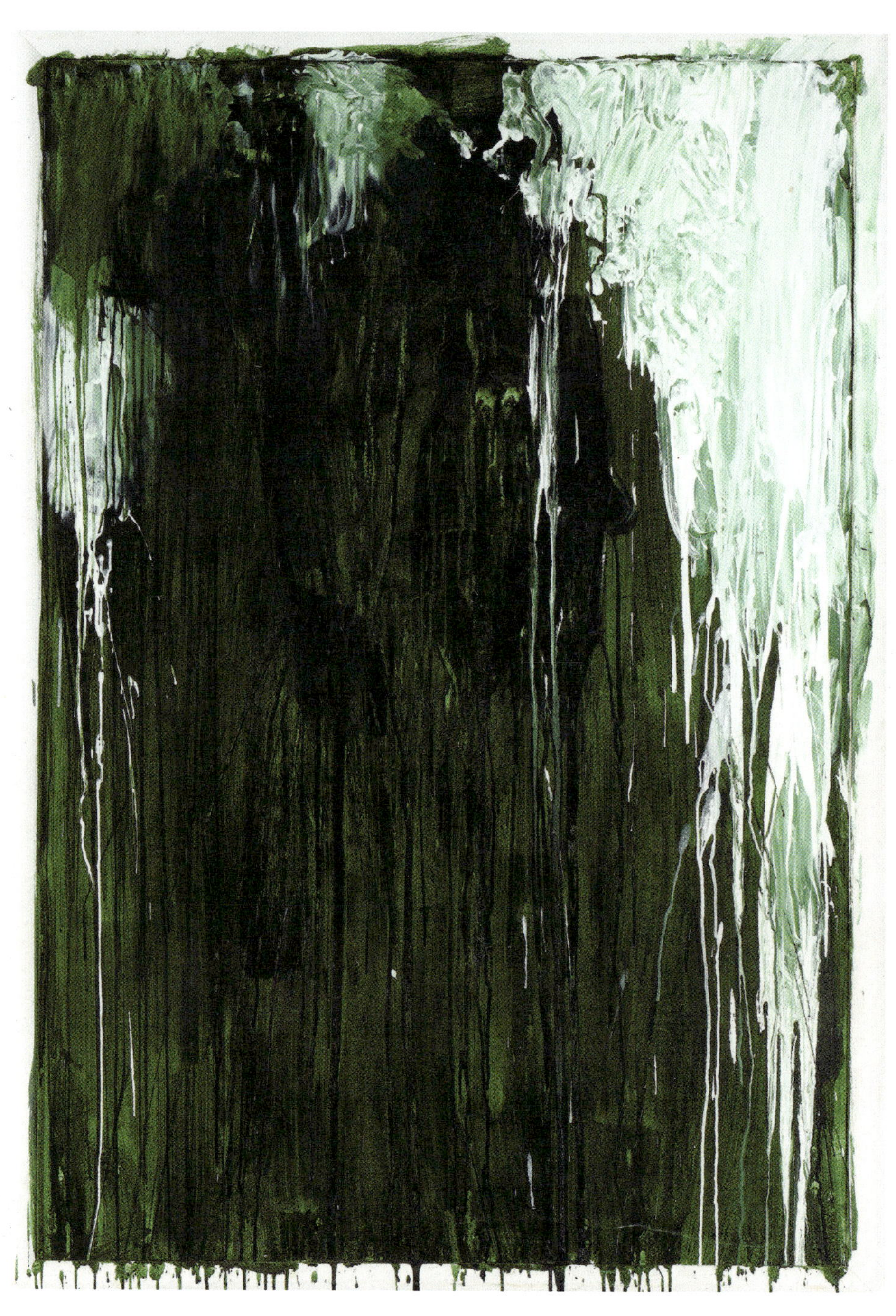

CY TWOMBLY

Untitled IV (Green Paintings)
[A Painting in Six Parts]
2002/03

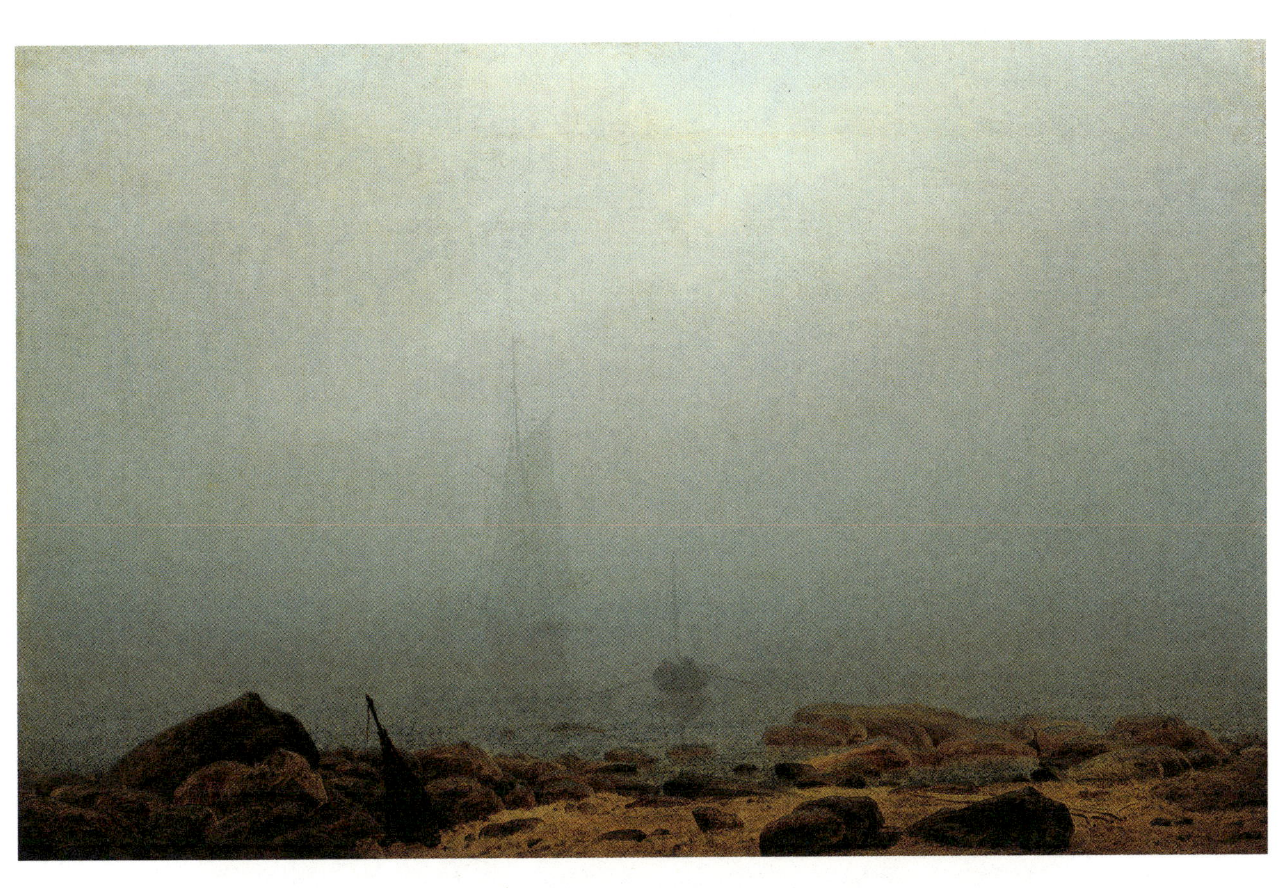

CASPAR DAVID FRIEDRICH

Seashore in the Fog
c.1807

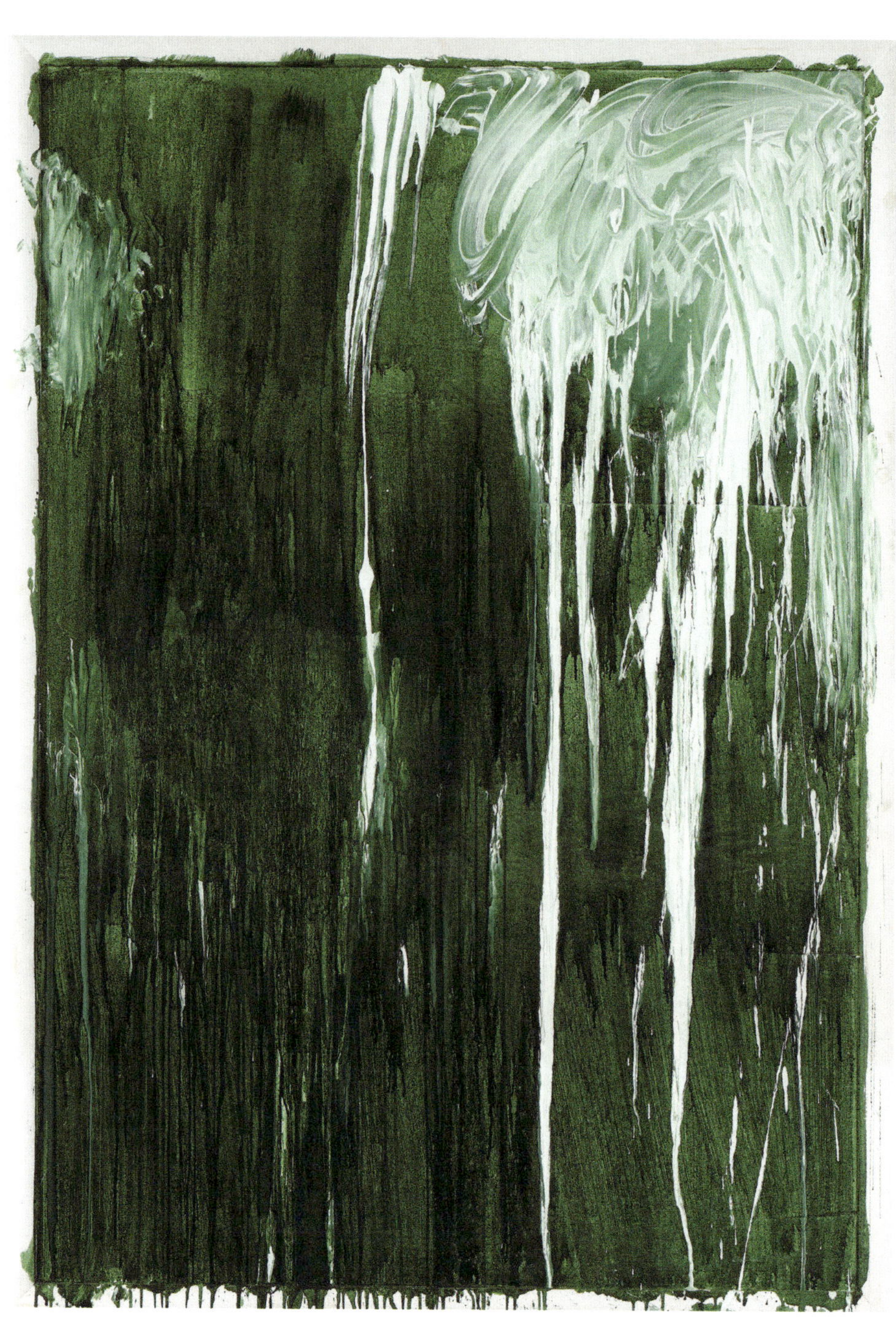

CY TWOMBLY

Untitled V (Green Paintings)
[A Painting in Six Parts]
2002/03

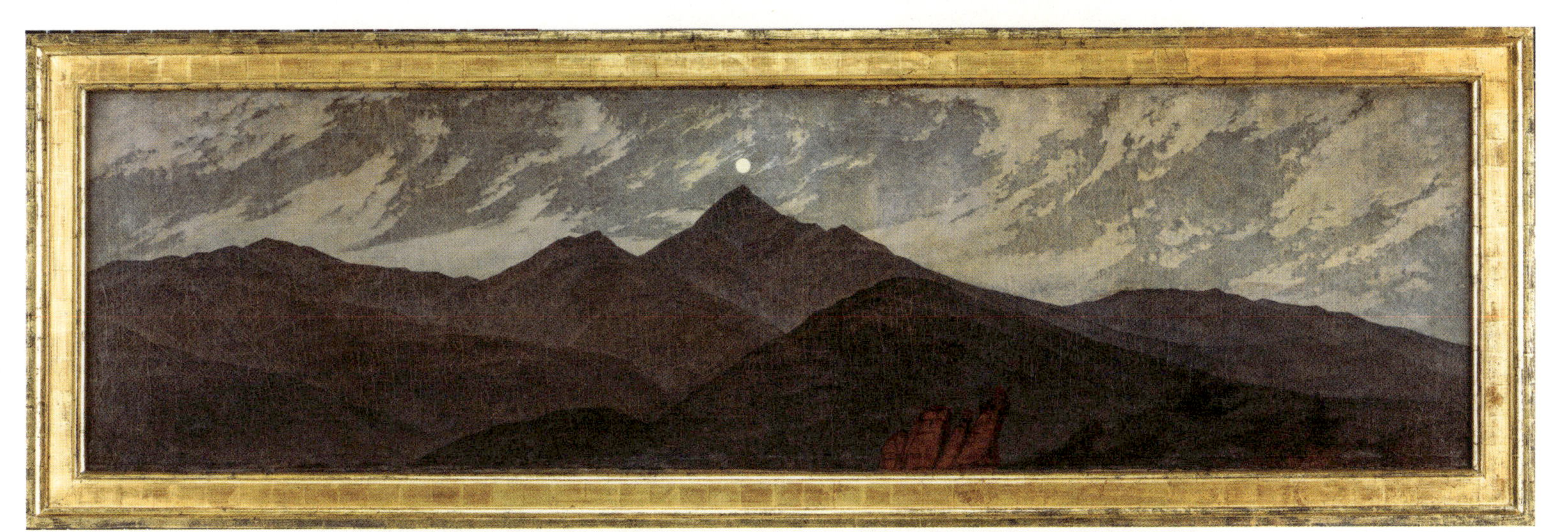

CASPAR DAVID FRIEDRICH

Moon above the Riesengebirge
c.1810

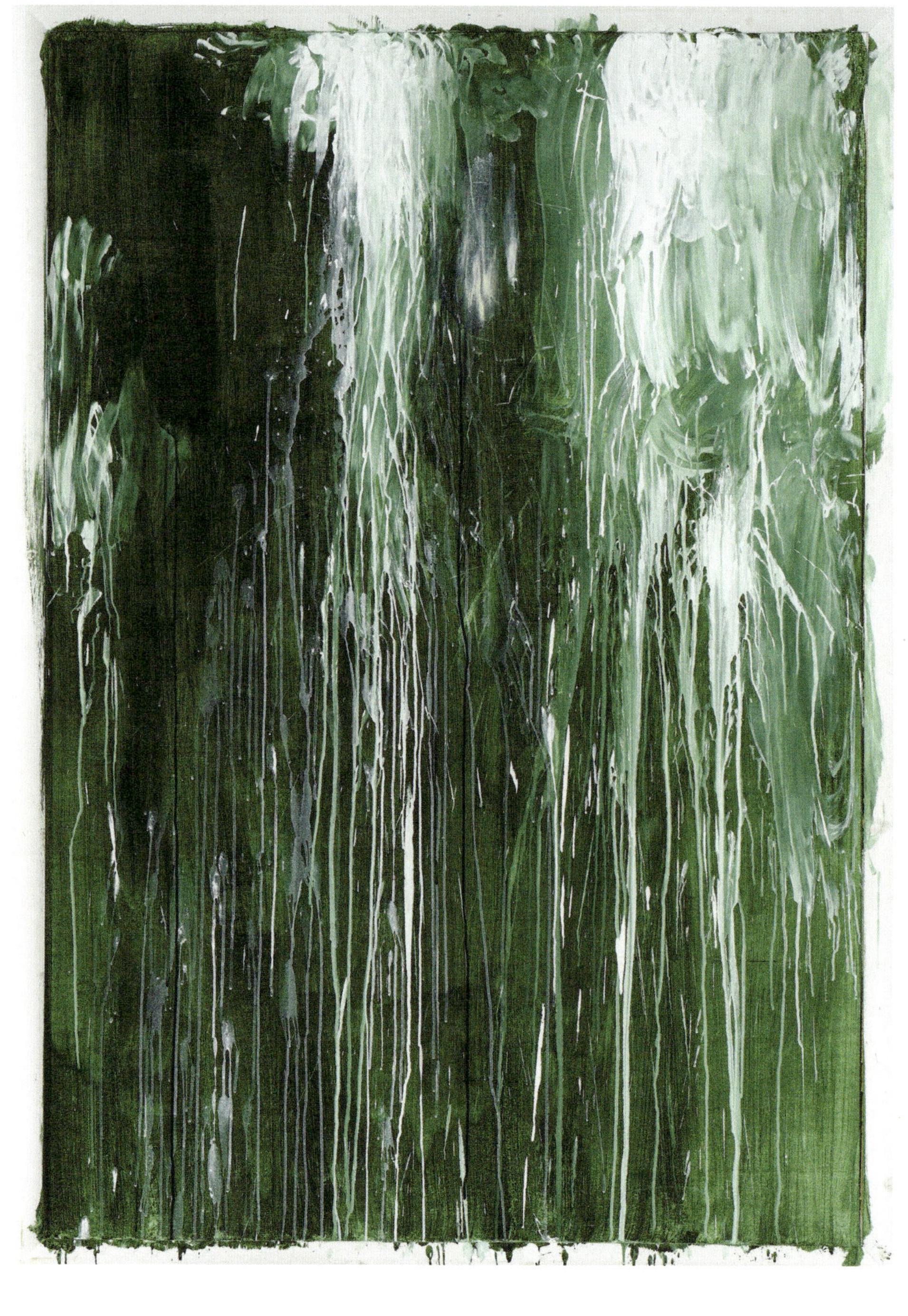

CY TWOMBLY

Untitled VI (Green Paintings)
[A Painting in Six Parts]
2002/03

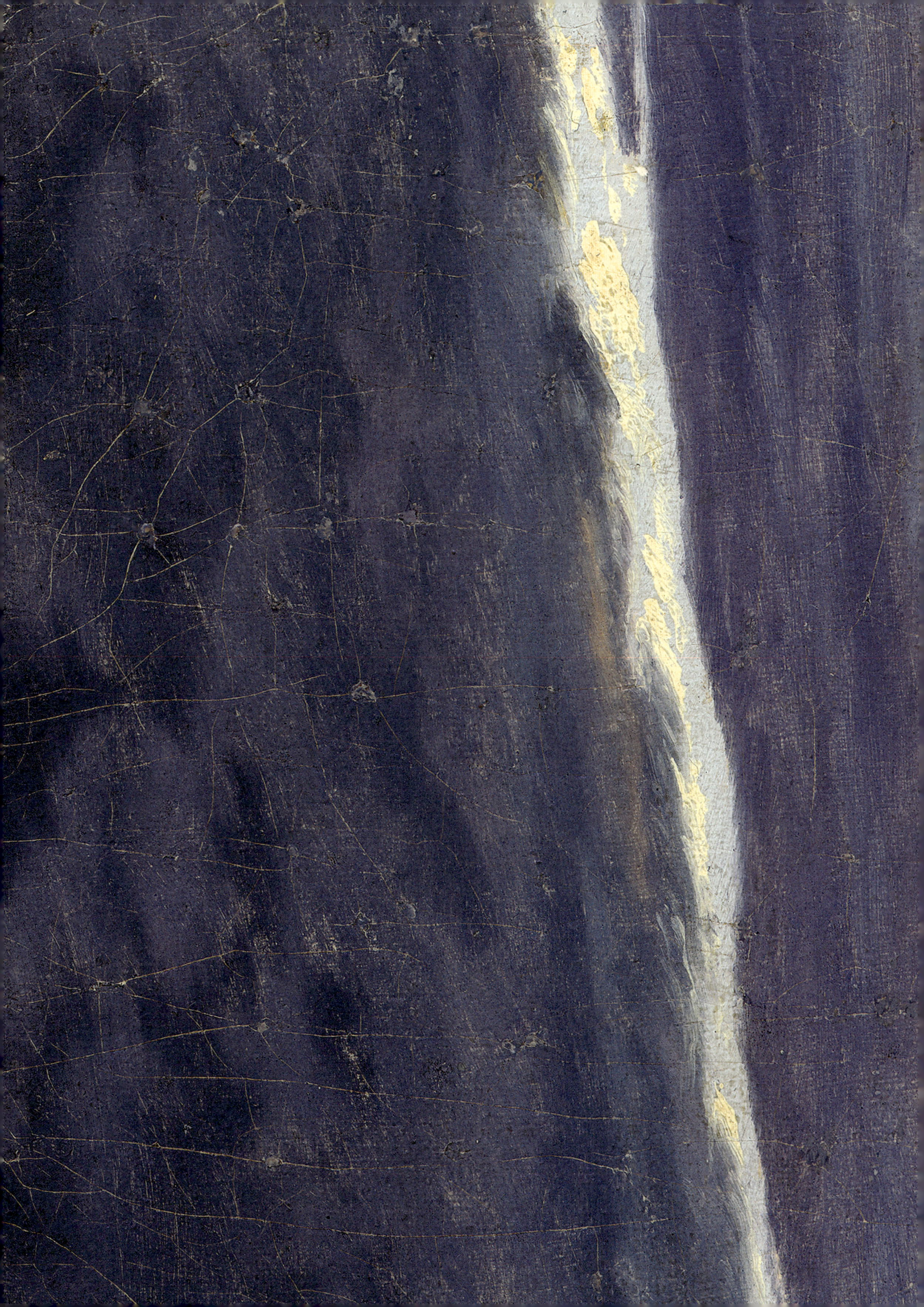

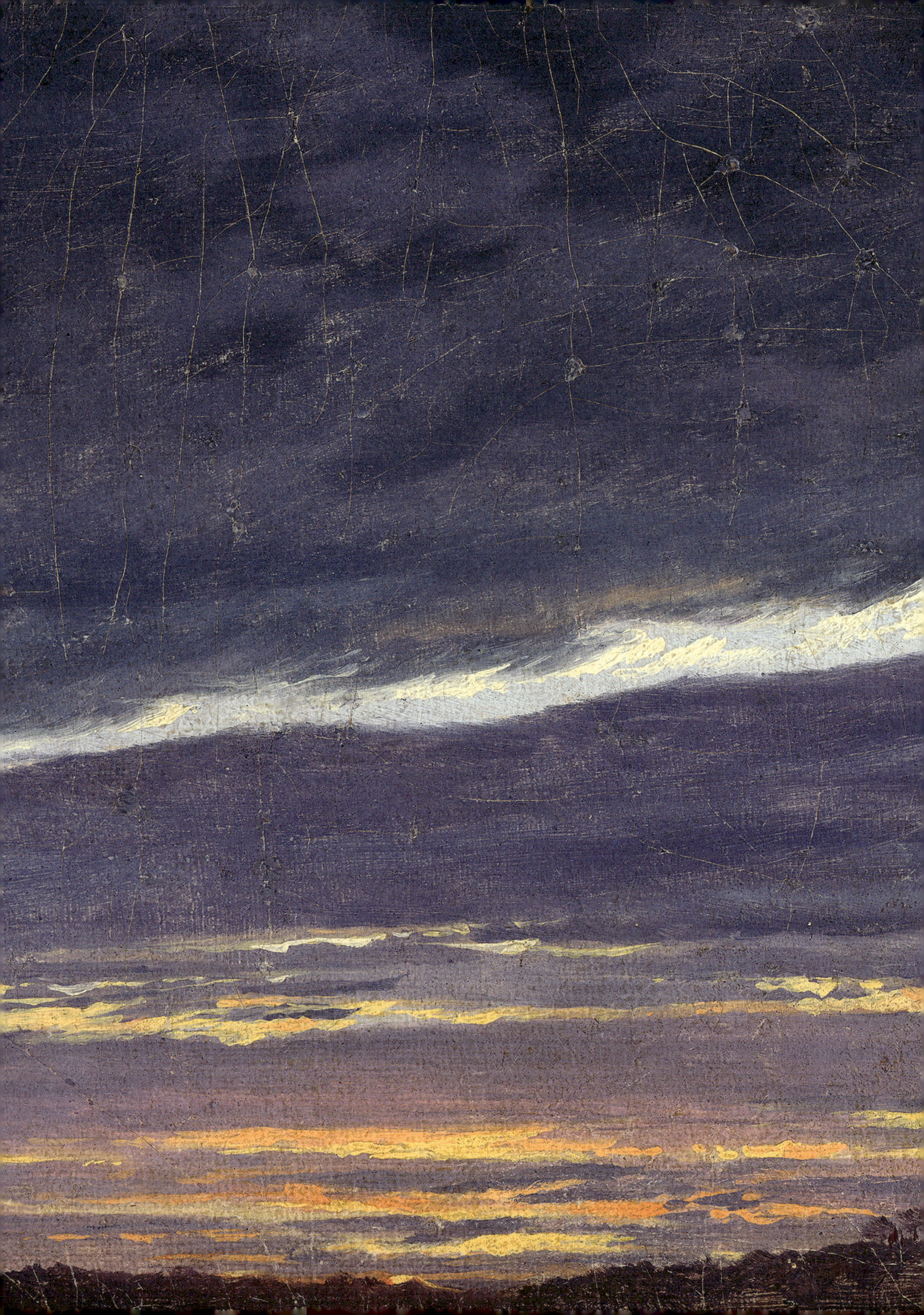

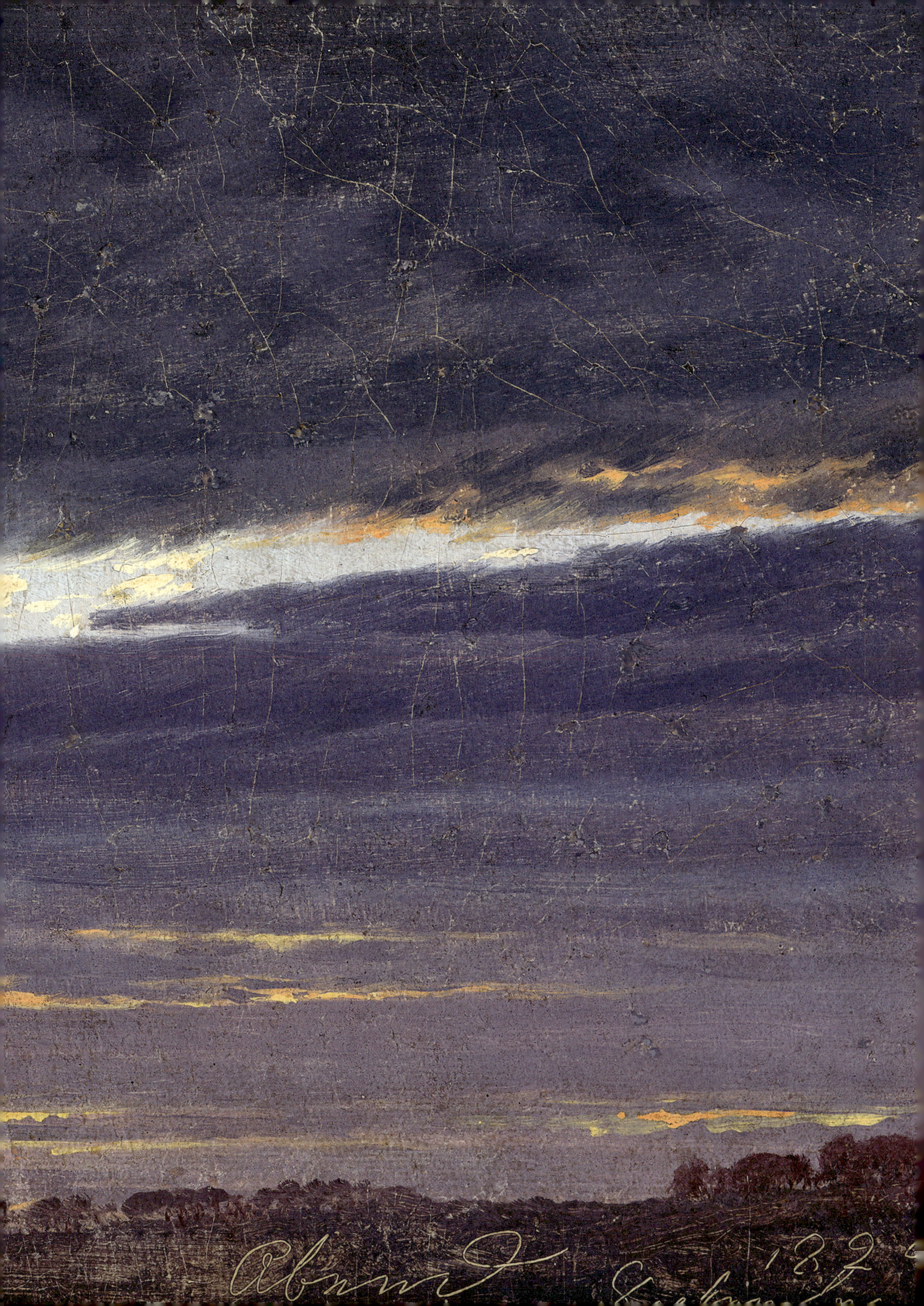
Abend

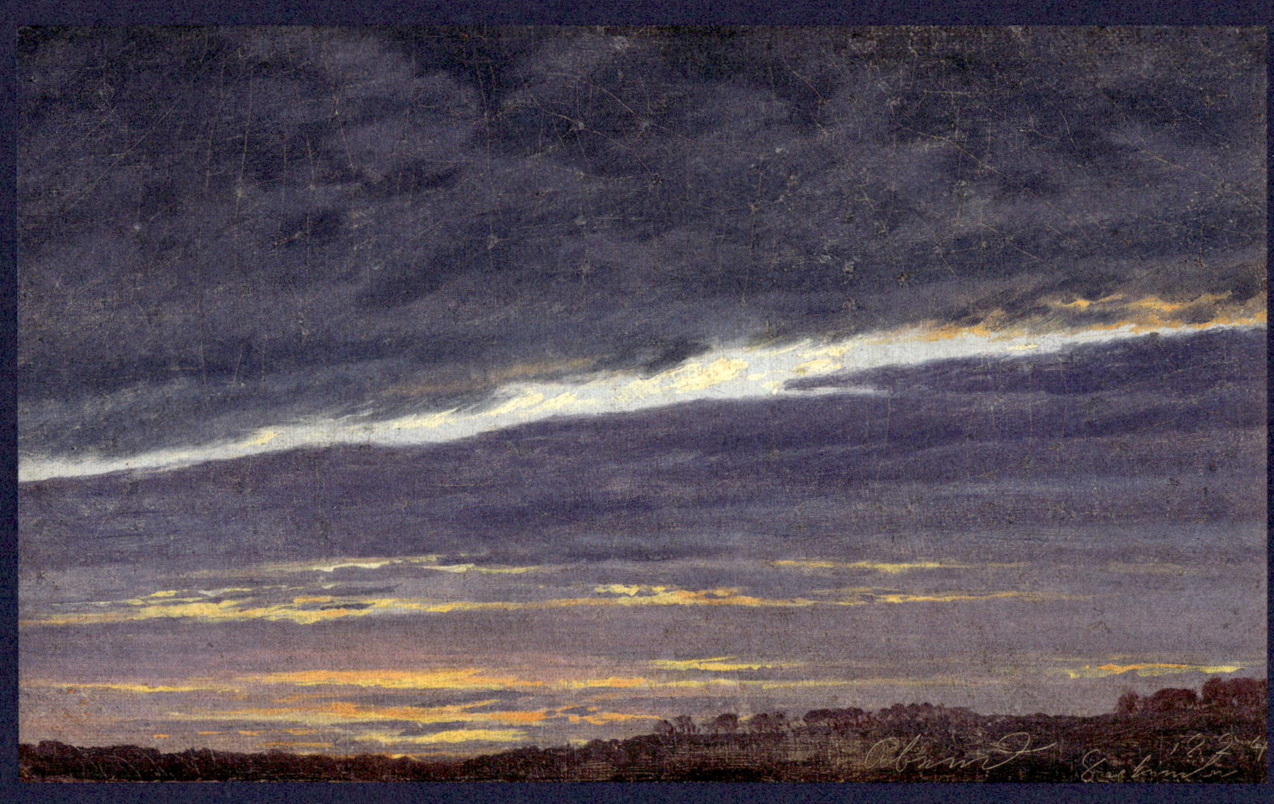

CASPAR DAVID FRIEDRICH, CLOUDY EVENING SKY, 1824

PHILIPP HAUSS

Without Words

Declaration of Envy No. 1

Beethoven is arguably one of the most theatrical composers. Not only do we find an explicit reference to *The Tempest*, not only do we have his various pieces of incidental music – he also displayed a certain thespian vocation which one could almost put into words, though ultimately it cannot quite be pinned down. For there is the Beethoven who sits down at the piano and plays in order to comfort a recently bereaved lady of his acquaintance – through music rather than words.

And the String Quartet in F, op. 135, for example – the final movement of which is inscribed with the question 'Muss es sein?' ('Must it be?'), followed by the answer given twice: 'Es muss sein!' ('It must be!') – ultimately goes beyond all that is said and implied in that question and answer: it spells out what lies in the innermost recesses of feeling, and yet it remains inconclusive. When reflecting on Beethoven, the 'berserker of emotions', it became clear to me that all professionals of the theatre – actors, directors, playwrights – are so very envious of musicians. Now this has not so much to do with Beethoven in particular as with the art form as such.

A work of music is incredibly thoroughly defined. This is especially so in Beethoven's case – right down to the metronome markings and the myriad indications of expression – though not in his case alone. Unlike a word, a musical note has a predefined pitch and a duration that stands in a clear relationship to the rest of the work. The tempi may be modified, notes may be played in a lighter or darker timbre, but none of this alters in any way the internal relationships within a given work. If minims in a specific passage have a certain length, then that has direct implications not just for all the crotchets, quavers and semiquavers in their vicinity but also for the following movements, for the beginning as well as for the end. That is a musical truism which, in fact, also applies to stage plays, though there it has much more to do with things that lie below the surface, that are open to question and a matter of individual taste.

Musicians, moreover, are able to produce with precision. As far as the envious theatre community is concerned, the fascination exerted on it at the most basic level by musicians perhaps rests chiefly on their 'know-how'. By this I mean that their art can be gauged not only subjectively but, up to a point, also objectively in terms of technical execution – in short, of skill. What is to be played in the case of a musical work does not simply depend, as in the performance of a play, on the chronology of words and on the revelation of emotions; rather, the sequences, duration and pitches of the notes are known: they are plain for all to see in the score.

DECLARATION OF ENVY NO. 2

One might be able to cope with that first tug of envy, were it possible for one to regard musicians as mere executors whom one could then compare unfavourably with the interpretative originality of an individual director, actor or even the chorus. But envy wells up a second time, for, despite all the machine-like precision and dexterity of the 'cogs' in the 'mechanical' ensemble as they mesh together, an experience is created that transcends the spoken word. We have here the apparent contradiction between craftsmanship and an artistic experience that, in coalescing, grows beyond itself. This contrast is not easy to bear; it elicits yearning glances from those working in the theatre.

For it happens to be the ideal of a stage performance: all those involved know what is to be done, what is to be played, and they are actually able to pull it off thanks to the skills they have acquired over many years. All the musicians are immersed in the task before them, yet at the same time they are receptive enough to be able to listen in all directions, to communicate with one another through glances and to look ahead. And all these playing units come together and produce something that is more than the sum of its parts – something the origin of which remains a mystery to everyone, and yet which gets through to the spectator or, rather, listener and takes possession of him or her. To quote Oscar Wilde: 'This is the reason why music is the perfect type of art. Music can never reveal its ultimate secret.'

Beethoven seems not to have quite trusted in the ability of his performers to translate emotions into tones, and so in his movement headings he urged them to play with great expression and feeling. Nevertheless, I cannot deny that even harmonies played without feeling, even pieces performed by mediocre youth orchestras or run-of-the-mill musicians still manage to move one. It is as if an algorithm were at work that is able to arouse emotions and create experiences that cannot be conveyed verbally. Again, quoting Oscar Wilde: 'Music creates for one a past of which one has been ignorant, and fills one with a sense of sorrows that have been hidden from one's tears.'

A DRUG

This applies not only to the performers: audiences, too, seem to be so much more willing to let go of themselves.

No one – not even the most qualified expert – expects to listen rationally to music, to take it in with cold intellect. One has only to let one's eyes wander during a concert and it becomes clear that the incredible freedom in composing which Beethoven personifies like no other seems to call forth an incredible freedom in listening. If you close your eyes in the theatre and let go of yourself, then, as far as you are concerned, the performance is over. Not so for people in a concert hall. They take their seats, the music begins, and they close their eyes and abandon themselves to their thoughts and feelings. In spoken theatre that would mean the performance had failed. At a concert, by contrast, people will cry without knowing why.

Words can be written down and grasped; they are able to indicate meaning and are comprehensible, no matter how strained their comprehensibility may sometimes be.

Musical sounds are ephemeral and ambiguous. Like colours? Yes, in that respect there is a closer connection between the visual arts and music, albeit with one major difference, namely, that in an image everything is already there. In great paintings various narrative discourses exist simultaneously, whereas in music even simultaneity can only be narrated through a temporal sequence. A tone may be a moment and no more, but it needs to have a duration. In that sense, images have no duration. Music is even more elusive, even more detached from materiality. It is pure vibration.

Besides, one cannot shut one's ears. While the eyelid is able to remove the world from our sight, the ear continues to hear. How ironic, though, to bring that up in the context of Beethoven, whose deafness left him with no other recourse but his inner hearing.

If one were to look down on the earth from high up, one might well see scenes in the theatre that were indistinguishable from real life – scenes in which one would at least be able to recognize familiar surroundings, passions and goings-on. By contrast, to someone who had no ear for music, to someone in whom harmonies did not awaken any emotions, concerts would probably be as baffling as would, for a non-skier, the thought of spending one or two weeks speeding down a mountain only to be hauled back up again.

'POSTERITY WEAVES NO WREATHS FOR THE ACTOR' (SCHILLER)

The final humiliation for the stage artist concerns the ability to leave a mark. That a work may be immortal – or at least that it endures for a long time – is true of literary texts. Similarly, acting performances may survive in the medium of film and be revisited repeatedly. However, neither the one, nor the other applies to the individual performance of a play – not even to a production as a whole. For who actually watches recordings of theatre productions? And not just once but over and over again? Such recordings are, truth to tell, intended primarily for members of the profession, apart perhaps from a few diehard fans.

Musicians achieve the leap from the present to posterity – that hurdle which drives theatre professionals to despair – and, what is more, they achieve it without having to renounce the moment of performance. Musical recordings are listened to again and again; even after many years, people will dig them out once more. It is a reunion with old acquaintances, as Beckett might have said. Thus, to use a term coined by Walter Benjamin, the 'tiger's leap' succeeds: surrender to the present moment in a manner calculated to last.

VINDICATION OF THE THEATRE

I do not know whether this envy is reciprocated. I do not know how many orchestral musicians secretly wish they could deviate from the score; how many times the same thing has to be repeated in order for the desire for change – for something different – to spill over. Is music-making unfree? Or is it a craft that takes pleasure in operating within marked-out channels? I am reminded of Bruce Naumann who, when asked how he had arrived at the idea for his simple, repetitive performances, replied that he wanted to set himself tasks he could accomplish. Does, then, the trick in music-making lie in knowing the task so well that one can accomplish it?

Finally: what about speech? Is speech a surrogate of art, a stage in its development? Or a child of music, from the spirit of which tragedy is said to have been born? Speech itself can 'be music'. But above all, we just cannot do without speech. We need it, if only to produce empty spaces – those spaces where words are no longer sufficient and which must be filled by music.

'MUST IT BE IT MUST BE IT MUST BE' (BECKETT)

In June 2019, I had another encounter with Beethoven – once again with his last completed work, the String Quartet, op. 135, and specifically with the final movement. It was at the funeral service for a dear friend and colleague. After the funeral orations there was just this music. Until then, death had had another tonality for me, namely that of Dinu Lipatti playing Bach's *Jesus bleibet meine Freude* (Jesu, Joy of Man's Desiring). While there we find consolation and deliverance, what remains at the end of Beethoven's music is agonizing loneliness. 'Muss es sein?' – 'Es muss sein! Es muss sein!'

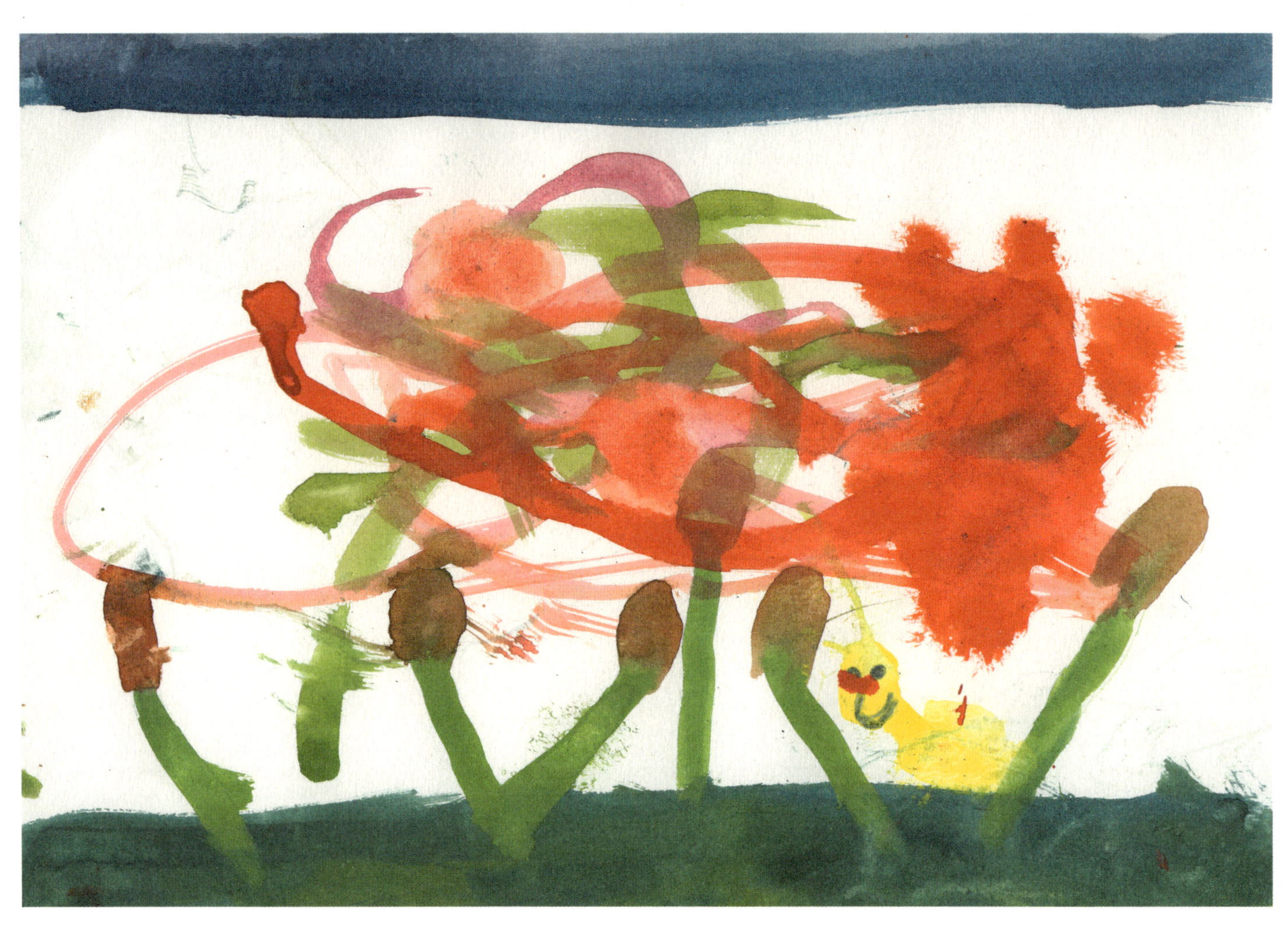

MAGDALENA GRAUSAM

Symphony No. 1 in C major, op. 21
2019

AKIRA KASAI

Oh Beethoven!

A sainted musician walks with God towards the perfection of God's creation. If you had not lived, surely the scales of human history would have been out of kilter. Like a dancing Indian god, you continue to dance on the stage of history through your music.

You gave us so much more than the joy of music that you brought to humanity to blessedly rain down on us. Yes, you were a musician, but even more, you were a great revolutionary. The revolution you incited was not the creation of something for the future here on earth; it was a sacred dance spinning within the core of your person, striving for a transformation of the soul.

Music is born within dance and dance is born within music. Music and dance are like the embrace of Adam and Eve; the moment of creation. Just like Prometheus when he stole fire from the realm of the Gods and bestowed it upon humankind in all our wretchedness, your music generously confers the entire dancing cosmos upon us humans.

What was it that surged through your body, your soul, like a cosmic heart to drive you on? Surely I cannot delve into the essence of your volition. Yet your limitless energy to compose derives from within that vortex. I cannot grasp the kind of process that lets a completed composition arise from that vortex of volition. If your revolutionary will had been bestowed upon you in another life, you might have been a knight leading on the battlefield, or a wandering minstrel endlessly spinning verse.

The extent of the revolution you begat for us is yet to be revealed. Your music is a coded record of the cosmos that is still not unravelled. Like a secret door that slowly swings open, your intentions will gradually be revealed as we earnestly endeavour to decipher your music.

I need to listen to your music through the ears of my heart to reveal the code of the unheard world at the very centre of the soul that you tried to discover day by day. This is truly a delicious act of dance. It leads me to suffer the same anguish that you suffered. Your music cannot be heard without this delightful suffering. It is an inevitable pain that leads to great joy. This joy reverberates in every note of the fourth movement of your Ninth Symphony.

Music and dance developed in unison in forms such as the pavane, sarabande, gavotte, minuet, chaconne and waltz. The dance of sound is music and the music of the body is dance, like a couple bound by love at first sight. Your music perpetually calls people back to the origin of dance and music. That makes you the dancer of sound. Indeed, you continued to compose German dance music throughout your life. It is not in your dances where we find that fundamental connection between dance and music most strongly, however: it is so much more apparent in your piano sonatas and your nine symphonies.

The chords you fashioned render every sound an individual dancer in your music. Major and minor keys transfigure into male and female dancers. A total embodiment of Pythagoreanism, it is the miracle whereby celestial music transforms into dance.

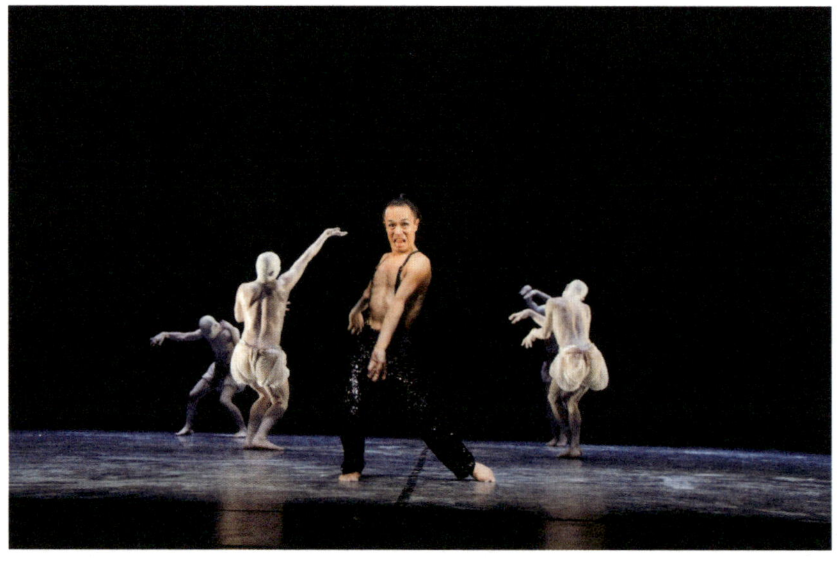

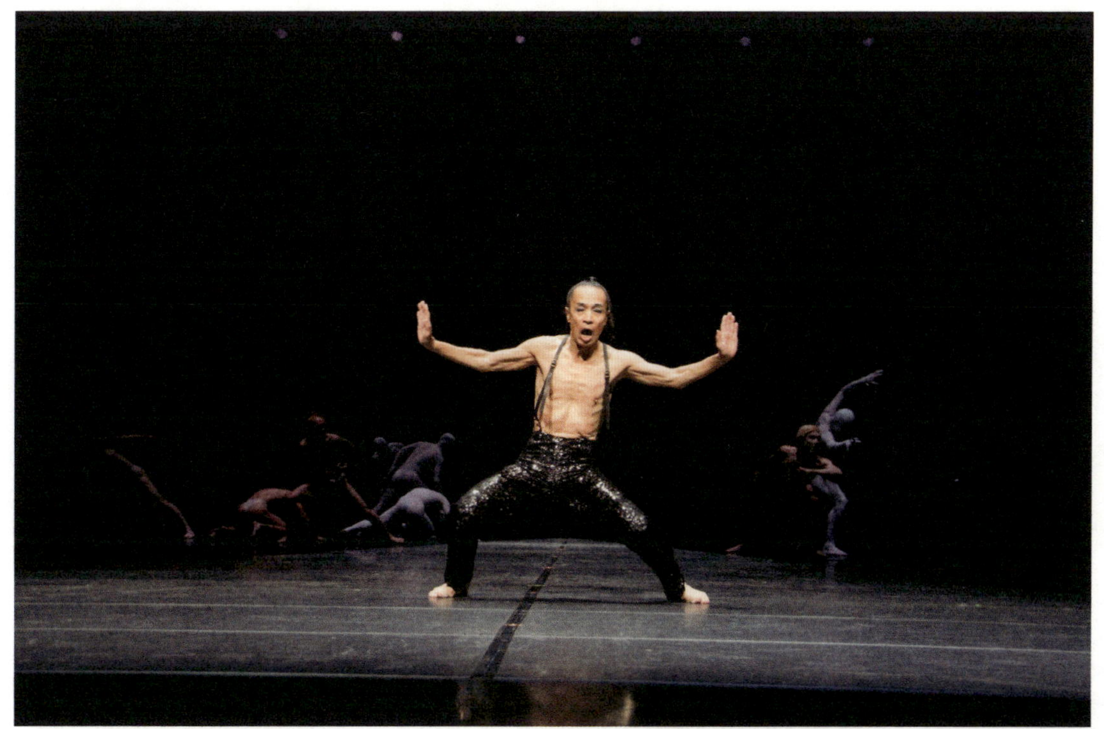

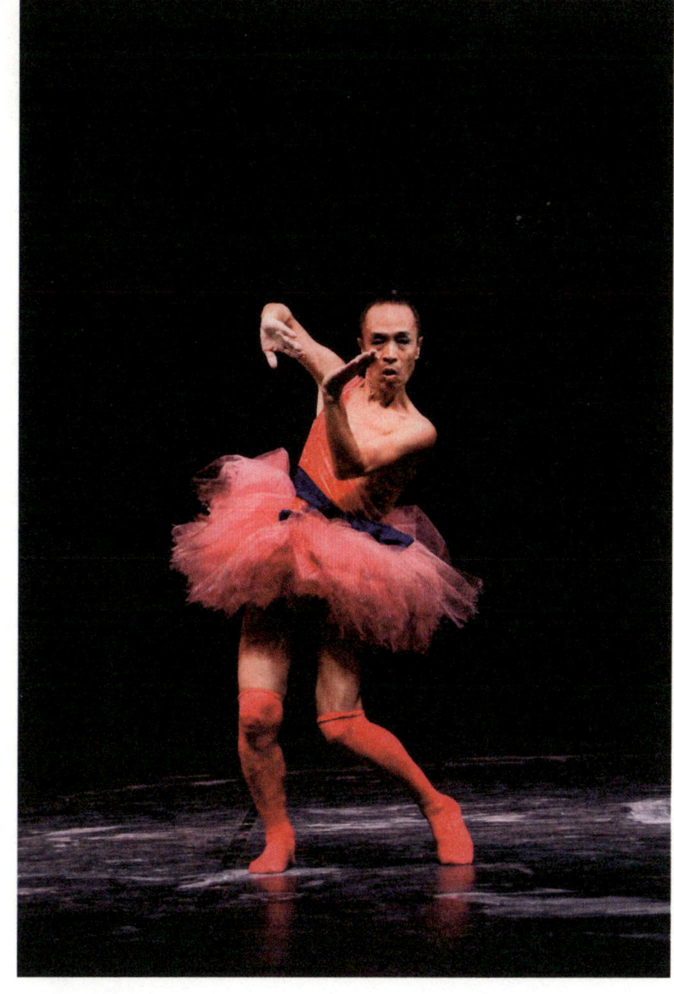

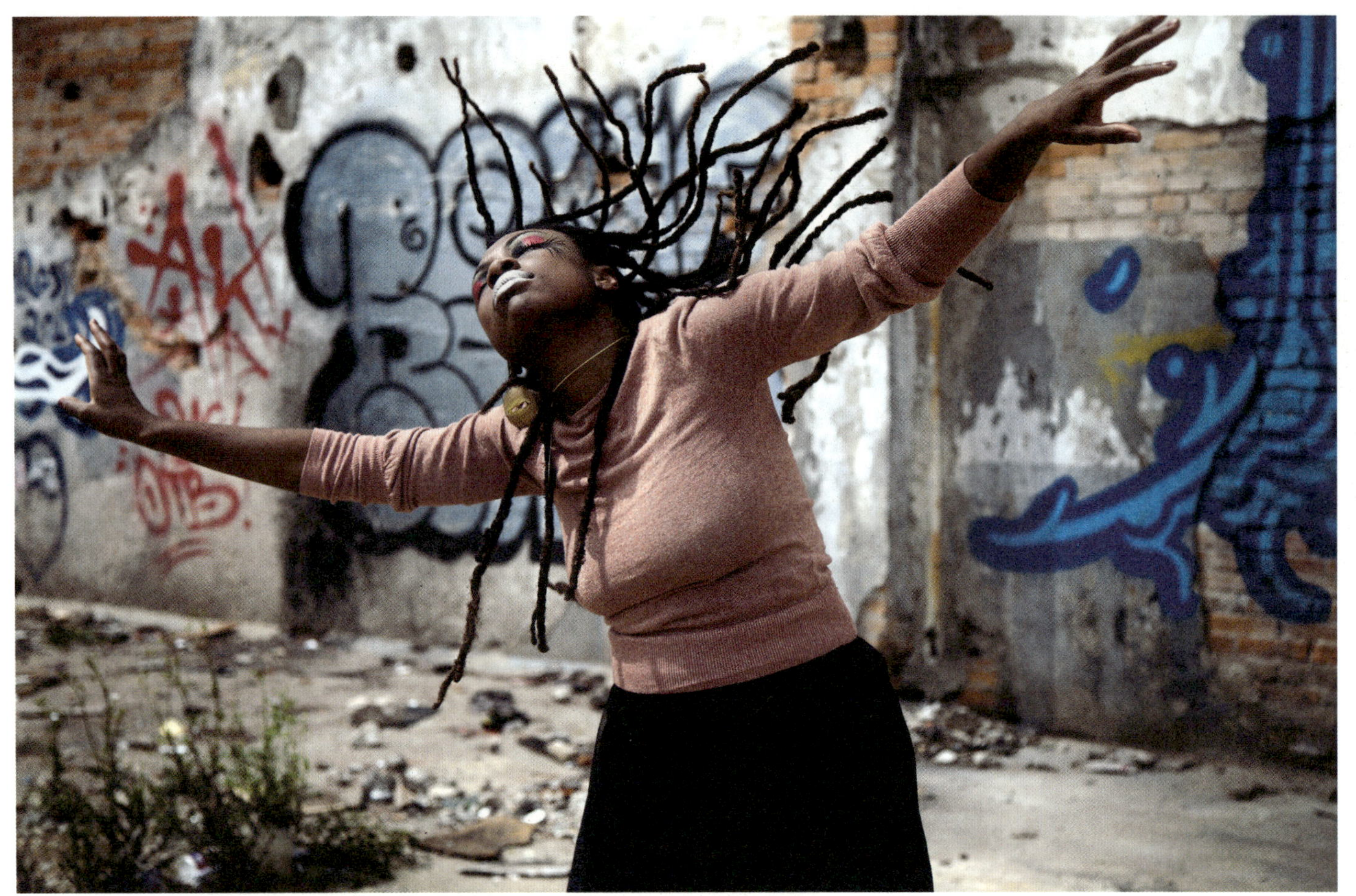

'This work deals with the ancestry inherent to a Brazilian black person's body in the context of the African diaspora. Historically, millions were exiled from West Africa and forced to work in the American colonies; the roots of these people are ingrained in the land. In this context, dance is a place of reconnection of what is below the earth with those who step on it.'

RENATA FELINTO

Danço na terra em que piso (I Dance at the Ground on Which I Step) 2014

Throughout his career, Beuys was motivated by the utopian belief in the power of human creativity to bring about revolutionary change. Beethoven adhered to a similar romantic ideal as epitomized by his ambitious compositions, such as the *Missa Solemnis*. Although both artists lived over a century apart and worked in two different mediums – music and the plastic arts –, they shared the same position regarding the social purpose of art.

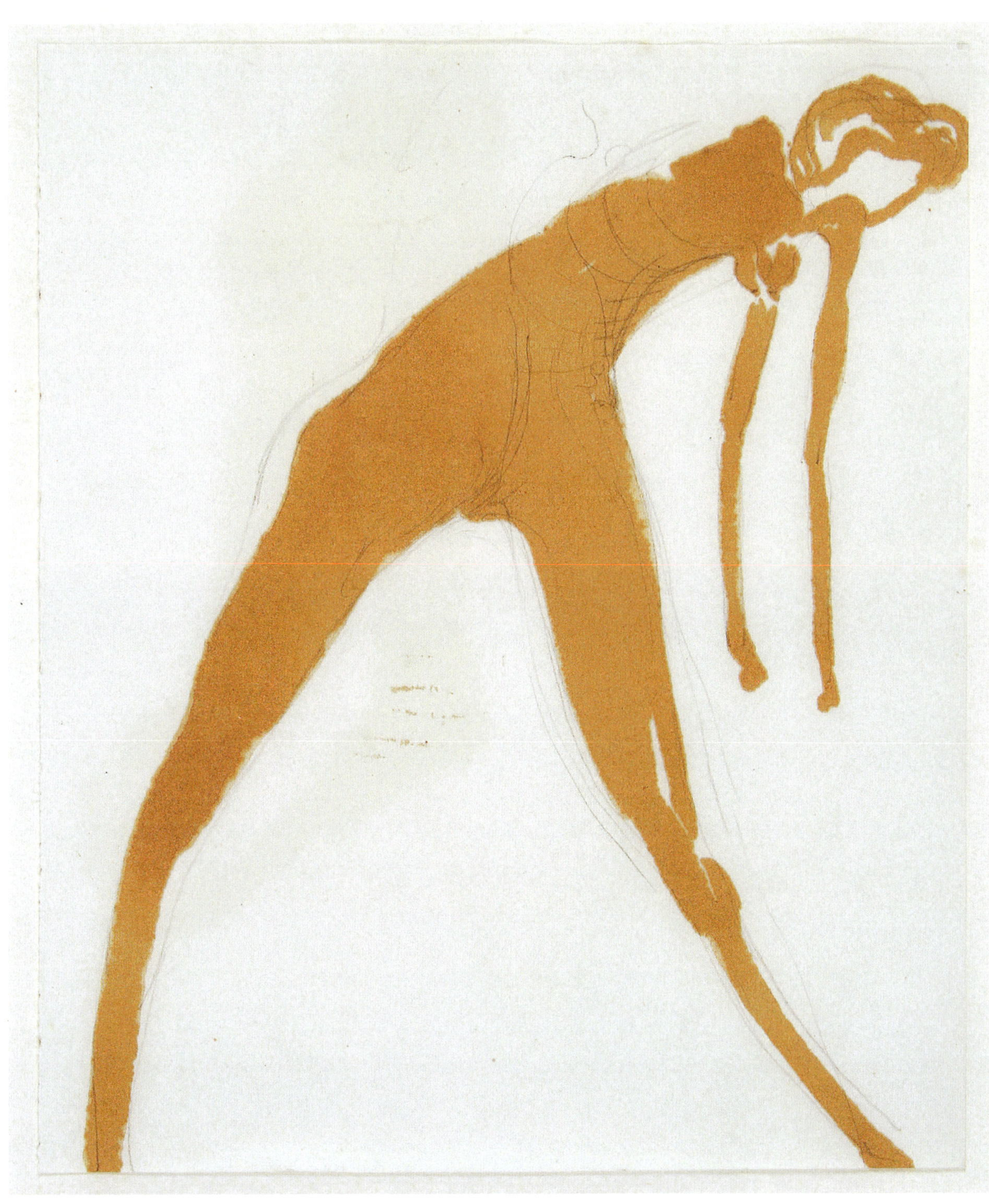

JOSEPH BEUYS

Dancer
1954

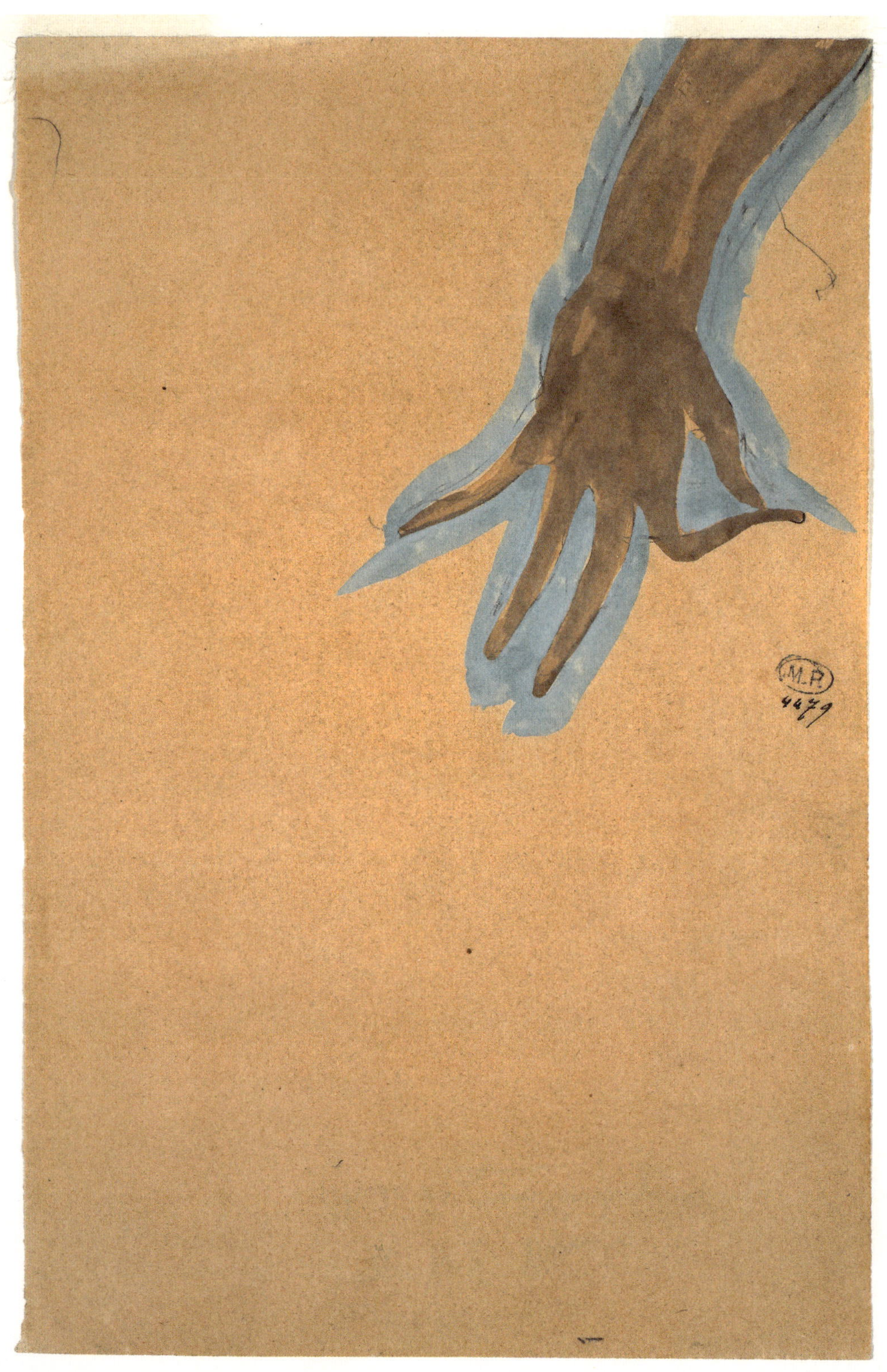

In 1906, Rodin came across the Cambodian Royal Ballet in Paris, whereupon he was immediately struck by the timeless nature and elegant movements of Khmer dance. In just one week after following the troupe, he made about 150 drawings, with an obvious fascination for the arms and hands of the dancers.

AUGUSTE RODIN

Study of a Cambodian Dancer's Hand
1906

CHRISTOPHER ROTHKO

Beethoven and Stillness

Stillness. Not the first word that comes to mind when one mentions Beethoven. More typically our thoughts jump to the bold, at times irascible, figure with unkempt hair and little patience for pleasantries or social conventions.

Or the dauntless firebrand, staunchly devoted to his artistic and humanistic vision, railing against gods and tyrants – or any others – who would suppress it. His music is inspired by heroism and inspires it by turns. Who can fail to be stirred by the Allegro con brio movements of the Seventh Symphony, or the 'Serioso' Quartet?

Oh, but Beethoven was an artist, not a soapbox orator, and his music moves us not simply because he knows how to make our pulses race but because he knows the many contradictory corners of our souls. Many times, when we least expect it, he brings us up short with movements of unalloyed tenderness, with musical confessions of genuine doubt, or simply with moments of deep reflection before once again launching forward. Such passages remind us that he possessed a complicated and sensitive soul too. I write this as I listen to the Adagio sostenuto of the 'Hammerklavier' Sonata, more than a quarter hour's pondering of a question too important to put aside. And it is not at all clear from the ensuing Largo that the answer so hard won was by any means definitive. Indeed, even when the Largo breaks into the Allegro risoluto, Beethoven treats his new subject fugally, which in my personal musical vocabulary means taking the question and looking at it from every possible angle – again.

Beethoven sought quieter, contemplative spaces throughout his career, but they become more frequent, more expansive, seemingly more necessary in his late works. In his earlier compositions, he could create a sense of hushed stillness, but ironically always in the presence of a constant, if quiet, pulse: a feeling of perpetual motion that never entirely recedes. I am thinking here particularly of the Andante cantabile of the Sonata 'Pathetique', or the dreamy opening movement of the Sonata 'Pastorale', though there are, of course, many other examples. It is a tribute to his greatness that he can create a sense of repose in the context of this unwavering reminder of his irrepressible energy.

In the works of his last years, however, Beethoven learns not only how to set his music free from that pulse, he also often liberates it from a clear melodic course, while journeying through the most ambiguous harmonic territory. It is music that becomes truly unhinged, ungrounded, questing in directions that even after repeated listening remain conjectural. One of the most striking examples is the Sanctus of the *Missa Solemnis*. Here time all but stops in the transitional material between the Sanctus and Benedictus. The solo violin emerges unexpectedly from the silence and wends its way along its own path, in no particular hurry, with no clear goal. Indeed, that solo voice appears to exist outside of time. Even when the chorus enters in the Benedictus, the pervading sense of calm remains. The violin returns in the second Hosanna, restoring the serenity and carrying the choir to a peaceful resolution of the movement.

For me, the meaning of this movement, despite the presence of a traditional religious text, remains inscrutable. Beethoven, on a truly personal journey. There are other places, even in late Beethoven, however, where the stillness he finds is clearly a gathering of self and thought, on the cusp of a declamation of great drama and urgency. Perhaps most famously, the Adagio of the Ninth Symphony introduces an elegiac, reflective moment just before the heavens open in the finale with a chord so wrenchingly dissonant that two hundred years later, it still sends shivers down the spine. The Adagio is a necessary pause to take stock so that a few minutes later (or is it a lifetime?), he can proclaim 'Freude!' with all of his being. Beethoven's String Quartet in F, op. 135, his final major composition, contains a slow movement with an apparently similar purpose. The Lento assai pulls us deeply inward for a period of quiet introspection before the trials of the affectingly titled *Der schwer gefasste Entschluss* (Difficult Decision). Stillness, palpable, before emotional unrest.

Beethoven's five final quartets serve as a fitting capstone to a career of impassioned composition. As so often with last works, however, particularly when intimations of mortality have risen well above the level of a psychological whisper, these pieces involve as much contemplation as animation. His penultimate string quartet, the A minor, op. 132 includes the frankly confessional *Heiliger Dankgesang eines Genesenen an die Gottheit* (Convalescent's Holy Song of Thanksgiving to the Deity). Homophonic and chordal, effectively a hymn for string quartet, the movement is daringly simple, the composer casting a spell of time-slowing melodic stillness. If not the utter suspension of time we find in late Schubert, this is Beethoven stopping to recognize what nearly just became of him and what is soon to come.

Ultimately, for me, it is this often-quiet music, marked and indeed shaped by questions, that yields Beethoven's most revolutionary moments much more than the bold proclamations of the Fifth and Ninth Symphonies do. Indeed, his last two quartets involve a radical assertion of subjectivity, his fierce individualism revealed not by a shout, but by laying bare his own vulnerability. Subtitles like 'Convalescent's Holy Song' and the 'Difficult Decision' take us directly into his thought process, engraving for his public the very struggles he is engaging with as he attempts to find their expression in musical language. It is a daring insertion of self into a process that had hitherto, in western classical music, remained Apollonian in the detachment between creator and receiver, composer and listener.

Perhaps more than Beethoven's daring harmonic language and genre-straining expansions of form, this personal gesture signals the great dawn of Romanticism, which will proceed to embrace that subjectivity in ever-greater emotional outpourings through sound. Notwithstanding forays into serialism, neo-classicism, functionalism, chance music, optics, etc. the history of all the arts over the next two centuries has been focused most centrally on the expression of, celebration of and, yes, obsession with the artist's subjectivity, the artist becoming subject and often object of the work. Perhaps we should curse Beethoven as well as praise him, for this explicit injection of self into a process that in so many ways rises to something far greater and more universal than that mere focus. Naturally, it was Beethoven who dared to name the elephant in the room that had always been dancing directly in front of us. Now, if only all of us were able to make it dance as he does.

Suggestions for further listening: Ludwig van Beethoven, 'Waldstein' Sonata: Adagio molto; Piano Sonata no. 31, Adagio ma non troppo; Quartet op. 130: Cavatina; Violin Concerto: Larghetto; 'Geister' Trio: Largo assai ed espressivo; Franz Schubert, String Quintet in C: Adagio; Piano Sonata in B flat, D. 960: Molto moderato

TINO SEHGAL

This joy
2020

This new work was commissioned by the Kunsthistorisches Museum on the occasion of the exhibition *Beethoven Moves.* It was conceived over a period of several months in 2019/20, and draws on a number of compositions by Beethoven arranged for voice. These include the 1st movement of Symphony No. 5, the 1st movement of Symphony No. 6, the 2nd movement of Symphony No. 7, the Overture to Egmont and an adaptation of the 4th movement of Symphony No. 9.

The work was developed with and is enacted by Alexandre Achour, Moss Beynon Juckes, Margherita D'Adamo, Sandhya Daemgen, Hanako Hayakawa, Leah Katz, Justin F. Kennedy, Vera Pulido, Lizzie Sells.

JOHN BALDESSARI (National City 1931–2020 Los Angeles)
Beethoven's Trumpet (with Ear) Opus # 132 [pp. 11–14]
2007
Resin, fiberglass, bronze, aluminium, electronics
L 179 cm, W 110 cm, H 42 cm (ear); L 224 cm, W 130 cm (trumpet)
New York, Beyer Projects, inv. nos. BEY 252.1, BEY 252.2
Courtesy of Beyer Projects and John Baldessari © Photo: KHM-Museumsverband/Thomas Ritter

LUDWIG VAN BEETHOVEN (Bonn 1770–1827 Vienna)
Piano Sonata No. 15 in D major, op. 28, autograph
1801
26 individual sheets, bound with cover
Bonn, Beethoven-Haus, inv. no. BH 61
© Beethoven-Haus Bonn, Sammlung H. C. Bodmer

'Ouvertura del ballo intitolato Prometheus', overture to the ballet The Creatures of Prometheus, op. 43, instrumental parts for the orchestra of Prince Lobkowicz
1801
Nelahozeves, The Lobkowicz Collections, Nelahozeves Castle
© The Lobkowicz Collections

Piano Sonata No. 21 in C major, op. 53, 'Waldstein', autograph
1803–05
32 individual sheets, bound
Bonn, Beethoven-Haus, inv. no. HCB Mh 7
© Beethoven-Haus Bonn, Sammlung H. C. Bodmer

Symphony No. 3 in E flat major, op. 55, 'Eroica', manuscript score [p. 147]
1804
Beethoven's personal copy, 1st volume, open on the title page with the dedication to Napoleon Bonaparte erased
Vienna, Gesellschaft der Musikfreunde in Wien,
Archiv – Bibliothek – Sammlungen, Sign. A 20
© Gesellschaft der Musikfreunde in Wien, Archiv – Bibliothek – Sammlungen

Sketches for String Quartets (in F major, E minor and C major), op. 59, dedicated to Count Andrei Razumovsky, autograph [pp. 42, 66]
1806
Vienna, Gesellschaft der Musikfreunde in Wien,
Archiv – Bibliothek – Sammlungen, sign. A 36, pp. 8–9, 28–29
© Gesellschaft der Musikfreunde in Wien, Archiv – Bibliothek – Sammlungen

Symphony No. 5 in C minor, op. 67, instrumental parts for the orchestra of Prince Lobkowicz
1804–08
Prague, The Lobkowicz Collections, Lobkowicz Palace, Prague Castle
© The Lobkowicz Collections

Piano Sonata No. 26 in E flat major, op. 81a, 'Les Adieux', 1st mvt, autograph
Dated 4 May 1809
Vienna, Gesellschaft der Musikfreunde in Wien,
Archiv – Bibliothek – Sammlungen, sign. A 1
© Gesellschaft der Musikfreunde in Wien, Archiv – Bibliothek – Sammlungen

Overture to Egmont, op. 84, instrumental parts for the orchestra of Prince Lobkowicz
1809/10
Nelahozeves, The Lobkowicz Collections, Nelahozeves Castle
© The Lobkowicz Collections

Piano Sonata No. 32 in C minor, op. 111, autograph
1821/22
Bonn, Beethoven-Haus, inv. no. BH 71
© Beethoven-Haus Bonn, Sammlung H. C. Bodmer

Sketches for the Choral Finale of Symphony No. 9 in D minor, op. 125, 4th mvt, autograph [p. 157]
1823/24
Vienna, Gesellschaft der Musikfreunde in Wien,
Archiv – Bibliothek – Sammlungen, sign. A 50, pp. 2–3
© Gesellschaft der Musikfreunde in Wien, Archiv – Bibliothek – Sammlungen

Sketches for Six Bagatelles for Piano, op. 126, nos. 1–3, autograph [p. 129]
1824
Vienna, Gesellschaft der Musikfreunde in Wien,
Archiv – Bibliothek – Sammlungen, Sign. A 50, S. 14–15
© Gesellschaft der Musikfreunde in Wien, Archiv – Bibliothek – Sammlungen

Heiligenstadt Testament
1802
Hamburg, Staats- und Universitätsbibliothek

BRAND & BAROZZI
9., Schwarzspanierstraße 15, Beethoven's last apartment
1903
Matte collodion paper on supporting cardboard
25.7 × 32.2 cm to 29.7 × 41.5 cm
Vienna, Wien Museum, inv. nos. 28147/9–14
© Wien Museum

Living room and bedroom [p. 85]
Study [pp. 86–87]
Hall
Room facing the alley (?)
Living room and bedroom facing the study
Servants' quarters [p. 88]

JAN COSSIERS (Antwerp 1600–1671 Antwerp)
Prometheus [pp. 139–142]
1636–38
Oil on canvas
182 × 113 cm
Madrid, Museo Nacional del Prado, inv. no. P001464
© Photographic Archive. Museo Nacional del Prado. Madrid

AYSE ERKMEN (b.1949, Istanbul)
esile rüf [p. 4]
2020
Sound installation, 2:49 min
On loan from the artist and from Galerie Barbara Weiss (Berlin), Barbara Gross Galerie (Munich) and the Dirimart gallery (Istanbul)
Photomontage: polyform, Berlin; Photo: Christian Mendez

CASPAR DAVID FRIEDRICH (Greifswald 1774–1840 Dresden)
Seashore in the Fog [p. 189]
c.1807
Oil on canvas
34.2 × 50.2 cm
Vienna, Belvedere, inv. no. 3700
© Belvedere, Wien

Seashore with Fisherman [p. 183]
c.1807
Oil on canvas
33.5 × 51 cm
Vienna, Belvedere, inv. no. 3701
© Belvedere, Wien

Moon above the Riesengebirge [p. 191]
c.1810
Oil on canvas
47.5 × 167 cm
Weimar, Klassik Stiftung Weimar, inv. no. G 689
© Klassik Stiftung Weimar, Museen

Billowing Clouds [p. 185]
c.1820
Oil on canvas
32.5 × 42.4 cm
Hamburg, Hamburger Kunsthalle, inv. no. 1056
© Hamburger Kunsthalle/bpk

Rocky Landscape in the Elbe Sandstone Mountains [p. 187]
1822/23
Oil on canvas
94 × 74 cm
Vienna, Belvedere, inv. no. 2589
© Belvedere, Wien

Cloudy Evening Sky [pp. 193–196]
1824
Oil on canvas
12.5 × 21.2 cm
Inscribed on the bottom right: 'Evening, September 1824'
Vienna, Belvedere, inv. no. 2379
© Belvedere, Wien, Photo: Johannes Stoll

Fishing Boat between Two Rocks on a Baltic Beach
c.1830–35
Oil on canvas
22 × 31.2 cm
Madrid, Museo Nacional Thyssen-Bornemisza, inv. no. CTB.1994.15
© Carmen Thyssen-Bornemisza Collection on loan at the Museo Nacional Thyssen-Bornemisza, Madrid

Ruins at Dusk (Ruined Church in the Woods)
c.1831
Oil on canvas
70.5 × 49.7 cm
Munich, Bayerische Staatsgemäldesammlungen, Kunstareal München, inv. no. 9872
© bpk/Bayerische Staatsgemäldesammlungen

FRANCISCO DE GOYA Y LUCIENTES (Fuendetodos 1746–1828 Bordeaux)
Los Caprichos
1799
Etching, aquatint
Approx. 216 × 151 mm each
Vienna, Albertina
© The Albertina Museum, Vienna

Works from the series shown in the exhibition:
El amor y la muerte (Love and death), inv. no. DG1935/23
Estan calientes (They are hot), inv. no. DG1935/26
Aquellos polbos (These specks of dust), inv. no. DG1935/36 [p. 102]
Chiton! (Hush!), inv. no. DG1935/41
Por que fue sensible (Because she was susceptible), inv. no. DG1935/45
Las rinde el sueno (Sleep overcomes them), inv. no. DG1935/47
Mala noche (A bad night), inv. no. DG1935/49
De que mal morira? (Of what will he die?), inv. no. DG1935/53
Ni mas ni menos (Neither more nor less), inv. no. DG1935/54
El sueño de la razon produce monstruos (The sleep of reason produces monsters), inv. no. DG1935/56
Hilan delgado (They spin finely), inv. no. DG1935/57
Soplones (Tale-bearers – Blasts of wind), inv. no. DG1935/61
Duendecitos (Hobgoblins), inv. no. DG1935/62
Y aun no se van! (And still they don't go!), inv. no. DG1935/72
Buen viage (Bon voyage), inv. no. DG1935/77 [p. 101]
Linda maestra! (Pretty teacher!), inv. no. DG1935/81
Si amanece, nos Vamos (When day breaks we will be off), inv. no. DG1935/84
Ya es hora (It is time), inv. no. DG1935/93 [p. 103]

REBECCA HORN (b.1944, Michelstadt)
Concert for Anarchy [pp. 33–36]
2006
Grand piano, hydraulic rams and compressor
L 150 cm, W 106 cm, D 155 cm
Rebecca Horn Studio, inv. no. T07517
© 2020: Rebecca Horn/Bildrecht, Vienna 2020. Photos: Attilio Maranzano

IDRIS KHAN (b.1978, Birmingham)
Struggling to Hear.... After Ludwig van Beethoven Sonatas [p. 133]
2005
Lambda digital C-print mounted on aluminium
258 × 192 cm
London, Victoria Miro, inv. no. IK 14 AP
© Idris Khan
Courtesy of the artist and Victoria Miro, London/Venice

ANSELM KIEFER (b.1945, Donaueschingen)
The starry heavens above us, and the moral law within [pp. 115–118]
1969–2010
Photograph on paper with overpainting
63 × 83.2 cm
Edinburgh, National Galleries of Scotland, inv. no. AR01164
ARTIST ROOMS Tate and National Galleries of Scotland. Acquired jointly through The d'Offay Donation with assistance from the National Heritage Memorial Fund and the Art Fund 2011.
© Anselm Kiefer

AUGUSTE RODIN (Paris 1840–1917 Meudon)
L'Âge d'airain (The Age of Bronze) [pp. 40–41]
1877
Plaster, gum lacquer varnish
H 184 cm, W 68.5 cm, D 54.5 cm
Le Havre, Musée d'art moderne André Malraux (MuMa), inv. no. 2014.0.2
© MuMa Le Havre/Charles Maslard

TINO SEHGAL (b.1976, London)
This joy
2020
Production: Cora Gianolla

JOSEPH MALLORD WILLIAM TURNER (London 1775–1851 London)
Vale of Heathfield Sketchbook [p. 164, top (inv. no. D10256), bottom (inv. no. D10257)]
c.1809–16
Watercolour on paper, sketchbook
181 × 228 mm
Tate: accepted by the nation as part of the Turner Bequest 1856.
Inv. nos. D10256, D10257
Photo © Tate

Skies Sketchbook [p. 162 (inv. no. D12467); p. 163 (inv. no. D12486)]
c.1816–18
Watercolour on paper, sketchbook
125 × 247 mm
Tate: accepted by the nation as part of the Turner Bequest 1856.
Inv. nos. D12467, D12486
Photo © Tate

Fire at the Grand Storehouse of the Tower of London [p. 159, top (inv. no. D27848), bottom (inv. no. D27849); p. 160, top (inv. no. D27850), bottom (inv. no. D27852)]
1841
Watercolour on paper
235 × 325 mm
Tate: accepted by the nation as part of the Turner Bequest 1856.
Inv. nos. D27848, D27849, D27850, D27852
Photo © Tate

JORINDE VOIGT (b.1977, Frankfurt/Main)
Ludwig van Beethoven Sonata 1 to 32 [pp. 57–60, 83–84]
2012
Ink, pencil on paper
865 × 1,400 mm each
Berlin, Studio Jorinde Voigt
© Jorinde Voigt/Bildrecht, Vienna 2020

GUIDO VAN DER WERVE (b.1977, Papendrecht)
Nummer acht, *everything is going to be alright* [pp. 173–176]
2007, Gulf of Bothnia, Finland
16mm film to HD
10:10 min.
New York, courtesy of the artist and Luhring Augustine
© Guido van der Werve; Courtesy of the artist and Luhring Augustine, New York

FLOOR FROM BEETHOVEN'S APARTMENT IN THE SCHWARZSPANIERHAUS [p. 113]
1780–1800
Parquet floor
Approx. 32 m²
Vienna, Wien Museum
© Franz Bauer

EAR TRUMPET OWNED BY LUDWIG VAN BEETHOVEN [pp. 104–105]
After 1812
L 58 cm, H 11.5 cm, D 11.5 cm
Cardboard, wrapped in black leather
Vienna, Gesellschaft der Musikfreunde in Wien,
Archiv – Bibliothek – Sammlungen, Sign. ER Beethoven 8
© Gesellschaft der Musikfreunde in Wien, Archiv – Bibliothek – Sammlungen

LUDWIG VAN BEETHOVEN (Bonn 1770–1827 Vienna)
Sonata for violin and piano No. 9 in A major, op. 47, 'Kreutzersonate' [cover]
1802/03
Courtesy of the Juilliard Manuscript Collection

MAGDALENA GRAUSAM (b.2012, Vienna)
Piano Sonata No. 23 in F minor, op. 57, 'Appassionata' [p. 19]
2019
Watercolour on paper
21 × 29.7 cm
Private collection

ERNST SCHWITTERS (Hannover 1918–1939 Oslo)
Ur Sonata Performed by Kurt Schwitters [Series I] [p. 26]
1944
Photograph, gelatin silver print
22.8 × 30 cm
Hannover, Sprengel Museum, inv. no. 2008.11.13.006
© Bildrecht, Vienna 2020

ULF AMINDE (b.1969, Stuttgart)
Life is not a Musical Request Show [p. 32]
2006
12-channel SD video installation, colour, sound
Between 1:00 min. and 18:00 min.
Installation view, 4th Berlin Biennale 25 March–5 June 2006
Berlin, Galerie Tanja Wagner
Courtesy Galerie Tanja Wagner, Berlin; Photo: Uwe Walter

DICK HIGGINS (Cambridge 1938–1998 Québec)
Symphony no. 76 in Memoriam Henry Cowell: Allegro [p. 51]
Symphony no. 76 in Memoriam Henry Cowell: Funeral March [p. 52]
Symphony no. 76 in Memoriam Henry Cowell: Triumphal Jig [p. 53]
1968–1991
Mixed media on music paper
57.5 × 44.5 cm
Colceresa, Fondazione Bonotto
Courtesy Fondazione Bonotto

ROBERT RAUSCHENBERG (Port Arthur 1925–2008 Captiva)
Automobile Tire Print [pp. 54–56]
1953
Paint on 20 sheets of paper mounted on fabric
41.9 × 726.4 cm
San Francisco, San Francisco Museum of Modern Art,
Purchase through a gift of Phyllis C. Wattis, inv. no. 98.296
© Robert Rauschenberg Foundation Photo: Don Ross
© Untitled Press inc. / Bildrecht, Vienna 2020

MARCELLO MERCADO (b.1963, Chaco)
Bestiary of the Minds of the 21st Century: Genomic Opera (page from the Opera-Artist's Book) [p. 67]
2015
Gouache, acrylic paint and pencil on transparent paper
40 × 60 × 30 cm
Photo: Tilman Peschel Courtesy Digital Synesthesia, Digital Art Department of the University of Applied Arts Vienna

CYMATICS RESEARCH
Piano note C1 made visible by CymaScope instrument [p. 70]
Courtesy www.soundmadevisible.com

PAULA NOLL (b.2016, Tulln)
Piano Sonata No. 16 in G major, op. 31, no. 1 [p. 73]
2019
Watercolour on paper
21 × 29.7 cm
Private collection

NASA
Voyager 1, Voyager Golden Record [p. 74]
1977
Courtesy NASA/JPL-Caltech

Pale Blue Dot [p. 75]
1990
Courtesy NASA/JPL-Caltech

KATIE PATERSON (b.1981, Glasgow)
Earth-Moon-Earth (Moonlight Sonata Reflected from the Surface of the Moon) [pp. 76–77]
2007
Giclée prints on Hahnemuhle Photo Rag 308g Fine Art Paper A3
50 × 33.37 cm
Photo © Blaise Adilon, 2015
Exhibition view Frac Franche-Comté

DORIT MARGREITER (b.1967, Vienna)
Experimental Noise [pp. 91–93]
2016–2019
Pigment print on aluminium
150 × 112.5 cm
Vienna, Charim Galerie, inv. no. Ed. 3 + 1 AP
Courtesy Charim Galerie Wien

VIJA CELMINS (b.1938, Riga)
Desert [p. 94]
1971
Lithography on paper
31.5 × 41.6 cm
London, Tate, inv. no. P78337
© Vija Celmins, Photo © Tate

CHRISTINE SUN KIM (b.1980, Orange County)
The Sound of Inactivity [p. 106, top]
The Sound of Obsessing [p. 106, bottom]
The Sound of Passing Time [p. 107, top]
The Sound of Temperature Rising [p. 107, bottom]
2017
Charcoal on paper
125 × 125 cm
Courtesy of the artist, François Ghebaly, Los Angeles, and White Space, Beijing
Photo: Rubin Museum and David de Armas

ISHA BØHLING (b.1970, Watford)
Silence [p. 108]
2002
Acrylic and wax on wood
20 × 10 × 5 cm
London, Central Saint Martins, inv. nos. PA.98.1.CC/PA.98.2.CC
Courtesy of the artist

LAURENCE STEPHEN LOWRY (Stretford 1887–1976 Glossop)
The Grey Sea [p. 114]
1964
Oil on canvas
75 × 100 cm
Private collection
© The Estate of L.S. Lowry. All Rights Reserved/Bildrecht, Vienna 2020

ALFRED EISENSTAEDT (Dirschau 1898–1995 Oak Bluffs)
The Room in Which Beethoven Was Born [pp. 126–127]
1934/1979
from: Alfred Eisenstaedt, *Eisenstaedt on Eisenstaedt: A Self-Portrait* (London, 1985), pp. 108–109

RONJA SPERNEDER (b.2011, Vienna)
Overture to Egmont, op. 84 [p. 128]
2019
Watercolour on paper
21 × 29.7 cm
Private collection

EMMA FRANCIS (*1975, Southampton)
2004
Oil on board
© The artist. Photo credit: Southampton Solent University

Bruiser [p. 137, bottom]
20 × 25.4 cm
Southampton, Solent University, inv. no. SI/04/0639

Crack [p. 137, top]
86 × 84 cm
Southampton, Solent University, inv. no. SI/04/0637

Lost [p. 138]
25.5 × 20 cm
Southampton, Solent University, inv. no. SI/04/0638

JEAN-MICHEL BASQUIAT (New York City 1960–1988 New York City)
Eroica II [p. 148]
1988
Acrylic, crayon, canvas
230 × 225.5 cm
Private collection
© Estate of Jean-Michel Basquiat/Bildrecht, Vienna 2020
Licensed by Artestar, New York

Eroica I [p. 149]
1988
Acrylic, crayon, canvas
230 × 225.5 cm
Private collection
© Estate of Jean-Michel Basquiat/Bildrecht, Vienna 2020
Licensed by Artestar, New York

Eroica [p. 150]
1987
Acrylic, crayon, canvas
228.5 × 271.5 cm
Private collection
© Estate of Jean-Michel Basquiat/Bildrecht, Vienna 2020
Licensed by Artestar, New York

OLAFUR ELIASSON (b.1967, Copenhagen)
Colour Experiment no. 58 [p. 158]
Colour Experiment no. 61 [p. 161]
2014
Oil on canvas
ø 190 cm
Private collection
Courtesy of the artist; Tanya Bonakdar Gallery, New York/
Los Angeles; neugerriemschneider, Berlin
Photo: Jens Ziehe, 2014

ALFRED STIEGLITZ (Hoboken 1864–1946 New York City)
Songs of the Sky in Five Pictures (No. 1) [p. 170, top]
1923
Photograph, gelatin silver print
11.7 × 9.2 cm
Boston, Museum of Fine Arts, inv. no. 24.1733.1
© Georgia O'Keeffe Museum/Bildrecht, Vienna 2020

Songs of the Sky in Five Pictures (No. 2) [p. 170, bottom]
1923
Photograph, gelatin silver print
9.2 × 11.7 cm
Boston, Museum of Fine Arts, inv. no. 24.1733.2
© Georgia O'Keeffe Museum/Bildrecht, Vienna 2020

Songs of the Sky in Five Pictures (No. 3) [p. 171, left]
1923
Photograph, gelatin silver print
11.7 × 8.9 cm
Boston, Museum of Fine Arts, inv. no. 24.1733.3
© Georgia O'Keeffe Museum/Bildrecht, Vienna 2020

Songs of the Sky in Five Pictures (no. 4) [p. 171, right]
1923
Photograph, gelatin silver print
11.7 × 8.9 cm
Boston, Museum of Fine Arts, inv. no. 24.1733.4
© Georgia O'Keeffe Museum/Bildrecht, Vienna 2020

Songs of the Sky in Five Pictures (no. 5) [p. 172]
1923
Photograph, gelatin silver print
11.7 × 8.9 cm
Boston, Museum of Fine Arts, inv. no. 24.1733.5
© Georgia O'Keeffe Museum/Bildrecht, Vienna 2020

JAMES ABBOTT McNEILL WHISTLER (Lowell 1834–1903 London)
Nocturne in Black and Gold: The Falling Rocket [p. 179]
1875
Oil on panel
60.2 × 46.7 cm
Detroit, Detroit Institute of Arts, inv. no. 46.309
© Detroit Institute of Arts/Gift of Dexter M. Ferry Jr./Bridgeman Images

CY TWOMBLY (Lexington 1928–2011 Rome)
Untitled I (Green Painting) [A Painting in Six Parts] [p. 182]
Untitled II (Green Painting) [A Painting in Six Parts] [p. 184]
Untitled III (Green Painting) [A Painting in Six Parts] [p. 186]
Untitled IV (Green Painting) [A Painting in Six Parts] [p. 188]
Untitled V (Green Painting) [A Painting in Six Parts] [p. 190]
Untitled VI (Green Painting) [A Painting in Six Parts] [p. 192]
2002/03
Acrylic on plywood panel
194 × 134.5 cm
New York, Cy Twombly Foundation
© Cy Twombly Foundation. Courtesy Archive Nicola Del Roscio

MAGDALENA GRAUSAM (b.2012, Vienna)
Symphony No. 1 in C major, op. 21 [p. 200]
2019
Watercolour on paper
21 × 29.7 cm
Private collection

RENATA FELINTO (b.1978, São Paulo)
Danço na terra em que piso (I Dance at the Ground on Which I Step) [p. 204]
2014
Performance in São Paulo, Brazil
Courtesy of the artist

JOSEPH BEUYS (Krefeld 1921–1986 Düsseldorf)
Tänzerin (Dancer) [p. 205]
1954
Pencil, stain on writing paper
15.9 × 13 cm
Bedburg-Hau, Museum Schloss Moyland, inv. no. MSM 00267
© Bildrecht, Vienna 2020
Photo: Stiftung Museum Schloss Moyland/Maurice Dorren

AUGUSTE RODIN (Paris 1840–1917 Meudon)
Etude de main de danseuse cambodgienne (Study of a Cambodian dancer's hand) [p. 206]
1906
Vellum paper, graphite pencil, gouache
31 × 20 cm
Paris, Musée Rodin, inv. no. D.04479
© Musée Rodin – Jean de Calan

Image credits/Comparative images

ESSAY LODES
Fig. 1a, b [p. 21]
© Keresztény Múzeum, Esztergom. Photograph by Attila Mudrák

Fig. 2 [p. 22]
© Albertina, Vienna

Fig. 3 [p. 23]
© Landesmuseum Württemberg, Stuttgart (2020)

Fig. 4 [p. 23]
© Beethoven-Haus Bonn

Fig. 5 [p. 23]
© Bibliothèque nationale de France

Fig. 6 [p. 24]
© Beethoven-Haus Bonn

ESSAY ZAPKE
Fig. 1 [p. 28]
© Bayerische Staatsbibliothek München

Fig. 2 [p. 28]
Private collection

Fig. 3 [p. 29]
Private collection

Fig. 4 [p. 30]
© Beethoven-Haus Bonn

Fig. 5 [p. 30]
© Biblioteca Beethoveniana – Carrino Collection, Muggia (Trieste)

Fig. 6 [p. 30]
Private collection

ESSAY WYSS
Fig. 1 [p. 44]
© bpk/Bundesstiftung Aufarbeitung/Klaus Mehner

Fig. 2 [p. 45]
© Beethoven-Haus Bonn, Sammlung H.C. Bodmer

Fig. 3 [p. 45]
© Beethoven-Haus Bonn

Fig. 4 [p. 45]
Private collection

Fig. 5 [p. 45]
© Universitätsbibliothek Heidelberg

Fig. 6 [p. 46]
© bpk/Staatsbibliothek zu Berlin

Fig. 7 [p. 46]
Amsterdam, Rijksmuseum. Gift of J. Fekkes

Fig. 8 [p. 46]
© Ernst Barlach Stiftung Güstrow

Fig. 9 [p. 46]
© Graphikantiquariat Koenitz, Leipzig

Fig. 10 [p. 47]
The Andy Warhol Museum, Pittsburgh; Founding Collection, Contribution The Andy Warhol Foundation for the Visual Arts, Inc.; Accession Number 1998.1.2497.1/ Licensed by Bildrecht, Wien 2020

ESSAY GADENSTÄTTER
All figs [pp. 63–65]
Courtesy of the author

ESSAY RONGE
All figs. [pp. 79–81]
© Beethoven-Haus Bonn

ESSAY BUSCH
Fig. 1 [p. 98]
© Albertina, Vienna

Fig. 2 [p. 98]
© bpk/The Metropolitan Museum of Art

Fig. 3 [p. 99]
© Albertina, Vienna

Fig. 4 [p. 99]
© Albertina, Vienna

Fig. 5 [p. 99]
© Albertina, Vienna

Fig. 6 [p. 100]
© Albertina, Vienna

Fig. 7 [p. 100]
© Albertina, Vienna

ESSAY MÜLLER
Fig. on p. 120
© AF archive/Alamy Stock Photo

Fig. on p. 121
© AF archive/Alamy Stock Photo

Fig. on p. 123
© Moviestore Collection Ltd/Alamy Stock Photo

Fig. on p. 124
© Photo 12/Alamy Stock Photo

ESSAY ZHOU
All figs. [pp. 151–153]
© Yanming Zhou

ESSAY KIRILLINA
Fig. 1 [p. 166]
© Beethoven-Haus Bonn

Fig. 2 [p. 167]
© Beethoven-Haus Bonn

Fig. 3 [p. 167]
© bpk/Kupferstichkabinett, SMB

Fig. 4 [p. 168]
Photo © The State Hermitage Museum, St Petersburg. Photograph by Aleksey Pakhomov

ESSAY KASAI
All figs. [pp. 202–203]
© Akira Kasai

ARTIST ROOMS Tate and National Galleries of Scotland. Acquired jointly through The d'Offay Donation with assistance from the National Heritage Memorial Fund and the Art Fund 2011.

Bad König, Rebecca Horn Workshop

Berlin, Jorinde Voigt

Bonn, Beethoven-Haus

Le Havre, Musée d'art moderne André Malraux (MuMa)

London, Tate

London, Victoria Miro

Madrid, Carmen Thyssen-Bornemisza Collection on loan at the Museo Nacional Thyssen-Bornemisza

Madrid, Museo Nacional del Prado

Munich, Bayerische Staatsgemäldesamlungen, Kunstareal München

Nelahozeves, The Lobkowicz Collections, Nelahozeves Castle

New York, Beyer Projects

New York, Luhring Augustine

Prague, The Lobkowicz Collections, Lobkowicz Palace, Prague Castle

Weimar, Klassik Stiftung Weimar

Vienna, Albertina

Vienna, Belvedere

Vienna, Gesellschaft der Musikfreunde in Wien, Archiv – Bibliothek – Sammlungen

Vienna, Wien Museum

Assmann, Aleida. Anglicist, Egyptologist, literary and cultural scientist. Germany

Assmann, Jan. Egyptologist, religious studies scholar, cultural scientist. Germany

Busch, Werner. Art historian. Germany

Cai, Jindong. Conductor, Director of the US-China Music Institute at Bard College. China

De Waal, Edmund. Artist, writer. United Kingdom

Flor, Olga. Writer. Austria

Gadenstätter, Clemens. Composer. Austria

Hauß, Philipp. Actor, director. Germany

Kaiser, Vea. Writer. Austria

Kasai, Akira. Butoh dancer (Jap. 舞踏, butō), derived from: ankoku butō (暗黒舞踏, 'dance of darkness'). Japan

Kawano, Sakoto. Tanka poet (Jap. 短歌, 'short poem'). Japan

Kirillina, Larissa. Musicologist. Russia

Lodes, Birgit. Musicologist. Germany

Macho, Thomas. Cultural scientist, philosopher. Austria

Mahler, Nicolas. Cartoonist. Austria

Melvin, Sheila. Writer, China expert. United States of America

Müller, Jürgen. Art historian. Germany

Naitō, Hiroshi. Architect. Japan

Ronge, Julia. Musicologist. Germany

Rothko, Christopher. Writer, Rothko custodian, music critic. United States of America

Suda, Norio. Car dealer. Japan

Trojahn, Manfred. Composer, director, writer. Germany

Wyss, Beat. Art historian. Switzerland

Zapke, Susana. Musicologist. Spain

Zeman, Barbara. Writer. Austria

Zhou, Yanming. Photographer, journalist. China

Rachid Abu-Hassan, Ben Adler, Götz Adriani, Jane Alison, Marie-Louise Arndt, Herrmann Arnhold, Tamio Aoyama, Martha Auer, Eva Badura-Skoda, Dita Baker, Jonathan Barnbrook, Franz Bauer, Lara Verena Bellenghi, Steven Beyer, Rebeccah Blum, Otto Biba, Gisela Capitain, Jade Bouchemit, Charlotte Bochet, Dieter Buchart, Caroline Burghardt, Isabel Bennasar Cabrera, Anne Campman, Martine d'Anglejan Chatillon, Katie Chester, Anne Cikanek, Marcus Dekiert, Liliana Dobner, Marcin Dobosz, Clémence Ducroix, Vladimir Erdeg, Thomas Fheodoroff, Regina Fiorito, Friederike Forst-Battaglia, Paul Frey, Ingrid Fuchs, Sophie Führer, Clemens Gadenstätter, Ann Gallagher, Maria Gattringer, Andreas Gegner, Andrea Glatz, Dietmar Götzelmann, Nikolaus Gräser, Victoire Guéna, Rico Gulda, Julia Haimburger, Alice Harnoncourt, Maximilian Harnoncourt, Meike Hartelust, Julia Häußler, Marianne Hergovich, Miriam Heschl, Ann-Kathrin Hitz, Claudia Hogl, Albert Hosp, Judith Hummer, Amanda Hunter, Miro Janczyk, Peter Karlhuber, Norbert Kettner, Angelika Klammer, Evelyn Klammer, Monika Klotz, Florian Köhler, Lisa Kohli, Larissa Kopp, Florian Kramer, Manuel Kreiner, Carmen Lenoir, Kiki Lippert, William and Alexandra Lobkowicz, Birgit Lodes, Veronika Lux, Bernard Maaz, Siobhan Maguire, Karin Maierhofer, Marie-Pauline Martin, Andrea Marbach, Ingrid Marsoner, Marie-Pauline Martin, Rosie Martyr, Una Matanovic, Paul Mayr, Apo Melitos, Christof Metzger, Katrin Middel, Alexandra Müller, Erika Neufeld, Ilona Neuffer-Hoffmann, Ryu Niimi, Elisabeth Noggler-Gürtler, Michaela Noll, Anna Nowak, Magdalena Ölzant, Maximilian Pavlovics, Franziska Piesk, Sascha Pirker, Sandra Pisot, Adrian Porikys, Pauline Portrait, Eva Reithofer, Marco Antonio Ricci, Stella Rollig, Julia Ronge, Thaddaeus Ropac, Benjamin Rowles, Jürgen Ruck, Jessie Fortune Ryan, Rana Saner, Mike de Schit, Birgit Schmidt, David Schreier, Sabine Stanek, Peter Steinacher, Eva Stiegler-Wilfert, Francesco Stocchi, Sarah-Jane Stockings, Helmut Stollhof, Monica Strinu, Selin Stütz, Christine Surtmann, Andrea Tarsia, Kristina Tencic, Claire Tillotson, Martina Tionova, Wolfang Tobler, Alexander Trewby, Elke Tschaikner, Alejandro Vergara, Elisa Wagner, Linda Wagner, Matt Watkins, Peter Weyrich, Rolf Wienkötter, Richard Winkler, Ronald Winter, Agnes Wolf, Susana Zapke, Stefan Zeisler

Partner

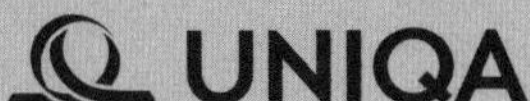

Sponsors

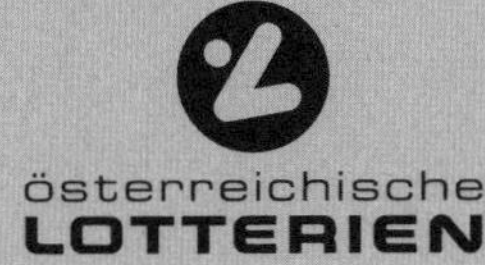

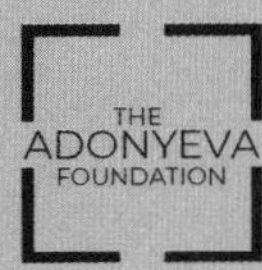

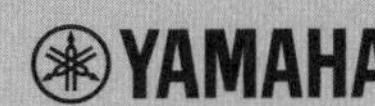

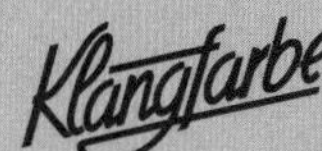

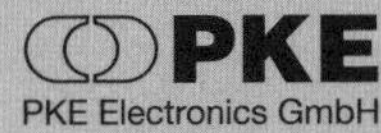

Media partner

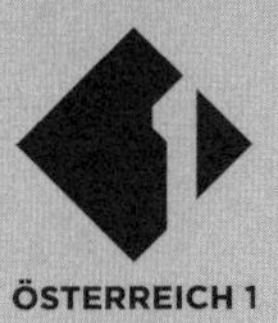

This book is published on the occasion of the exhibition

Beethoven moves
25 March to 5 July 2020

Kunsthistorisches Museum Wien
www.khm.at

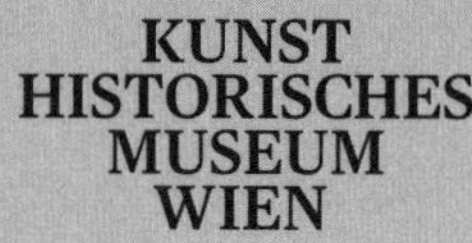

In collaboration with the Archiv der Gesellschaft der Musikfreunde in Wien

GESELLSCHAFT
DER MUSIKFREUNDE
IN WIEN

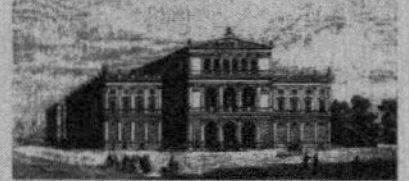

EXHIBITION

Director General
Sabine Haag

Curators
Andreas Kugler
Jasper Sharp
Stefan Weppelmann
Andreas Zimmermann

Curatorial assistance
Giulia Mangone
Hannah Marynissen

Exhibition management
Stefan Weppelmann
Esther Hatzigmoser

Exhibition design
Dani Mileo, Joris Nielander (Tom Postma Design, Amsterdam)

Construction
Martin Vonmetz (Bruckschwaiger GmbH)

Arthandling and exhibition installation
vienna arthandling GmbH

Exhibition graphics
polyform, Berlin

Light
Gustavo Allidi Bernasconi with Bertrun Kos, Maximilian Pavlovics and Roel Smit

Media
Peter Gregorc
Kunal Kumar

Sound design & audio engineering
Rachid Abu-Hassan (Platform78)
Martin Plötzeneder (Klangfarbe)

Facility management
Bertrun Kos (exhibition engineering)
Angelika Polster (air-conditioning)
Elvir Osmanovic (security)
Peter Tampier (security)

Conservation
Dominik Cobanoglu
Andrea Glatz
Eva Götz
Petra Gröger
Helene Hanzer
Ina Hoheisel
Elke Oberthaler
Nadja Pohn
Georg Prast
Petra Süß

Education
Andreas Zimmermann
Barbara Herbst
Rotraut Krall
Daniel Uchtmann
and a team of art educators

Audioguide
Natalie Lettner (texts)
Alexander Smith (engineering)
Andreas Zimmermann (direction)

Corporate design and campaign design
Katrin Middel, Robert Haselbacher (polyform, Berlin)

Press and publicity, online communication and social media
Nina Auinger-Sutterlüty
Sarah Aistleitner
Kristina Königseder
Angelika Kronreif

Legal department
Verena Eisner

Advertisement
Ruth Strondl
Elena Eiböck
Gudrun Hatvagner

Development
Bärbel Holaus-Heintschel
Verena Baumgartner
Jonas Jünger
Katrin Riedl

Events
Alexander Kimmerl
Victoria Kohout
Edyta Kostecka
Tina Madl

PUBLICATION

Editors
Andreas Kugler
Jasper Sharp
Stefan Weppelmann
Andreas Zimmermann

Editorial coordination
Rafael Kopper
Hannah Marynissen
Benjamin Mayr

General Manager of Publications
Franz Pichorner

Copy editors
Nadezda Kinsky Müngersdorff
John Nicholson

Translations
Robert Crow
Caroline Frantzen
Susanne Karau
Evelyn Saito Lackner
Wayne Lammers
Luis Sundkvist
Isabel Wolte
Shaun Whiteside

Graphic design
Robert Haselbacher (polyform, Berlin)

Image rights and coordination
Hannah Marynissen

Image editing
Thomas Ritter
Michael Eder

Printed and bound by
Printer Trento s.r.l., Trento

Paper
Munken Print White 1.5, 115 g/m²
Arena Natural Smooth, 300 g/m² (museum edition)
Condat Perigord Matt, 200 g/m² (museum edition)

Published by
Hatje Cantz Verlag GmbH
Mommsenstraße 27
10629 Berlin

www.hatjecantz.de
A Ganske Publishing Group Company

Bibliographic information published by the Deutsche Nationalbibliothek
The Deutsche Nationalbibliothek lists this publication in the Deutsche Nationalbibliografie; detailed bibliographic data are available online at http://dnb.d-nb.de.

Short title
Kugler et al. (eds.)
Beethoven Moves
Exhibiton catalogue of the Kunsthistorisches Museum Vienna
Vienna 2020

ISBN 978-3-99020-202-9 (museum edition)
ISBN 978-3-7757-4749-3 (trade edition)

Printed in Italy

Ludwig van Beethoven. Sonata for violin and piano No. 9 in A major, op. 47, 'Kreutzersonate'. 1802/03. Courtesy of the Juilliard Manuscript Collection

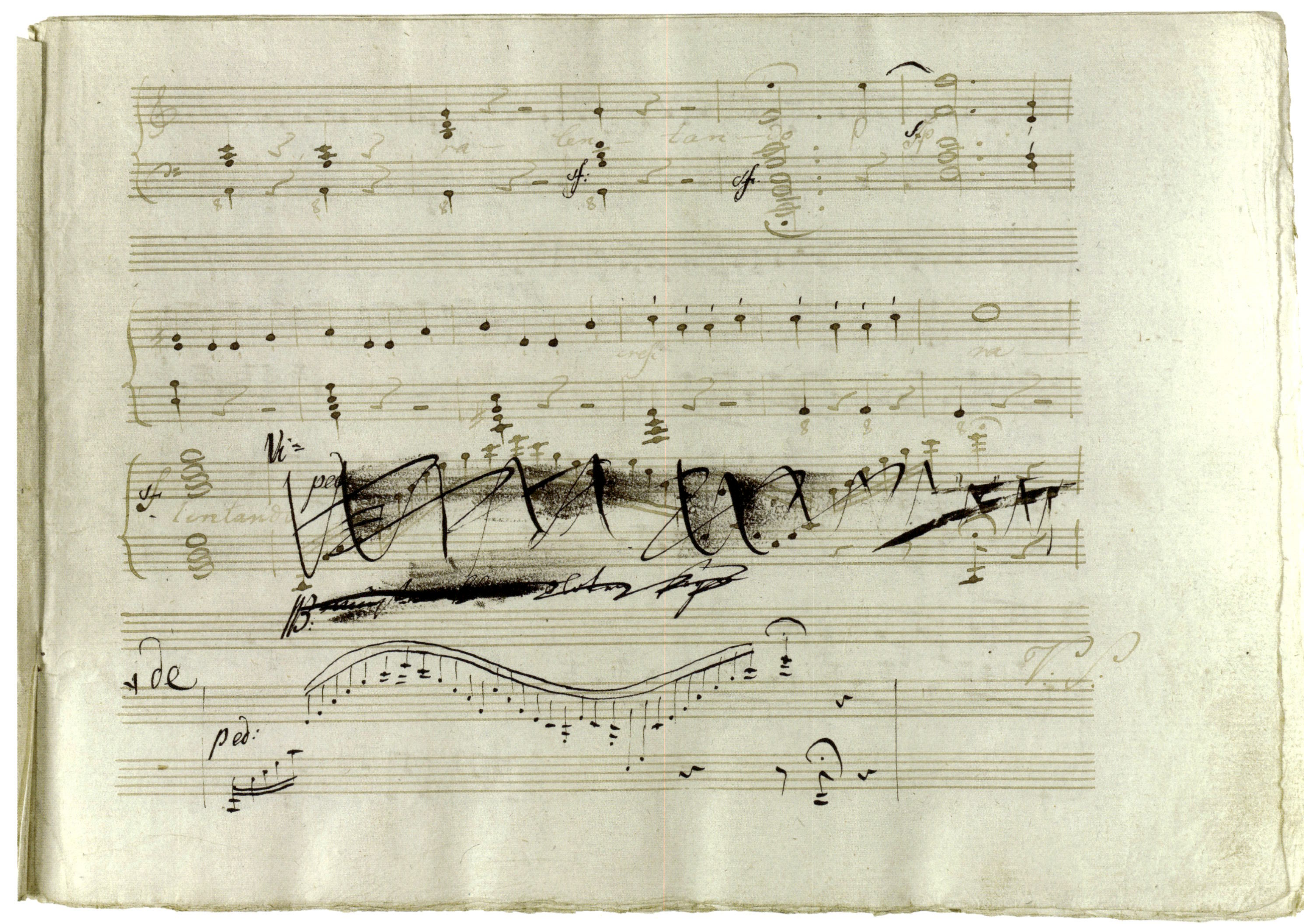